1 MONTH OF
FREE
READING

at

www.ForgottenBooks.com

By purchasing this book you are eligible for one month membership to ForgottenBooks.com, giving you unlimited access to our entire collection of over 1,000,000 titles via our web site and mobile apps.

To claim your free month visit:

www.forgottenbooks.com/free173799

ISBN 978-0-265-17929-1
PIBN 10173799

SPEECHES

ON QUESTIONS OF PUBLIC POLICY

BY

JOHN BRIGHT, M.P.

EDITED BY

JAMES E. THOROLD ROGERS

IN TWO VOLUMES

VOL. II.

'BE JUST AND FEAR NOT'

SECOND EDITION

London

MACMILLAN AND CO.

1869

OXFORD:

BY T. COMBE, M.A., E. B. GARDNER, E. P. HALL, AND H. LATHAM, M.A.,

PRINTERS TO THE UNIVERSITY.

CONTENTS OF VOL. II.

REFORM.

REFORM.

B

REFORM.

I.

BIRMINGHAM, OCTOBER 27, 1858.

[In the autumn of the year 1858, Mr. Bright, having recovered from a serious
illness which had compelled his absence from the House of Commons during
the sessions of 1856 and 1857, visited some of the principal towns in Great
Britain, and made several important speeches on Parliamentary Reform.
In the spring of the next year Lord Derby introduced his scheme. It was
rejected, and a dissolution followed, which put Lord Palmerston at the head
of affairs. During his life the question slept. On Lord Russell's accession
to office in the latter part of the year 1865 the question was revived, and
the Bill of 1866 was produced. This was lost, through a coalition of the
Tories and the 'Adullamites,' and Lord Derby came into office again. In
1867 a Reform Bill was carried.]

IF I exhibit embarrassment in rising to address you, I must
ask for your forbearance, for, in truth, as I cast my eyes over
this great assembly, I feel myself almost bewildered and
oppressed with a consciousness of my incapacity to fulfil
properly the duty which devolves upon me to-night. It is now
nearly three years since I was permitted, and, indeed, since I
was able, to stand upon any public platform to address any
public meeting of my countrymen; and during that period I
have passed through a new and a great experience. From
apparent health I have been brought down to a condition of

weakness exceeding the weakness of a little child, in which I could neither read nor write, nor converse for more than a few minutes without distress and without peril; and from that condition, by degrees so fine as to be imperceptible even to myself, I have been restored to the comparative health in which you now behold me. In remembrance of all this, is it wrong in me to acknowledge here, in the presence of you all, with reverent and thankful heart, the signal favour which has been extended to me by the great Supreme? Is it wrong that I should take this opportunity of expressing the gratitude which I feel to all classes of my countrymen for the numberless kindnesses which I have received from them during this period—from those high in rank and abounding in wealth and influence, to the dweller on one of our Lancashire moors, who sent me a most kind message to say that he believed where he lived was the healthiest spot in England, and that if I would come and take up my abode with him for a time, though his means were limited and his dwelling humble, he would contrive to let me have a room to myself? I say, looking back to all this, that if I have ever done anything for my countrymen, or for their interests in any shape, I am amply compensated by the abundant kindness they have shown to me during the last three years. And if there be any colour of shade to this picture, if there be men who subjected me to a passionate and ungenerous treatment, when I was stricken down and was enduring a tedious exile, though the best years of my life were engaged in the defence of their interests, I have the consolation of knowing that their act was not approved by the country, and that when my cause came up, by appeal, to a superior, because an impartial tribunal, their verdict was condemned and set aside by the unanimous judgment of the electors and population of this great central city of the kingdom.

I shall not attempt, by the employment of any elaborate phrases, to express to you what I felt at the time when

you conferred upon me the signal honour of returning
me as one of your representatives to the House of Commons.
I am not sufficiently master of the English language to
discover words which shall express what I then felt, and
what I feel now towards you, for what you did then, and for
the reception which you have given me to-night. I never
imagined for a moment that you were prepared to endorse all
my opinions, or to sanction every political act with which I
have been connected; but I accepted your resolution in choosing
me as meaning this, that you had watched my political career;
that you believed it had been an honest one; that you were
satisfied I had not swerved knowingly to the right hand or to
the left; that the attractions of power had not turned me
aside; that I had not changed my course from any view of
courting a fleeting popularity; and, further, that you are of
this opinion—an opinion which I religiously hold—that the
man whose political career is on a line with his conscientious
convictions, can never be unfaithful to his constituents or to
his country.

At the time of my election, you will remember that some
newspapers which commented upon it, took the liberty of
saying that I had had a good deal of time for reflection; that I
had been taught a wholesome lesson; and that I had changed
or modified my views with respect to recent public policy.
I have had no proper opportunity before to-night to refer to
that statement, and I beg leave to tell those gentlemen that
they were, and are, if they still hold the same opinion,
entirely mistaken; that whether I was wrong or right, I
acted according to what I believed to be right, and that all
the facts and all the information which I have since received
have only served to confirm me in the opinions which I had
previously expressed. I wish now, too—and all this is rather
preliminary—to refer to one ingenious misrepresentation,
which it was of no use attempting to meet when passion was
at its height, and when public clamour prevented any calm

argument upon the question then before the country. All
who read the newspapers at the time will recollect that it was
said of me, and of others who thought and acted with me—
but more of me than of any other person—that my opinion
upon such a question as the right or wisdom of any particular
war in which the country might be engaged was, after all, of
no kind of value, because whatever was the war, whatever
were the circumstances, I should have taken exactly the same
course, and therefore that argument upon a particular war
was of no avail, and was totally unnecessary. Now I beg
leave to say that this was a misrepresentation which no person
had a right to make.

I shall not trouble you more than a moment or two on this
point; but permit me to say that the first time I spoke in the
House of Commons on the subject of the Russian war, was on
the 31st of March, 1854, when a message from the Crown
came down announcing that the calamity of war was about to
befall the country. In the very opening of my speech were
these short sentences, which, if you will allow me, I will
read to you. I said : — 'I shall not discuss this question
on the abstract principle of peace at all price, as it is termed,
which is held by a small minority of persons in this country,
founded on religious opinions which are not generally received; but I shall discuss it entirely on principles that are
held unanimously by the Members of this House. When we
are deliberating on the question of war, and endeavouring to
prove its justice or necessity, it becomes us to show that the
interests of the country are clearly involved; that the objects
for which the war is about to be undertaken are probable, or,
at least, possible of attainment, and that the end proposed to
be accomplished is worth the cost and the sacrifices which we
are about to incur.' And I went on to say that I hoped if a
noble Lord, who was then a Member of the Government,
rose to make any reply to my observations, he would not run
away from the subject before the House, but would meet me

fairly as having discussed the question in that way, and that way only. Well, I now tell you, what it ought not to be necessary to say, that from that time until the time when I last spoke on the subject of the Russian war, I confined myself entirely to those points; my facts, my arguments, and my case were drawn from the despatches and Blue Books which the Government for their justification laid before Parliament; and therefore, I repeat, it was not open to any one who opposed me to oppose me on the ground that my opinion on the Russian war was worth nothing, because whatever might have been the cause of war, I should have held exactly the same language.

Now, after all is over except the tax-gatherer, and the sorrows of those who have lost their friends in the war, I will just in one sentence say that I am still unable to discover what compensation England has for the hundred millions of money she expended, or what compensation Europe has for the three hundred millions squandered by all the parties engaged in that frightful contest. It is not easy to say how much; but of this we may be sure, that the squandering of 300,000,000*l.* sterling by the nations of Europe in that struggle has had a great influence on the enhanced price of money during the last few years, and greatly aggravated the pressure of the panic through which we passed twelve months ago. The 40,000 lives which we lost in the Russian war some persons hold cheap; I do not. I think that the grown men of Birmingham from eighteen years of age to fifty (and there are, probably, not more than 40,000 of them) are something worth looking at by the statesman and the Christian; and I say that the 400,000 lives which were lost to Europe deserved to be considered before we rushed blindly into a war with Russia. For myself, therefore, all I wish to point out to you is this, that the man who hesitates before he squanders so much blood and so much treasure has at least a right to be received with a moderate amount of tolerance and forbearance.

I shall say no more now on this subject, for I intend to take an early opportunity of going into the general question of foreign policy at a greater length than would be proper this evening.

I am afraid to say how many persons I now see before me who are by the present constitution of this country shut out from any participation in political power. I shall take this opportunity of discussing, and, as far as I am able, with brevity and distinctness, what I think we ought to aim at this moment, when the great question of Parliamentary Reform is before the country. I think we may fairly say that that question occupies now something like a triumphant position, and at the same time a position of great peril— triumphant, inasmuch as it has now no open enemies— perilous, inasmuch as, for the moment, it is taken up by those who, up to this hour, have been, for the most part, the uncompromising opponents of Reform. We have had four Governments pledged to Parliamentary Reform within the last few years. Lord J. Russell, as Prime Minister, introduced a Reform Bill, and afterwards, in the Government of Lord Aberdeen, Lord J. Russell introduced another Reform Bill, and the least said of these two Bills, especially of the latter, the better. The Government which has recently been overthrown pledged itself to the country and the House of Commons to bring in a Reform Bill, but at the time when it came to an unexpected, but a not undeserved end, no Bill had been prepared, so that we knew nothing of the particulars of which it was to be composed. We have now a Government under the chieftainship of Lord Derby, who, during his short term of office in 1852, stated, if I remember right, that one of the chief objects of his Government would be to stem the tide of democracy. Now, it may be that Lord Derby has entirely changed his mind, that he is as much converted to Parliamentary Reform as Sir R. Peel, in 1856, was converted to Corn-law repeal. If he is so converted, then our question may be in good hands, but if he is not (and he has never yet acknowledged his conversion), then I think it is but reasonable of us to view his course with some suspicion, and to look upon the position of the question in his hands with some alarm. All parties now pretend to be in love with the question of Reform, but still they do not tell us much about it. They remind me, in the few speeches which they have made upon the question, of the condition of that deplorable Atlantic cable, of which I read the other day in the newspapers, that 'the currents were visible, but the signals were wholly indistinct.'

But having admitted that Parliamentary Reform is necessary, they thereby admit that the present House of Commons does not satisfactorily represent the nation, and it is one step in advance to receive that admission from all those persons, from among whom it has hitherto been supposed that Governments could alone be formed in this country. Now, I do not believe that the Parliament, as at present constituted, does fairly represent the nation, and I think it is capable of most distinct proof that it does not. Before I proceed to figures, I will mention one or two general proofs of that assertion. In the year 1846, when the great question of the repeal of the Corn-laws was under discussion, it required something like an earthquake to obtain for the people the right to buy their bread in the world's markets; it required a famine in Ireland, which from 1845 to 1851 lessened the population of that country by 3,000,000; it required the conversion of a great Minister, the break-up of a great party, the 'endangering of the Constitution,' and all those mysterious evils which official statesmen discovered when the poor artisan of Birmingham or Manchester, or the poor half-starved farm-labourer, asked this only, that where bread could be had best and cheapest in return for his labour, he might be permitted to buy it. But coming down to 1852, when Lord Derby was in office, he dissolved the Parliament, and the great question proposed to the constituencies was Protection. Parliament re-assembled, and Protection and Lord Derby were defeated by a majority of nineteen; but when you had only a majority of nineteen in the House of Commons against the re-establishment of Protection, nineteen-twentieths of the people of England were determined that they never would have anything of the sort again.

Take again the questions which affect the Established Church. Probably many persons in this meeting are not aware that, according to the return of the Registrar-General, only one-third of the people of this country have any connection with the Established Church. In Scotland, one-third only of the population are connected with the Establishment; in Ireland, five out of six, in Wales, eight out of ten, have no connection at all with it. And yet the Established Church is paramount in both Houses. If the House of Commons fairly represented all the people of the United Kingdom, the Established Church (it is as a political institution that I speak of it, I say nothing of it as a religious institution) would be much more modest, and we should probably get some changes much more readily than we have ever got any before.

Again, you are aware, probably, that up to 1853, if a man received landed property by inheritance, if it were left to him by will, or came to him as heir-at-law, it paid no legacy-duty —I speak of freehold property. In 1853, Mr. Gladstone, by an effort which was considered superhuman, prevailed upon the House of Commons to pass a law to impose a succession-tax, as it was called, or a legacy-duty on real property. I will tell you how they did it. You know that if a man in Birmingham comes into possession of leasehold houses, or machinery, or shares in the North-Western Railway, or shipping, or any other property not called real property— though, by the way, when a man gets hold of it, it is surprising how real he finds it—if he be no relation to the

person who left it to him, he has to pay a legacy-duty of ten
per cent., and a different degree of per-centage according to
the degree of relationship in which he may stand to the
testator.   In the case of land—the best of all property, with
regard to its durability and certainty, for a man to have left
to him or to possess—the law is of a different kind.   A friend
of mine, a Member of the House of Commons, was fortunate
enough to have left to him by a person who was in no way
related to him a landed estate of about 700*l.* a-year.   This was
worth in the market thirty years' purchase, or 21,000*l.*
There was timber on the estate to the value of 11,000*l.*, which,
added to 21,000*l.*, made the whole bequest 32,000*l.*   If it
had been leasehold houses, or stock-in-trade, or machinery, or
shares, or shipping, or in the funds, my friend would have
had to pay 10*l.* per cent. on it, that is to say 3,200*l.*   But
what did he pay?   The calculation was this:—My friend
is of a certain age—I do not know what, and it is not
material; the tax-gatherer or the people at Somerset House
look into a table, which shows the probable length of life
of a man of that particular age, and instead of paying
10*l.* per cent. on 32,000*l.*, he is taxed upon the annual income of the estate multiplied by the number of years which
according to the tables he may be expected to live.   It
ended in this way, that instead of paying 3,200*l.* to the
State, to bear your burdens and to pay for your wars, he paid
700*l.*, or rather less than one-quarter of that sum.   Do you
think that if the House of Commons fairly represented the
lawyers, merchants, manufacturers, shopkeepers, artisans, and
all the rest of the population, such an Act as that could have
passed that House, or that if it had existed it could continue
to exist for a single session?

I could show you inequalities as great and scandalous in
the manner in which the income-tax, so grievously felt by
owners of certain property in Birmingham, is imposed and
presses upon the owners of the soil and those engaged in

professions and trades chiefly carried on in towns, but I will not enter into that matter. Your own experience must have shown you how unequal that tax is. You know how entirely every Government has swept aside all proposals to make it more equal and just.

And now we come to the question of figures. I think it is very easy to show that if the present House of Commons represented equitably or even honestly the population of the country, figures would be of no avail in this discussion; but the figures prove conclusively that such is not the case. I will not trouble you with a heap of statistics which you cannot remember, but will give you as a proof one or two cases. Take the greatest county in England. Yorkshire shows you an existing inequality which is absolutely fatal to all fair representation. There are in Yorkshire 10 small boroughs which return to Parliament 16 Members—there are other 8 boroughs in Yorkshire whose Members altogether are 14. Now, the 10 boroughs returning the ·16 Members have not more than a population of 80,000, while the 8 boroughs with the 14 Members have a population of 620,000. Now, whether you take the amount of population, the number of houses, the sum at which they are rated to the income-tax, or the number of electors, the proportion is in the same way,—the large boroughs with the smaller number of Members have seven times the population, seven times the number of houses, seven times the amount of income-tax to pay, and seven times the number of electors. I must ask your attention to one other comparison, and it relates to your own town. The present Chancellor of the Exchequer, you know, represents the county of Bucks. That county has a population of 164,000, which is not much more than half the population of Birmingham, and yet, Bucks with its boroughs has not less than 11 Members in the House of Commons. 164,000 persons in Bucks return 11 Members, while Birmingham, with not less than 250,000, and probably much more, only returns

2 Members.   I will give you another illustration, which refers
to your own town.   In Dorsetshire, Devonshire, and Wiltshire
there are 22 boroughs, which return 34 Members to Parliament.   Compare the population and political power of those
22 boroughs, returning 34 Members to Parliament, with the
population and political power of Birmingham.   You have
nearly twice the population, but you have only 2 Members to
represent you in Parliament.

I could furnish you with pages of illustrations of this kind
to show you that our whole system of representation is
unequal and dishonest.   But one more proof only, and then
I will quit the figures, for I think the case will be sufficiently
clear.   There are in the House of Commons at present 330
Members (more than half the House) whose whole number of
constituents do not amount to more than 180,000, and there
are at the same time in Parliament 24 Members whose constituents are upwards of 200,000 in number, and, while the
constituents of 330 Members are assessed to the property-tax
at 15,000,000*l.*, the constituents of the 24 Members are
assessed to the same tax at more than 24,000,000*l.*   There is,
besides, this great significant fact, that wherever you go in
Great Britain or Ireland, five out of every six men you meet
have no vote.   The Reform Bill, which I am not about to
depreciate, since I know what it cost to get it, and I know
something of what it has done—was so drawn as purposely to
exclude from the list of electors the great body of the working
classes of this kingdom.   But supposing that out of the
6,000,000 of grown-up men in the United Kingdom 1,000,000
had the suffrage, as is now the case, and supposing that
1,000,000 returned the House of Commons by a fair distribution of Members according to numbers, there would, in
all probability, be a fair representation of the opinions of the
6,000,000, because the opinions of the 1,000,000 would to
a considerable extent reflect and represent the opinions of
their fellow-countrymen.   But that is not the case.   The law

has selected 1,000,000 to be the electors of Members of Parliament, but, having got that 1,000,000, it has contrived —partly by accident it may be, but very much by intention— that the political power of the majority of that 1,000,000 is frittered away, is fraudulently disposed of and destroyed by the manner in which Members are distributed among the 1,000,000 electors composing the electoral body. Now, I wish to ask this meeting—and let us try to take a judicial and dispassionate view of the question when we talk of Reform—What is it that we really want? I hold it to be this—that we want to substitute a real and honest representation of the people for that fraudulent thing which we call a representation now.

But there is a very serious question to be decided before we can almost take a step. When you are about to reform the House of Commons, are your eyes to be turned to the House of Peers, or to the great body of the nation? The House of Peers, as you know, does not travel very fast—even what is called a Parliamentary train is too fast for its nerves; in fact, it never travels at all unless somebody shoves it. If any man proposes to reform the House of Commons just so much as and no more than will allow it to keep pace with the wishes of the House of Lords, I would ask him not to take any trouble in the matter, but just to leave it exactly where it is. If you want it to represent the nation, then it is another question; and, having come to that conclusion, if we have come to it, there is no great mystery, I think, as to the manner in which it can be brought about. The question between the Peers and the people is one which cannot be evaded. It is the great difficulty in the way of our friends at head-quarters who are for Reform, but do not know how to meet it. It was the difficulty which Lord John Russell felt. Lord John Russell—I believe you may take my word for it—has probably, from association, from tradition, from his own reading and study, and from his own just and honest sympathies, a more friendly feeling towards this question of Parliamentary Reform than any other man of his order as a statesman. But, having said this, I must also say—what he, too, would say if he thought it prudent to tell all he knew—that this is the great difficulty with him—How can I reconcile a free representation of the people in the House of Commons with the inevitable disposition which rests in a hereditary House of Peers? Now, we must decide this question. Choose you this day whom you will serve. If the Peers are to be your masters, as they boast that their ancestors were the conquerors of yours, serve them. But if you will serve only the laws, the laws of your country, the laws in making which you have been consulted, you may go on straight to discuss this great question of Parliamentary Reform.

I am not going to attack the House of Lords. Some people tell us that the House of Lords has in its time done great things for freedom. It may be so, though I have not been so successful in finding out how or when as some people have been. At least since 1690, or thereabouts, when the Peers became the dominant power in this country, I am scarcely able to discover one single measure important to human or English freedom which has come from the voluntary consent and good-will of their House. And, really, how should it? You know what a Peer is. He is one of those fortunate individuals who are described as coming into the world ' with a silver spoon in their mouths.' Or, to use the more polished and elaborate phraseology of the poet, it may be said of him—

> ' Fortune came smiling to his youth and woo'd it,
> And purpled greatness met his ripened years.'

When he is a boy, among his brothers and sisters he is pre-eminent : he is the eldest son ; he will be ' My Lord;' this fine mansion, this beautiful park, these countless farms, this vast political influence, will one day centre on this innocent boy. The servants know it, and pay him greater deference on account of it. He grows up and goes to school and

college; his future position is known; he has no great incite-
ment to work hard, because whatever he does it is very
difficult for him to improve his fortune in any way. When
he leaves College he has a secure position ready-made for
him, and there seems to be no reason why he should follow
ardently any of those occupations which make men great
among their fellow-men. He takes his seat in the House of
Peers; whatever be his character, whatever his intellect,
whatever his previous life, whether he be in England or ten
thousand miles away, be he tottering down the steep of age,
or be he passing through the imbecility of second childhood,
yet by means of that charming contrivance—made only for
Peers—vote by proxy, he gives his vote for or against, and,
unfortunately, too often against, all those great measures on
which you and the country have set your hearts. There is
another kind of Peer which I am afraid to touch upon—that
creature of—what shall I say?—of monstrous, nay, even of
adulterous birth—the spiritual Peer. I assure you with the
utmost frankness and sincerity that it is not in the nature of
things that men in these positions should become willing
fountains from which can flow great things for the freedom
of any country. We are always told that the Peers are
necessary as a check. If that is so, I must say they answer
their purpose admirably.

But when we come to consider the question of a reform of
the House of Commons, which the Constitution does not
recognise as the House of Commons belonging to the Peers,
but to the nation, we will allow the House of Peers to go for
awhile into something like obscurity, and discuss it as if our
sole object were to make it what the Constitution supposes it
to be—a complete representation of the people in Parliament.
With regard to the question of the Suffrage, which is one of
the chief points on which I should insist, I have no doubt
there are persons who, on reading my speech, will say, 'Subversive doctrine, violent language this. The change which

you propose would endanger many things which we highly value.' Now, I beg to assure all those timid people that I do not wish to endanger or to move any of the ancient landmarks of our Constitution. I do not want to disturb this question of the franchise beyond what has been already sanctioned by Parliament and the country. I do not want to introduce any new principle or theoretical opinion which it may be found difficult to adopt. There are many men probably among those whom I see before me who are of opinion that every man should have a vote. They are for what is called 'universal suffrage,' or 'manhood suffrage'—something which means that every man of twenty-one years of age who has not forfeited his right by any misconduct, should have a vote. Let me say that, personally, I have not the smallest objection to the widest possible suffrage that the ingenuity of man can devise. At the same time, if I were now a member of a Government, and had to arrange a Reform Bill for next session, I should not act upon that principle. I will tell you upon what principle I would act. I find in the country great diversities of opinion. There are the Peers, of whom I have already spoken. They are citizens with ourselves, and have therefore a right to be considered. There are the rich and influential classes, who, as wealthy men are generally found to be, are a little timid of the great bulk of the people who have not many riches. There are thousands—scores of thousands—who imagine that they could not sleep safely in their beds if every man had a vote. We are surprised that children sometimes cannot sleep in the dark—that they fancy something dreadful will happen to them, and there are actually rich people in this country who believe that if every man had a vote it would give him a weapon wherewith to attack their property. There being all these diversities of opinion, it clearly is the duty of Government, and of Parliament too, to frame a measure which shall fairly represent what may be called the Reform opinion of the whole country. What have we at present in the way of franchises? We have the parish franchise. For generations, for ages past, there has been an extensive franchise in all our parishes. We have poor-law unions which have worked, on the whole, satisfactorily to the country. We have a franchise in our poor-law unions. We have a corporation franchise, and that franchise may be said to have worked to the satisfaction of the country. I will ask any man here whether he believes that in all the parishes, all the poor-law unions, and all the corporations, men have not conducted themselves with great propriety, and managed the affairs of their parishes, unions, and corporations satisfactorily? And I should like to ask him whether he would object to have the same franchise conferred upon them for the election of Members to the House of Commons. There is one great point gained in such a franchise—your registration would be easy and inexpensive. There is another point—that whatever its omissions, whatever its exclusions, they would not be directed against any one particular class. It would admit the working people to electoral power just as fully as it would admit the middle, or what may be called the higher and richer classes. Therefore, as regards class and class, it would remove a great defect of the Reform Bill, and would give a suffrage so wide that I believe no one would suppose it did not afford a fair representation of all classes. I do not want anybody for a moment to suppose that this particular franchise is better than manhood suffrage. I am only speaking of what Government might do, of what it ought to do, and of what it might do, moreover, in accordance with the vast majority of opinion which exists in this country on this question.

With regard to the counties I shall say little. I know no good reason why the franchise should not be as extensive there as in the boroughs; but there appears to be a general understanding that the next step in counties shall be one short of that. But I think it is of great importance that the 40s. franchise should be extended to all parts of the United Kingdom as fully as it is to the people of England and Wales.

I now come to the question which I believe all persons who have studied the matter will readily agree is one of great importance to the country—how your Members shall be allotted to the various constituent bodies. I will ask you this simple question. What is the obvious rule which would recommend itself to every man when first about to arrange this allotment? Would he not argue in this way? The law has given certain persons the right of voting, and it presumes that every person who has that right is capable of deciding how he shall vote. Every elector, therefore, is of the same importance in the eye of the law, and why then should not every elector vote for the same portion of the whole Parliament? I shall be told that I am not to go to the United States for an illustration of this. I will not. I will go a little nearer home. Take the kingdom of Sardinia. I was in Turin last year, and I made inquiries as to the mode of election and the distribution of Members there: and I found that Genoa, with a population of 140,000, returned seven Members to the Sardinian Parliament. Sardinia is not a Republic, it is a limited Monarchy like our own. Let us go to the colonies of Australia. Take New South Wales. The capital — Sydney — returns eight Members to the New South Wales Parliament. In Victoria, the city of Melbourne returns thirteen Members to Parliament, and by the Bill now introduced by the Ministry of that colony, the number thirteen is about to be increased to eighteen. I believe that in Belgium and in Canada, both countries under a limited Monarchy, the same rule applies, and we know that throughout the whole of the United States, the number of Members is allotted according to the population, and that once in every ten years this scale is re-arranged; in fact, it works itself.

I do not for a moment argue that it is necessary that we should get an actuary to apportion the number of Members exactly according to his calculations of the number of the population, but we have a fair right to an honest approximation, and without it there can be no fair representation of the people.   Look at London, putting aside the City.   If you were to divide the six boroughs of which the metropolis is made up, you would still have 12 boroughs with 300,000 population each (larger than the population of Birmingham), and constituencies of 10,000.   Divide them again, and you would have 24 boroughs, each of 150,000 population, with 5000 electors; and when the franchise is extended, the number will be still greater.   I say that the metropolitan boroughs and all large boroughs ought to be divided, or subdivided; they ought to have double, or treble, or quadruple their present number of Members.   What a miserable delusion it is that this great capital of your midland industry, with its 250,000 or 300,000 inhabitants, sends only two Members to the House of Commons!   But if every man I see here before me had a vote, or if every man outside had a vote, how will he be better off if he sends only two Members to the House of Commons, while some boroughs of 10,000 inhabitants, equal to one of the small corners of your city, have a right to return the same number?   The whole thing, as at present arranged, is a disgraceful fraud.   It ought to be put an end to, and, if it is not put an end to, your representation will remain for the future very little better than a farce.

If you look at the county seats you will find that the object of the present Government, and, in fact, of any Government in which the aristocracy has so great a power, and where landowners are so predominant, must be to greatly increase the number of Members for counties in the distribution of seats. The Chancellor of the Exchequer is a very ingenious gentleman. At this very moment in all probability he has got before him rows of figures which he hopes may enable him to prove that the proper way of reforming Parliament is to increase the number of landed gentry in the House of Commons. I recollect, on one occasion, that he referred to the county of Chester, and showed that there were three boroughs in that county which returned six Members, while the two divisions of the county only returned four, and that the four Members represented far more electors and population than the six Members of the towns. Now, it will be unfortunate for the Chancellor of the Exchequer if he ventures upon the ground of arithmetic in connection with this question. We are for arithmetic in connection with Reform, and if he proposes to deal with it in that way, we have no objection to carry out the principle fully.

But now let me turn your attention once more to the House of Peers. You know that the House of Peers is a body composed entirely of landowners, with the exception of a few lawyers and a few successful soldiers. Have you ever been to the botanical gardens in some of our towns, where a board is put up with the words, 'No dogs admitted here'? There is a similar board at the door of the House of Peers, though you cannot see it with the outward eye, and it says, 'No traders admitted here.' The House of Peers is a house for the great proprietors of the soil. The county of Chester, to which Mr. Disraeli referred, is very strongly represented in the House of Lords. There are the Marquis of Westminster, Lord Combermere, Lord Stanley of Alderley, and, no doubt, another peer or two, if our acquaintance with them was only a little more extensive. Take Lancashire. We have the Earl of Burlington, now the Duke of Devonshire, the Earl of Derby, the Earl of Sefton, and the Earl of Wilton. They come up from their great landed properties in Lancashire, and sit in the House of Lords. Let us come to your own county. You have the Earl of Warwick, Lord Leigh, Lord Craven I think, Lord Calthorpe, and one or two others, for in a county so charming as this, there are sure to be many estates and mansions belonging to the aristocracy of England. The time was when both Houses of Parliament sat together. They meet together now, but in different chambers, under the same roof, and no law can pass, not the smallest modicum of freedom or of justice come to you, until it has gone through the very fine meshes of the net of the House of Lords. Well, then, I say that if the landed proprietors of England insist upon a great addition to their power in the House of Commons, the inhabitants of the towns and the traders of the country will be obliged to ask, 'How is it that we have not our share of power in the House of Lords?'

Only one word more on the question of distribution of Members. Whenever a Reform Bill is brought into the House of Commons by any Government, be as watchful and exacting as you like on the subject of the franchise, but never, I beg, take your eye for one moment from the question of the distribution of the Members, for in it lies the great subject of dispute, and unless you guard your rights you will have to fight your battle over again, and to begin it the very day after the next Bill has passed.

There is one other point to which I must refer, and it is one upon which I presume I shall have the cordial assent of this meeting. I believe it is the opinion of the great body of the Reformers of the United Kingdom, that any Reform Bill which pretends to be generally satisfactory to Reformers must concede the shelter and protection of the ballot. I shall not discuss that question or argue now in its favour. I am quite sure that in the minds of the electors of England it has long been decided, and it has also been decided in the House of Commons. Those who are for the ballot are for it mainly because they wish free elections. Those who are opposed to it, are opposed to it chiefly because they believe it would liberate the great body of the constituencies from the control and influence of the rich. The *Times* newspaper and others, but particularly the *Times*, in discussing this question, treat it as if it were a question to be despised, and tell us that it is mean and unmanly to ask that men should go to the poll and give their votes in secret. The very man who writes thus in the *Times*, writes his article in secret, and publishes it in secret, and if any person says that he ought to affix his name to it— which, mind, I do not say at all—what is his answer? He replies, 'I am performing a great public duty; I am obliged, in the discharge of that duty, to comment with great severity upon Ministers and public men, and to expose abuses, and in doing this it is necessary that I should have the shelter of anonymous writing.' Well, I do not dispute that, but if it is wise and just for a writer in the *Times* to have that shelter in the performance of a public duty, I say it is especially wise and just that the humble elector in every county and every borough should have from the law, if the law can give it, an equal protection in the exercise of his franchise. I believe that when the franchise is thus extended, when the apportionment of Members to the constituencies approximates to a just arrangement, and when you have the protection of the ballot, you will have that kind of representation in the House of Commons which will give to every man who sits there a real constituency, and will fix him with a real responsibility.

I believe there is no country in the world that pretends to regular government where there is less of real responsibility among high officials than there is in England. There is one case which I cannot resist the temptation of citing as an illustration of what I mean. During the Russian war, there were two points on which the interest of Europe was centered; one was Sebastopol, the other the city of Kars. I hope we have not forgotten all the geography we learnt during those calamitous times, for I believe it is the only really valuable thing we got by the war. You recollect that the city of Kars was besieged by the Russians, and that it was defended by Turkish troops, assisted and commanded, I think, by an Englishman—Colonel Williams. You have heard, and I am

not at all prepared to dispute it, that Colonel Williams behaved, I do not say with great bravery, for that is common
to almost all Englishmen—and, indeed, to the majority of
men everywhere—but with great sagacity and prudence, and
showed the qualities of a commander. Eventually he was
obliged to capitulate, and those who capitulated were treated
in the most honourable manner by the Russians, who obtained
possession of the town. At that time a nobleman of very
high rank—no less a personage than Lord Stratford de Redcliffe—was Ambassador from the Queen of England at the
city of the Sultan. He had been there for nearly twenty
years. During the siege of Kars Colonel Williams wrote and
forwarded to Lord Stratford at Constantinople more than
sixty letters or despatches with reference to his position,
stating how they were worn out with sorties and the attacks
of the enemy; how long their provisions and ammunition
might last, and urging him to take any steps which might
be possible for the purpose of making a diversion in his
favour, or of sending relief. All that was proper for Colonel
Williams to write and communicate to the Ambassador of the
Queen at Constantinople, he did write and communicate; but
do you recollect the striking fact that Lord Stratford de
Redcliffe did not reply to—did not acknowledge or take the
smallest notice of—any one of these sixty or seventy despatches? He treated them as waste paper. He had been
years at Constantinople, quarrelling with every European
minister there, and bullying the ministers of the Sultan; but
when his own countrymen and their allies were shut up in
the fortified town of Kars, besieged by a powerful and overwhelming force, driven at length to starvation, and finally to
capitulation, this great official treated the whole thing as
utterly beneath his notice. Subsequently, Colonel Williams
came to England and was made a baronet; Parliament passed
an Act granting him a pension of 1000*l.* a-year, and the
Marquis of Lansdowne, one of the Cabinet Ministers of the

day, brought him into the House of Commons for his pocket borough of Calne, in Wiltshire. Colonel Williams has never opened his mouth in public in England on the subject of his treatment by Lord Stratford de Redcliffe; while that noble-man, who had been guilty of this great neglect—I say this enormous crime—has since taken his seat in the House of Lords, has become a great authority, and has now been sent by the Government on a special mission to Constantinople.

I need not tell you that I was not in favour of any of that Eastern policy, but I presume Lord Stratford was; he was one of the great authors of it, and I say that any man who takes office from his sovereign and his country as he took it, with a salary of 10,000*l.* a-year, and expenses of almost an equal amount, for the Embassy at Constantinople, is guilty of a scandalous abandonment of the duty he owes to the Queen and to the country if he pays no attention to such letters as those which Lord Stratford received from an officer of the Queen shut up with our allies in Kars. If Lord Stratford had been a Russian noble and had so behaved, before taking his seat in the House of Peers and going on a special mission to Constantinople, he would have had the advantage of being sent on a special mission to Siberia; while if he had been an Am-bassador of the United States of America—but I cannot follow out the illustration, because in the United States there is no family influence, there is no power such as that wielded by our great territorial potentates: there is nothing in that country to shield an officer of the State from public reprobation, and therefore I am quite certain that no person deputed from the United States could by any possibility be guilty of the aban-donment of duty which was manifested by Lord Stratford de Redcliffe. Whenever you get a House of Commons that fairly represents the nation, with a Cabinet that fairly repre-sents the House of Commons—if there be any other Lord Stratford I would not like to predict precisely what will befall him; but I believe that such a man, with such a temper—for it was a question of temper—will not receive under such circumstances high and continuous employment from the Government of this country. I say we have a right, be it in peace, be it in war, when we employ men in the service of the Crown and of the State, and pay them for their labour, to all their energies and to all their devotion[1].

This question of Parliamentary Reform, then, is a great and serious question. I want to give a word of warning to those persons who are now engaged, if there be any engaged, in constructing a Reform Bill for the next session. Let them not bring in a delusive and sham measure. Universal suffrage, equal distribution, vote by ballot—any of these points may or may not be perilous; but if there be one thing more distinctly perilous than another to the ruling classes in this country, it is that now, when they are committed to at least a temporary (I wish it were a permanent) settlement of this great question, they should bring forward and pass a Bill which, while it pretends to offer you something great in the way of constitutional freedom, is found immediately after it has passed to be nothing but a delusion and a sham. It will disappoint everybody; it will exasperate all the Reformers; it will render a feeling, which is now not bitter, both bitter and malignant, and within twelve months after the Bill has passed, and the cheat is discovered, we shall be entered in all probability upon another agitation, but an agitation of a very different character from any we have yet seen. Let us have a real Bill, a good Bill, or no Bill at all.

The question at this moment is in the hands of the enemy. We stand the risk of having brought before us what I will describe as ' a country gentlemen's Reform Bill.' The country

---

[1] Mr. Bright discovered that he was in error in describing Colonel Williams's letters as having been written *during* the siege of Kars. They were written before the siege began, and during Colonel Williams's preparations to resist the progress of the Russians in Asia. The facts are not literally exact, but the charge against Lord Stratford loses none of its gravity when the correction is made.

gentlemen have not been notorious for their sympathies in favour of Reform. We have always been carrying on, for the last thirty years and more, a steady and perpetual war against the predominance and the power of the country gentlemen in Parliament. If we look at their past policy we shall not have much confidence in their proposed measure. Their wars, their debts, their taxes, placed upon the bulk of the people, their stout opposition to the Reform Bill of 1832—all this leads us greatly to suspect them; and I confess for my own part I wish the question of Reform were in the hands of Reformers—in the hands of men of whose sympathies with respect to it we could not have, from their past lives, the shadow of a doubt. I have great fears that until you have a Ministry in which there are men who are really in favour of Reform, and of an honest Reform, you are not likely to get any such measure as the most moderate among us ought to be in the least satisfied with.

I must warn you against one phrase which I find our friends (we cannot now call any of them our opponents), the bewildered Reformers, are beginning to use. They say we must not on any account 'Americanize' our institutions. Now, I know only one institution in America of which the Americans need to be very greatly ashamed; and that institution was established under the monarchy, although unfortunately it has lived and flourished under the republic. They tell us in America numbers overwhelm property and education. Well, but numbers have not overwhelmed property and education in England, and yet look at legislation in England. Look at our wars, look at our debt, look at our taxes, look at this great fact—that every improvement of the last forty years has been an improvement which numbers, and numbers only, have wrested from the property, and what they call the education of the country. Our education is fairly represented by our Universities, but I say now, as I have said before, that if the Legislature of

England, if the Parliament of England, had been guided for thirty years past according to the counsels of the representatives from the Universities, England, instead of being a country of law and of order, would have been long before this a country of anarchy and of revolution.   America is a strange bugbear.   There are thirty-two at least, if not thirty-three, independent and sovereign States in the United States of America.   Now, I am not one of those who believe that you cannot be free and happy under a monarchy such as ours. I am not proposing—I am the last person to propose—that the institutions of this country should be modelled upon the plan of some other country, because it is the plan of some other country ; but I say, that if we are at liberty to draw science, products for our manufactures, and literature from every country in the world, why should we not, if we see anything good in the politics of another country, be equally at liberty to take a lesson in that respect also ?

Speaking generally, in all the sovereign and independent States of America there is a franchise as wide as that which I have proposed to-night ; there is an exact and equal allotment of members to the electors ; and there is, throughout most of the States, the protection of the ballot.   Yet in America we find law, order, property secure, and a population in the enjoyment of physical comforts and abundance, such as are not known to the great body of the people in this country, and which never have been known in any country in any age of the world before.   Will any man dare to tell me, in the presence of this audience, that the English nation in England is a worse nation than the English nation in America?   Are we less educated, are we less industrious, are we less moral, are we less subject to the law, are we less disposed to submit to all the just requirements of the Government ?   If we are so, and if the English nation in America excels us in all these particulars, does it not look very likely that the institutions in England are not as good in the training and rearing of a nation as the institutions in the United States? I do not say that; but those persons who say that the franchise, the distribution, and the ballot, which operate so well in America, would be perilous in England, do what I will not do—they libel the people of this country, and they libel our institutions.

Now, I have a suggestion to make, which I hope somebody will act upon. The Reformers now are more numerous than ever they were before. Why should they not, by some arrangement, have their own Reform Bill; have it introduced into Parliament, and supported with all the strength of this great national party; and if it be a Bill sensibly better than the Bill that is being prepared for us in Downing Street, why should we not, with all the unanimity of which we are capable, by public meetings, by petitions, and, when the proper time comes, by presenting ourselves at the polling-booths, do everything in our power to pass that measure into law? I say that we are great in numbers; that, united, we are great in strength; that we are invincible in the solidity of our arguments; that we are altogether unassailable in the justice of our cause. Shall we then, I ask you, even for a moment, be hopeless of our great cause? I feel almost ashamed even to argue it to such a meeting as this. I call to mind where I am, and who are those whom I see before me. Am I not in the town of Birmingham—England's central capital; and do not these eyes look upon the sons of those who, not thirty years ago, shook the fabric of privilege to its base? Not a few of the strong men of that time are now white with age. They approach the confines of their mortal day. Its evening is cheered with the remembrance of that great contest, and they rejoice in the freedom they have won. Shall their sons be less noble than they? Shall the fire which they kindled be extinguished with you? I see your answer in every face. You are resolved that the legacy which they bequeathed to you, you will hand down in an accumulated wealth of freedom to your children. As for me, my voice is feeble. I feel now sensibly and painfully that I am not what I was. I speak with diminished fire; I act with a lessened force; but as I am, my countrymen and my constituents, I will, if you will let me, be found in your ranks in the impending struggle.

REFORM.

II.

MANCHESTER, DECEMBER 10, 1858.

[At the general election in 1857, the Right Hon. T. Milner Gibson and Mr. Bright were defeated in the contest at Manchester. This speech was delivered at a great meeting in the Free-trade Hall, to which they were invited by their old friends and supporters in the Manchester constituency.]

I CANNOT tell you how much I rejoice in being permitted to meet so large a number of those whom I must describe as my old and dear friends in the Liberal cause. I fear, however, that the reception which you have granted to us to-night, and which you have but at this instant given to me, is calculated in some degree to disturb the balance of the mind, and to interfere with that calm judgment which is demanded by the circumstances under which we are met together, and by the gravity of that great question which is now being discussed in every part of the United Kingdom. I know not whether there be persons who will look upon this meeting in the light of the commemoration of a defeat which we have sustained. To me, it wears far more the aspect of the celebration of some great success. And may we not say that we are successful—that notwithstanding the vicissitudes which wait upon the

career of public men, and upon the progress of public questions in a free country, we find as we look back over a' term of
years, that those beneficent principles which we have so often
expounded and defended on this ground, are constantly making
progress and obtaining more and more influence on the minds
of all our countrymen ?

Forty years ago, the spot where we are now assembled
became famous. Thousands of the population of Manchester
and its neighbourhood assembled here—not in this magnificent building, but under the wide canopy of heaven. They
met only to plead with the Government and the Parliament
of that day, that they might be permitted some share in the
government of their country, and that they might be permitted further to possess that natural right which one would
think no man would ever deny to another—the right of disposing of the produce of their labour in the open market of
the world, in purchase for their daily bread. That meeting
was dispersed by the rude arm of military power. The tragedy
of that day proved at once the tyranny and brutality of the
Government, and the helplessness and humiliation of the
people. Now, you have seen a Ministry representing and
supported by the political party that committed that iniquity—you have seen such a Ministry voting in the House of
Commons in favour of a resolution which declared that the
repeal of the Corn-laws had been a great blessing to the
country; and after having twenty-six years ago obtained one
instalment of Reform, you have now the amazing spectacle of
a Ministry representing and supported by that same political
party, engaged at this very hour in the arrangement of the
clauses of another Bill, which shall still further extend political
rights to the great mass of the population of this country.
Seeing this, then, who will despair? Since I have been able
to think maturely upon public questions, since I have been
able and have been permitted to open my mouth in these the
open councils of my countrymen, I have never for one moment

despaired; and when I look around me, and see this magnificent—I will say this all-powerful—assembly, my hopes, my faith, all are confirmed, and I gather fresh strength for whatever struggle is before us.

My right honourable Friend in his speech has almost entirely abstained from entering into details connected with the question of Parliamentary Reform. Now, I think that at this moment, wherever men assemble to discuss political questions, it would be a great misfortune if some one present did not go into some portion of the detail connected with that question. And perhaps in the peculiar position which I am now placed in with regard to it, you will not expect that I should leave it altogether untouched. Let us recollect that whatever is said upon this question will meet with much hostile criticism from those who are not present with us. You know that I have recently, a few weeks ago, addressed large audiences of my constituents in Birmingham, upon this question; and you know to what kind of hostile criticism my speech or speeches on that occasion have been subjected. It is not in human wisdom to make speeches to please everybody; and it is not in human wisdom to attempt to do it. I shall take the course of addressing myself to that question, according to the light I have with regard to it from great study, from much consultation with others, and from an honest wish that I have, that the subject of Reform should be rightly viewed by every intelligent man amongst my countrymen.

Now we will mention two or three things that we do not want. We do not propose in the smallest degree to call in question or to limit the prerogatives of the Crown. I believe we are prepared to say that if the throne of England be filled with so much dignity and so much purity as we have known it in our time, and as we know it now to be, we hope that the venerable monarchy may be perpetual. We do not propose to discuss even, much less to limit, the legal and constitutional privileges or prerogatives of the House of Peers. We know, everybody knows, nobody knows it better than the Peers, that a house of hereditary legislation cannot be a permanent institution in a free country. For we believe that such an institution must in the course of time require essential modification. Last year, or the year before, the Queen herself proposed to nominate persons to life peerages. That was deemed an essential change by the present members of the House of Peers, and in a manner that was not gracious to the Queen, that was not respectful to the nation, they 'almost insolently rejected the attempt of the Crown, and the Ministers of the Crown, to introduce into the House of Lords a member whose peerage should exist only so long as his life.

I do not want to discuss that question now. We want to discuss the question which is immediately before the country— which the Government has brought before the country—for we do not bring it before the country on this occasion—and a question in which we are deeply and closely interested. The House of Commons is so called, I presume, because it is understood and intended to represent all those portions of the people—the vast majority of the people—who are not included in the privileged and titled classes. The constitution, if I know anything about it, intends that that House should fairly, openly, and widely represent all the vast interests of all the vast population who are called upon to obey the legislation which is mainly enacted by that House. Now, I wish to ask you this simple question. Do you believe, after examining the figures that have been placed before you for months and for years past, that the House of Commons does at present fulfil honestly its intended place in the Constitution, or is the organ of the expression of the opinions of all classes of the population of Great Britain and Ireland ? You may have a. shadow and form of representation, as of anything else. You know very well that you may have gorgeous temples— you may have in wonderful ostentation all the outward semblance of religion—yet there may be wholly wanting the life of Christianity itself. And you may have electors, a million or more, and you may have canvassing, and nominations, and polls, and returns, and houses of legislation, and speeches, and the contention of parties, and divisions, and laws enacted, and yet there may be only the form of representation, and its life and spirit and reality may be altogether absent. All this we had previous to 1832; yet nobody says now that we had representation before then. All this existed, or nearly all, in France, previous to the year 1848. A great deal of it exists there at this moment, and yet there is a general impression that representation is not free there. There is a general belief that it was not free here previous to the passing of the Reform Act.

I should like to put, in as few words as I can, exactly what we think the House of Commons should be. It should be a House composed of men sent by the free election of so many of the people, voting with such an equality of power as shall give a real expression to the opinions of the people. If anybody says that we are for levelling doctrines—that we intend to have a President instead of a Queen—which is a favourite theory with some few people, you at least will not believe them. I ask them again and again, if they choose to read once, to read again, that they may not misrepresent that which I am now proposing. Now, what is the British Constitution? I never saw it. I never heard of anybody who had handled it. It is not, in very few words, in any of the books. But there is, notwithstanding, something that we all understand by the British Constitution. It is not a thing meant entirely for the Crown. The Crown has its limits by Act of Parliament, and by custom. Nor is it intended entirely for the hereditary peerage. The House of Lords has its pre-rogatives and its privileges well defined. But the Constitution does not confine itself to care for the monarch on the throne, or for the peer in his gilded chamber. The Constitution regards the House of Commons as well. It regards you and me, and all the people of the United Kingdom. And it professes to take within its pale all these populations and these interests, and to give them as complete a shelter and as complete a voice as it gives to the Queen or to the peerage. But if you want the House of Commons elected by so many of the people as shall give a fair expression of the people's wishes, can any living man say that we possess it when five out of six of all the men he will find if he traverse every county from John O'Groat's to the Land's End, and from Cape Clear to the Giant's Causeway,—when five out of every six of these men have no more vote at the poll for a Member of Parliament than if they lived in some foreign land; when their utmost privilege at an election is to look on, to hold up their hands, and to shout for one candidate or the other?

But if you think it necessary that your Members should be elected by some fair number of votes, that votes should be given with something like an equality of power, how far are you from this, when you hear that 330 Members of the House of Commons—more than one-half of the whole number—are returned by less than one-sixth even of that small number of persons to whom the franchise is entrusted? You give votes to a million out of six millions, and half the House of Commons is elected by less than 200,000 of those electors! And then, if bribery be somewhat common, and if intimidation, wherever it can be practised, is almost universal, how can you come to the conclusion that there is any real freedom of election whatsoever, when you survey the whole representation of the counties and boroughs of the kingdom?

I would ask your attention for a moment to those counties, to which your attention has been already turned by my right hon. Friend. The counties, as you know, return their Members by the votes, chiefly, of two classes—freeholders, and occupiers of lands or houses of the value of 50*l.* and upwards. Of these 50*l.* occupiers and upwards, there are about 200,000; but of occupiers between 10*l.* and 50*l.*, I see by a return recently made to the House of Commons, not less than 400,000. But the 400,000, by the present law, are entirely ignored and excluded; and the 200,000, being to a very large extent occupiers of land, and occupiers for the most part without leases, are to a large extent dependent upon the good-will of their landlords, and their votes, speaking generally, are employed to swell the power of the great landed proprietors in all the county elections of the kingdom. Now, Lord Derby, the present Prime Minister, is a man who has the power of expressing very accurately what he means; he is a great master of the English language; and he once gave us an illustration of what is understood in England by county representation. He said that, if anybody would tell him what were the politics of three or four of the great landed pro-prietors of any county, he could tell at once what were the politics of the Members for that county. We might fancy, if we did not know something about it ourselves, that this was some conjuring trick, but it is in point of fact nothing but that which we all know. The 'three or four great proprie-tors' are the constituents of the county, and the Members are the representatives of those great proprietors. They have, as you know, unfortunately for us, small sympathy with com-merce, and they have never manifested, at least for the last sixty years, any sympathy whatever with Reform of any kind. How should they? They are connected with the peerage, and with the great territorial power. The members of their fami-lies, generally speaking, do not come into the operations of trade. They find employment—at least they find salaries— in the military or naval service, or some other service of the country; or they take shelter from the storms of life in some snug family living in the Church.

I venture to say that, if it were possible to have an accurate account of the receipts and payments of those families, there are many hundreds of them—I believe there are some thou-sands—who receive more in the way of emolument, and salaries of one kind or other, from the public revenues, from the sixty or seventy millions of taxes which you annually raise, or from that portion of the public estate which for the time is entrusted to the Established Church—I believe they receive far more than the whole of the taxes which they annually pay to the expenditure of the State.

But we do not find fault only with the counties; the boroughs are not at all in a satisfactory state. I was looking down a list, the other night, beginning with the Tower Hamlets, the largest population, and coming down to some one which is the smallest, I forget its name; but I found that there were 71 boroughs, not one of which had a population of 10,000 persons. I think 10,000 is about one-third the average size of the several wards in Manchester. The whole population of the 71 boroughs is only 467,000, which is not very much more than the present population of Manchester and Salford; and yet these 71 boroughs return 117 Members to the House of Commons, while Manchester and Salford return only three Members. But if you go a little lower, to 8,000 as a standard, you will find not less than 54 boroughs, and their whole population is exactly 316,000, which is also exactly the population of the city of Manchester at the census of 1851; but these 54 boroughs return 89 Members, while Manchester returns only two. If Manchester and Salford, by some tradition of the past, or by some accident or other, returned 117 Members, or if Manchester returned 89 Members —if the conditions which I have stated were just reversed— do you not think that we should have from other parts of the country—probably from the landed gentry—a very violent assertion that we were favoured in the representation, and that the condition of things was monstrous and intolerable, and must be put an end to?

But there is another point which you do not find out from the population tables. That is this—that whereas the boroughs of Manchester and Salford can do as they like, acting wisely at one time and foolishly at another—at least they are free to follow their own information, their own light, their own convictions; these little boroughs are not so free, being, I dare to say, very little better than what we used to describe by the unpleasant term of 'rotten.' They are under influence of some kind or other. A very little clique, indeed, two or three persons, in a very small borough, can have a great influence. A neighbouring landowner—some subtle and not very scrupulous lawyer—by turning the 'screw,' can, if he likes, turn the scale. But these boroughs are not only so small in population, but for the most part they cannot pretend to the power of free election in any way whatsoever.

I come now to the result of all this—that a House of Commons so formed, becomes for the most part, as we know it is, a sort of deputy to the House of Lords, and an organ of the great territorial interest of the country. It hates changes, with an animosity that nothing can assuage. It hates economy. Let any man propose in the House of Commons that there shall be a fair committee appointed, to which shall be submitted those enormous estimates of which we have so much reason to complain, and you will find that very few persons in the House will vote for such a committee, and it will be stoutly resisted by the Government, whether formed from the Conservative or the Whig section of the House. The House hates equality of taxation. The succession-duty is a glaring instance of it. The income-tax is another instance scarcely less glaring. It gives to property vast influence in the government of the country, and it perpetually shields property from its fair burden of taxation. It was the same before the Reform Bill as it is now.

Some people are of opinion that we have had much better legislation since the Reform Bill than we had before. I do not deny it; but I believe it is owing much more to the general intelligence of the people, an intelligence which has penetrated even into the House of Commons and into the

House of Lords, than to any more exact representation of the influence of the constituencies, or to any change that took place by the Reform Act.   You know that before the Reform Bill, Catholic Emancipation was granted, when a civil war was about to break out in Ireland.   You know that the Reform Bill itself was granted when an insurrection, perhaps a revolution, was at the door.   And you know that in 1846 the repeal of the Corn-laws was granted, not because the House of Commons or the House of Lords wished to grant it.   By no means.   For I believe that not more than one hundred Members had ever voted for Mr. Villiers' motion for the repeal, until it was granted in 1846, because a portion of the kingdom was visited with a famine so intense, that Lord John Russell, in order to describe its magnitude and its severity, compared it to the famines which are recorded to have desolated parts of Europe during the thirteenth century.   It required a famine, not a scarcity.   There had been many scarcities, as you know.   There had been a scarcity for years. On more than one occasion thousands and hundreds of thousands of families had been pressed into penury, and not a few into premature graves.   And yet the Corn-law was not repealed.   To quote two lines of the unhappy Chatterton—

> 'The civil power then snored at ease,
> While soldiers fired to keep the peace.'

And it was not till the famine became so sore in the land that all Europe and the civilized world were startled with the horrors that floated across every ocean and in every gale, that the Parliament of England at last consented to take their hand from the food of the people.   And you know that a large party—a party who are now in possession of the Government—assailed and denounced Sir Robert Peel as a traitor and a coward, because he did not make a still greater fight on behalf of the most odious monopoly that ever existed in any country.

And now they do not give you the Ballot; not because they

do not understand it as well as you do, but precisely because they do understand it. Do you suppose there would be such a whip in the House, such a steady and powerful phalanx of Members brought up, county Members especially, to vote against the Ballot, if they did not believe all we say in favour of the Ballot? You have had it discussed since the Reform Bill. The argument has been already exhausted for twenty years, yet for all that they do not give you the Ballot.

Take the question of church rates. A Bill to repeal the church rates has just passed the House of Commons. But how many years has it been discussed? The arguments were the same before I went into the House of Commons that they were last session. Take the question of the game laws. Would it be tolerated—would it be tolerated by the people of this country, if they were fairly polled, that there should exist laws whose object is to promote, to the greatest possible extent, the preservation of wild animals for the sport of the territorial and wealthy classes? The law has never yet said that game was property. It treats it as something else. It dare not say that game is property, and it cannot say so. But we have several Acts of Parliament—clauses of the utmost complication —traps of every kind, as many to catch the poacher as the poacher has to catch the game. And you have in this civilized and Christian country—we are not at all discussing the United States—in this civilized and Christian country, with an ancient monarchy, an hereditary peerage, an Established Church, and all that can be necessary to preserve law and order, according to the opinion of some of those who criticise what I say; yet you have, in the months of November and December particularly, in every year, men going out armed, not to protect cows, and sheep, and poultry, which are recognised and understood as property—for nobody attempts to meddle with them—but to preserve that which the law dare not designate as property, and the preservation of which it dare not commit to the ordinary guardians of the public peace. And you have further from your towns and from your villages, and from your country parishes, bands of men armed to the teeth, instigated it may be occasionally by want, more often probably by the love of adventure—you have bands of men of this kind prowling about in almost every county endeavouring to destroy this game; and you have outrages such as we have had described to us within the last month, in which several of our fellow-creatures have fallen victims, and have been murdered. No; the dukes, and lords, and county Members, and great men of any name, must not tell me that a Parliament and a House of Commons that perpetuates this enormity represents the intelligence and the morality of the Christian population of this country. And to show you how little a Prime Minister even is master of his own actions in the face of that great territorial interest, let me tell you that when I, some years ago, and before I had any political connection even with Manchester, when I gave notice of a motion in the House of Commons for a Select Committee to inquire into the operation of the game law—to inquire merely—such was the anxiety, such was the trembling terror of these gentlemen, that Sir Robert Peel was obliged to call his followers together in Downing-street, and there to reason with them, and to obtain their co-operation in the course which he felt himself bound to pursue, which was to consent to the Committee for which I was about to move. I need not tell you that the Committee produced very little result. Committees of the House of Commons very seldom do yield much result. For what the House is, Committees generally are; and if a Committee does happen to stumble upon something valuable, it is generally distasteful to the House, and is immediately rejected by it. I believe that no great measure passes the House of Commons merely because it is just. It passes sometimes because the people are restive; sometimes because the exigencies of party require that something should be done. But it does not pass—I state it fearlessly after.

fifteen years' sitting in that House—a great measure of justice does not pass because it is just.

Then I come to the conclusion that Reform is necessary. But I can show you further that it is inevitable. The Government is at a dead lock without Parliamentary Reform. The only great result of the. Reform Bill, in the House, has been this, that it has introduced about one hundred men who do at times show some amount of independence, and they act free from the shackles of the Tory or Whig sections of the aristocracy. And it is we—it is by our work, it is by our speeches, by our votes, that we transfer the Government from one party to the other. But we make it impossible for either of them to conduct the Government upon those antiquated principles which we and the people of England are ready to abolish. Now I will ask you another question. What is the obvious, the simple, in fact the only mode by which you can reform the House of Commons? If a man is hungry, he eats; if he is thirsty, he drinks; and if he is cold, he puts on an extra coat or goes nearer to the fire. If the number of electors is too small, extend the suffrage. If it be intolerable that more than half the House of Commons shall be returned by one-sixth of the electors, or that a population equal to that of Manchester should return 89 Members in other parts of the country, while here it only returns two, the obvious remedy is to take from one scale and put into the other. And if there be this bribery and this intimidation, the remedy which every man who has considered the question, and who wishes for freedom of election, the remedy which he points to, is the remedy of the Ballot.

You have read, I have no doubt, some, I hope not all, of those interminable leading articles which have been written since I was at Birmingham. You have read some speeches, probably, which have commented on what I said. I was charged with wishing to adopt republican institutions, levelling principles, introducing something or other wholly destructive of everything good, and noble, and admirable in this country. Well, I find the suffrage in the boroughs is 10*l.* What did I propose? I did not propose to put it to 9*l.* That would have been to be laughed at. These very writers and speakers would have said, 'What a lame thing this is— dissatisfied with 10*l.*, happy with 9*l.*!' I did not ask for 8*l.*, nor for 7*l.*, nor for 6*l.* The Reform Bill, stopping at 10*l.*, drew a line, on one side of which were the constituencies as we now have them, and on the other side the great body of the working classes. The working classes were purposely excluded by the adoption of the 10*l.* franchise. But the 9*l.* would not have admitted them, nor the 8*l.*, nor the 7*l.* The 6*l.* would have admitted a considerable number, and the 5*l.* probably would admit nearly all of them that can be admitted. I felt that it was not worth while making, as the saying is, 'two bites at a cherry.' If you wish to admit the working classes—for that is the question—if you wish to admit them, you must bring your suffrage down to the point that will admit them, or else you are only practising upon them precisely the same sort of legislation that they complain of with regard to the Bill of 1832.

But then I find a most admirable thing all ready at my hands. I find in all our parishes from the time of Queen Elizabeth, and for anything I know from the time of Alfred— I do not know how many hundred years it has lasted—a franchise which everybody has been contented with, and nobody has condemned, and which has done no harm to law, or order, or security of property. I find that when Parliament came to legislate for Poor-law unions, it adopted this same franchise as the basis of the union franchise. When it came to legislate for corporations, it adopted, with some restrictions, the same franchise as the basis. Why tell me that this franchise does not act properly in the United States? For my argument, I do not care a farthing whether it does or not. We have tried it here, in our parishes, our unions, our corporations; and I say, if it acts on the whole justly, in those three departments of representation, it may be trusted, without danger, in that more important representation which concerns our Imperial Legislature. I am in favour of authority, particularly when it agrees with my own opinion. I will read from an authority which is not one that the Whig party ought to think lightly of. In the year 1797—sixty-one years ago—Mr. Grey (afterwards Lord Grey of the Reform Bill) brought forward a motion in the House of Commons for a Bill to establish household suffrage in all the boroughs of the kingdom. I will not give you what Mr. Grey said about it, for I do not happen to have any portion of his speech with me; but I will give you the words of Mr. Fox—Charles James Fox—the greatest light, I presume, which the Whig party has ever offered to the country. Charles James Fox said this :—

> 'I think that to extend the representation to housekeepers is the best and most justifiable plan of Reform. I think also that it is a most perfect recurrence to first principles—I do not mean to the first principles of society, nor to the abstract principles of representation, but to the first known and recorded principles of our constitution. According to the early history of England, and the highest authorities in our parliamentary constitution, I find this to be the case. It is the opinion of the celebrated Glanville, that in all cases where no particular right intervenes, the common law right of paying scot and lot was the right of election in the land. This was the opinion of Serjeant Glanville, and of one of the most celebrated committees of which our parliamentary history has to boast ; and this, in my opinion, is the safest line of conduct that you can adopt.'

Now, what is it that I propose? That every householder, of course, because every householder is rated to the poor, shall have a vote; and if a man be not a householder strictly, but if he have an office, or a warehouse, or a stable, or land—if he shall have any property in his occupation which the Poor-law taxes, out of which he must contribute to the support of the poor, then I say I would give that man a vote. Now, sixty years is a long time. We have members of the aristocracy of this country exhibiting themselves frequently upon platforms on various occasions. They tell the people how wonderfully education has advanced; how much Parliament grants every year, and how much voluntary effort does; what a great step the people have taken forward. I wish they would come to the legitimate conclusion after all this praise of the people. Your statisticians tell you that two millions of the people are subscribers to benefit societies, and that their funds amount to more than nine millions sterling. Is that no proof of providence? Is that no proof of improvement and advancement? Who is the man that dare stand before any considerable number of his countrymen, and libel them by saying that the right which Mr. Grey, and which Charles James Fox, advocated for you in 1797, you are still so degraded that you are not fit to be trusted with in the year 1858? And of course with regard to your small boroughs, you must take some point of population, and you must cut off all those below it. You must allow their present electors to merge, as they would necessarily merge, in the 10*l.* franchise, which in all probability you will establish for your counties.

But still I know exactly how we shall be met—'You are going to Americanise us.' Nothing is so dreadful to an Englishman who is thinking of emigrating across the Atlantic, as that we should be Americanised in England. That is a phrase invented by some cunning knave, intended to catch a good many very simple dupes, and no doubt it will catch some of them. But I should like to ask these gentlemen, whether representation is not an English custom and an English principle? They were Englishmen who first took it to the United States. It is said that wherever an Englishman goes, just as he takes with him his white skin, he takes with him the foundation of representative institutions. He has taken them already to the Cape; he is already as busy as possible in building up four or five monarchical republics in Australia; he has carried the representative system to Canada; he carries it wherever he goes. The

Bill of 1832 was a desperate measure in the direction of Americanising us. It took some boroughs, where twelve members of a corporation returned the Members to Parliament, and it gave the suffrage to 5,000 of the people. That was Americanising such boroughs with a vengeance. The more you extend your representation, the more, of course, you become like that systematic and theoretically perfect representation which exists in the United States of America.

It is curious how free countries, and countries that we deem not free, often exhibit the same kind of thing at the same time. You know that lately a most distinguished Frenchman wrote a pamphlet about England—about a debate in the English Parliament. He was charmed with the freedom of debate; he was charmed with the absence of all kind of difficulty in expressing our opinions, and he went away full of this impression; and he wrote a pamphlet in burning words, describing what he had seen in England, and by inference, of course, saying something that was not palatable to those who are the present directors of the Government in France. Well, what was done? It was found out that it was an indictable offence, and the advocate for the prosecution said in so many words, 'You praised England, and in doing so you humiliated France.' An humble individual like myself comes before his constituents, and he finds a nation of twenty or thirty millions, chiefly of Englishmen, on the other side of the Atlantic. He finds that with some small exceptions, in two or three of the transatlantic cities, which are more German and Irish than American, he finds there in all the Free States law and order and security of property, equal to that which is found in the course of years in any other country in the world. And he says that to his constituents. He is not indicted for it; they do not give him so many pounds' fine, and so many months' imprisonment; but some scores of writers for the press, men who, or some of them, pretend to be in favour of liberty in England, but men who, if they were dressed in the garb that

most becomes them, would be. dressed in plush—these men
assail me ; and, probably, if I were in France, and they were
in France, they would do their best to indict and prosecute
me.

One word more upon this. I have said over and over
again, that, perhaps, I am the very last man in England who
would propose any institution here because I found it elsewhere. I am not insensible to some things that appear to me
to be errors in principle, some that are errors in practice, in
the constitution and the customs of the United States. But
I protest against our being shut up to take nothing from
America but cotton, and rice, and tobacco. And, in fact, we
do take a good many other things. I am told that my friend
Mr. Platt, a member of a very eminent firm, has a wonderful
machine from America with which to make bricks. We know
that the agriculture of this country has been greatly advan-
taged by the importation of reaping machines from America.
We know that those persons who are going about so appre-
hensive of an invasion, have particular reason to be delighted
with America, because they have received from that country
the invention of the revolver. At this moment, in the
Government small-arms establishment at Enfield, they have
patent machinery from America for making gun-stocks. They
can turn out a gun-stock, I am told, in twenty-two minutes,
fit for the barrel. What a dreadful thing to think of ! And
I am sure that Mr. Miles, if his Protectionist principles have
not long ago deserted him, will be horrified to hear that they
have actually brought Americans over to show the English
how to work them. But there is much more behind.
The *Times,* the *Morning Star,* the *Daily Telegraph,* and the
leading newspaper in this district, the *Manchester Daily
Examiner,* with, I believe, two or three of the widely-circu-
lated London weekly papers, are all printed on machines
which were either made in America, or, being made in this
country, were made on the American patent. And further

than this, do you not remember that the West Enders, including even ladies, have been subscribing ten guineas apiece
to invite a clever farmer from Ohio to show them how to tame
a horse? Anything but politics. You may delight yourself
with their charming poets—with Bryant, and Whittier, and
Longfellow; you may interest and instruct yourself by their
great historians—Bancroft, and Prescott, and Motley; but
if you ask how free popular institutions are working among
your own countrymen on the American continent, you are
denounced as unpatriotic, and charged with treason to the
House of Lords.

I will read a passage that was particularly galling to those
gentlemen, from the report of my speech at Birmingham. It
is very short. I said :—' Generally, in all the sovereign and
independent States of America, there is a franchise as wide as
that which I have proposed to-night. There is an exact and
equal limit of Members to the electors ; and there is, throughout many of the States, the protection of the ballot; yet in
America we find law, order, and property secure, and a population in the enjoyment of physical comforts and abundance
such as are not known to the great body of the people of this
country, and which have never been known in any country in
any age of the world before.' Now, Lord John Russell a
short time ago was at Liverpool, at a meeting of the Social
Science Association, and he made a speech, many parts of
which, I think, were admirable and instructive. He referred
to America in two particulars, and showed how, in the
States of New York and Louisiana, the laws had been
codified and simplified. He said that with a few days' study
a man might make himself perfectly acquainted with the
laws with regard to land and landed property. He did
not see (and Lord John Russell is not afraid to look abroad
on a matter of this kind) why an old country—I do not
quote his exact words—should be compelled to continue a
system which was not necessary, and which it was found so

advantageous to dispense with in a new country.   But he
said this :—

'It is education which enables the United States of America to proceed in
their wonderful career, upheld by the most popular institutions, without
serious disturbance of law and order.'

I quote another nobleman—a most estimable man too—a man
who has done in his time great justice to the people and the
institutions of the United States—the Earl of Carlisle.   Eight
years ago, when the state of America was fresh in his mind,
he delivered a lecture, from which I have taken two extracts.
Speaking of their elections, he says :—

'Elections may seem the universal business, the topic and passion of life ;
but these are, at least with but few exceptions, carried on without any
approach to tumult, rudeness, or disorder ; those which I happened to see
were the most sedate, unimpassioned processes I can imagine.   In the Free
States, at least, the people at large bear an active, and I believe, on the
whole, a useful part in all the concerns of internal government and practical
daily life.'

And then speaking of the condition of the people he said—
and you will know how far it corroborates, how far it exceeds
even, what I said :—

'The feature which is the most obvious and, probably, the most inevitable,
is the nearly entire absence, certainly of the appearance, in a great degree of
the reality, of poverty.   In no part of the world, I imagine, is there so much
general comfort amongst the great bulk of the people ; and a gushing abundance struck me as the permanent character of the land.'

And then with his own generous sympathy, he went on to
say :—

'It is not easy to describe how far this consideration goes to brighten the
face of nature, and give room for its undisturbed enjoyment.'

I cannot, of course, help the fact that Lord Carlisle for a
moment has fallen into rather a foolish panic since I undertook to address my constituents at Birmingham.   I can assure
him I do not wish to introduce American institutions here.
But I want to argue this point—that the people of England
are now in a condition wherein it would be just to them, and

safe for all classes in the country, that they should be widely
entrusted with the possession of the elective franchise.

Now I want to ask you, before I sit down, whether we
can realise, or whether we can do anything towards realising,
such a project of reform as that of which I have given you
the very faintest sketch to-night? There is a danger awaiting
us. It is quite possible, I think it is not wholly improbable,
if the present Government should introduce a Bill very
ineffectual, wholly falling short of what we have a right to
expect, that there should be some combination of the most
unworthy portion of the Whig party with the present Government, for the sake of carrying that Bill. It would be
a great misfortune to us if any such thing should happen.
But that misfortune would be but temporary. It would be
a fatal act on the part of the Whig party to take any such
course as that. They would bring about this great result,—
that the aristocracy who were wholly opposed to free Parliaments in this country, would sit on one side of the House,
and that we, who may be considered of the more Democratic
party, would take our seats on the other side of the House.
But I will undertake to say that if that division should once
take place in Parliament, every election would increase the
power of the Democratic section; and that the remembrance
of the treason to the people which would be effected by
conduct such as this would create an animosity towards the
ruling class, against which I believe they would be wholly
unable to contend.

I have come to the conclusion of the observations I intended to offer you upon these questions. Of myself I must
add one or two words. My position in reference to this
question is just now, as you know, one of heavy responsibility. I feel it to be so. I know it to be so. I have
been requested by those who believed they represented a
large amount of public opinion, to undertake the preparation
of a Bill to be submitted to the House of Commons during

the coming session. I have not sought the office. I did everything I could to decline it, without being guilty of an absolute desertion of what appeared to be my duty. I am told—some that are not friends of mine and some that are my friends tell me—that I hazard whatever little reputation I have with the public in taking this course. If it be so, I can only say that the creation or the sustaining of a reputation has never been the great motive in my political life. I have said before, and every day I am more sensible of it, how ill qualified I am, in many respects, for the work which I have undertaken, and I am more and more sensible of the almost insurmountable obstacles which lie in the path before me. But I know that the cause is a just cause. I know that its success is necessary to the great future of this country; and I am perfectly certain that, sooner or later, it must prevail. From this platform I do not speak to you only—I speak to all my countrymen. If they wish for Reform,—if they think me honest, informed, capable on this question—if they have any confidence in those with whom I am associated,—then let them meet in their cities, their towns, their villages,—in country parishes even, where free speech is not forbidden,—let them meet and speak; let them resolve, and let them petition. If they do this, I think I can promise them that before long they will be in full possession and in free exercise of those political rights, which are not more necessary to their national interests than they are consistent with the principles of their boasted Constitution.

REFORM.

III.

GLASGOW, DECEMBER 21, 1858.

[Mr. Bright visited Scotland, and spoke at Edinburgh and Glasgow in the
winter of 1858, on the subject of Parliamentary Reform. At the same time
he drew up a Bill, for the amendment of the representation, the main
features of which were—the borough franchise was conferred on all who
were rated to the relief of the poor, and on all lodgers who paid a rent of
ten pounds; no more freemen were to be created; and the county franchise
was reduced to 10*l*. rental. The Bill put the returning officer's expenses on
the county or borough rate; prescribed that votes should be taken by
ballot; disfranchised fifty-six English, twenty-one Scotch, and nine Irish
boroughs; and took away one Member from thirty-four other boroughs.
The seats obtained by these disfranchisements were to be distributed according to population among the larger towns, counties, and divisions of counties
in the United Kingdom. The Bill was not brought into Parliament, but
the provisions of it were well known, and discussed at the time.]

WHEN I look upon these great meetings, at several of which
I have been permitted recently to be present, I cannot help
asking myself, What is the question—what is the matter—
which appears to be stirring to their very innermost depths
the hearts of my countrymen? Is it some sudden frenzy,
some fanaticism which wise men must rather be sorry for
than rejoice over? Is it some phantom which you pursue
and never overtake? Judging by the looks of expectation and

hope—even of assurance of success—which light up the countenances of so many before me, I must believe you have at least some great and worthy object which has brought us together. I believe no more worthy object can assemble the citizens of any free nation; for here we are met to discuss the great question of Constitutional Reform, and to consider how far it may be possible to confirm and give greater permanence and security to whatsoever portion of liberty we have derived from our forefathers. Let me remind you that when you discuss questions connected with the House of Commons, you are discussing that branch of the Legislature which is far the most important to liberty—without which, in fact, liberty cannot exist. You may have liberty with a monarchy, as you have in this country, but you may have a monarchy without liberty, as you see in many other countries of Europe. You may have liberty, as we have here, even with a portion of the legislative power in the hand of hereditary legislators; but you might have hereditary legislators and no liberty whatever. But that branch of the Legislature which we are about to discuss is not only consistent with the existence of liberty, but it is inseparable in this country from the existence of liberty.

One of the greatest men, one of the brightest names in the muster-roll of English worthies — the illustrious founder of the colony and province of Pennsylvania—gives this definition of freedom. He says, ' That is a free country where the laws rule, and where the people are parties to the making of the laws.' And we are assembled to-night, I hope, in the full understanding of the magnitude of the question before us, and with the resolve in our hearts that we will, if we can, by the extension and improvement of our representative system, confirm and secure permanently, as far as lies in our power, that which is the greatest guarantee of freedom which we in this country possess. Now, in the discussion of this question, we are in a very different position from that in which we

found ourselves when I was here before. It is generally con-
ceded that the figures are all on our side. You recollect that,
twelve or fourteen years ago, there were orators almost innumerable going about the country—there were some scores of
them—who attacked us with figures without end on the policy
of Protection. I do not intend to dig up these from the
oblivion which the orators themselves now wish they should
be buried in, but I turn to them for the purpose of pointing
out that nobody gets up to tell us, and to prove from the
multiplication table, that the people are fairly represented in
the House of Commons.

But there is one charge brought against us that it is difficult
to escape from. I am told that I use the same figures and
facts in my various speeches. What should I be told if I used
different figures and facts each time I spoke? It is the same
case and the same grievance, and I speak to men of the
same order on each occasion, and who are to be appealed to
and roused by the same facts and statements, and therefore
I cannot be expected to say something wholly different to
that which I have said on other occasions. For instance, if
I tell you that the whole body of electors of the United
Kingdom amounts only to one-sixth portion of the whole
adult men of the United Kingdom, and if I tell you that
one-sixth of these electors—that is, one thirty-sixth of the
adult men of the United Kingdom—return more than one-
half of the Members of the House of Commons, I shall find it
difficult to convey a clear idea of that fact, unless I make
that statement; and although I may grieve our terrible critics,
who watch over everything which I say, yet I am bound to
explain this matter to my countrymen, wherever I meet them,
and whenever they are willing to hear. Putting that statement into another form, we have at least six millions of grown
men in the United Kingdom, yet we have not more than one
million who have votes, and I find by the Parliamentary
returns that 200,000 electors of that million return more than

half of the Members who sit in the House of Commons.   The
fact is, that it is easy to show that the electoral body is so
grouped and managed, and the whole machine is so ingeniously contrived, that almost the whole objects for which
such an assembly should exist are frustrated under the system
which prevails among us.

There is another illustration which has occurred to me.   I
have imagined that all the men over twenty-one years of age
of the United Kingdom were assembled on Salisbury Plain,
or, not to go so far, in some wild and desolate part of your
own country, although I should hesitate to take you there
even in imagination, for fear we should be charged with
disturbing those sacred animals, the grouse and the deer.
But for the sake of this illustration, we will imagine ourselves
so assembled, and that the framers of our Parliamentary
arrangements address these six millions of men, and say to
five millions of them—comprising almost the whole body of
the working classes, and a large portion of the middle classes
—they say to them, 'We don't want you, you may return to
your homes, and then we who are left will do your business
for you.'   Well, there would remain a million who would
compose the electoral body.   Let us make another separation.
Take all the boroughs which compose the metropolis of the
kingdom, seven great boroughs, and their seven great constituencies; then add to them the constituencies of the seven
next largest boroughs—Liverpool, Glasgow, Manchester, Birmingham, Leeds, Dublin, and Edinburgh.   It would require
you to take 200,000 from this million to form the constituencies of London and the other great constituencies.   And
when you have formed them, you would find they were
permitted to return thirty Members to the English Parliament.   But in another part of the plain you find 200,000
men taken out of the group, and they are permitted to
return one hundred and twenty-six Members to the House
of Commons.

We see at a glance that although Parliament must do something when it is sitting, and must pass, sometimes bad and sometimes good measures, and the good ones with difficulty, we cannot but be sensible that, not as a machine for carrying out views on particular questions, but for sustaining the character of the country in the Legislature, it would be impossible to devise any plan more clumsy and more untrustworthy with reference to the purpose for which it exists. Those boroughs which I have mentioned, namely, Manchester and the other seven great cities, have a population of nearly 3,000,000, and yet they only return thirty Members to the House of Commons. Of these 200,000 electors you have not heard the last. You do not know so much of it in Scotland as we do in England. Those 200,000 we left together are in groups, and are scattered up and down the country—many in Ireland—very many in England—with constituencies as low as eighty-six in number, and others, a considerable number, with two hundred and three hundred electors. The bulk of these have only a small body of electors compared with the large towns and constituencies. Now, when you have a small number of men together they can hardly keep themselves warm, and they cannot preserve their independence; and the nobles or landholders, and two or three lawyers, or two or three anybodies, who choose to combine and act with a fair amount of unity and subtlety, will control the representation of these small boroughs—and the Members who go up to the House of Commons from them are often, and generally, not earnest men, not anxious to carry out any great public principle, or any principle at all; for the House of Commons is a convenient club, and a nice lounge, and affords a pleasant means of filling up their time; and the most of them being men of no business, they still want something respectable to be engaged in, that they may pretend not to be absolutely idle.

Well, it follows from all this that the general result of

what we call our Parliamentary representation is not found efficient as the guard of our national interests. It does not respond with any heartiness or any willingness to the aspirations of the people for better government, but it is found to be in sympathy—not with you, but—with the ruling class, and is infinitely more careful to preserve monopolies and privileges than the general rights of the great body of the nation.

But to-morrow morning, somebody who is probably now, or will soon be sitting pen in hand, will say, with a show of reason, that I am arguing entirely upon the question of the magnitude of populations. That is not true; but still he may assert, that, in a country like this, numbers simply should not decide this great question, and he will say that property ought to be taken into consideration as well as population. Well, let us test the worth of that appeal. Take your two foremost cities, and compare them with other cities which enjoy an unfair share of the representation. Let us take your two cities of Edinburgh and Glasgow. I have the taxable property of these two cities. Take Schedule A of the income and property tax, which means lands and buildings, things which you can see, and take Schedule D, which means profits on trades and the income of professions—then the taxable property of these two cities is 7,800,000*l.*, leaving out odd sums. There are one hundred and one boroughs in Great Britain and Ireland, whose taxable property is 7,434,000*l.*, some 350,000*l.* less than the taxable property of Edinburgh and Glasgow. But, then, which has most of the representation? The larger amount of that taxable property returns altogether only four Members to the House of Commons, and those other boroughs, with the smaller amount of taxable property, no less than one hundred and twenty-six Members to that House. Let me make this explanation on the Bill which Lord John Russell, acting in Lord Aberdeen's Government, brought before Parliament in 1854, and which did not become law. He proposed to disfranchise all boroughs with populations less than 5000, and where the number of electors was less than three hundred. Now, I believe if the line is drawn at 7000, it will leave this amazing disparity, that 7,800,000*l.* of taxable property will be represented by four Members, and that a smaller amount of taxable property will be still represented by one hundred and twenty-six Members in the present House of Commons. Take another illustration on that point, namely, the annual sums paid by the people of Edinburgh and Glasgow in taxes, including income-tax and property-tax in the two Schedules referred to ; including also house-duty, assessed taxes, land-tax, and the whole of those direct taxes paid by the population of Edinburgh and Glasgow,—the amount is 556,000*l.*, represented by four Members ; while the sum which the one hundred and twenty-six Members represent in the annual direct taxes paid by their constituents is 568,000*l.*, being 11,000*l.* more than is paid by the populations of Edinburgh and Glasgow. In short, my investigations lead me to this conclusion, that whether we take numbers, or industry and wealth, or what we comprehend as political independence—I do not care by what test you try it—you come to the same startling, the same impressive result, that these great populations and great interests are most inadequately represented in the House of Commons under our present system of representation.

Well, having got thus far, we must have a change ; and the question is, what change ? I have a great suspicion of those men who profess great anxiety for something to be done, but who constantly assail those who are attempting to do something. You are aware that less than two months ago I had the privilege of addressing on two occasions very large meetings of the constituency of Birmingham. You remember the howl of astonishment which arose. I do not complain of the Tory papers, because they are labouring in their always unsuccessful vocation ; but of that which

was set up by papers calling themselves Liberal, but which
are written by men who seem to be manacled by the triumph
of 1832, but who are not so far advanced now as at the
time of the Reform Bill. I say to any of you who read
leading articles, and who invariably believe them—and I
have not the slightest doubt that this kind of faith may be
prevalent among some here—it is impossible, I believe, for
anybody to compare the speech at Birmingham with that
at Manchester, or the two speeches with the speech in
Edinburgh, and to discover the slightest possible, abandonment of any one single sentiment that I uttered on the first
occasion. Do these men suppose that I have the effrontery
to stand before many thousands of my countrymen, after days
and weeks of notice that I am to appear before them, and
that I come, then, to speak merely the temper, the passion,
and the sentiments of the hour? They little know, if they
dream of this, the sense of responsibility under which, I think,
every man should speak who offers himself on any occasion
as the expounder of the opinions, or to be the guide of the
deliberations, of his countrymen.

Nearly thirty years ago the sentiments that I have uttered
upon this great question of Parliamentary Reform were proclaimed to thousands of our countrymen by Lord Durham.
My opinions with regard to the franchise are not novel.
I stated in Manchester that they were but the opinions
which Mr. Fox and Lord Grey proposed to the House of
Commons in 1797. I am no conjuror, I have no specific
for national happiness, I offer you nothing made up of
conundrums and tricks, but I bring before you what I believe to be a rational and substantial project for the arrangement of our representation, which, I venture to say, has had,
during the last sixty years, the sanction and approval of many
of the greatest minds and of the greatest patriots of our
country. Well, then, what is this change which is to swamp
everybody, and that men stand aghast at? Is it that the

elective franchise, which is now, both in England and Scotland, confined, in boroughs, to occupiers of a house valued
at 10*l*., should be lowered so as to take in, in reality, all the
persons who are householders and occupiers of premises which
are rated to the relief of the poor? Your system of rating
is much more modern in Scotland than ours in England, but
I learn that, with two or three inconsiderable exceptions, it is
now become uniform throughout the whole of your country.
The main reason that I propose this franchise is this. Unfortunately in this country—I mean in Great Britain and Ireland
—there is a very large class, which constantly requires the
assistance of their fellow-men. There must needs be levied
throughout the kingdom, a rate that does not amount to less
—at least, in 1856, it amounted to more—than the enormous
sum of 7,000,000*l*., raised for the express purpose of giving
relief to the poor. Now, I think there is not one of your
artisans who, in his walk of life, works hard from morning till
night, six days in the week, who may have heavy demands at
home in his own family, who is called upon to perform all the
duties of citizenship, who is called upon also to contribute
from his own earnings to the support of some feeble, some
sick, it may be some dissolute and profligate man, who is not
able to support himself,—I think there is not one of these who
is thus called upon to be taxed on his weekly and annual
earnings for such purposes, that has not some claim to be
considered a citizen, and to be admitted to the rights of
citizenship.

I have been attacked, I am told—for I have not had time
to read half of the attacks which I understand have been
made upon me—I have been attacked as having been guilty
of misrepresentation in stating the custom in England with
regard to the question of the franchise. I have said that in
England, in our parochial government, in Poor-law Unions,
and in our municipal governments, the system of rating forms
the basis of the elective franchise; and I could see no reason

why it should not also form the basis of the franchise in the election of Members of Parliament. I am told that with regard to Poor-law Unions, and in some cases of parishes, but not universally, there is a mode of voting by which men give votes somewhat in proportion to their property in the parish; where one man can give one vote, and another four or six votes. This is not very pleasant, wherever it is practised, to those having a smaller number of votes; but the defence and the pretended justification of it is that this is a question of expenditure in the immediate locality, in the making of roads, in a variety of objects which are required to be attended to by our various local governments, and that it might possibly end in throwing a great inequality of expenditure and taxation upon a particular number, or on a few individuals in parishes or districts: but when you come to the question of Parliamentary Reform, where not only taxes are to be considered, but interests and personal rights, and not taxes only and personal rights only, but all questions affecting the great policy of the country both at home and abroad, I say it would be to cast a most deadly and ineradicable insult upon the working classes of this country if anybody, for one single moment, urged that I should propose to give six votes at the poll for a Member of Parliament, while an operative at my side should be only allowed to give one vote. Until you are prepared to do full justice to the great portion of the unenfranchised classes, I would advise you to allow matters to remain as they are. I am sure that opinion is growing, intelligence is growing, power is growing, combination is growing, and before long it will be seen to be the interest of all those who value the tranquillity of the country and the contentment of the people, that political rights should be widely and honestly distributed among all classes of our countrymen.

There is one other question of the suffrage which, I believe, I have never yet touched upon in any preceding speech, that is, with regard to the possibility of conferring the franchise, in some shape or other, upon those who are not householders, and are not rated, but are what are called lodgers. In England we have no such franchise; in Scotland you have. A person may live in lodgings, for which he pays, when unfurnished, the sum of 10*l*. per annum, which is the rental required for houses to give a vote. In such a case that lodger can claim to have his name put upon the register, and I am told that in Edinburgh about thirty persons are enrolled who are in that condition. If that be so, I suppose there cannot be a difficulty in reducing the sum to some smaller amount, which shall become in some degree accordant with the principle of a general franchise, so based as to place persons of this description on the electoral register.

We come now to the question of the county franchise, in which we have in England a great advantage over you in Scotland. Here the limit is a 10*l*. property and a 50*l*. occupation franchise; but in England we have freehold franchise as low as 40*s*. a-year. I think he would be a most fastidious mortal indeed who thought that the constitution of the British Empire and the safety of anybody would, in the smallest degree, be jeopardised by extending the 40*s*. franchise to Scotland.

One has to go with remarkable precision over the various topics of this great question, for if, by any chance, I say any-thing that is not fully explained, it is sure to be explained in a manner favourable to some inconsistency, and if any point is omitted it is generally insinuated that I have seen reason to change my opinions. In Edinburgh, my voice was very bad and the room was densely crowded, and I was anxious not to make a long speech, and I said nothing on the question of the Ballot. It was instantly supposed that I did not hold the same opinions in Edinburgh that I did in Manchester and Birmingham. We will not altogether leave out the Ballot to-night. If the franchise in your boroughs be reduced so much as to double the whole number of your electors, and if it be reduced so much in your counties as to increase by, probably, more than one-half all the number of electors in those counties, I think, if there be any call now for the adoption of the Ballot, that call will be more strong and imperative after such a change in the franchise has been made. I am quite certain that in the district I came from, the county of Lancaster, there is but one opinion on this point amongst the great body of those persons who are hoping, by any Reform Bill, to be admitted within the pale of the Constitution of this country. I think that they would to a very large extent implore the House of Commons not to confer upon them the right of the franchise, unless they conferred upon them also the power which, I believe, the Ballot alone would give them, of exercising that franchise in accordance with their own convictions.

I cannot comprehend why any man should oppose the Ballot. I can understand its importance being exaggerated, but I cannot understand the man who thinks it would be likely to inflict injury upon the country. Every good influence, every legitimate influence, would still exist. The rich man would still be rich and would still be powerful; in the nature of things it must be so. The educated man, the intellectual man, the benevolent man, the man of religious and saintly life, would continue to exercise a most beneficent influence, which the Ballot, I believe, would not in the slightest degree impair; but the influence of the landlord, of the creditor, of the customer—the influence of the strong and unscrupulous mind over the feeble and the fearful — that influence would be as effectually excluded as I believe it could be by any human contrivance whatsoever.

But there is another aspect of the question of the Ballot, which I think is more important than its political one, that is, its moral aspect. How would canvassing be conducted under the Ballot? I do not know how you conduct the canvassing of electors in this great city; I suppose it is not accurately conducted at all; but I will tell you how it is managed in small and moderate boroughs in England. The candidate goes to see as many electors as possible. In calling on any particular elector, the canvassers endeavour to find out his employer, his landlord, some one who has lent him money, or done a kindness to some of his friends, or who has some influence over him, and half a dozen meet together, and though there may be nothing said, the elector knows very well there is somebody in that small number who has done him a benefit for which he expects a return, somebody who has power over him and who expects to be obeyed, and while the object is professedly that of a canvass, it is little better than a demonstration of force and tyranny. Every man who, for want of the Ballot, votes contrary to his convictions, is a demoralized and degraded man. If not so before, he would feel it necessary, for the sustaining of his character, that he should turn round and belie the principles that he has up to that moment held and declared—and assert that he holds contrary principles now, and therefore did not vote against the convictions of his conscience. There is no portion—I can assure this meeting there is not one of the propositions for Reform that have been submitted to the public—there is no other portion that is received with such unanimity, such enthusiasm of resolution, throughout all the meetings in England, as the proposition that the Ballot shall form a portion of the coming Reform.

We come now to that question which, after all, is more difficult than any to which I have referred, and much more difficult of obtaining or carrying through Parliament— viz. the determination as to the mode in which Members shall in future be allotted to electors and constituencies. I presume that any Reform Bill will draw some line, and below that line will disfranchise a number of boroughs, assuming their population to be too small, and the number of electors too limited, and the interests too circumscribed, to justify them in returning a Member to Parliament, and the more

of these boroughs that are thus cut off, the larger number
of members or seats will Parliament have to distribute
among other constituencies.   Now, what shall be done
with such a borough as Glasgow?   Are you content to go
on with your brethren in Edinburgh, with a population
approaching to half a million—will you go on contentedly
returning only four Members to the House of Commons to
represent your vast and annually increasing interests and population, whilst a population no greater than yours shall return, as the case may be, fifty, eighty, or a hundred Members
elsewhere?   You are not the lovers of freedom I take you to
be—you do not understand the question as well as I am
satisfied you do—you have not resolved to brace yourselves
up for this great contest, as I hope this night you will—if
you are content to go on in the same condition of things
under which you have been for some time past.   I am not
about to state what I think is the limit that ought to
be taken.   Lord John Russell would not continue representation to boroughs with a population under 5,000.
Others have proposed that in the case of boroughs with
a population under 10,000 they should be merged in the
counties, and the electors in boroughs become electors in
counties,—which would be a vast improvement to the
county representation.   I will leave this point, for I believe
that with regard to my Bill it is not a settled question,
and I do not know the intentions of the Government or
of anybody else who may take a prominent part in introducing any measure to the House of Commons and the
country.

Now, bear in mind, it is possible to make great changes in
the representation without the smallest improvement.   At
a dinner you may go from one bad dish to another; you
may go from one unpleasant street to another, from one
unprofitable business to another; you may make a very
important change in respect to the franchise without any

sensible relief; and it is precisely thus we˜ must warn each other about these points of Reform, because it is quite possible that the Government, hampered by their own prejudices and dispositions, hampered by their followers, and conscious that there are some of their opponents who do not want much Reform; it is quite possible that Government may attempt a measure which, while seeming to reform, will leave the state of the representation quite as unsatisfactory as at present. Thus, I maintain, there can be no Reform except on such, or on something like the basis which I have endeavoured to lay down; and I state this the more particularly because I am anxious that all my countrymen who have not investigated the question shall, when any measure is really before them, be in a condition to form an intelligent opinion of it At present the great body of the working classes of the country are excluded, and I have shown you, from the mode in which electors are crippled and managed, that the great body of the middle classes, if not excluded, are so arranged that they may be said to be almost altogether defrauded. I want to know why the working classes and the middle classes—and I wish we had no such terms, or that we had some better terms, but I mean by them all those persons who compose the vast population of the country below the great privileged and titled classes of society—I want to know why they should not all unite fairly in behalf of the great measure of political Reform to which we are looking forward? Depend upon it a real measure of Reform is as much wanted for the security and for the welfare of the middle classes of society as it is for the operative classes.

There is a great attempt constantly made to frighten the middle classes. They are told that working-men will not be inclined to listen to the advice of those above them in condition, circumstances, and education. Some of you recollect forty years ago, when such a thing as a public political meeting could not be held in Scotland. The ruling classes then held that political meetings were dangerous, that they were absolutely treasonable, that public tranquillity and the security of Government were impossible if Englishmen and Scotchmen were permitted to meet and discuss public affairs. But Reform was carried, and after many years' experience of it, we find that public tranquillity is more firmly established now than at any former period of the history of this country. Twenty-seven years ago the Reform Bill passed. What said the great peers then, some of whom appear to have been recently startled from their somnolent security? What did they say? They said the King's Government could not be carried on, and that from the time when that moderate but great measure of Reform was passed there would be an end of the greatness and glory of this powerful nation. But what has been the result? Every one of these predictions has been utterly falsified. Twelve or fourteen years ago, when I was here last, what did they tell us of that simple measure of the repeal of the Corn-laws? One great Peer told us that he should leave the country; and one of the labourers who was at the meeting asked, would his lordship take his land along with him? And we are told that not agriculture alone, but manufactures, and all the commerce of the country would be crippled if not destroyed, and that your splendid river, bearing the leviathans of noble architecture constructed on its banks, would return to its former state of a small and pleasant stream,—and, I suppose, that men could catch trout and salmon from the bridge that crossed it. This kind of argument is what Jeremy Bentham has happily described as the hobgoblin argument, a great trick now-a-days to frighten people, lest they should do themselves some good.

Yet to the middle classes—to you, who twenty-seven years ago were pronounced utterly unworthy of the franchise, to you they now say, 'You are the bulwark of our

constitution.' You can live in a 10*l.* house, but if you
go below to 9*l.*, if you go to 8*l.*, if you go to 7*l.*, the
case is considered bad, but it becomes more desperate at
6*l.* and 5*l.*, and the rating franchise is positively revolutionary. I confess I do not believe this. The number
of electors under this rating franchise has been very
much exaggerated by those who have not examined it. It
was stated at a meeting in Edinburgh the other night, by
a gentleman whose authority will not be disputed, that the
franchise that I propose would raise the number of electors
in Edinburgh from 8,000 to nearly 17,000. I presume
that in your city you have a greater population than Edinburgh has; but whatever it be, I am satisfied that if we
are to take any step, if we are ever to change our represcutation, I say to every man of the middle classes, to every
man who wishes for the stability of institutions,—I say,
let us treat the great body of the population with a magnanimous generosity; that our fellow-countrymen of twenty
years hence may make an unanimous acknowledgment that
generosity in the year 1859 was the path of true statesmanship and of wisdom.

But I observe in some newspaper, I am not sure whether it
was one in your city,—it is said that I have failed to show to
the working classes how giving them a vote could be of the
smallest advantage to them. I believe that it would be of
one advantage to them in the way of raising their self-respect.
I have seen thousands of men who have no votes, at the nomination of candidates, attending polling-booths, with looks of
great anxiety, and often with looks of great dejection. I
believe that if the major part of those men were enfranchised,
the effect upon their minds and morals and general condition
would be obvious and signal. The great secret of raising any
man who has been brought up to what may be called the
inferior occupations of life, is to find out something to
increase his self-respect. If a man becomes possessed with

that feeling—if a man sees any way among his fellow-workmen, and in your numerous societies, benevolent or otherwise, by which he can make himself of use—you will at once see the change in the character of the man, and that what was before either stupid or low in his nature seems to be removed or diminished, and you will find that the man has become wiser, and nobler, and happier. I believe that when you admit the general body of our artisans upon the roll of electors, when they can not only attend nominations and hold up their hands and cheer for the successful or the popular candidate, but can also go one by one to the polling-booth, and register their votes for the man who shall represent the great interests of Glasgow ; my honest, conscientious opinion is, that you will do as much to raise their self-respect, to give them at least the rudiments and elements of the higher class of citizenship, as you can do by all the other means that you now have in operation with a view of improving the condition of the working classes.

But there are other results that will come to this country in case you ever obtain a fair representation of the people. I have been in Scotland a good deal for the last three or four years, and often before then. I have found, in travelling over your country, that your land is not the land of the people of Scotland, but that it is in a position—in a manner exclusive—which is not found to be the case with regard to any other property. It is found in the possession —in comparison to the whole body of the people—of a small handful of proprietors. Let no man say that I am about to assail any landed proprietors in Scotland. I have received many courtesies from them, and not a few courtesies from the most eminent and distinguished among them ; I speak only of the system which arises from a Legislature that is diametrically opposed to all the great principles of political economy, which we and you struggled for so many years to place on our statute books in the shape of a wiser legislation in matters of

trade. Land is the basis of your industry. Is there any
reason why land should not be as free as machinery, or ships,
or household furniture, or cattle, or the goods and manufactures in your warehouses ? If freedom be the law of right
and of wisdom with respect to all these kinds of property,
how should the reverse of freedom be any other than the law
of mischief and injury when applied to land ? You may
travel—I was going to say, 'from the rising of the sun to
the going down thereof'—on some single estate in Scotland,
north or south, east or west—wherever you go you ask whose
land you are on, and you are told that it belongs to some
marquis or some duke. They are happy mortals, it will
be said, who possess this great territory; and so, probably, they would be, if it were possible for any man, however well disposed, to adequately answer the responsibilities
which such possessions lay upon him. You find on these vast
estates very few tenants, and generally very few of an agricultural population at all. There is little social freedom, there
is little industrial freedom, and there is still less political freedom in districts such as those which I am describing. I do not
know very well how men can breathe freely when they find
themselves continually on a soil not one morsel of which
they can call their own, or can ever hope to call their own,
until they take their last long sleep in that portion of it
which shall finally be allotted to them.

I am no advocate for a law to force the division of land.
I do not want any landlord to be compelled to have a greater
or smaller number of tenants; but I say that the system of
legislation in regard to primogeniture, and on entails and
settlements, which is intended to keep vast estates in one
hand through successive generations, to prevent that economical disposition and change of property which is found
so advantageous in every other kind of property—I say
this state of things is full of the most pernicious consequences, not only to the agricultural classes, but to all

other classes of our countrymen, since all are affected by it.
I recollect one evening seeing a farmer ride away from
an hotel in the Highlands, and I asked his name. I was
told that he was a farmer in some neighbouring glen,
where he had a prodigious farm; and my informant said
that there were once fourteen good farms on what is now
one farm, and that each of the fourteen families always
managed to send at least one of its sons to obtain a first-
class University education. Now, I do not want any law
to strip that one farmer of his farm; but the law which
interferes with the free course of transactions in land,
which multiplies and keeps up these vast estates, which
gives to one man power over a whole territory, whereby
he has at his disposal tenant and labourer alike, is not
such a law as is consistent with that freedom to which
the people of England and Scotland are entitled. Your
agricultural labouring population have no chance of rising
in the world. They can come to Glasgow, as scores of
thousands of men have come from the Highlands and from
Ireland, or, forced by the unfavourable circumstances in
which they find themselves, they may become exiles from
their native country, and form colonies in the far Pacific, or
beyond the wide Atlantic.   But I think we are bound as free
men—and we townsmen are especially bound, for we only
have the power to take the initiative in this great question—
we are bound, so far as we are able, by our representatives in
Parliament (and I have no doubt it will be one of the couse-
quences of a real Reform Bill), to apply those great principles
of political economy, which are the gospel and the charter of
industry, as fully to property in land as we have already
applied them to property engaged in trade.

There is another point to which I must call your attention
in answer to the question, ' What is the good which the
working classes, or any other class, can hope for from a wide
extension of the franchise ? '   Now there is one great question

over which the public has no great hold, and that is the question of the public expenditure. The present Chancellor of the Exchequer, Mr. Disraeli, an eminent member of the House of Commons, a leading member of the Government, and a man of genius, whose present position, I must say, is a proclamation to the world of the incompetency of the Conservative aristocracy and country gentlemen of the United Kingdom; and, what is still more to be remarked, is an evidence of the humility which adorns their character in thus admitting it,—Mr. Disraeli said, on more than one recent occasion, that expenditure depended on policy—by which he meant that our public expenditure depended on our foreign policy. Now, our past foreign policy has been of a very questionable character. It has entailed upon us the permanent payment, from which there is no honourable escape, of a sum of 28,000,000*l.* per annum; and our present foreign policy, and matters connected with it, involve us in the present payment of 22,000,000*l.* per annum for our great military and naval preparations and expenses. I am not about for a moment to discuss the question, whether our foreign policy has been, or is now, good, bad, or indifferent, because that does not very much affect the question to which I wish to call your attention. In our home affairs we have a very open system of government. If the Home Office is about to do anything, somebody hears of it, and somebody approves of it, or somebody objects to it. In all matters connected with our personal freedom, with the administration of justice, in all things which may be called internal, we have the freest opportunity of obtaining information, expressing our opinion, and enforcing our views on the Government.

But when you come to our foreign policy, you are no longer Englishmen; you are no longer free; you are recommended not to inquire. If you do, you are told you cannot understand it; you are snubbed, you are hustled aside. We are told that the matter is too deep for common understandings like ours—

that there is great mystery about it.   We have what is called
diplomacy.   We have a great many lords engaged in what
they call diplomacy.   We have a lord in Paris, we have
another in Madrid, another in Berlin, another (at least we
had till very lately) in Vienna, and another lord in Constantinople ; and we have another at Washington ; in fact, almost
all over the world ; particularly where the society is most
pleasant, and the climate most agreeable, there is almost
certain to be an English nobleman to represent the English
Foreign Office, but you never know what he is doing.
You have three or four columns every other day in most
of the leading London papers—not a little of which is
copied into the provincial journals—all about our foreign
affairs, and yet, notwithstanding this, you are not a bit better
acquainted with the matter when you read it, if you do read
it at all, than you were before.   Yet you have the great fact,
that you have paid 28,000,000*l.* a-year for more than forty
years, and, since the year 1815, more than 1,000,000,000*l.*
out of the industry of the population.   And out of all this
comes the supposed necessity of armaments twice as large as
were necessary twenty-five years ago ; and yet you have no
control over, and know nothing of the matter.   There is not
a population equal to this in Russia, Austria, or France, that
knows less of the foreign affairs of any of those countries than
this meeting probably knows of the foreign affairs of England.

Lately, our Minister for Foreign Affairs was candid enough
to tell you that Government drifted into war, and you know
what is meant when a ship drifts.   And other Foreign
Ministers have drifted us into a great many wars ; and I
expect, if some change be not made with regard to this question, that they will either find it convenient, or that they
cannot avoid it, from some cause or other, to allow us to drift
into a war at some future period.   I will not talk of what war
is—we have had a specimen of it.   Be it necessary or be it
unnecessary—be the quarrel just or be it unjust—be it for the

rights of the nation or to gratify the stupidity of a monarch or the intrigues of a minister—war, nevertheless, is one of the greatest calamities that can afflict any kingdom or the human race; and you, the people, are ignorant of the steps by which you are drawn into war. A Scotch Duke—and, by the way, rather a sprightly Duke he is too—lately took me to task for something that I had said. I had called in question the wisdom of the policy which compels this vast expenditure abroad, while the people of Ireland were working at one shilling a day for wages, and the people of your own Highlands were living upon three meals of oatmeal a day! What was the triumphant refutation of my argument? This only, that oatmeal was a most wholesome article of diet. If I had said that the Duke's dogs, at Inverary Castle, had been fed upon oatmeal three times a day, the answer would have been perfectly satisfactory.

But I am told further by these authorities, though the country does occasionally become involved in war, that the people desire it, that they are as fond of it as their rulers. Well, if the Peers did sorrow for the late war, they never told their grief. Are the people, are the nation, to have the blame of those calamities thrown upon them when they do occur? Who form your Cabinet? Not the merchants of Glasgow—not the shopkeepers nor the artisans—no, but the members of the peerage of the United Kingdom. Half of your Cabinets are formed from the House of Lords, and the other half from the House of Commons are so directly connected with the peerage that they may be regarded as belonging to that class. Do not let the conduct of public affairs remain with a few leading families, who enjoy all the emoluments and all the power; and when such an one as myself steps forward to point out the blunders they commit, and the crimes they are guilty of, if I tell them of the sufferings which my countrymen have endured, sufferings, the full measure of which never will be known or revealed to us, and which will be known only in eternity, do not let us have it said that the people are in favour of wars, when they have in reality so little to do with them.

It is a curious thing to observe the evils which nations live under, and the submissive spirit with which they yield to them. I have often compared, in my own mind, the people of England with the people of ancient Egypt, and the Foreign Office of this country with the temples of the Egyptians. We are told by those who pass up and down the Nile, that on its banks are grand temples with stately statues and massive and lofty columns, statues each one of which would have appeared almost to have exhausted a quarry in its production. You have, further, vast chambers, and gloomy passages ; and some innermost recess, some holy of holies, in which, when you arrive at it, you find some loathsome reptile which a nation reverenced and revered, and bowed itself down to worship. In our Foreign Office we have no massive columns ; we have no statues ; but we have a mystery as profound ; and in the innermost recesses of it we find some miserable intrigue, in defence of which your fleets are traversing every ocean, your armies are perishing in every clime, and the precious blood of our country's children is squandered as though it had no price. I hope that an improved representation will change all this ; that the great portion of our expenditure which is incurred in carrying out the secret and irresponsible doings of our Foreign Office will be placed directly under the free control of a Parliament elected by the great body of the people of the United Kingdom. And then, and not till then, will your industry be secured from that gigantic taxation to which it has been subjected during the last hundred and fifty years.

There is much in this country, notwithstanding, of which we may be proud. We can write freely, we can meet as we are met now, and we can speak freely of our political wishes and our grievances. The ruling classes, with a wise sagacity, have yielded these points without further struggle; but we are so delighted with our personal freedom, we are so pleased that we can move about without passports, and speak, write, and act as freely as a free man requires to do, we are so delighted with all this, that we are unconscious of the fact that our rulers extract from our industry a far larger amount than any other Government does, or ever did, from an equal number of people. Dr. Livingstone, the African traveller, if I am not mistaken, is a native of this neighbourhood, and you no doubt identify his reputation in some degree with your own. He gives, in his interesting and charming book, many anecdotes of the various creatures which he saw and heard of during his travels. He describes in one place, I remember, a bird, which he calls a dull, stupid bird, a kind of pelican, which occupies itself with its own affairs on the river side. This pelican catches fish, and when it has secured them it puts them into a pouch or purse under its bill, instead of the ordinary accommodation which anglers have in Scotland for their prizes. Dr. Livingstone tells of another bird which is neither dull nor stupid, which he calls the fish-hawk. This hawk hovers over the pelican, and waiting patiently until the latter has secured the fish, he comes down upon him with a swoop and takes the fish from the purse, leaving the pelican delighted that the hawk has not taken him bodily away, and setting to work at once to catch another fish.

I ask of you whether you can apply this anecdote to your own case? You are told that your Government is a Government which allows you to meet, and that it lets every man say anything short of absolute treason, at least in times of tranquillity; it permits your leading-article writers to denounce, at will, every member of the Government; and like the pelican, you are so delighted that you are not absolutely eaten up by it, that you allow it to extract from your pockets an incalculable amount of your industry, and you go to work just as the pelican does, until this great Government fish-hawk comes down again upon you. What I want is, that all the people should examine the question thoroughly for themselves. Rely upon it, your present and future welfare as a nation are bound up with it. Many persons suppose that because some people pay but little in the shape of taxation, that it matters nothing to them what taxes the Government imposes upon the nation. Every man who drinks tea, or consumes any exciseable articles, pays taxes; but apart from this view of the question, I would have you to understand that everything which the Government expends, supposing it was all to come from the employers' pocket, would be a diminution of that great fund of capital out of which wages were paid. Every man, therefore, whether he pays taxes or not—more so, of course, if he does—every man, if he is not mainly living upon the taxes, has a most direct interest in establishing that representation of the people that will give the nation a firm control over the expenditure of its money.

I have devoted many years of my life, I have spent much labour in advocating a greater freedom of the soil. I believe that it would work better and prove more profitable to the landed proprietors themselves. I think that free land, greater economy in the public expenditure, with the growing intelligence which we see all around us, and the improvement which is taking place in the most temperate habits of the people, all these things together fill me with the hope that whatever we have in the annals of the past of which we can boast, there is still a brighter future in store for this country. I come amongst you not to stir up animosity between class and class; that is the charge brought against me by men who wish that one class may permanently rule over every other class. I come amongst you that we may deliberate on those great questions on which our success and our prosperity depend. You know, at least if you do not know it I will tell you, that I am no frequenter of Courts. I have never sought for office or the emoluments of place.

I have no craving for popularity. I think I have little of that which may be called the lust for fame. I am a citizen of a free country. I love my country, I love its freedom; but I believe that freedom can only be extended and retained by a fair and honest representation of the people; and it is because I believe this, that I am here to-night to ask you, through the power of your intelligence and your numbers, to step into the position which now opens up before you.

REFORM.

IV.

LORD DERBY'S BILL.

HOUSE OF COMMONS, MARCH 24, 1859.

From Hansard.

[The Bill proposed by Lord Derby's Government in 1859 introduced certain 'fancy franchises' in boroughs, giving a vote to persons having 10*l*. per annum in the Public Funds, Bank Stock, or India Stock, or 6*cl*. in a Savings Bank; and to recipients of pensions in the Naval, Military, and Civil Services, amounting to 20*l*. a-year. Dwellers in a portion of a house whose aggregate rent was 20*l*. a-year could have a vote. The suffrage was also to be given to graduates of the Universities, ministers of religion, members of the legal and medical professions, and to certain schoolmasters. The Government recommended an identity of franchise in counties and boroughs, and therefore proposed to reduce the occupation franchise in counties to 10*l*. The Bill proposed the use of voting-papers, and the disfranchisement of such freeholders in towns as voted for counties. The Government Bill was defeated on April 1 by a majority of 39 (291 votes for the second reading, 330 against), and a dissolution followed.]

In the observations which I am anxious to address to the House I shall endeavour to keep myself strictly to the question before it. I shall not attempt any answer to some, perhaps well-intended, but rather feeble, assaults which have been made upon me during this debate, and I shall not attempt any explanation in answer to what was said by the hon. and learned Gentleman the Solicitor-General the other night when he spoke of an alliance between the noble Lord

(J. Russell) and myself. That which is purely imaginary is not easy to explain. The House I believe will give me credit when I say that if I am found acting with the noble Lord it is because I think the course he is taking is advantageous to the country, and I hope if I have hereafter occasion to differ from him they will give me credit also, and will presume that I differ from him only because my convictions lead me to do so.

There are two questions before us — the Bill of the Government and the resolution of the noble Lord, and in addition to these the great question of Parliamentary Reform, which has been more or less discussed by every Member who has addressed the House. With regard to the Bill there is a singular unanimity of feeling. With the exception of Gentlemen on the Treasury bench, who may be considered in the light of professional witnesses, I believe there is no single Member who has spoken who has not expressed strong repugnance to some main point or principle of the measure. A remarkable speech has been delivered by a right hon. Gentleman on this side of the House. He denounced the Bill as much as if he had been the greatest opponent of hon. Gentlemen opposite, but he was vehemently cheered by the other side of the House throughout almost the whole of that speech. Seeing that he turned the measure inside out, it was rather remarkable that his speech should be so relished by hon. Gentlemen opposite, and considering some of the observations which he made, the right hon. Gentleman certainly suggested a course the most extraordinary. He denounced the Bill as treason, not to the Crown, but to the people, and he proposed to inflict upon it something like the barbarous punishment with which our law, I believe, still visits those who are guilty of this great crime; and yet, after calling on the House to go with him in taking out the heart of the measure, and, for aught I know, in disembowelling it, he comforted himself with the belief that the Government would accept and assist in carrying the Bill.   He appeared to forget that the Government had parted with two eminent Colleagues on the very points of difference which he was discussing.   He seemed to forget that if the Chancellor of the Exchequer adopted this proposal he would lay himself open to the unfortunate suspicion that a suggestion, to which he would not consent at the instance of two of his late distinguished Colleagues, he would accept rather than have a vote of this House against the Government with the consequences which are likely to follow. I certainly was astonished that a man so acute as the right hon. Gentleman, after having spoken in such glowing language, and with an eloquence rarely heard in this House, of the priceless honour of our public men, should suggest such a course to the Government.

I shall not follow the right hon. Gentleman who has just spoken on the details of the Bill to the extent to which he has entered upon them.   I shall confine myself to the two principles which, after all, are at this stage of the Bill only before us, being brought specifically under discussion by the resolution proposed as an amendment by the noble Lord.   I should like to ask the House—because I think there is some disposition to evade this question — what is it that people understand by a measure of Parliamentary Reform?   I mean people out of doors, of whom hon. Gentlemen are likely to hear a good deal before this matter is settled.   They understand it should mean two things—first, an extension of the franchise to considerable classes, not now enfranchised; and, at the same time, that it should give to the country larger and freer and more independent constituencies.   Now, I want to ask how this Bill meets such a demand, because if it does not it is no Reform Bill, the Government had no right to propose it in answer to that demand, and the House of Commons will fail in its duty if it gives any countenance to such a measure, or passes it into a law.

In the counties at this moment, confining myself to

England and Wales, to which alone this Bill refers, there are, in round numbers, 500,000 electors, 400,000 of whom are freeholders and 100,000 occupying tenants above the value of 50*l*. Now, is there any doubt upon this point—that if any gentleman were asked to put his finger upon that description of elector in the counties which is most independent, he would say the freeholder; if upon the least independent, he would say of necessity the 50*l*. occupier? Without saying anything against tenant-farmers or the owners of farms themselves, I think this is a description which the House will admit to be fair. Well, the Bill proposes first of all to get rid from the counties of one-fourth, 100,000, of the most independent class, the freeholders. I am not now speaking of disfranchising them, but of getting rid of them from the counties, and mixing them up with another class of electors. Everybody will see at a glance that if 100,000 of the most independent class of electors are taken from the counties, the less independent class must necessarily be made more powerful.

The Bill makes, to my mind, another proposal of a most insidious character. The boundaries of boroughs are to be altered in a very remarkable fashion. The framers of the Bill seem to imagine that it is necessary for some object of theirs to include within the boundaries of boroughs every individual whom by any pretence they can lay hold of and separate from the county, if they suspect him to be infected with the prevalent opinions of the towns. By this means, of course, they would after the passing of their Bill diminish still more whatever there may be of the independent element in the county constituencies. But now observe the cunning—will right hon. Gentlemen forgive me the expression?—perhaps it was a mistake, like the disfranchisement of 50,000 men—observe the mistake, then, involved in the plan which is to be referred to our intelligent and impartial friend Mr. Darby. I understood that Mr. Darby, the head of the Enclosure Commission, is to appoint a Commission for this object.

The question, then, will be referred to him or to somebody. I will admit, if you like, that the Commission is as good as I or anybody in this House could wish. This Commission is not to examine the case of all boroughs. It is merely intended, as I understand it, to shut up within the borough boundaries all the suburbs of our cities and towns, and all immediately contiguous villages. But the Commissioners have no charge to go to another description of borough, and shut up the country parishes within the boundaries of counties. Now, surely, if it was a fair thing to go to any large town and say, 'All these streets and villages shall be comprised within the borough; none of these 10*l.* occupiers shall vote for the county,' it would be a fair thing to go to agricultural boroughs and to say, 'My good fellows, farmers, and so forth, in all these country parishes we are about to make a clear distinction—perpetual enmity between town and county; everybody near a town is to be shut into that town; you must be shut out of the borough, and into the county.'

I will tell the House what will be the result of the proposal in one or two cases. There are at this moment, within the limits of boroughs, farms the rental of which exceeds 2,500,000*l.*, and yet these are called boroughs. We will take the borough represented by the First Lord of the Admiralty. He will speak in this debate, and can correct me if I am wrong. In Droitwich there is an assessment to the income-tax under Schedule A of land and buildings to the amount of 56,000*l.* a-year, of which 39,600*l.* is an assessment of land and farms. There are four town parishes and twelve rural parishes. The town parishes contain one hundred and sixty electors, the rural two hundred and thirty-two electors. In point of fact, therefore, the right hon. Gentleman does not represent a town at all. No, the large majority of his supporters and constituents are farmers and persons as much connected with rural affairs as if they were in the centre of the county and

miles away from any towns or villages. I say, if this line is
to be drawn, it must be drawn in all cases. Take the case of
the borough of Petersfield, which is also represented by an
hon. Baronet on the Treasury bench. In that town the case
is still more glaring. There is 31,000*l.* assessed in land and
buildings in the borough, but of that, 24,000*l.*, or more than
four-fifths, is in respect of land and buildings in agricultural
parishes. I am not now complaining of those parishes being
added to the town; but the Government has no right to propose,
and Parliament will never pass, a Bill the only object of which
will be to shut as many as possible in the borough in the one
case, but not to interfere in the other, and thus to diminish
that great variety of suffrages and of interests which it is
desirable that every Member in this House shall represent.

The noble Lord the Secretary of State for India said with
regard to the great measure of disfranchisement, that it was
a mistake, and that he was sorry the clause was not originally
introduced into the Bill which was afterwards laid on the table
of the House by his hon. Friend. Again, the Secretary of
State for the Colonies, when he was charged with the faulty
character of the clause extending the 10*l.* franchise to counties,
made rather a staggering admission that this was also in the
nature of a mistake, and if it was wrong, that we could
likewise go into the question in Committee. But I find
everything that has been done has one direction, and one only.
I cannot understand the Chancellor of the Exchequer, when
speaking of the painful anxiety with which this Bill has
been brought forward, he has not, in all that anxiety and
deliberation, discovered that he was going to disfranchise
50,000 of the best electors of the kingdom.

Now, what is the main object of this measure? It is
evidently to make the representation of the counties, if
possible, more exclusively territorial than it is at present.
I ask the House to consider whether that is a desirable object
for us to attempt? Ask Lord Lyndhurst—long a leading

statesman, acting with gentlemen opposite; ask Lord Aberdeen. Sir Robert Peel is not here, and you cannot ask him; but you can ask the right hon. Gentleman the Member for Carlisle, and the right hon. Gentleman the Chancellor of the Exchequer could add his impressive testimony, whether it has not always been the chief difficulty of the Cabinet sitting on that side of the House—I mean with Gentlemen opposite, for many years, far longer than I have been a politician—that they were supported by one hundred and fifty or more Gentlemen representing the counties, and elected very much in the way described by Lord Derby, and, being supported by that party, whether they have not found it utterly impossible, without doing that which was very unpleasant, or without ruining themselves, which is unpleasant to a Government, to propose or carry any of those measures which were made necessary by the opinions and demands of the country.

Do not let Gentlemen opposite suppose that I am finding fault individually with any one of them in this matter. From 1842 to 1846, what was the difficulty which the Government of Sir Robert Peel constantly found in its way? Of that, I dare say, the right hon. Baronet the Member for Carlisle could give us a graphic and instructive description. What became of that Government of 1846? There was a disruption which resulted in years of anarchy in this House. But go back to the experience of the Chancellor of the Exchequer in 1852. The then Government was broken up by a majority of nineteen votes in this House after a general election, because it was necessary, in order to satisfy the expectations and demands of that same party sitting behind them, to propose a Bill with regard to the malt-tax, for which, on the whole, the country certainly made no demand, and to which the House was not willing to consent. I was then very sorry for Lord Derby, and I never, except once, gave a vote which I more regretted to have to record than on that occasion; but the Government could not alter or withdraw their propositiou, because the one hundred and fifty Gentlemen behind them thought it necessary that such a measure should pass, and now we find the right hon. Gentleman in the same position.

Does any man believe that this is the sort of Bill that the Chancellor of the Exchequer thinks best for the country? Does any one suppose that a man with his intellect, and who understands all the bearings of this question, approves of—I will not say the 'deplorable rubbish,' but the grievous and fatal mistakes to be found in the clauses of this Bill? He knows that this Bill in its present shape is a Bill framed to satisfy the prejudices, the scruples, the convictions, if you like, and the fears of the one hundred and fifty country Gentlemen who sit behind him. I should think it a great misfortune to have one hundred and fifty Gentlemen here, representing only iron-works, or only ships, or only the cotton and woollen factories of Lancashire and Yorkshire. I believe it is almost essential to a good Member of this House, so far as it depends on external circumstances, that he should have among his constituents a variety of what the Chancellor of the Exchequer would call 'interests,' persons of various classes, occupations, and opinions. I think they keep him better to his duty, modify his opinions, and make him a more valuable Member of the House than he is likely to be if he represented only some special interest.

I must say one word about that charming part of our institutions of which the right hon. Gentleman (Mr. Walpole) has spoken in such affectionate terms. I mean the small boroughs. They are the jewels of our representative system. Putting the case in the smallest number of words, you say that they send men into Parliament who cannot get in anywhere else. In one of them a boy was put in at nineteen. That is considered a great argument for perpetuating such a system. These boroughs form, in point of fact, a refuge for the politically destitute; and all that I have heard in their favour is that the persons who find shelter in them are what would be called 'deserving objects.' Now, the right hon. Gentleman, I dare say, reads the papers as well and as studiously as I do ; and he will perhaps recollect a case or two which I will state to the House. There was an election at Harwich the other day. It is not long since there was an election there, and I remember a statement made at the time. It was said that Mr. Bagshaw—not now a Member of this House—had discharged a drunken gardener. There were two free-traders who had carried out their principles further than the law sanctioned, and were imprisoned for smuggling. A respectable parson of the parish, who had not been out of his room for two years, was brought down (by the aid of cordials, stimulants, and a sedan-chair) to the poll, and those four individuals influenced the result of the election. Now, go to another borough. I recollect an election for the borough of Carlow. There were two troops of dragoons, two companies of infantry, and one hundred and fifty police ; the whole of this force having, during the period of the election, been engaged in keeping the peace in a town which comprised only two hundred electors. Now, notwithstanding the picture which I have drawn of these small boroughs, I must not be understood as saying that virtuous elections do not take place in some of this class, and that they do not still retain some remnant of freedom. But if there be any virtue or freedom left in them, the right hon. Gentleman the Chancellor of the Exchequer, not content with corrupting and maltreating them in every way, defaces the fair form of your county representation, and lays his sacrilegious hands upon those very spots about which everybody but myself just now speaks in such very high terms.

I should like to give the House an instance of the justice of what I state. There has been an election at Banbury. It is but the other day that the hon. Gentleman who represents that place took his seat in this House. Banbury is a borough which I do not propose to disfranchise, but it is one which everybody who knows its size must admit to be possessed of singular independence of action in political affairs. I believe the hon. Gentleman who at present represents it will admit that to be the fact. Now, just imagine what the proposition of the right hon. Gentleman the Chancellor of the Exchequer will lead to in the case of Banbury. Imagine, if you can, the people of that borough making speeches, canvassing, explaining their political views, and resolving upon the proper fulfilment of their political duties. Well, all this is taking place, but at the critical moment you may see a man— for aught I know he may be the concocter of this Bill—for it appears to me to be not so much the Bill of a statesman as of some party electioneering agent—you may see, I repeat, a man of this description, emerging after dark from the Carlton Club, proceeding to a pillar letter-box which stands quite near it upon the opposite side of the street, and dropping into it— unless, indeed, he should find it necessary to go as far as Charing Cross for the purpose of registering them—some ten or twenty letters about nine or ten o'clock in the evening, while the unfortunate people of Banbury are labouring under the delusion that they are carrying on a great constitutional contest. Unhappy men, they little know that the resistless locomotive engine has been set to work; that it is rushing down through county after county; and that they will awake the next morning only to find out that, through the instrumentality of a leathern bag, which has just been deposited at the post-office, somebody is returned as their representative who has not the slightest sympathy with their interests.

But this is no new thing. If anybody will turn to the report of the Municipal Corporation Commissioners in 1834, he will there find a statement made by Mr. Austin in reference to the borough of Carmarthen; in which he gives the number of resident and non-resident freeholders not of the value of 40s., but of 4l., and, in addition, the number of 10l. occupiers.

The number of burgesses in the borough he sets down at 646; resident in the borough, 178; outside the borough, but still within the county, 257; in the county of Pembroke, 108; in Glamorgan, 31; in Cardigan, 25; in Brecon, 12; and outside the limits of South Wales altogether, 35: so that, while the number of resident was 178, the number of non-resident electors was 468. Mr. Austin then gives a list of voters at a contest which had taken place for the election of sheriffs, when 131 votes were recorded in favour of the corporation candidates, against them 51; thus giving a majority in their favour of 80, of which majority 75 were non-resident electors. The commissioner then goes on to say, ' In effect, therefore, the constant majority is a majority of non-residents, who, with rare exceptions, are supporters of the corporation party.' Now, let me ask if this system prevailed in the case of a 4*l*., is it not likely to prevail in the case of a 2*l*. freehold? It must also be observed that in the former instance the votes could not be recorded by letter. The voter had to appear in person at the place of election; but if this system of voting-papers be adopted in addition to non-residence, I know no limit whatever to the amount of corruption which it may occasion. You cannot therefore, in my opinion, too strongly express your sense of the entire extinction of freedom which this scheme is calculated to produce in all the small boroughs of the country.

There is also another point which a large portion of our fellow-countrymen regard as of the utmost importance, and to which I may be permitted briefly to refer. I allude to the borough franchise. I have endeavoured to show that the effect of the Bill as it now stands will be to render counties more exclusive, and to hand over the small boroughs to rottenness and complete dependence; for the only independence they could possess must rest upon the opinions and wishes of non-resident electors. I am not going to discuss this question in any different tone from that which has hitherto marked this debate; but I would ask the House whence comes it that we

are here to-night discussing the question of Reform at all?
There are plenty of other things for us to do. Why, then, is
this question thrust upon us by Minister after Minister?
Some persons say that the noble Lord the Member for London
is entirely in fault. Hon. Gentlemen may say whatever they
like, but such an assertion as that goes but a very little way
indeed. The noble Lord has no particular desire, any more
than I have, to disturb the great question. Its settlement,
however, has become a necessity, and will continue to be a
necessity to the existence of every Government until it is set
at rest in a manner that will be satisfactory to the country.
[Cheers.] Do hon. Gentlemen by their cheers mean to show
us that they do not want Reform? The Government have not
touched this question simply in obedience to the commands of
their followers, although they have brought in this Bill in
accordance with their prejudices and their fears. The farmers
do not ask you for Reform, although there are, no doubt,
some respects in which they desire it. The farm-labourer
does not press it upon your attention. No, the demand
for Reform comes from all your towns and cities; nor is
the cry heard from the mouths of the unenfranchised alone,
but, in point of fact, from the great majority of the electors
themselves.

It is not an uncommon thing to hear it asserted—as several
hon. Members have asserted in this House—that the electors
of this country do not care for Reform. ['Hear, hear.']
Those hon. Gentlemen who cry 'Hear, hear,' do not know
quite so much as I do about the sentiments of people residing
in towns. When the electoral power was in the hands of a
few corrupt corporations the case may have been otherwise, for
they turned their electoral privileges into a means of annual
profit, and did not like to share them with their fellow-townsmen. But I never heard it made a charge against the
electors in boroughs, at the present day, that they were
anxious to retain the franchise for fear of admitting others of

their fellow-countrymen to be sharers, or rivals, or partici-
pators with them in the advantages which it comprises. The
Government, it seems, do not think it necessary to make any
change in the borough franchise. We all know that the line
which was drawn in 1832 was drawn in direct and almost absolute exclusion of all that class of persons who live by wages.
Has it been a source of satisfaction to them ? Have there not,
upon the contrary, been constant protests against it? Have we
not seen and heard—when there was great depression in trade,
and a great scarcity of food, which now, happily, is not the
case—these constant protests aggravated into something like
incipient insurrection ? That such has been the case is not to
be denied. Well, and what is that you now do? Twenty-
seven years after the passing of the great Reform Bill, and
after a whole generation has passed away, you propose to continue, it may be for twenty-seven years longer, that exclusion
against which the great body of the unenfranchised population
of the country have been lifting up their voices ever since
1832.

What is it that Her Majesty's Ministers say to us in introducing this measure ? What will this House in effect say
if it passes it into a law in its present shape ? You proclaim, in a voice which will reach the furthest corner of the
land, that will enter not only into the ear but into the heart
of the inhabitants of every home of the class of which I
am speaking in England—that we have something in our
legislature which they cannot comprehend and must not inter-
meddle with. You will in effect say to them, ' We do not
trust you, you are as ignorant, as dangerous, as little to be
relied upon now as you were twenty-seven years ago.' And
what will be the result ? They will come to the conclusion
that upon the same principle upon which you now act you will
act for the next twenty-seven years; using precisely the same
arguments and pursuing the same course.

And now let me pause for one moment to ask what sort of

a generation that has been which is just passing, or has passed,
away?   My answer is, such a one as was never known before.
You have had under its auspices a longer period of peace than
you ever previously enjoyed.   The humbler classes have had a
larger proportion of the comforts and necessaries of life than
at a preceding period.   They have improved at a rate of which
your grandfathers scarcely dared to dream.   You have a free
press—though there may be something still to be done in
order that it may become completely unfettered—a subject to
which the right hon. Gentleman the Chancellor of 'the Exchequer will be good enough to turn his attention when he
gets out of the little difficulty in which he is now placed.
You have not only the ordinary number of public journals,
but you have 300 newspapers published at the price of 1*d*.,
circulating all over the country.   All this has been accomplished; yet you propose to exclude the members of that
class to whom you are indebted for much of your prosperity—
with the exception of the trifling numbers whom the Chancellor of the Exchequer, in his small mercy, proposes to admit
under the savings-bank clause—from the exercise of the
franchise.

I saw a statement the other day, to the effect that the
operation of such a clause applied to Scotland would be to
give Edinburgh about 300, and all Scotland not more than
600 additional voters. The borough electors are 50,000, and
this extraordinary extension of the franchise will admit $2\frac{1}{2}$
per cent. increase, and that is all the small dole which the
Chancellor of the Exchequer and his friends offer to the great
body of the working classes of that country.   Scotland is a
frugal country; its people are industrious and saving to a
degree which is hardly comprehended here, and yet this boon
will only enfranchise some 1,200 persons there.   I am prepared to assert that this is not a Bill of Reform at all.   It is,
in point of fact, that which, in electioneering phrase, is considered a complete case of personation.   It is not the genius

of Liberty that comes before us in the shape of this Bill, but it is something which the people of this country had hoped they had seen and heard of for the last time in our history. I think if it were to pass, that it would be held by the whole population of the country to be nothing better than a complete delusion, disappointing every class, and tending to create discontent, which this House would have great difficulty hereafter in allaying.

There is one point which has been dwelt upon by the right hon. Gentleman opposite and others, in which I do not feel the same extraordinary interest which some Members appear to feel, and that is as to the uniformity of franchise. I do not say that it is necessary—I do not say that there is any advantage in it—but I do not see the great disadvantages which have been ascribed to it. It has been represented to me as a very democratic proceeding. I am not myself very democratic—therefore I can assure the House the scheme has not on that account any charms for me. I think it would have been just as well not to have had this uniformity; but I do not see any harm there is in it. There is only one reason why we should complain of it, and that is, that it would not be so easy again to move the whole franchise hereafter as it would be if the county franchise were different from that of the boroughs. But I can assure hon. Members that if they tie the two together, there is no power in this House to keep the borough franchise at 10*l*., and unless they give up the idea of uniformity the county franchise must come down with that of the boroughs. However, that is a matter for hon. Gentlemen opposite to consider, and no doubt it has been considered by Her Majesty's Government.

But if I have no alarm about that, there is one thing that I have some alarm about, and that is the manner in which some Members of the House seem disposed to treat this question. I refer particularly to my hon. Friend near me (Mr. Horsman), the right hon. Gentleman the Member for Wilts

(Mr. S. Herbert), and the right hon. Gentleman the Member for Coventry (Mr. Ellice), who has not spoken in this debate, but who wrote a letter to his constituents upon the subject. The right hon. Gentleman is an extraordinary instance of what I may call hallucination. He represents the greatest number of working-men to be found in any constituency— out of a population of 40,000 there are 6000 electors, which is a far larger number than I thought of proposing to the House. My right hon. Friend says there is no constituency that he knows which equals his in independence, in intelligence, in virtue. I cannot admit all that. I know something of Coventry—my father was born there—but I never heard nor ever observed that the people of that town were upon the whole very superior. I believe they are in no degree inferior to the same classes in other manufacturing towns. My right. hon. Friend says he is in favour of household suffrage, but as the people are not ready for that, he will do nothing,—he will have household suffrage or nothing; which, after all, is very much like the suffrage proposed in what was called the ' People's Charter.'

I am alarmed that the right hon. Gentleman, like -the Members for Wilts and Devonport, should, in the face of a hundred meetings held spontaneously within the last month, delude himself with the idea that nobody, beyond the 650 Gentlemen in this House, cares anything about this question, and that we may comfortably get rid of it in some way here, by digging a hole in the floor of the House and burying it, as nobody cares about it. The right hon. Gentleman the Member for Cambridge University (Mr. Walpole) has the same notion. He thinks it must be settled this session— that it can be—that it is necessary that it should be settled. Why ? For this reason, because you know that the form in which you propose to settle it will not be satisfactory to the people. You know well—I think the right hon. Gentleman has confessed it, as some have—that during the autumn you may have meetings—during the winter you may have agitation. And, what would this country have been without meetings, without agitation? We boast that we have abolished our ancient and barbarous mode of making extensive revolutions and changes in our political system, but if you have done with war and bloodshed for these purposes, do not imagine that those changes which become necessary from time to time can be accomplished without the healthy operation, in some cases perhaps of a rude, but still a refreshing and strengthening agitation.

Some Gentlemen opposite seem to forget some things that happened fifteen years ago. Then their organisation was complete. They had farmers' meetings everywhere. And, not content with farmers' meetings, they had an office in Old Bond-street, and a Publication Committee, and they had every description of instrument for an irritating and exasperating agitation which they could possibly devise. I do not imagine for a moment that this question can, in the present temper of the House, be settled satisfactorily to the people. Are you quite sure that there is nothing in what is going on out of doors? I met a right hon. Gentleman the other day near the House, and he said to me as a great secret, 'You know, of course, that nobody does care about Reform?' I did not agree with him upon that point. I happen to have been to some of the largest towns of this country, and I have seen meetings exceeding in number and exceeding in influence, I believe, almost every meeting that was held by the Anti-Corn-law League during the agitation for the repeal of the Corn-laws.

The populations you are about to disappoint and defy,— what have they done? They have conquered everything they have grappled with hitherto. I do not speak of distant realms conquered under your banners, but of arts and manufactures, and all that tends to wealth and civilisation. Do you think that this population will not also conquer a much

larger share of their political rights than in your present
mood you appear disposed to give them? There was a speech
made by the hon. Member for Dorset, and I agree with
those who have expressed regret that that Gentleman does
not speak more frequently; but, in that speech the hon.
Gentleman said, 'I am not afraid of the people of this
country.' And he gave a very powerful, and eloquent, and
just rebuke to a Gentleman who, in a thoughtless moment,
cheered his observation in a sneering manner. I tell the
House frankly that they do not well understand the great
populations of this country, especially of the manufacturing
towns.

I have seen great mistakes made. I remember, in 1848,
when the right hon. Gentleman above me (Sir G. Grey) was
Home Secretary, there was a great panic on the 10th of
April—or rather before the 10th of April, for by that day
the panic was laughed at. And, what was done? I
do not know what was done at the Bank, but I am told
that at the British Museum that institution was actually
garrisoned. There were no Minié rifles or Armstrong guns,
perhaps, but there were a hundred or two hundred tons of
paving-stones, or boulders, taken up to the roof of the
Museum. Not only was it garrisoned, but, very properly,
the commissariat was attended to, and provisions for three
days were laid in, and I am told the steps leading to the
rooms where the medals and most precious articles are kept
were cut away. The British Museum was not assaulted,
but the garrison, I believe, managed to consume the three
days' provisions before Sunday.

Now come to a later time — the period of the Exhibition in Hyde Park in 1851. There was then alive a
man who stood pre-eminent in this country, the Duke of
Wellington. He was terrified—a man who was supposed
never to have been alarmed, — he was alarmed at the
people of his own country. He urged upon the Government,

who of course agreed with him, to draw near the metropolis a large number of troops in case of emergency. If half-a-dozen foreigners had attempted to get up an insurrection in London they would have been put into the reservoirs in Trafalgar Square by the people themselves, and yet it was considered necessary to bring these troops near to London, to be ready in case of disturbance. I remember the noble Lord the Member for Tiverton (Lord Palmerston) once gave us an account of what some foreigner told him as to the conduct and deportment of the masses of the people. The noble Lord knows a good deal of the character of the people, and he said, 'All this order is the result of a sense among the people that they have a Government which, upon the whole, does not intend to oppress them; that they are a people good in themselves, intelligent, and orderly, and that a policeman among them is an authority of high dignity, whom they at once obey.' The remark is creditable to the noble Lord's good taste, and is perfectly just to the people of this country.

I ask hon. Gentlemen opposite why they are so afraid of the people? The manufacturing, the employing class, does not fear them. At the Bradford meeting there were present when I moved the resolution, Mr. Titus Salt and Mr. Crossley, the brother of the Member for Halifax. Those Gentlemen conduct vast manufacturing and commercial undertakings. There are no men more prosperous, and none have more confidence in the people. Those two Gentlemen agreed cordially with every proposition I made as to an extension of the suffrage. The meetings at Rochdale, Bury, Blackburn, and Bolton were attended by Gentlemen almost equally eminent; at the meeting at Bolton there were four Gentlemen who employ not less than 6,000 or 7,000 people, and who own property of not less than a million sterling; one of those Gentlemen thought my proposal as to the suffrage was not sufficiently extensive. Why is it they do not regard the people with

the same fears that you do ? They must know what they are
about ; they know that any convulsion or disturbance in
society would touch them first. Your landed estates are
much more permanent as property than our manufactories.
Any disturbance or violent action of a democratic nature
would be more dangerous to us than to you. Yet a large
proportion of the employers of labour favour a large extension
of the suffrage, and believe it would prove for the safety
of their property; for the working-men, in thinking over
this question, feel they are distrusted, that they are marked
as inferiors, that they are a sort of pariahs. In that position,
should there be an opportunity, great discontent and tur-
bulence might arise; but if you give them a vote they will
have more self-respect, more elevation of mind.

I will read an extract from a letter I have received from
a working-man—I believe a stonemason—on the question
whether or not working-men have any interest in the country.
He says :—

'But some say that we, as working-men, have no stake and no interest in
the country. I hardly know what is meant by these assertions ; but if to
make sacrifices for the good of our country be any proof of an interest, I
believe the working classes can clearly show greater sacrifices, and fairly
claim to have greater stake and interest both in the country and in good
government. I had three uncles who all lost their lives fighting for their
country ; I had three brothers, two of whom served under Lord Wellington
throughout the Peninsular campaign ; and my third and youngest brother lost
his life in the Indian war, and now lies buried at Kurnaul. I had two
nephews, one of whom died of the cholera at Varna, and the other, after
serving throughout the Crimean war, was raised from the ranks, and is now a
lieutenant. No doubt but very many working-men could tell of even greater
sacrifices and similar tales of their families, except the last. To these statements I would only add, that if the working classes have no stake and no
interest in their country, they must be wonderful lovers of their country for
nothing.'

There is only one other point to which I will allude; it
was touched upon by the Solicitor-General when he referred
to the state of Europe; he warned the House to beware what
it was about to do in regard to this question. I draw quite

a different lesson, a different conclusion, from what he said of the state of Europe. In 1830 there was also a state of Europe and especially of France that was not satisfactory, and it had great effect on the legislation of this House, in the course of the two succeeding years, on the question of Reform. In 1848 the state of Europe was again unsatisfactory, and was it not a subject of congratulation that two years before the Corn-laws had been abolished, and one great cause of discontent removed? I assure you that resistance is not always Conservative. I profess to be, in intention, as Conservative as you,—I believe, infinitely more so, if you look forward twenty or thirty years into the future. Was not Free-trade Conservative? And yet you resisted it to the last. I recollect occasions when the Chancellor of the Exchequer told us of the cruelty practised on the ruined and betrayed agriculturist. I recollect he addressed us on the condition of the farm labourer two or three years afterwards; and since that time his condition has been improving rapidly. Is not prosperity Conservative? Is not peace Conservative? Any energies I possess I have devoted to their advance; I have endeavoured to stand on the rules of Political Economy, and to be guided by the higher rules of true Morality; and when advocating a measure of Reform larger than some are prepared to grant, I appear in that character, for I believe a substantial measure of Reform would elevate and strengthen the character of our population; that, in the language of the beautiful prayer read here every day, it would tend 'to knit together the hearts of all persons and estates within this realm.' I believe it would add to the authority of the decisions of Parliament; and I feel satisfied it would confer a lustre, which time could never dim, on that benignant reign under which we have the happiness to live.

REFORM.

V.

BIRMINGHAM, JANUARY 18, 1865.

[This speech was spoken in the Town Hall of Birmingham at a meeting when, according to annual custom, the Members for Birmingham met their constituents to discuss the political questions of the day.]

WHEN my honourable Colleague and myself had the pleasure last year of meeting you in this hall, there was one subject which was pressing upon the minds of all of us, and causing us great disquietude. We were encompassed by rumours of war. A small State in the North of Europe was surrounded by difficulties—mainly, I am afraid, of its own creation—and it was assailed with what, in this country, we thought almost a savage vindictiveness by a powerful people comprising one vast empire and several kingdoms. We were not disposed to go into the contest, and to mingle in that war; and you will recollect that my honourable Colleague spoke in the most emphatic language against the idea that we should enter into a war—first, with Germany, and perhaps, afterwards, with some other States of Europe, on behalf of Denmark. And, following him, I used these words—speaking now from my recollection of them—I said that any Government in England that plunged us into war for the sake of Denmark would deserve not only the condemnation but the execration of the people.

But still, although we took so decided a view, we cannot conceal from ourselves that there was a certain restlessness in the public mind; it was observed that those newspapers in London particularly which are supposed to represent the Government, were strongly urging the country to war, and the papers which are supposed to represent the Opposition were urging the Government to the same course, no doubt with the kindly intention of embarrassing and destroying the Ministry. But we had to recollect that at the head of the Government, as it exists, are two very ancient states-men — the Prime Minister and the head of the Foreign Office; and, remembering that but ten years ago they were the Ministers mainly responsible for the war with Russia, we could not but feel that the danger which impended over us was not wholly imaginary. How we escaped the war people seem hardly to know. Some say that the Queen was very much opposed to a war with Germany — as doubtless she would be opposed to any war which she believed could possibly be avoided—and, if we owe our chances of peace to the opinion of the Queen, for my part, I say with gladness that I am grateful to the Queen. Some say that we owe peace to the younger members of the Cabinet, led chiefly by Mr. Gladstone, who were opposed to the war. If that be true, I tender my thanks to the majority of the Cabinet. And some say that the unusual speculative monetary engagements and investments of last year made all the moneyed interests of the country look on the prospect of war as something absolutely appalling and ruinous. If that be so, I tender my thanks to the moneyed interests of the country.

But, during the session, this question was incessantly discussed, and the Government exhibited its usual feebleness, and the Opposition its usual folly. Nobody could get the

Government to say whether it was for peace or war. If a question was asked about the station, or movements, or destination of the fleet, an answer was given which might be read one way or the other; and if the Opposition was not in favour of war—as they afterwards declared they were not—they showed it by an incessant attempt to drive the Government to some act which should make hostilities inevitable. Towards the end of the session, if you are readers of the debates in Parliament—and I hope you do not wholly neglect them—you would see that there was a very long, and what was called a great debate, and then the feebleness of the Government and the folly of the Opposition were manifest, and the two sides of the House had to make some ridiculous recantations of all the policy that in past times they have appeared to advocate. There were remarkable speeches on the Opposition side, one made by General Peel, another made by Lord Stanley; and there was a speech of remarkable ability, and in every way admirable, made by Mr. Hardy, the Member for Leominster. Now, I am not charging General Peel, or Lord Stanley, or Mr. Hardy with recanting as far as regards their individual opinions; but speaking—if they did speak—on behalf of their party, I say that their speeches contained a general and wholesale repudiation of the whole foreign policy of this country, as regards the continent of Europe, from the time of William III to the reign of Victoria.

They did not say, perhaps, as I once said in this hall—and some men criticised what I had said with a severity that would have been perfectly just if what I had said had been untrue—they did not say, as I had said, that the foreign policy of this country for the last 170 years has been a system of gigantic out-door relief to the English aristocracy, but they admitted this—and I am willing to accept it, if they will, in place of my statement—that it had been a cause of enormous burdens and sacrifices to the people of England. I could

not help, during these discussions—in which I took no part,
for this reason, that, finding it my duty to vote against
the Opposition, I hardly trusted myself to make the speech
which, if I had risen to address the House, I must have made
against the policy and the conduct of the Government. I
thought of the position of those ancient statesmen to whom
I have referred. Now, do not imagine that I am speaking
disrespectfully of Lord Palmerston or of Lord Russell, but I
am speaking to my fellow-countrymen on a question of the
most stupendous importance to their present and future
interests. I say that these two statesmen have in past times
held or professed opinions which I think altogether unsound,
and pernicious to the nation.

Going back to the time just before the Russian war—to the
year 1853—I will give you an extract from a speech made by
Lord Russell at the town of Greenock, in Scotland, on the
duty of England with regard to its foreign relations, and I
will show you what a change has taken place from that day to
this. Bear in mind this was just before the opening of the
Russian war, and when that question was being discussed,
and when that horrid shape of carnage was appearing above
the horizon, and every thoughtful man looked at it with
dread. Lord Russell said this to the Baillies and other
sensible inhabitants of Greenock. He said :—

'It is likewise to be considered—and I trust we shall none of us forget it—
that this country holds an important position among the nations of the world ;
that not once, but many times, she has stood forward to resist oppression, to
maintain the independence of weaker nations, and to preserve to the general
family of nations that freedom, that power of governing themselves, of which
others have sought to deprive them. I trust that character will not be forgotten, will not be abandoned by a people which is now stronger in means,
which is more populous, and more wealthy, than it ever has been at any
former period. This then, you will agree with me, is not a period to abandon
any of those duties towards the world, towards the whole of mankind, which
Great Britain has hitherto performed.'

Now you see what Lord John Russell at that day proposed for us to do. You, hard-working men—and every man

who receives his wages at the end of the week, be his labour what it may—were here pledged by Lord John Russell not to abandon any of those duties towards the world, towards the whole of mankind, which Great Britain has hitherto performed. We were to defend all weaker nations, and to take care that nobody was molested in any part of the globe.

I read this passage in order that you may see the sort of thing which, only twelve years ago, ·was spoken by a Cabinet Minister, to a meeting of what are generally reputed to be sensible Scotch people. But if I were to take Lord Palmerston's speeches, I dare say I could find a cartload of rhetorical rubbish of exactly the same character. During many years these statesmen have been making their popularity upon such a theory as that, and their newspapers have been reviling Mr. Cobden and myself for a different view, and now you find that Parliament, by an unanimous vote, has discarded and abandoned and overturned the whole of this policy, and has sent the whole thing—lie and superstition and all—into that receptacle to which all lies and superstitions will ultimately go.

I think myself that Lord Palmerston and Lord Russell, in their now mature age, must feel that either they have been themselves greatly deceived, or they have done much to deceive their countrymen; and I think my country-men will derive from what I have said this lesson, which they may learn on many pages of history,—that it is not always certain that men are great statesmen because they happen to fill great offices.

But now if Denmark was allowed to be dismembered, I do not know why Holland, or Belgium, or Portugal, or Turkey—[A Voice: 'Or America']—I am confining myself, as you will observe, to Europe—I cannot see the probability of that state of things arising to which my honourable Col-league has referred, when the principle of non-intervention

will require to be departed from. I agree with him that the country has other interests than its commercial interests, and that it would be a mean and a base thing for the
of England to do, as I am sorry to say our Government has often done, to determine what was the exact gain or loss commercially in the conquest of an island, or upon the opportunity of trade, before it determined to go to war or to maintain peace. My own opinion is that, taking the events of the last few years—the war in Italy, in which we took no part, the war in Denmark, which we abstained from meddling in—the debate of last Session—and the great division which took place upon this question,—I think I am not much mistaken in pronouncing the theory of the balance of power to be pretty nearly dead and buried. You cannot comprehend at a thought what is meant by that balance of power. If the record could be brought before you—but it is not possible to the eye of humanity to scan the scroll upon which are recorded the sufferings which the theory of the balance of power has entailed upon this country. It rises up before me when I think of it as a ghastly phantom which during one hundred and seventy years, whilst it has been worshipped in this country, has loaded the nation with debt and with taxes, has sacrificed the lives of hundreds of thousands of Englishmen, has desolated the homes of millions of families, and has left us, as the great result of the profligate expenditure which it has caused, a doubled peerage at one end of the social scale, and far more than a doubled pauperism at the other. I am very glad to be here to-night, amongst other things, to be able to say that we may rejoice that this foul idol—fouler than any heathen tribe ever worshipped—has at last been thrown down, and that there is one superstition less which has its hold upon the minds of English statesmen and of the English people.

And if this be true, surely my hon. Friend need not be so very careful to guard his observations with regard to the diminution of armaments; for if it be now determined that we are not to send armies to the continent of Europe, and fleets to blockade ports and people with whom we have no concern, and if the British North American Colonies are about to make themselves into a great and powerful confederation still in friendly alliance with this country, and if the colonies of Australia are so distant and so powerful that nobody can molest them, and if the people of these islands are better fed—as I believe they are better fed than they have been for the last eighty years—I say, that if they are more loyal to the law and more friendly to every good institution of the country, there is no necessity whatsoever to extend the annual military expenditure, which is double that which the Duke of Wellington and Sir Robert Peel thought necessary five and twenty years ago.

There is one other thing to say. If we are not this next session to discuss the question of Denmark, the question of Italy, and the question of America, what are we to discuss? It is quite clear to me that whether we have more disposition or not, we shall have a good deal more time to discuss our home affairs. Now what is the question which some gentlemen who have been eating a very good dinner and making very foolish speeches at Torquay,—what is the question which I think Lord Devon says—copying the language of his leader Mr. Disraeli—is 'looming in the not distant future?' what is the question that will not go to sleep? And, let me remind you of this, that really great questions that affect the true and lasting interests and rights of men, never can be laid fast asleep; they always, somehow or other, wake up again. There is a startling exemplification of this in what is now taking place in the United States. You know that for thirty years past the statesmen of the United States have voted the negro a very great nuisance; they said they would not talk about him; some of them would not have petitions about him in Congress; they swore each other to silence; the negro's business was to grow rice, and sugar, and tobacco, and cotton, but not to make his appearance on the floor of Congress, and therefore they determined to have done with him and to bury the question, and they congratulated the country that it was buried. And now after a few years you see North and South—both responsible for the oppression of the negro—in the most deadly conflict, and the negro stands forth in vast proportions before the world. He is rubbing the marks of the branding-iron from his forehead, the shackles which have bound him so long are dropping from his limbs, and the chattel which was bought and sold by these statesmen is now becoming every day a free man before the world.

Well, then, there is this question that will not sleep—the question of the admission of the people of this country to the rights which are guaranteed to them, and promised to them by everything that we comprehend as the constitution of this United Kingdom. In 1861, as my hon. Friend has described to you—and I listened to his observations with very great pleasure, because some persons may suppose that he takes a calmer view of this question than I do—that great question of Parliamentary Reform was also voted a nuisance; and it was betrayed, and it was slain, and they thought it was buried. And, when I use the word 'betrayed,' do not suppose I am using a word of improper harshness to the Minister or the Ministers concerned. My hon. Friend said truly enough that a measure of that kind being submitted to Parliament, the Minister or Ministers by whom it was presented should be prepared to stand or fall by it. I was reading only within the last few days a very interesting book, *The History of the Passing of the Reform Bill*, written by an estimable clergyman in my neighbourhood—Mr. Molesworth, son of the Vicar of Rochdale—a book which you would do well to look at if it comes in your way; and there I find that Lord Grey—the Lord Grey of the time—did not stand before the House of Lords, with a smirk, and that kind of look about him which led them to believe that he did not mean it, but told them, in language as distinct and emphatic as our English tongue affords, that the Ministry would stand or fall by that measure; and, more, that if it were their business and duty to bring in another Bill, if that should be rejected, it would not be less efficient than that which they were then discussing.

There is not a man in the House of Commons who was there in 1860, who knows anything at all of the manner in which Bills and questions are treated there,—and there is not a man in the present Cabinet, who does not know perfectly well that if Lord Palmerston had said on some one evening in the year 1860, that his Government would stand or fall by the Reform Bill then before the House, that Bill would have passed through the House of Commons without one single effective hostile division; nay, I have heard it from an authority, that I believe cannot err upon this question, that the sagacious leaders of the House of Lords had resolved that if the Bill did come up from the Commons they would not take the responsibility of rejecting it.

That Bill or question is not dead; it takes shape again, and you perceive that the Tories, and those Whigs who are like Tories—all Whigs are not like Tories, therefore I make the distinction—the Tories, and those Whigs who are like Tories, have an uncomfortable feeling which approaches almost to a shiver. What is this apparition which alarms them? If I were not wishful to say something different from that to which it would lead me, I should be tempted to read you those speeches at the Torquay dinner to show you what it is that they are afraid of. I will tell you what it is. They are afraid of the five or six millions of Englishmen, grown-up men who are allowed to marry, to keep house, to rear children, who are expected to earn their living, who pay taxes, who must obey the law, who must be citizens in all honourable conduct—they are afraid of the five or six millions who by the present system of representation are shut out, and insultingly shut out, from the commonest rights of citizenship.

We are proud of our country; and there are many things in it which, as far as men may rightly be proud, we may be proud of. We may be proud of this, that England is the ancient country of Parliaments. We have had here, with scarcely an intermission, Parliaments meeting constantly for six hundred years; and doubtless there was something of a Parliament even before the Conquest. England is the mother of Parliaments. I will undertake to say, with a little latitude of expression, that Lord John Russell, before he abandoned the cause of Reform—perhaps even since—talked very much in the daytime, and in all probability dreamt in the night, of the time when all countries in Europe would be strictly constitutional, and there would be a representative assembly after his own heart. If this be so, I ask you, men of Birmingham here—a fair representation of the great mass of the five millions throughout the United Kingdom—I ask you why you should be thus treated in your own land? You know the boast we have of what takes place when negro-slaves land in England; you know what one of our best poets has said, that if their lungs but breathe our air, that moment they are free; they touch our country, and their shackles fall. But how is it with an Englishman? An Englishman, if he goes to the Cape, can vote; if he goes further, to Australia, to the nascent empires of the New World, he can vote; if he goes to the Canadian Confederation, he can vote; and if he goes to those grandest colonies of England not now dependent upon the English Crown, there, in twenty free, and, in the whole, in thirty-five different States, he can give his free and independent vote. It is only in his own country, on his own soil, where he was born, the very soil which he has enriched with his labour and with the sweat of his brow, that he is denied this right which in every other community of Englishmen in the world would be freely accorded to him.

I agree very much with the gentlemen of the Torquay dinner, not as to the quality of the dinner, but as to that apparition which seemed to alarm even their formidable and robust digestion. This apparition is not a pleasant one. This state of things I hold to be dangerous, and one that cannot last. It may happen, as it happened thirty years ago, that the eyes of the five millions all through the United Kingdom may be fixed with an intense glare upon the doors of Parliament; it was so in the years 1831–32. There are men in this room who felt then, and know now, that it required but an accident—but one spark to the train, and this country would have been in the throes of revolution; and these gentlemen who are so alarmed now lest a man who lives in a 10*l.* house in a county, and a 6*l.* house in a borough, should have a vote, would have repented in sackcloth and ashes that they had ever said one word or given one vote against Lord Grey's Reform Bill. I say that accidents always are happening, not to individuals only, but to nations. It was the accident of the French Revolution of 1830 that preceded that great movement in this country. You may have accidents again, but I do not hold that to be statesmanship which allows the security, the tranquillity, the loyalty of a people to be disturbed by any accident which they are able to control. If the five millions should once unitedly fix their eyes with an intense look upon the door of that House where my hon. Friend and I expect so soon to enter, I would ask who shall say them nay? Not the mace upon the table of the House; not the four hundred easy gentlemen of the House of Lords who lounge in and out of that decorated chamber; not the dozen gentlemen who call themselves statesmen, and who meet in Downing-street; perhaps not even those more appalling and more menacing personages who have their lodgment higher up

Whitehall. I say there is no power in this country, as opinion now stands, and as combination is now possible, there is no power in this country that can say ' Nay' for one single week to the five millions, if they are intent upon making their way within the doors of Parliament. This is the apparition which frightens the gentlemen at Torquay— the climate of Torquay, I have always heard, is somewhat relaxing, and we may make a little allowance for that nervous excitement which was exhibited last week.

But it gives trouble, this apparition gives trouble in other quarters, to which I would pay more respect. It is evident from the books, and the pamphlets, and the letters that are written, and the speeches that are made upon it. Everybody who does not want Reform says that nobody wants Reform, and though this is a subject which they say the people do not care about, they immediately begin upon it and make it the staple of their own speeches. Two gentlemen have recently come before the public on this subject, whom I would not class with those of whom I have been speaking. One is Mr. Charles Buxton, the Member for Maidstone; he is a very honest and excellent person, but, after the proposition he has made, I should be slow to affirm that he is a robust politician. Mr. Buxton has put forward a scheme which I will pass from after one sentence, and that is that two of your townsmen shall go up to the poll at the next election, and one of them shall give one vote to Mr. Scholefield and myself, or to any two candidates he may prefer; and the other shall give two votes to each of such candidates as he shall prefer; and the only justification is that one lives in a house above 10*l.* rental, and the other in a house below 10*l.* I was very much surprised that any man in political life should have propounded such a scheme. He found, what he ought to have thought of before, that no one was in favour of it.

The other gentleman on whom I would make an observation

is a Member of the House of Lords, the son of that Lord Grey of whom I have been speaking—the Lord Grey of the present time. Now Lord Grey is an eminent and a very capable man; everything that he says at least demands an examination. I have a great respect for Lord Grey for two special reasons. I heard him make a speech in the House of Commons, when he was there as Lord Howick, against the Corn-law, and he quoted a grand and solemn passage of Scripture against that atrocious law—and the Protectionists said that it was very vulgar to quote Scripture on such a subject. Lord Grey again made a great speech in the House of Lords against the Russian war, and that showed some moral courage, and from my view of that question, I think it showed both intelligence and patriotism. Therefore I come to the consideration of anything he says with the most favourable feeling towards him.

Lord Grey, I said, is very capable—that is, capable with things that are possible, but like myself, or like you, he is not capable with the impossible—and his undertaking is this, to reconcile something which he thinks will be, or will appear like justice to the people, with the non-disturbance of the existing supremacy of his order. Now, it is no use attempting great political changes without disturbance; the object is to disturb something. The Reform Bill which his father brought in, and which will make him renowned through all English history, disturbed the borough-mongers to a remarkable degree. And the Bill which repealed the Corn-law which Lord Grey so honourably approved, disturbed landlords and farmers, and did them nearly as much good as it did the people. Therefore, I do not care a bit about political change. I have no hostility to it because it makes some disturbance; that is precisely what we want.

What then do you think Lord Grey has proposed? I wish you to observe it minutely, to see what it is that one of the most acute minds in the country can propose in opposition to the plain and simple proposition to which my hon. Friend has given his warm approval to-day, and so often before. Lord Grey—I am quoting, not from his book, but from a friendly criticism in the *Spectator,* which newspaper proposes that votes should be given after the cumulative fashion. Now I must explain that—[Uproar in the hall]—and if the gentleman there, who is rather pressed in the crowd, will only listen, he will hear the most amusing proposition he has ever heard in his life. Lord Grey, as I understand, proposes that when there are two candidates to be elected, or three, or any number—(I will take two for the sake of the simplest illustration)—that any man coming to vote, instead of giving one vote for Mr. Scholefield and another to me, might give both to Mr. Scholefield or both to me. Now, let us see how it would work. Take your last election : there were three candidates, and two Members to be elected. I will assume, for the sake of illustration, that this borough had a number of electors equal to 10,000, and that 6,500 were Liberal, and would support us, and 3,500 would have been disposed to support Mr. Acland, when he was a candidate, though that, as you know, is a very wild supposition. Look how it would work. The 3,500, we will suppose, kept well together, and instead of giving 3,500 votes, which we now call plumpers, each man would give him (Mr. Acland) two, which would make 7,000; so Mr. Acland would stand on the poll with 7,000 votes. If the remaining 6,500 who were Liberal kept together, and had an equal regard for Mr. Scholefield and myself, and voted steadily for him and for me, we should have 6,500 each, and if one more voted for Mr. Scholefield than for me, of course Mr. Scholefield would be at the head of the poll as regards myself, and Mr. Acland would be at the head of the poll as regards both; and thus the gentleman who came into your town upon principles which are repudiated by two-thirds or the vast majority of the electors would, under this ingenious scheme, be returned by our worthy Mayor the next day at the head of the poll. That is what they call, I suppose, not disturbing anything. We have heard of races—I have heard of donkey races, where the last wins. So in this case, the slowest animal would run off with the prize.

That is not all, because Lord Grey has several other propositions. One is that Members should be given to Universities. I happen to know that the Universities which are now represented could not at any time during the last sixty years—during which Lord Grey and his father (one or the other) have been statesmen—have been induced to return either of them to Parliament. Lord Grey proposes, further, that professions, such as lawyers and doctors, should have representatives in Parliament; not from them as citizens, as we have now, but from them as lawyers and doctors. I have had the misfortune of late years to fall very unfortunately into the hands of the lawyers, and hardly anything, I assure you, can be more painful or more costly. Then, occasionally, we all of us have to fall into the hands of the doctor; and, though we feel grateful to him, we would much rather see him in our houses as a friend than in his professional character. If I wanted law I should go to the lawyer, and if I wanted medicine or surgery I should go to the physician or the surgeon; but I should not like the public and political interests of the people of this country to go into the hands of a class of men because they were lawyers or because they were doctors. In fact, there is nothing like this that I recollect, except the proposition of old Mr. Weller, who, when his son was engaged in some legal business, recommended him to consult a friend of his because he was a very good judge of a horse.

But I have not done with Lord Grey's proposition. He proposes that the House of Commons itself should have the authority on certain occasions to nominate as Members of its own body certain prominent men from amongst its number. For example, if a Member of the House, a prominent man, from some cause or other had failed of his election, that the House of Commons should have the right to give him the nomination of a perpetual seat in that House, in order that the House might be sure to have a Member whom some great constituency had rejected. But now to you men—to the working-men of Birmingham—he offers another proposition, which is that there should be a register of trades, and that a certain number of Members should be elected by certain trades, enough to allow them to speak in the House of Commons; but rely upon it, not enough seriously to affect the decision of that House. I have always thought that it was one of the great objects of statesmen in our time not to separate the people into sections and classes, but rather to unite them all in one firm and compact body of citizenship, equally treated by the law, and equally loyal to the law and to the Government of the country.

But Lord Grey proposes some things that are right. He would extend the suffrage, and he would abolish many, if not all, the very small boroughs. But having made these concessions, he adds to them the propositions which I have described, and which more than neutralise the gifts which he would confer upon you; and I beg you to take the warning which my hon. Friend has given you, and which I will venture to repeat—to look with the greatest possible suspicion upon any of these fancy propositions of Reform. The question is a great question, and a simple question, and if any man comes before you with a complex and involved scheme which is difficult to understand, take note of this, that he does not offer you solid coin in payment of your claim, with the impress of the English Constitution upon it, but he offers you flash notes or coin of an inferior or worthless metal.

I am often charged, as you know, with having too little reverence for authority in this country. Some have even dared in public newspapers to charge me with disloyalty to the head of the executive in this country. There is one disloyalty which I hold to be worse than all other—worse than that which turns its back upon the Crown, or turns its back upon the peerage,—and that is disloyalty to freedom and to the people. If representation be not an evil—and who in this country shall say it is?—what is the use of all these tricks not to complete representation, but to avoid it and escape it? I want to ask what is this representation that we consider the foundation of liberty in this kingdom? If all the men in England, Wales, Scotland, and Ireland—6,000,000 or 7,000,000—were assembled on Salisbury Plain to determine on great public questions, the crowd would be too great for business, and chaos would come. It is therefore resolved, and has been resolved for six hundred years, that counties and boroughs and districts, and the people in their different localities, shall send up men in whom they have confidence, to meet at a certain time and place, and having the fear and the regard which I trust we all have for those who send us there, to act honourably in the face of God and of our conscience, and honourably in the face of our country, on behalf of the true and solid interests of the nation. But if you did decide on Salisbury Plain with that vast multitude, clearly the majority must carry the day; and if you split the nation up into constituencies, clearly if you are to have any representation at all, the majority must carry the day.

There is a great fear of majorities amongst these people. The people of Torquay did not go into much detail, and therefore they did not say much on that point, but they have a great fear of what they call 'numbers,' and of election and legislation by majorities. What is a majority in Birmingham? It holds one opinion, and we are supposed to represent it; but the majority in Liverpool—a town bigger than Birmingham—in the present state of the constituencies, holds a different opinion, and it sends one man who agrees with us, and another man who always contradicts him. The minority in Birmingham is in a certain sense represented by the majority of Liverpool, and taking the majorities in some districts, and the minorities in others, if there be an opinion that is worth anything which is held by any constituency, as a matter of course it has its representative, who can speak on its behalf in that House; but surely nobody in his senses would ask that in a representative country the minorities in all the constituencies should send Members to Parliament, and that their business when they got there should be always to say 'No' when the majority said 'Ay.'

I want to know whence this fear of the people is. Will somebody undertake to tell us why is this fear of the people? It does not exist elsewhere. It does not exist in the various countries of Europe, where representative systems are being daily established. It does not exist anywhere amongst Englishmen, except in these two islands. I have spoken to you already of Australia. The franchise in Australia, doubtless, is lower than it is in this country : but Australian Governments legislate in accordance with the opinions of the Australian people. As to Canada, I have here a little extract which I will read to you. You know that the province of Canada—of the two Canadas—New Brunswick, Prince Edward Island, Nova Scotia, and I suppose Newfoundland and all the British North American provinces, are about to make a Confederation —a State of considerable magnitude; and they wish our Parliament, this present session, to pass a measure which shall be the foundation and constitution of that future Confederacy. Here is an extract from the speech of Mr. George Brown, who is at this present moment the most prominent of Canadian Ministers, explaining the scheme :—

'The duration of Parliament will probably be limited to five years, and of course it will be composed of two branches—a legislative Council appointed by the Government of the day on the principle of equality of the sections, and a House of Commons, in which we are to obtain that so long desired, so long earnestly contended for Reform—Representation by Population.'

Therefore our Parliament is this session about to pass a Bill

affecting the British North American provinces which these
gentlemen tell us will be wholly destructive if applied to
this country. I want to ask you, the men of Birmingham,
who have recently been reading the papers a good deal,
especially with regard to what is taking place in the United
States—and I shall, like my honourable Friend, avoid any
allusion to that terrible revolution which is taking place
there—if you have observed that in the State of New York
alone 700,000 men voted at the last Presidential election, and
that throughout the whole of the Free States not less than
4,000,000 votes were given, and that they were all given with
the most perfect order and tranquillity throughout the whole
of the States?

But perhaps our friends who oppose us will say, ' We do not
fear about elections and order. What we fear is this—the
legislative results of this wide extension of the franchise.'
I am ready to test it in any country by the results of
legislation. I say, whether you go to South Africa, or to
Australia, or to the British North American provinces, or
to the States of the American Union, you will find—ex-
cluding always those States where slavery injures the state of
society—you will find that life and property are as secure,
you will find that education is much more extended amongst
the people, that there is quite as wide a provision for their
religious interests, that the laws are as merciful and just, that
taxes are imposed and levied with as great equality, and that
the millions of your countrymen who are now established in
those countries are at least as well off in all the circumstances
of life as are the people of this country whom they have left
behind them. I confess that I never yet heard of a man who
returned to this country from any of those countries under
the impression that he would be more secure here than he
would be there.

I have a very intelligent friend in London—he is an eminent
man, whose friendship I consider a great honour and advantage

to myself—who wrote to me the other day, and said, 'I do not think it is good tactics at present, in discussing the question of Reform, to make any reference to the United States.' But I am not asking you to follow the example of the United States. I am only showing you that there, and in the Canadian provinces, and in Australia, Englishmen can vote in perfect order in vast numbers, and that they can legislate with all the justness, and all the fairness, and all the good to their people which we, even speaking in the most favourable language, can ever gain from the legislation of the Government of this country. But still, I ask you to answer me this question if you can. There is something— tell me what it is—that these people at Torquay are afraid of. They talk about our institutions; and if I were to read you the report of one of these speeches which I have here, you would find in every sentence that there was something said about 'our institutions,' and it comes out that the 'institutions' are what they call Church and State. It is not very distinct, but because we have heard it for fifty years—some of us—we begin to have a kind of glimpse of what it means. It does not mean the House of Commons, and it does not mean chapels, and what is more, it does not mean churches in any other sense than the political sense, for a man must be a fool who supposes that any extension of the suffrage in this country, or any democratic form of government, would lessen by one single brick or stone or piece of timber or scantling any place of worship of any sect or church in this country; and more than that, he must be a blockhead beyond all power of argument to suppose that in this great community the ministers of your various free churches and dissenting sects would be less thought of than they are at present, or that the gentleman whom I saw on this platform to-night (Dr. Miller) would have less respect or influence here than he has at this moment.

But this, I suspect, is what they fear. I have sought a

good deal into this question, and it seems to me as if they had a notion that in this country we have some institutions which have come down to us from the middle ages—from what some people call the dark ages—and that these institutions may not permanently harmonize with the intelligence and the necessities of the nineteenth century in which we live. The 'institutions' are truly safe enough if the Government be in the hands of the institution; and if the Peerage and the Established Church are to rule in England, then I presume that the Peerage and the Established Church, in their present condition, will be permanently safe; and if the great patronage of our vast expenditure is to be dispensed perpetually amongst the ruling class, the ruling class as a matter of course will take extreme care of the patronage. There is something very sacred in that patronage. There are many families in this country with long lines of ancestry, who, if patronage were curtailed, would feel very much as some of us feel in Lancashire when the American war has stopped our supplies of cotton. They look upon patronage as a holy thing, not to be touched by profane hands. I have no doubt they have in their minds the saying of a great friend of mine, though he is an imaginary character —I mean Hosea Bigelow, the author of the *Bigelow Papers.* He says —

> 'It is something like a fulfilling the prophecies,
> When all the first families have all the best offices.'

But, Sir, I protest against this theory. I protest against the theory that the people of this country have an unreasonable and violent desire to shake or overturn institutions which they may not theoretically approve of. What are these people admitting by making these statements and expressing these fears? Are the people really against the House of Lords? [A Voice: 'No.'] They say—I am constantly told—the people like the Lords very much.

I never think it worth my while to deny it; for I am perfectly content to live under the institutions which the intelligence, and the virtue, and the experience of my countrymen fairly represented in Parliament shall determine upon. I was told when this Government was formed— you must recollect that some people did me the honour to suppose that I should be asked to take office in Lord Palmerston's Government, along with my friends Mr. Gibson and Mr. Cobden. Mr. Cobden was in America at the time,— I suppose they did not like him much better than they liked me, but it is possible they disliked him rather less. Mr. Cobden did not take the seat which was offered him for reasons which were then made public, but the statement which was made to me—which came from Lord Palmerston to be conveyed to me—was this, that I had expressed opinions in recent speeches with regard to institutions, or an institution, which the majority of Englishmen deemed essential, which would make it impossible for him to offer me a seat in his Government.

I had attended meetings—you must recollect—in fact, the first I attended here after I was elected one of your representatives. I afterwards went to Glasgow, and to Edinburgh, and to Manchester, and to Bradford, and the largest room in all these places could not contain one-half of those who wished to come to hear something said on the question which I was discussing, and the speeches which were then made were supposed to be tainted with rather less reverence for the House of Lords than some persons think proper; and therefore, though I was fit to be your representative, and was applauded by listening thousands of my countrymen, I was not qualified to take office in her Majesty's Government.

But is it true that the people are against the Church? Do they ever, in the slightest degree, abstain from giving respect and honour to any minister of that Church who acts even though it be with the feebleness which belongs

to all efforts in that character—who acts in any degree
consistent with the position of a Christian minister?
Besides, if the Church is the poor man's Church, surely
the poor man must know it; and, therefore, who could
imagine for a moment that the people of this country,
acting fairly through their representatives, would do anything as regards that Church which would damage its
usefulness as a Christian institution, or make it less honoured
or less influential in the spread of Christianity amongst the
population of these islands? Why are they, then, afraid of
the people? If a million more electors—I believe the last
Bill only proposed to add half a million—were admitted, is
there any single interest that deserves one moment's consideration that this million of new electors, joined with the
present million of electors, would combine in Parliament to
uproot and destroy? I am not one called upon to defend our institutions. It is not my business, because they
are not attacked; but I will assert this, that the Crown—
which is the most venerable of the institutions to which
it is supposed democracy could be hostile—that the Crown is
not opposed to the admission of this million or half million,
and that the Queen of these realms has more than once from
her own lips declared to Parliament her free consent to the
admission of this number of people to the franchise.

It follows, then, I say, that the institutions which people
are so much afraid of are in themselves unpopular or hurtful,
or else that the people themselves are grossly slandered. I
would insist on this; since the power of the Crown was
limited two hundred years ago, and since the power of the
nobles was limited thirty years ago, good government has
gained greatly in this country, and the people are in all circumstances better, and I am quite sure that the respect shown
to the Crown is more general by far than it was at an earlier
period. But our Constitution involves necessarily the representation of the people, and in calling for this representation

we stand upon a foundation from which no argument and no
sophistry can ever remove us. The House of Commons is in
reality the only guarantee we have for freedom. If you
looked at any other country, and saw nothing but a monarch,
he might be a good king and might do his best, but you
would see that there is no guarantee for freedom—you know
not who will be his successor. If you saw a country with no
Crown, but with a handful of nobles, administering the
government of the country, you would say there is no
guarantee there for freedom, because a number of individuals
acting together have not the responsibility, or the feeling of
responsibility, that one man has, and they do things which
one man would not dare to do. If there be a man here
who feels himself and his prejudices rise up against the
statements I am making, he, at least, will admit that the
real and only permanent foundation for political freedom
in any country is in the establishment and maintenance of
a system of political representation — in your Houses of
Parliament.

At that dinner at Torquay, a nobleman presided whom
I had the pleasure of knowing a little when he was a
Member of the House of Commons, and another nobleman
whom I have also known there made the principal speech,
and what do you think they did? They had a number of
toasts—which is a thing I do not recommend because they
do not drink them in cold water—and they proposed, first,
what are called the ceremonial toasts—though one would
hope they are not altogether ceremonial—and amongst them
the House of Lords. The toast was responded to in a long
speech by Lord Devon. And what did they propose next?
Not the House of Commons, but 'The Conservative Party in
the House of Commons.' They did not propose 'The Conservative Party in the House of Lords.' Perhaps they
thought the whole House of Lords was a Conservative party,
or else they thought that the Liberal party in the House of

Commons was really not worth remembering, except it may be to wish that it did not exist. These gentlemen do not comprehend our Constitution at all. They do not know, apparently, that it is only because there is something which the people still believe to be in some degree a representative body, and which stands between them and monarchical and aristocratic despotism—that it is only the existence of that House which makes the institution they are so fond of safe and permanent at all—and they are afraid that the five millions somehow or other will get into it. Now, I beg to tell them that the five millions will get into it, though they may not get into it all at once; and perhaps few men desire that they should, for I am opposed myself to great and violent changes, which create needless shocks, and which are accepted, if they are accepted, with great alarm.

But I will undertake to say that some portion, a considerable and effective portion, of those five millions will before many years are passed be freely allowed to vote for Members of the House of Commons. It is not the democracy which these gentlemen are always afraid of that is the peril of this country. It was not democracy in 1832 that was the peril. It was the desperate antagonism of the class that then had power to the just claims and rights of the people. And at this moment, when they dine and when I speak, I tell them that Conservatism—they give it that name, but it is worthy of a very different name—that Conservatism, be it Tory or be it Whig, is the true national peril which we have to face. They may dam the stream, they may keep back the waters, but the volume is ever increasing, and it descends with accelerated force, and the time will come when, in all probability, and to a certainty, if wisdom does not take the place of folly, the waters will burst their banks, and these men, who fancy they are stemming this imaginary apparition of democracy, will be swept away by the resolute will of a united and determined people.

For one moment cast your eyes over the face of Europe. You will find that there are now only two considerable States that have not representative institutions—Turkey and Russia; and Russia is making progress in freedom equal at least to the progress of any other State in Europe. Representation is found in Italy, in Austria even, in almost all the German States, in the Northern States, in Belgium, Holland, France, Portugal, and Spain. It is found also, as I have said, and as you know, all over the American continent. It is found, also, firmly settled as an institution in Australia. Englishmen, everywhere but at home, are received into the bosom of this great permanent undying institution, this safeguard for national, for human freedom. But here they are slandered, they are insulted, they are reviled, they are shut out. They are invited to half a hundred ways of amusing themselves; but if they stand at the hustings or at the poll, and see their richer brethren come up to vote, they are not allowed to register their names in favour of principles for which their fathers before them, and themselves, have sighed in many a bitter hour of disappointment.

Now, Sir, I would change all this. I speak out of no hostility to any class, or any institution. That man who proposes to exclude permanently five millions of his countrymen from the right which the Constitution of his country makes sacred in his eyes, I say that is the man that separates Englishmen into two nations, and makes it impossible that we should be wholly or permanently a contented people. I demand, then, this, which is but the right of our Constitution, that the House of Commons shall be made freely and fairly to represent the Commons and the people of the United Kingdom. England has long been famous for the enjoyment of personal freedom by her people. They are free to think, they are free to speak, they are free to write; and England has been famed of late years, and is famed now the world over, for the freedom of her industry and the greatness and the freedom of her commerce. I want to know then why it is that her people should not be free to vote. Who is there that will meet me on this platform, or will stand upon any platform, and will dare to say, in the hearing of an open meeting of his countrymen, that these millions for whom I am now pleading are too degraded, too vicious, and too destructive to be entrusted with the elective franchise? I at least will never thus slander my countrymen. I claim for them the right of admission, through their representatives, into the most ancient and the most venerable Parliament which at this hour exists among men; and when they are thus admitted, and not till then, it may be truly said that England, the august mother of free nations, herself is free.

REFORM.

VI.

THE REFORM BILL OF LORD RUSSELL'S ADMINISTRATION.

ON THE MOTION FOR LEAVE TO BRING IN THE BILL.

HOUSE OF COMMONS, MARCH 13, 1866.

[On the death of Lord Palmerston, Lord Russell became Prime Minister, and on the meeting of Parliament, a Bill for the improvement of the Representation of the People was introduced by Mr. Gladstone, on behalf of the Government. The Bill did not pass, and the Russell Administration retired from office in June, 1866.]

ALTHOUGH in the course of this debate I have been the subject of much remark, and of not a little that may be fairly termed unusual attack, I beg to assure the House that I have not risen for the purpose of defending myself, since I am ready to leave my course in this House and my political character to the impartial view of Members of the House, and to the just judgment of my countrymen outside the House. Nor have I risen for the purpose of entering into an elaborate defence of the Bill introduced by the Chancellor of the Exchequer. I think, however, that there has been so much said which is not to the point that it may be advantageous if I endeavour to explain to the House what I understand the Bill to be—to state some of the grounds on which it appeals to us for support, and to ask the House whether, under the circumstances of this question, and in the existing condition of the country, it is the duty of Parliament to permit it to pass into a law.

One thing in the Bill is highly satisfactory to me—that both in what it does and the manner in which it proposes to do it, it is distinct, clear, without any tricks—without semblance of giving something in one clause, and then under a feeling of alarm withdrawing that something in the clause that follows. I have always been in favour of meeting this question and dealing with it in such a manner that every person in the country who is now an elector, or who is to be included in the Bill, should comprehend that it was a measure, so far as it went, fair and generous to the people whom it was intended to enfranchise.

I think I can show reasons—if we can for a moment get rid of the notion of party combination — why this House should readily, and without hesitation, agree to this Bill. One portion of it will recommend itself, I am quite certain, to all Gentlemen who are enthusiastic admirers of the Bill of 1832—and on this point I can confidently ask for the support of the right hon. Gentleman the Member for Calne—that is the portion of the Bill which is intended to remove all legal obstacles or difficulties by which many persons who were intended to be enfranchised by the Reform Bill have been up to this time deprived of their votes. The Reform Bill proposed to give a vote to every occupier of a 10*l.* house in a borough. It is shown, partly it may be by the wording of the Act, partly by the decisions of judges and courts, that this extension of the franchise was never complete; that by the operation of clauses which made it necessary to pay rates, and which made it necessary almost in effect that the occupier himself should pay the rates, many thousands—I know not the number—will have been disfranchised from 1832 up to the very hour at which this Bill shall pass into law. In Scotland there is no such disqualification as that which this Bill proposes to remove, for there they have no rate-paying clauses, and they have no system of compounding which would juggle men out of their franchise; and the object of this Bill is to assimilate our law in this respect to the law of Scotland, and to give to the Reform Act of 1832 the same efficacy which the people expected from it when it passed both Houses of Parliament. I suppose, although Gentlemen may not admit it by any outward expression of opinion, they are not against such an improvement of the Reform Act as will give the vote which this part of the Bill is intended to give. The right hon. Member for Calne can certainly not refuse his assent, because if there be one thing except the classical times of antiquity to which he is more devoted than another it is clearly the Bill of 1832.

The next point to which I shall ask the attention of the House is that which the Bill proposes to do in respect to the county franchise. Here I must say, at the risk of saying what is not complimentary to the Chancellor of the Exchequer and his colleagues, that I think the Government have shown a remarkable feebleness, which lays them open to great blame, not only on the part of the House, but of almost every person in the country who has expected a Bill on the subject of Reform. They propose to bring the franchise down from a 50*l.* occupation to one of 14*l.* The occupation franchise in counties was a measure of your own carrying in 1832. I do not say that to touch it would not have been necessary now, if you had not then disturbed the ancient franchise of the counties; but when the county occupation franchise was fixed at 50*l.* and the franchise in boroughs at 10*l.*, he must have been a very dull man indeed who could not have foreseen that the county franchise must at some time not remote be greatly reduced. The right hon. Gentleman the Chancellor of the Exchequer spoke encouragingly in that Reform discussion many years ago, when the House carried the third reading of the Bill introduced by my hon. Friend the Member for East Surrey; but from that time to this there has been a good deal more done on this question. The right hon. Gentleman the Member for Buckinghamshire, and his Cabinet—the noble Lord the Member for King's Lynn being very intimately concerned with the then leader of the House in manufacturing a Reform Bill—had not had much experience, and it was not to be wondered at that they made mistakes. They brought in their Bill—a Bill containing some good things and some bad things—and among other things proposed a 10*l.* franchise in counties. They took, however, a considerable compensation by attempting to withdraw all freeholders within the limits of boroughs from the county franchise—transferring them to the electoral body within the limits of boroughs. But that does not in the slightest degree change this fact—that they did with due deliberation come to the opinion that 10*l.* occupiers in counties were fit and proper persons to exercise the elective franchise. You do not suppose that they proposed to put persons on the county lists of whose fitness they were not well assured, and then endeavoured to compensate for this by their proposal with regard to the freeholders in the boroughs. They believed, and believe now, no doubt, that 10*l.* was a proper and fitting franchise for the counties in England and Wales; and I should be glad to find them, when the House shall be in Committee on this Bill, proposing to reduce the sum of a 14*l.* franchise to a 10*l.* one. If they wish to have an easy victory over the Government, and to prove themselves consistent, and to extend the range of the county registration, I and a good many Members in this part of the House will be extremely happy to give them our cordial support; and I can promise them the support of the right hon. Gentleman behind me (Mr. Lowe), because he has fixed his affections on a 10*l*. rental franchise. If he were to say he approved a 10*l*. household franchise in boroughs he must do so also in the counties, because we all know that the 10*l*. householders in counties are generally men in better pecuniary circumstances than those of equal rental in boroughs.

So far as I have gone, I hope I have persuaded Gentlemen opposite, and the right hon. Gentleman the Member for Calne, from any opposition to the Bill of the Government with regard to these two portions of it. I may say further, with respect to this proposition of the Government, that there was one illustration the learned Gentleman (Mr. Whiteside) might have made in his amusing speech, for however much the country is going to ruin, he can always be amusing in this House—there is one illustration he might have given us. He said that in Ireland they had a 12*l*. rating franchise for the counties, and that is as near as may be in value to a 14*l*. rental franchise. Therefore, the proposition of the Government—although I disapprove it—still has the sanction of the course which has been taken in Ireland, and this, I have heard from Irish Members, is considered a not unsatisfactory condition of the county franchise. But, with the experience of a great number of years of this franchise in Ireland, I think the Member for Calne may screw up his courage to support this proposition of the Bill.

I now come to the only point on which there is any great difference of opinion. I think the world has never shown an instance of a legislative assembly such as this making a great disturbance among themselves, exciting themselves, getting into a violent passion, pouring out cataracts of declamation like those we heard last night, and all upon the simple question whether the franchise in boroughs shall remain as now at 10*l*. or shall be fixed for a time at 7*l*. Hon. Gentlemen opposite appear to be surprised at the frankness with which I speak. The head of the present Government was

laughed at for years because he spoke of finality in connection
with the Bill of 1832. I should be very happy if it should so
happen, as the right hon. Gentleman has suggested in his
fervid imagination, that the working classes would in great
numbers surmount the barrier of $7l.$, and that ultimately
it should be even equal to a household suffrage in the
country. But does any Gentleman opposite believe that he is
carrying a Bill—did any Gentleman sitting in this House
ever vote upon any measure of arrangement and organisation like this, and confidently assure himself that the
measure should be final? He must have a very poor notion
of what our children will be if he thinks them less competent to decide such questions for themselves than we are
at present to decide them. Therefore do not think that
because I use the phrase 'for a time,' I am not of opinion
that this Bill, if it be carried, will in all probability put an
end to Bills having reference to the suffrage—for such portion
of time, at least, as this Bill will be found to meet the views
of the intelligent—[loud laughter and cheers]—allow me to
finish the sentence—of the intelligent population of this
country.

The Bill of the Chancellor of the Exchequer proposes,
in addition to the $7l.$ franchise, what he calls a lodger
franchise. The Member for Buckinghamshire in his Bill
proposed something of the same kind, but with a $20l.$
qualification, while the present Bill proposes a $10l.$ qualification—$10l.$ being very nearly the same for a holding of
this kind as $7l.$ would be for a house. But the right hon.
Gentleman opposite proposed provisions in his measure which
would be extremely difficult, and I think would lead to
great perplexity. I have no doubt that the proposition now
made by the Government is simpler than his, and likely to
be carried out with less difficulty and more satisfaction to that
class of persons in this metropolis who are chiefly interested
in this part of the Bill. With regard to the $7l.$ franchise,

let us examine it for one moment. Somebody has said, and many persons have written, that this Bill is my Bill—that the Government made this Bill at my recommendation. [' Hear.'] I thought somebody would say this. I have not been able to find a point of the Bill which I have recommended. I never was in favour of a 6*l.* franchise, and I should never have proposed it. I believe in a household franchise for the boroughs of this country. But when I found a powerful Government like the last—and it was not as honest as it was powerful—proposing a 6*l.* franchise, with the expectation that it would carry it, I was not to stand in the way of a considerable enfranchisement of the people merely because I had an idea that household suffrage would be better. A 7*l.* franchise is a proposition I have never said one syllable in favour of, and it never entered into my mind that the Government would split hairs in this fashion, and would leave the 6*l.* franchise, their own former proposition, and which nearly everybody in the country who has asked for a Reform Bill has expressed himself ready to accept, and would offer the House a 7*l.* franchise. But here it is offered, and unfortunately, beggars in the House of Commons, like beggars outside of it, cannot be choosers, and we are sometimes in a position to take only what is given.

When the Bill of the right hon. Gentleman opposite was brought in, a very remarkable thing happened. Two eminent Members of the Government seceded from it, and took their seats on the third bench behind, and I think I see one of them sitting there at this moment. They both made what we call a personal explanation to the House, and the explanation was that they differed from their colleagues on this question of the suffrage. They did not approve that the suffrage in counties should be brought down to the rate of the boroughs, and that the suffrage in the boroughs should be continued at the same rate which was fixed at the time of the Reform Act. I am not sure whether these right hon. Gentlemen coincide in the opinion that the county franchise should be brought down to 10*l.* I think the right hon. Gentlemen expressed some dissent—at least they were of opinion that the franchise in the boroughs ought to be reduced; and I know the Member for Oxfordshire, in the words which have often been quoted since, expressed himself in favour of establishing a borough franchise at 8*l.* Now when the Government have been splitting hairs with regard to 6*l.* and 7*l.*, I hope the right hon. Gentlemen on that side of the House will not split hairs between 8*l.* and 7*l.*, because surely after the discussion this question has undergone — after the mode and manner the House has been brought into difficulty by past transactions—after the great expectations which have been raised throughout the country, I think it would show very ill statesmanship on the part of those right hon. Gentlemen and a mere obedience to the cause of party—it would hardly be becoming in them—if they were not willing to make the small concession of 1*l.* in answer to the concession of 1*l.* which I am willing or forced to make, and join with me in giving at least a friendly if not an enthusiastic support to the Bill of the Government.

And, after all, this 3*l.*, what is it? The right hon. Gentleman behind me has conjured up a frightful apparition. The 10*l.* is the salvation of the country. For thirty-four years its operation has been such as to extort from him unlimited approval. I do not know whether he will think 9*l.* perilous or 8*l.* in any degree of doubtful utility, but 7*l.* he considers to be actually destructive to the interests of the country; and he has shown moreover that it would destroy the connection between the Executive Government and the House—that it would add greatly to all the evils which are supposed to exist in connection with the present Bill, without any of its advantages; in fact, I know not whether a more gloomy, discouraging, and appalling picture of the future of the House and the country was ever drawn by any Member of the House. And all the foundation of these horrors is that it is proposed to reduce the franchise in the boroughs by 1*l*. lower than was recommended by the Member for Oxfordshire and by his colleague the Member for the University of Cambridge. Now, I appeal to Gentlemen opposite whether they will allow themselves, considering the position of this question, to make it impossible that the question of the suffrage should be got out of our way during this present session of Parliament. If they do make it impossible—I am not much given to prophesy, but I venture to predict that there are many on those benches now who will live to regret the course they are about to take.

There is one other proposition—it is made in this Bill—which I hope the House will not listen to for a moment, and that is the Savings-bank franchise. I think the Member for Buckinghamshire had something like it—perhaps the very same thing—in his Bill. I disapproved of it then. I have no objection to enfranchise those who may be enfranchised by it; but I think it is the very worst of all the fancy franchises ever proposed. It will be unequal to the last degree, and it will be, I believe, the source of every kind of fraud. I agree with the right hon. Gentleman the Member for Wick, who, I think, in speaking of it said he did not see why the investment of 50*l*.—the saving of it in a Savings-bank—should give a man a higher social and political position than the investment or saving of an equal sum in any other description of property where the investment could be fairly ascertained. I object altogether to giving the franchise to one man and shutting it out from another—that second man, it may be, being far more heroic than the other. For example, a man may have to provide a humble equipment for a daughter's marriage, a small sum for a son's apprenticeship—something may be taken out of his earnings for the education of his children, he may have under his roof an aged parent, and he may be performing to that parent the most sacred and most holy of duties, and these may cause him to withdraw 5*l*. or 10*l*. from his little fund in the Savings-bank, or may prevent his having any fund there at all, and the law steps in, and for doing so much, which in every rank of life is so honourable and so exemplary, his name is to be erased from the electoral list of the town in which he lives. I protest against this Savings-bank franchise. I think also it would be liable to great fraud, because three or four members of a family may invest in a Savings-bank in one name and so give to that one person a vote. I do not in the least object to any one person having a vote, but I do object to giving it under a system which, altogether apart from the general processes of our enfranchisement, is liable to the utmost inequality, and to a species of fraud which cannot be prevented.

Now I have gone through the Bill in its main provisions, and I would ask the House what they think of it. The Chancellor of the Exchequer tells us—in fact, we well know —that we have in England and Wales about five and a half millions of men. Under this Bill he further tells us we should have 900,000 electors. [A Voice from the Treasury Benches: ' 1,300,000.'] But not 1,300,000 when the double qualifications are taken off. Whatever that be, it will place within the franchise perhaps a little more than one in five, leaving out four millions of grown men in England and Wales who will still not have the franchise. Of those he says there will be 330,000 working-men. This is a very —as I am quite confident whenever the matter is fairly looked into will be found out—exaggerated estimate. The right hon. Gentleman included 60,000 who now live in 10*l*. houses be- sides those referred to in the Blue Books. And more than that, he included every man between 10*l*. and 7*l*., although the experience of every one tells us that is not correct; and as to all these working-men brought forward in these Blue

Books, except the Members for Coventry, I will undertake to say that there is scarcely a single Member of the House, looking to his own canvass and his own constituency, who is not prepared to say that the estimate is a delusion and a snare.

I should only be too glad if it could be honestly ascertained that so many working-men would be placed upon the register; at least I think it would do something towards confirming hon. Gentlemen in the view they entertain that the conduct of so many of those men as possess the franchise has hitherto been most exemplary in their exercise of it. Now, I appeal to hon. Gentlemen—I am very earnest in my wishes upon this question, because, notwithstanding the unkind allusion and imputation thrown upon me some time ago by a right hon. Gentleman on this side of the House, there is nobody who has a greater interest than I have, in a certain sense, in a fair and early settlement of this question. I have had as much to do with it as any one, I think, in discussing it publicly out of the House and in the House. I have discussed it frankly, and whatever hon. Gentlemen may think to the contrary, I never spoke on any question in which I took a greater interest, or with a deeper conviction that I was serving the true interests of their class as well as those of my countrymen at large.

I do not know whether I can appeal to certain Members of the House. The right hon. Gentleman the Member for Calne has shown that nearly everything the Bill proposes is really that which is bound up in some shape with the Bill of 1832, or with the propositions in which he has been concerned. I have got here—it is really curious how things drop into your hands when you want them — here is a paper, the *Norfolk News*, of the year 1859, and I have certain extracts which I have taken from the paper. These are extracts from election addresses. The first is from the election address of Lord Palmerston, who said there must be a Bill to alter the law regulating the representation of the people in

Parliament. Then Lord John Russell said we should have to consider the great question of the amendment of the represcutation of the people in Parliament. Sir George Grey said that at the earliest period consistent with duty, the Government would be prepared to deal with the question of Parliamentary Reform. Then there were similar extracts from the speeches of my right hon. Friend the President of the Board of Trade, from the speeches of the Attorney-General of that day, and of the Solicitor-General. There is then an extract headed, 'Right Hon. Robert Lowe, Vice-President of the Committee of Council on Education.' And what does he say in 1859, before the Government of the right hon. Gentleman opposite was discharged from the service of the House and of the country? The Right Hon. Robert Lowe says:—

'It will be the duty of the Government to prepare a measure of Reform, and I have every confidence that it will be one which if not fully satisfying men of extreme opinions, will be acceptable to the great body of the people.'

I think the right hon. Gentleman has a very short memory, or else he trifles with this House. Is it conceivable that a man who wrote that in his election address in 1859 should stand up to-night and deliver such a speech as we have heard from him for an hour and a half? I am afraid, Sir, that when under these circumstances men change their opinions after they are fifty years of age, there is not much expectation of turning them back again. I feel that I could not with much hope appeal to the right hon. Member for Calne, or to his colleague the right hon. Member for Stroud; I do not know that I should appeal to the noble Lord the Member for Haddington (Lord Elcho), who, with the exception of the hon. Member for Salisbury, is the only Member at this side of the House who cheers the sentiments of either of the right hon. Gentlemen.

What is the reason, I ask, that Gentlemen who have been holders of office take this course with regard to the Bill of

the Government? I will not deal in any insinuations, but
I will say that, from Gentlemen who have held office, but
who happen to have been left out of what may be called
the daily ministrations, we have a right to expect a very
minute account of the reasons why they change their opinions
before we can turn round and change with them. These are
the Gentlemen who all at once start up as the great teachers
of statesmanship to the House and the country. Are they
what the right hon. Baronet the Member for Droitwich spoke
of in the recess—are they the foremost statesmen in the
country? and if so, is there to be a bid for them to take the
place of Gentlemen who have not much succeeded as statesmen when in office? In office these right hon. Gentlemen
are as docile as any other Gentlemen in office, but I fear,
notwithstanding the ideas some people have of my influence
with Earl Russell, that I am not able to offer them any arguments on his part that will tell upon them. I do not object
for a moment to a Member of this House being fond of office.
The Chancellor of the Exchequer probably lives much more
happily in office than he would live if he were out of it,
though I do not think he will live quite so long. I do not
complain of men who are fond of office, though I could never
comprehend the reason they like it so much. If I may
parody, or if I may make an alteration in a line or two
of one of the most beautiful poems in our language, I might
ask—

> ' For who, to dumb forgetfulness a prey,
>   That pleasing, anxious office e'er resigned,
> Left the warm precincts of the Treasury,
>   Nor cast one last, long, lingering look behind.'

What I complain of is this, that when place recedes into
the somewhat dim past, that which in office was deemed
patriotism vanishes with it; and we have one howl of
despair from these right hon. Gentlemen because it is proposed to diminish the franchise in boroughs from 10*l.* to 7*l.*,

and to add by so small a proposition as that something to the freedom of the people of this country.

The right hon. Gentleman below me (Mr. Horsman) said a little against the Government and a little against the Bill, but had last night a field night for an attack upon so humble an individual as I am. The right hon. Gentleman is the first of the new party who has expressed his great grief, who has retired into what may be called his political cave of Adullam, and he has called about him every one that was in distress and every one that was discontented. The right hon. Gentleman has been anxious to form a party in this House. There is scarcely any one on this side of the House who is able to address the House with effect or to take much part in our debates, whom he has not tried to bring over to his party or cabal; and at last the right hon. Gentleman has succeeded in hooking the right hon. Gentleman the Member for Calne. I know there was an opinion expressed many years ago by a Member of the Treasury bench and of the Cabinet, that two men would make a party. When a party is formed of two men so amiable—so discreet—as the two right hon. Gentlemen, we may hope to see for the first time in Parliament a party perfectly harmonious and distinguished by mutual and unbroken trust. But there is one difficulty which it is impossible to remove. This party of two reminds me of the Scotch terrier, which was so covered with hair that you could not tell which was the head and which was the tail of it.

The right hon. Member for Calne told us that he had some peculiar election experiences. There are men who make discord wherever they appear. The right hon. Gentleman on going down to Kidderminster got into some unpleasing altercation with somebody, and it ended with his having his head broken. But I am happy to say, and the House will bear witness, that with regard to its power, that head is probably as strong now as before he took his leave of Kidderminster and went to Calne—a village in the West of England. The right hon. Gentleman found on the list of electors at Calne, one hundred and seventy-four names, of whom, according to the Blue Book, about seven were working-men. I suppose three or four of them were probably keepers of shops, and some of those whom the Chancellor of the Exchequer I think improperly included in his list. When the right hon. Member went down there he found a tumult even more aggravated than at Kidderminster. They did not break his head, but they did something that in the eye of the law was much worse, for they shut up the police in the Town Hall, and the little mob of this little place had the whole game to themselves. The right hon. Gentleman told us of the polypus, which takes its colour from the rock on which it lives, and he said that some hon. Members take their colours from their constituencies. The constituency which the right hon. Gentleman represents consists of one hundred and seventy-four men, seven of whom are working-men; but the real constituent of the right hon. Gentleman is a Member of the other House of Parliament, and he could send in his butler or his groom, instead of the right hon. Gentleman, to represent the borough. I think in one sense—regarding the right hon. Gentleman as an intellectual gladiator in this House—we are much indebted to the Marquis of Lansdowne that he did not do that.

And now, Sir, I said that I wanted to explain the particulars of this Bill, and to appeal to the good sense and patriotism of hon. Gentlemen opposite. I ask them not to take that disparaging view of their countrymen which has been presented to them by the right Hon. Member for Calne and the hon. Member for Salisbury, who—I presume from their residence at the antipodes—seem to take a Botany Bay impression, and a Botany Bay view, of the character of the great bulk of their countrymen. The right hon. Gentleman some nights ago, when I was not here, said that I, even in the matter of the cattle plague, set class against class. ['Hear, hear!' from the Opposition benches, and laughter.] The hon. Gentlemen opposite, who from the ease with which they are amused must be a most amiable party, laugh at this observation. I ask any man in this House, is it possible to do a thing more perilous than that which is done by the right hon. Gentleman and his Australian colleague the hon. Member for Salisbury —namely, to make it appear that there is a gulf that shall not be passed by legislation between the highest and most powerful and a portion of the middle classes, and the great body of the working-people who are really the heart of this great nation?

The right hon. Gentleman tells us that by and by, if everybody will wait long enough, everybody will get over this barrier and be inside the franchise. But that is no great consolation, because he said that by the Bill of the Government we, or our children, shall be eaten up at some future time. Would it not be infinitely better to show our trust in the people now? Of all the follies and crimes which Governments commit, that of a constant distrust of their subjects, of their citizens, of their country, is about the wildest and most foolish. But the right hon. Gentleman the Member for Stroud and somebody else who followed him tell us that the people are very indifferent about this matter. I think I just caught the Member for Salisbury in the hubbub of the House as he rose to speak, making an observation about the number of petitions; and the right hon. Gentleman the Member for Calne said he thought their number was not more than four. But how many petitions were there previous to 1831? Bear in mind that Lord John Russell had for some time discontinued bringing forward his motion for Parliamentary Reform. In 1821 one petition was presented to the House in favour of Parliamentary Reform. In 1822 there were twelve, in 1823 there were twenty-nine; in the six years that passed between 1824 and 1829 there was not a single petition presented to this House in favour of Parliamentary Reform; and in 1830 there were fourteen petitions—ten more than those with which the right hon. Gentleman made himself merry to-night. And what took place in 1831-2? This,—some of you were fleeing for your lives in the midst of a storm which you had not foreseen, but which was as inevitable as any storm that arises in the heavens. It was an accident that brought it about—the French Revolution. Well, there are always accidents. A great portion of the things that happen in our lives, so far as we can judge, have the appearance of accidents. But with the accident there was material for a conflagration, and a conflagration arose.

I recollect that the late Francis Place and two or three others went to the Duke of Wellington as a deputation when he took office after the fall of Lord Grey's Government, and that they remonstrated with the Duke. He was not a man that liked remonstrances very much, but they told him what was going on, how dissatisfied the people were, and how perilous they thought the course of the Government in opposing Reform. And what did the Duke say? He was standing warming himself at the fire. He said to these gentlemen, 'You have got heads on your shoulders, and I would advise you to keep them there.' Two or three days afterwards the Duke of Wellington was driven from office. The popular feeling in the country and in the metropolis was such that this great soldier that knew no fear was obliged to resign, and Lord Grey was permitted to come back, and the Reform Bill was eventually carried.

Now I ask hon. Gentlemen if they think any accident will ever happen again. That accident was in Paris. But in 1848, only eighteen years afterwards, there was another accident in Paris, which was followed by a succession of accidents in other parts of Europe. I recollect at the time a noble Lord who was then a Member of this House was greatly alarmed. He came to me from that side of the House, and assured me that he had always been in favour of a great extension of the suffrage. I believe that he was not quite sure that I should not soon be a member of a Provisional Government. I ask hon. Gentlemen whether it is not better to accept a measure so moderate, and if you like, as may be said by many in the country, so inadequate, but still to some extent so good? Is it not better to accept this measure, and show your confidence in the people, than to take the advice of the Member for Calne—the most revolutionary advice that was ever given in this House—and shut your doors against five millions of people, and tell them that unless they can scramble over this 10*l.* barrier none of them shall ever find a direct representation in this House?

The Member for Stroud talked loudly last night about constitutional rights and constitutional principles. But who was it that made the present constitution of England more than any other men in our history? Surely the men of the first and second Parliaments in the reign of Charles the First. Is it not in the very journals of your House? The Clerk of the House could easily find and read to you the resolutions of the House, that wherever there is not some direct interdiction or contradiction of it, the ancient and common franchise of the people of this country in the towns is the householding franchise. And do you mean to tell me that Lord Somers, who was himself a great authority, and to a large extent one of the builders of our existing constitution, was wrong when he said that though no man by birth had any right to office, yet that by birth he had a right to vote, and that the possession of a vote was the only true security which an Englishman had for the protection of his life and property? I am not stating that as my opinion, I am giving you the opinion of one of the greatest men in the Parliamentary annals of this nation, and therefore I say you will not act constitutionally or wisely if you put any obstacle in the path of a Bill that is so moderate as this, and that may give great satisfaction to vast multitudes of the people.

If this Bill be rejected you will show that you are against

all Reform, you will show that you have no confidence whatever even in that portion of the population which lives in
houses between 10*l*. and 7*l*. rental.   And if you pass this Bill
you will show that you are not cut off altogether from sympathy with multitudes of your fellow-countrymen.   I say
there is peril in the present state of things.   You have
a population divorced almost entirely from the land, and shut
out from the possession of the franchise.   My hon. Friend the
Member for Brighton touched upon the question of emigration.   The right hon. Gentleman the Member for Calne spoke
of the intelligence of the people in this way—of their combinations and associations.   We all know that they are
reading, debating, thinking, and combining, and they know
that in all our colonies, and in the United States, the position
of their class is very different.   I believe that if you do not
moderate your tone and your views with regard to the great
bulk of the working classes, you will find your country gradually
weakened by a constantly increasing emigration, or you will
find some accident happening, when you will have something
to do more than you are asked to do to-night, under the
threat, and it may be under the infliction, of violence.

Now, Sir, I said at the beginning that I did not rise to
defend this Bill.   I rose for the purpose of explaining it.   It
is not a Bill which, if I had been consulted by its framers, I
should have recommended.   If I had been a Minister it is not
a Bill which I should have consented to present to the House.
I think it is not adequate to the occasion, and that its concessions are not sufficient.   But I know the difficulties under
which Ministries labour, and I know the disinclination of
Parliament to do much in the direction of this question.
I shall give it my support because, as far as it goes, it is
a simple and honest measure, and because I believe, if it
becomes law, it will give more solidity and duration to everything that is good in the Constitution, and to everything that
is noble in the character of the people of these realms.

REFORM.

VII.

THE REPRESENTATION OF THE PEOPLE BILL.—DEBATE ON
THE SECOND READING.

HOUSE OF COMMONS, APRIL 23, 1866.

From Hansard.

BEFORE I address myself to the question which is before
the House, there are two matters of a personal character
which I wish to dispose of. The right hon. Member for
Calne, on the first night of this debate, made a complaint to
the House that, in a speech out of this House, I had imputed
to him, or quoted as from him, words which he had not
uttered. The right hon. Gentleman was quite right to make
that complaint, if he thought it worth while to make it,
because there is no doubt—and I am sorry it so happened—
that some three or four words which he had not spoken in
that connection were added to the passage which he had
spoken. I regret the inaccuracy very much. I have the
satisfaction, however, of knowing or believing that I did the
right hon. Gentleman no substantial injustice.

The other point refers to the speech of the noble Lord the
Member for King's Lynn (Lord Stanley). He retorted on
me a charge of conspiracy with reference to two divisions
which took place some years ago in this House, one on the

China War, and the other on the Conspiracy Bill.   In neither
of these cases did the mover of the resolution obtain a seconder
from the opposite side of the House.   But with regard to the
first case, that of the China War, I was not in Parliament
during that session.   I was in bad health, out of the country;
and the first thing I knew of it was from reading an account
of what had taken place in this House in a public news-room
in the city of Rome.   With regard to the other case, that of
the Conspiracy Bill, Members who were then in the House
will recollect that on the first division, on the first reading of
the Bill, nearly one hundred Members—I think that was the
exact number, I am not sure—or ninety-nine, voted in the
division against the introduction or first reading of the Bill,
including Lord John Russell, the President of the Board of
Trade (Mr. Gibson), myself, and many others.   The noble
Lord's friends warmly welcomed and supported that Bill.
Before the second reading came on, my right hon. Friend the
President of the Board of Trade gave notice of a resolution, which was carried by the House; the noble Lord
with several of his friends, departing altogether from their
votes on the first reading, turned completely round upon
their own policy, supported my right hon. Friend, went into
the same lobby with him, and made a majority against the
Government of Lord Palmerston.   If there was any conspiracy
then, it was owing to the other side of the House; and if it
was a dirty conspiracy, the dirt was imported into it by the
noble Lord and his friends.   Now, these are inaccuracies
which may occur in debate, but I think it was necessary to
make an apology to the right hon. Gentleman, and to explain
the charge which the noble Lord had inadvertently brought
against me.

    I come now to the question before the House, and the
resolution which has been moved by the Member for Chester.
Whatever are the words in which a resolution or design is
wrapped up in this House, the true meaning of it generally

comes out during the debate; but the noble Lord the Member for Chester did not in the slightest degree leave us in difficulty with respect to his view; and there can be nothing more clear than this — I do not in the slightest degree blame him for it — he has a perfect right to his opinion — that he stands as the principal opponent of this measure, on the ground either that he is opposed to all Reform, or to such an extension of the franchise as the Government propose in this Bill; and I presume, if the truth were known, and judging from his speech, that if the Government would lay on the table of the House the Seats Bill, which may be as extensive with respect to that part of the subject as this measure of the franchise is on another part, it would meet with the strenuous opposition of the noble Lord. Thus the Bill that is not before us is made an excuse and weapon for destroying the Bill that is before us. That, I think, as far as I can judge, is a fair statement of the position of the noble Lord; but when the Seats Bill is laid on the table of the House we shall have an opportunity of knowing what is the course which the noble Lord will take upon it.

I come now to the speech made by the Member for King's Lynn, in seconding the amendment. His speech was much more ingenious, and it was much less candid; it was much less straightforward, but it lands us in the same position; and the noble Lord during his speech, twice at least, if not oftener, used the words the ‘balance of power’ in reference to the representation of the people in this House. We have done now pretty much with the balance of power on the Continent of Europe. I hope the time will come when we shall have no such phrase as the ‘balance of power’ in this House.

Sir, I think that this House should be a fair representation of the people of this country, and though it may not be desirable, and even if desirable it may not be attainable, that all persons should vote, yet, far short of that, I am persuaded that the representation may be so arranged that every person of every class will feel that his interests are fairly represented, and will be fairly consulted by the House. But the noble Lord is afflicted with a species of terror, or perhaps I should rather call it a feeling of no confidence, such as I have hardly ever seen before in this House. He has no confidence in the Government. That I have very often seen, and I have seen him in a Government in which the majority of the House had no confidence; but he has no confidence in the House. First of all the Government, through the Prime Minister and through the Chancellor of the Exchequer, have given the most distinct promise with regard to the Bill for the re-arrangement of seats; but the noble Lord has no confidence in that promise. The noble Lord has no confidence in the House, because if this Franchise Bill should pass, he thinks the House might do something very unwise in the matter of the Seats Bill. He has no confidence in the people, because the object of this Bill is to admit them to the franchise; and he has special terror of what might happen if the Franchise Bill should pass and the Seats Bill fail, and we should all be sent back to enlarged constituencies to be returned to a future Parliament. The noble Lord must know that, whatever be the re-arrangement of seats, it must lead to greater popular power in the House; and that whatever be the extension of the franchise, it must lead to the same result; and we all know that henceforth the Parliament which shall be elected on an extended franchise, or after a redistribution of seats, will be a Parliament of full authority in the country—that it will have power still further to extend the franchise, and still further to alter the distribution of seats, and to conduct all matters connected with the legislation of the Empire. And therefore the noble Lord, who was in such extraordinary tremor with regard to what may happen if this Bill pass or if the other fail, appears to me to present the most singular exhibition of political anxiety I have ever seen.

I thought that when the noble Lord concluded his speech, everything in it that was true was unimportant, and everything that seemed to be the least important was not true. But there is one thing important, and that is the opposition of the noble Lord to this Bill; and I hope that he and his colleague in proposing this resolution will forgive me if I say that I think it is a perilous thing when the heirs of two of the most ancient and the most wealthy and powerful of the houses of the English nobility oppose themselves to this moderate and just Bill, and have set themselves by a coalition in this House to drive Lord Russell from power—for this, and this only, offence—that he wields the authority of his great office to extend in what I believe to be a moderate and . conservative degree the franchises of his countrymen.

The noble Lord the Member for Chester blames the Government because it took advice from this end of this side of the House [below the gangway of the Ministerial side], and did not confine itself to the advice of powerful persons of the Whig party. I should think that a measure. which is supported by the House of Bedford, by the House of Devonshire, that has among its supporters the Howards, the Sutherlands, the Duke of Somerset, the Duke of Argyll, Lord Clarendon, Lord Granville, Lord Stanley the Post-master-General, and the right hon. Gentleman the Secretary of State for the Home Department—I think a measure that is supported by the Peers that I have mentioned cannot be said to be introduced to this House without some consultation with the Whig party. Now, if the noble Lord will allow me in a perfectly friendly manner to give him a little advice, I will do it in one sentence. The course that he is taking is a course which tends to separate important persons of the Whig party from the Liberal and popular party in this House and in the country, and if he should succeed in dissevering the most intelligent of the Whig nobility from the great popular party in the country, if he should transfer them to the other side, and put all the dukes and the nobles on one side of Parliament, and the popular party on the other—if the noble Lord knows anything whatever of history, he will know this,—that when the great popular party of a country are fighting by themselves against the nobles of a country, whatever their virtues and whatever their power—speaking of many of them—you may rely upon it that the popular party will win, and the nobles will go down.

The noble Lord and many hon. Members of the House during this debate have referred to the supposed influence I have had as to the mode in which this question has been brought before Parliament. Seven years ago, just about the time when the Government of Lord Derby was thrown out, in an accidental or incidental conversation with Lord Russell, I suggested to him that whenever this question was brought again before Parliament, the proper course to take was to introduce the Franchise Bill by itself. From 1860 until this hour I have only had one interview—a very short interview —and only one conversation of a political character with Lord Russell, and until he mentioned the matter at the meeting of his supporters the other day in Downing-street, I must confess to the House that I was totally in ignorance of the fact that the course of the Government in this matter had been in any degree influenced by anything I have said. It was at a meeting at Rochdale in January last that I advised not only the Government to take this course, but that I advised all persons who were in favour of Reform in the kingdom to consider the question and to support this course if it should be taken by the Government. I will tell the House with the most complete candour and fairness what were the reasons which led me to give this advice. I will assume that the House is in favour of Reform. I know what a stretch of imagination is necessary in order to come to that conclusion. But as I am speaking not only to Gentlemen in this House, but to some who are outside this House, I shall treat the question just as if we were all in favour of some measure of Reform, but differed a little as to the mode and extent.

When I suggested to Earl Russell six years ago that he should bring in a Franchise Bill first, he replied that if he did so the opponents of Reform would make use of that plan of action to oppose the Government altogether. They would submit a resolution to the House, in all probability, to the effect that they will not proceed with any measure to extend the franchise till they see before them everything that the Government has to propose on the subject of Reform. The noble Lord knows perfectly well the tactics of hon. Gentlemen opposite, but, notwithstanding that knowledge, he has thought it his duty to introduce the Franchise Bill first, and ask the House to take the question of the redistribution of seats at a later period. Now let us consider why he should do that. If you will carry back your recollection to the year 1848, when a resolution was proposed by Mr. Hume, and come down step by step from that period until the occasion of the introduction of the Bill of my hon. Friend the Member for Leeds last year, you will see that the great question, so far as it is to be regarded as a great popular question, and as it was discussed at public meetings, has all along been much more a question of the franchise than of the seats. The pledges of Governments and of Parliament have been not so much pledges to the middle classes that their share of political power should be rendered more equal by a redistribution of seats, but more distinctly and fully they have been pledged to the working classes, which are now excluded, that they should at some early day be admitted in some fair numbers to the franchise.

I agree with my hon. Friend the Member for Westminster (Mr. Mill), and I think all within this House will agree, that apart from any effect in respect to the choice of Members

which you may hope to produce by any measure for
the extension of the franchise, it is a thing desirable in
the highest degree that there should be an extension of the
franchise so far that the working-people might feel that
they were not purposely excluded. What I want is to
give the sense of justice to a great class now labouring
under a sense of long-continued injustice. And that is
essential to be done, although that might not change the
seat of any Member in this House, and although the distribution were as equal as it can be made, and there were
no other Reform necessary but on this single measure of
the franchise. The House will see that there is an essential
difference between the two questions. The extension of the
franchise affects a peculiar portion of the population, and
the redistribution of seats does not; it affects all—the higher,
the middle, and the lower classes (as to a portion of them)
alike. It is not a class question, and therefore is not pressed
with the same force and resolution, as a great measure of
justice, which the question of the franchise has received.

An hon. Gentleman who once sat on the other side
is of opinion that when you come to consider the redistribution of the seats you will find that a larger amount of
power ought to be given to the counties. No doubt the
counties ought to receive more Members, and so ought
some of the largest boroughs, and some new boroughs ought
to be created. All that is necessary for the fair representation of all classes, but not as matter of justice to any
special and peculiar class. The other matter comes before
us with a claim far more pressing. I will not say far more
righteous, but certainly far more urgent. Then another
reason why this course should be adopted is one which any
Member of the Government would see at once; and as a
supporter of the Government I will take the liberty of
stating it. It is very much more simple than 'if this
measure were mixed up with another great question. We

all know perfectly well whether in our view it is desirable to reduce the franchise or not, from 10*l.* to 8*l.* or to 7*l.* We can form an opinion on that point; and it does not matter for that purpose whether there is any redistribution of seats or not. I could frame a measure, and so could the right hon. Gentleman the Member for Buckinghamshire, which would give a vote to every man in the kingdom, and yet the re-distribution of seats could be so made that the representation should be infinitely worse than it is at present. When you have argued the question of the suffrage and settled it, you stand and will stand free to deal with the question of the redistribution of seats. And if you think to juggle the public by giving the suffrage with the one hand and with the other preventing the fair representation of the people by an unjust redistribution, you will not be reforming the constitution of this House, but you will be making the people more dissatisfied with Parliament than they have been in past times.

Another reason why I think the Government were justified in the course which they have taken, is that they did not wish to combine the various classes of opponents to the different branches of Reform into an opposition of the extension of the franchise. They thought that a Bill which would get rid of ten, twenty, thirty, or forty seats, would be a matter of great difficulty to those Members who represented seats that would be disfranchised by such a Bill. But yet they felt they might fairly ask the aid of the Members for the small boroughs to do justice to the excluded class, and open the franchise fully and fairly to the people. I have heard a rumour that amongst those who are likely to vote upon the amendment of the Member for Chester, with only one exception, there will not be a single representative of any small boroughs which are likely to be disfranchised by the Bill which the Government have promised to lay upon the table. Therefore, the Members for the small boroughs,

wherever they sit, and whosoever they are on this side of
the House, have not shown any hostility to an extension
of the franchise, whatever may be their course when the
Distribution of Seats Bill makes its appearance on the
table.

I shall have to appeal to the right hon. Gentleman opposite
on a point to which I am about to address myself. I think
that a Franchise Bill which does not adjust this question
for a period at least as long as the Bill of 1832 settled the
question of Reform, is a Franchise Bill which it is not desirable for this House to consent to. I think, further, that a
Distribution of Seats Bill which will not settle that question
as long as the Franchise Bill will settle the question of franchise, is not a desirable Bill for this House to pass. It seems
to me that after you have settled the franchise and come to
discuss the question of seats, Parliament and the public directing its eye to that one question, it would be much more likely
that the question of seats could be settled so far, that for
thirty, and it may be for fifty, years no further change would
be required. I believe that if Parliament were honestly disposed to amend the representation they could do it infinitely
better, more solidly, more satisfactorily to the people, with
greater duration to our legislation, by taking the course proposed by the Government, than by taking that proposed by
the amendment of the Member for Chester or the course
proposed by hon. Gentlemen opposite, which, I suppose, is
to get rid of this Bill and the Government by the same vote.
I believe that the argument which I have laid before the
House—not so clearly as I could have wished—had the effect
of inducing a great number of Reformers in the country to
approve of the course which the Government has taken; and
I believe now, that if I were addressing the hon. Gentlemen
opposite as friends of Reform, and if they were its friends,
that argument would be conclusive. But if they are not
friends of Reform, of course I must content myself with

saying what I have to say, and with leaving it to make a very small impression upon understandings not prepared, I fear, to receive the truth in this matter.

I said I must quote the right hon. Gentleman that I see opposite me. My own honest opinion is that the course which has been pursued by the Government is one of true Conservatism. I think nothing can be less Conservative than that Parliament should have these questions of representation, questions affecting the basis of power, discussed in this House during every session, and discussed throughout the country during every Parliamentary recess. There were some striking things said in this House on the 1st of March in the year 1859, when two right hon. Gentlemen (Mr. Henley and Mr. Walpole) who sit opposite withdrew from the Government of Lord Derby and explained to the House the grounds of that withdrawal. The Member for Oxfordshire made use of these observations :—

'If one thing can be more destructive to our Constitution than another it will be to have a Reform Bill every few years ; and that will be the case if you cannot settle your system upon such grounds that you can reasonably hope that it will stand, I do not say for a long time—finality is out of the question—but for a decent number of years. If you cannot do that, you will lay the foundation for revolution.'

The foundation for revolution in almost every country, unless history lies dreadfully, has been laid by those who have pretended to be specially Conservative. I agree with the right hon. Gentleman. I say there never was a sentence uttered in this House of more undoubted wisdom than that which he spoke on that occasion. I should like to ask the House why it is that we are now involved in this question of Reform. [Derisive cries from the Opposition.] Yes, I will answer hon. Gentlemen immediately. The reason is this—because there is a feeling universal throughout the country that the whole number of electors is much too small to afford a satisfactory representation of the people, and that the largest class in the country, that class which makes the nation, is specially excluded.

I shall show hon. Gentlemen opposite that this is so by referring to a Bill of their own leaders and of their own Ministry. It was on the twenty-eighth of February, 1859, that the Member for Buckinghamshire stood up at this table to propose a Reform Bill on behalf of the Conservative party, of which he is the leader in this House. He quoted on that occasion no less than three Queen's speeches, and he told us that three Prime Ministers had stated distinctly that it was necessary to do something on this question. And that there may be no mistake, for there is a peculiarity in the way the right hon. Gentleman has put it, I will read to you the question he asked of the House. After descanting on the previous attempts, which every Minister thinks it necessary to do—after quoting three Queen's speeches—he says:—

'Were you to allow this question, which the Sovereign had three times announced was one that ought to be dealt with, which three Prime Ministers, among the most skilful and authoritative of our statesmen, have declared it was their intention to deal with, to remain in abeyance?'

The answer he would give of course is—No; we could not let it remain in abeyance. But since then there have been three other Royal speeches in which the same thing has been said with increased emphasis, and three other Prime Ministers have declared their intention to deal with it.

What is the subject to which the right hon. Gentleman refers when he puts in this form the inquiry 'Are you to allow this question to remain in abeyance?' I maintain that it is the question of the suffrage—the question of the franchise. What did the right hon. Gentleman deal with? He gave, according to his own statement, a Franchise Bill of the largest proportions—so largely proportioned that it dwarfs the measure of the Chancellor of the Exchequer. What did the right hon. Gentleman do with regard to the seats? He altered fifteen seats. It was no redis-

tribution at all. It was a ludicrous attempt to arrange the
question of the redistribution of seats. Gentlemen opposite have forgotten these words of the right hon. Gentleman. They would be a great deal wiser if they remembered
some of the things which the Member for Buckinghamshire tells them. The right hon. Gentleman proposed that
the county franchise should be reduced to 10*l.*, and he
said it would extend the franchise in counties by not
fewer than 200,000 electors.   And 200,000 is the exact
number which the Chancellor of the Exchequer expects to
be added to the county electors by the Bill now before the
House. What did the right hon. Gentleman do with regard
to the borough franchise? He proposed that everybody who
had an income of 10*l.* a-year from the Funds, from Bank
Stock, or from East India Stock, or Bonds, should be enfranchised. It would be easy to show what a very foolish idea
of enfranchisement that was; because it is capable of distinct
proof that any man who chose to invest 5,000*l.*, or 6,000*l.*,
for which he would receive a steady interest, might enfranchise all his family, from his grandfather to his youngest
son, and even include all his uncles, nephews, and first
cousins. And those persons would be enfranchised by a
fraud it would be impossible to detect. He proposed that
every person who had invested 60*l.* in a Savings-bank, even
for one year, should have a vote. Thirdly, he proposed that
pensioners in receipt of 20*l.* should have a vote. Fourthly,
he proposed that persons occupying part of a house—that is,
lodgers paying a sum of 20*l.*—should have a vote. The right
hon. Gentleman also proposed that graduates of universities,
ministers of religion, members of the various branches of
the legal profession, medical men and schoolmasters having
certificates, should have votes.

We will not discuss whether that was a proper extension of
the suffrage. If you like I will admit that every person
included there—barring cases of fraud—would be suitable

persons. I am afraid of using the word 'suitable,' the hon. and learned Member for Belfast objects altogether to that—but I will admit that, according to my notion, and according to the notion of the majority of the House, all such persons, with the exception I have mentioned, would be proper persons to have votes. At what did the right hon. Gentleman estimate the number that would be added to the borough electors? At no less than 300,000. That is fifty per cent. more than is proposed to be added to the borough electors by the Bill now on the table—perhaps not exactly of the same class of persons. But whether you give the franchise to A or to B, it is equally an extension of the franchise. And when the Member for Buckinghamshire was asked, towards the close of the discussion on the first night, what he thought would be the total addition to the number of electors in England and Wales, he said the increase, no doubt, would be very considerable—exceeding half a million, he had no hesitation in saying. In answer to the Royal speeches, in deference to what three Prime Ministers had said, and in accordance with the inquiry 'Can the question any longer be left in abeyance?' what did the Government of Lord Derby do? They introduced a Franchise Bill, which I do not here undertake to approve or condemn—that is not necessary for my argument—they introduced a Franchise Bill that would increase the electoral body by not less than half a million— 100,000 more than the Chancellor of the Exchequer proposes to admit by the Bill which he has laid on the table. Am I not therefore justified in saying that the Bill of the Member for Buckinghamshire was in fact a Franchise Bill?

What did the right hon. Gentleman do with regard to the seats? He was very chary in telling the House what he wished to do with regard to the seats. He did not wish, I suppose, to shock the Members who represented boroughs he was going to disfranchise. He did not disfranchise the borough of Calne. He did not even disfranchise the borough of Portarlington, for which, after a very exhaustive poll of forty-six votes, my right hon. Friend the Attorney-General for Ireland has been returned to this House. Nay, the right hon. Gentleman defended the borough of Arundel in several sentences of his speech. He said that the noble Lord who represents the borough of Arundel sits here as the representative of 900,000 Catholics in England and Wales. But the borough of Arundel is as much a nomination borough as any in Schedule A of the Reform Bill.

The right hon. Gentleman touched the question of seats so gently that he took only fifteen seats of small boroughs having now two seats, and he made a distribution of them which I need not detail to the House. He distributed them in a way which I am willing to admit was a very fair and satisfactory distribution of them, because he gave four seats to the West Riding of Yorkshire, two seats to South Lancashire, two seats to Middlesex, and he proposed to create seven new boroughs from towns that have a population entitling them to representatives. Therefore I do not complain at all of the way in which he distributed the seats, but my argument goes to show that the Government of Lord Derby felt that the real question involved in their Reform measure was the question of the franchise, and accordingly Lord Derby's Government proposed by their Bill to admit 500,000 new electors and to distribute fifteen seats. I think then that nothing could be more absurd than to suppose that theirs was not a great Franchise Bill—or that it was a Bill for the settlement of the distribution of seats.

Now, if I were to ask the right hon. Gentleman why he touched the seats with so delicate a hand, and if he were to give me a candid and an honest answer, he would say that the difficulties attending the question of the distribution are very much greater than the difficulties attending the question of the franchise; and he would say, I am quite sure, that a Government having to deal with the question, than which none can be more important, and perhaps none can be more difficult, would be justified in taking that course which avoids difficulties as much as possible, and enables Parliament to deal fairly and simply at once with one important branch of it. I will ask hon. Gentlemen opposite and the House—I will ask those Gentlemen on this (the Liberal) side of the House, who are supposed, I hope untruly, to be about to vote with the Member for Chester—do they believe that if the right hon. Gentleman had passed his Bill admitting 500,000 electors, new voters, and distributing fifteen seats, the question of the arrangement of seats would have been settled for twenty, or ten, or for five years? Is not every man in the House convinced, and is not the right hon. Gentleman the Member for Oxfordshire convinced, that in the very next Parliament elected after the passing of that Bill there would have been propositions submitted to the House declaring that those small boroughs, which had not been touched, were not proper boroughs to return Members to this House, and that a certain number of them should be extinguished and their Members turned over to the populous counties and to the great and populous cities? We should have had exactly what the Member for Oxfordshire wants to avoid. We should have had every year a debate on a new Reform Bill, and a debate on the basis of power; and there would have been contentions between the landowners and the rest of the population who are represented, and probably the right hon. Gentleman who sits on that bench and I, both wishing to do fairly to all parts of the country in this matter, might not have seen distinctly whether more Members should be given to counties or more to boroughs. If the Chancellor of the Exchequer were to add to this Bill those fifteen seats of the Member for Buckinghamshire—that little clause of his in that very short Schedule—do you think the House would agree to pass it?

Will the noble Lord the Member for Chester (Earl

Grosvenor) and his colleague who seconded the amendment (Lord Stanley) frankly tell the House that if the distribution clauses of Lord Derby's Bill were added to the Bill of Lord Russell, they would give that Bill their support? If they will undertake to do that, although it might ruin the Government if I said it—still I would give them a little advice, and I would counsel them to take it. You know perfectly well that all this clamour you have been making about the distribution of seats—I am afraid, Sir, there is not exactly a parliamentary term that will enable me to express it with sufficient delicacy—but, at least, one thing you know, you do not impose upon us with that cry. I do not think I felt the slightest satisfaction when the Government proposed to lay upon the table of the House their Bill for the distribution of seats. If I had been a Minister, I think I should have recommended that the Member for Calne, for example, and the Member for Stamford—both of whom must know a good deal about the small boroughs—should have been requested to prepare clauses of disfranchisement for the fair consideration of the House.

It is obvious that if the arguments on which you have opposed this Bill are your honest arguments, you would not support the Bill though the Chancellor of the Exchequer were to propose to add to it the distribution clauses of the Bill of Lord Derby. And I think you would be wise in refusing it; because although that distribution is, I believe, perfectly satisfactory and fair as far as it goes, yet it would not in any degree settle that question; and I am convinced that the greatest error the House can commit is to agree to something on the question of the franchise and something on the question of the distribution of seats, by which neither the one question nor the other shall be settled. But, Sir, at this moment the Government is assailed by a united party on the other side of the House, with a few recruits from this side. I tell hon. Gentlemen opposite that they are not in very good hands. The Member for Buckinghamshire and the Member for King's Lynn are not, in my opinion, councillors to be followed implicitly on this question of Reform ; and if any-body doubts it I should call as witnesses the two right hon. Gentlemen to whom I have already referred.

You have before you the Bill of Lord Russell's Govern-ment, and you know exactly what it is. You may think quite honestly that the reduction of the franchise is some-thing more than is necessary, and you may even think it is something more than is safe ; but you know exactly what it is. ['No, no.'] You have listened with very small attention to the speakers on this side of the House if you do not, at least, know the worst of it. What was the Bill brought in by the Member for Buckinghamshire ?—and it had upon every clause of it the impress of his subtle under-standing. I will tell you what was said of it by the Member for the University of Cambridge (Mr. Walpole) on that night when he explained to us why he had withdrawn from the Government. He said that their scheme of suffrage was—

'A most dangerous innovation, by giving to temporary and fluctuating occupations a preponderating influence over property and intelligence, while it throws large masses into the constituencies who are almost exempt from direct taxation.'

That is exactly what your friends have been saying of the Bill of the Chancellor of the Exchequer. And, again, the Member for the University said, and this, I think, was in a letter which he wrote to Lord Derby, and which he read to the House :—

'The measure which the Cabinet are prepared to recommend [and in which he did not, as you know, concur] is one which we should all of us have strongly opposed if either Lord Palmerston or Lord Russell had ventured to bring it forward.'

The right hon. Gentleman knew exactly the character of his colleagues. It was prophetic of the course which they would take, and which they have taken now, in opposition to a Bill which only proposes to admit 400,000 electors, while

their own Bill proposed to admit 500,000. Now, the Member
for Oxfordshire on the same evening, with regard to the same
question, used these remarkable words :—

'I believe that identity of suffrage, which is the principle of the Government Bill, is fatal to the constitution of this country.'

I do not think that anybody in the House during this discussion has gone so far as to say that the reduction of 3*l.* in the
borough franchise would be absolutely fatal to the constitution of this country, seeing that five hundred years ago, and
less, every freeman being a householder in every borough had
a vote for Members to sit in this House.   But the two right
hon. Gentlemen expressed these opinions of the Bill introduced
by the Member for Buckinghamshire, and I say, therefore,
that the right hon. Gentleman and his colleagues, especially
the noble Lord the Member for King's Lynn, are condemned
out of the mouths of their former colleagues, and ought to
be put out of court as advisers on this question.

I shall now ask the attention of the House for a little
time to the Bill itself.   Hitherto I have been speaking
as to the mode in which the Government have proposed
to deal with this question.   As to the Bill itself, almost
everything that has been said has been said in connection with
the question of the borough franchise.   I omit altogether the
sort of frenzy into which the Member for North Staffordshire (Mr. Adderley) worked himself the other night when discussing the question of the county franchise.   For aught that
I know a 14*l.* rental franchise in counties may have a very fatal
effect in North Staffordshire.   I like to take the advice and
opinion of men of great experience and great moderation, and
it is for this reason that I ask the right hon. Gentleman the
Member for Oxfordshire to step for one moment into the
witness-box on this matter.   He said in the speech to which
I have referred :—

'Ever since the Reform Act of 1832 the working-people have been having
a less and less share in the representation. They had considerable represen-

tation before 1832 through the scot and lot voters and the freemen. They are gradually dying out.'

And turning to those about him he said :—

'I ask my honourable friends near me to consider, if they draw a hard line, and leave the working-people behind it, how long they think it will stand ?'

That was a wise saying, a pertinent question in the year 1859, and it is not less wise and worth considering in the year 1866.

But then the greater part of it is exactly what the Chancellor of the Exchequer has said. The right hon. Gentleman has told the House that the proportionate power of the working-classes in the constituencies has been diminishing since 1832. I believe there can be no doubt of it; and here I must tell the Chancellor of the Exchequer that my opinion is— and I think every Member of the House who represents a borough, excepting the borough of Coventry and perhaps one or two others, must know—that the figures which have been laid before the House by which the per-centage of working-men electors is put down at 25 or 26 per cent. are not in any degree to be relied upon, nor are they in any degree accurate. Now, hon. Gentlemen have a perfect right, of course, in assailing the Government, to fight upon the figures which they have laid before them, and the Government would find it very difficult to retreat from the position they have taken up upon those figures. I am not one of hon. Gentlemen opposite, and am not one of a Government responsible for those figures. I am here as an advocate, an honest advocate of a moderate and just reform, and, therefore, I must deal with this question from my own point of view, and speak of it in language based on the convictions which I hold. I will give the House only two cases, and I have not sought for them in the Blue Book or written about the country for them. The first has been presented to this House, I believe, in a petition by the hon. Member for Stoke-upon-Trent. Stoke-upon-Trent, as hon.

Gentlemen know, is a borough consisting of three or four neighbouring towns. One of them is the town of Burslem. The Blue Book says that Burslem is a constituency with 680 electors. Of that number 197 are represented to be working-men or artisans, and that they form 29 per cent. of the whole number. But what does this petition, which has been accurately prepared, and which gives the analysis of the register for Burslem, say? It says this: that of the 197 which the Chancellor of the Exchequer's figures represent to be working-men there is 1 publican and 40 beersellers. That is 41 to begin with. I would rather have 40 really hard-working, industrious artisans in any borough than 40 beersellers. But there are grocers and other shopkeepers to the number of 48. There are persons who are put down as cart-owners, cowkeepers, tradesmen with assistants, having profits from their capital in their trade, numbering 33; and adding these together and deducting them from the 197, there remain in the town of Burslem not 197 working-men on the register, but 75. You may bring if you like the whole staff of the Poor-law Board, but they cannot alter these figures, and it shall not be my fault if the House discusses this question and decides upon figures that are deceptive and delusive.

Next I will take one other town, and that is the borough of Wakefield. The Blue Book says there are 122 working-men, or rather over 11 per cent. in the borough of Wakefield. But if you will deduct the various classes to which I have referred with regard to Burslem, you will bring the number of 122 in Wakefield down to 35, so that instead of there being 11 per cent. of the present constituency working-men, there are not more than 3 per cent. I was talking the other day to a Member on this side of the House, the Member for Newark. I will not give the figures, for I have not them in my recollection, but I hope he will take some opportunity of stating them to the House. But the return from Newark was sent back, I think, twice, if not three times, for correction, and

I think at least one county magistrate was put down amongst the working-men.

The only figures with which I shall trouble the House are these. We have had the figures of the Chancellor of the Exchequer, and quite as many more from Gentlemen opposite, and I wish to give the House my figures in a single sentence. The Blue Book says that there are 126,000 working-men upon the register. Some bring these down to one-third that number, but, for the sake of being within the mark, I will call them half. The 126,000 is then brought down to 63,000. The Chancellor of the Exchequer calculated that by the repeal of the rate-paying clauses and the system of compounding, persons who pay 10*l.* a-year rent, who are now excluded, would be admitted to the number of 60,000. He put all these 60,000 as working-men. There is not a man in any borough in England that believes that is an accurate calculation. I put these down at one-third that number—namely, 20,000. The Chancellor of the Exchequer says that between 10*l.* and 7*l.* there will be admitted 144,000, and he estimates these as being all working-men. We all know that these persons within 7*l.* and 10*l.* are not, cannot, and never have been all working-men, and I reckon that if two-thirds are admitted as working-men that will be as fair a calculation as can be made.

Look at the result. The Chancellor of the Exchequer says when this Bill is passed there will be 330,000 working-men upon the register. I say there will be 179,000. Call them, for easier recollection, 180,000. The newly admitted by this Bill will be 116,000. What will be the gross effect? The whole number of borough electors in England and Wales, if this Bill should pass, upon the calculation of the Blue Book will be 691,000, of whom 180,000 only, or about one-fourth, will be working-men, and therefore that portion of the people which forms at least three-fourths of the whole population will only have one-fourth of the electoral power in the boroughs, and no power whatever worth reckoning in the constituencies of the counties. I shall say no more about these statistics. Having made my calculations, they are as proper to be placed before the House as those of the Chancellor of the Exchequer or any hon. Gentleman opposite. But, after all, there will be in England and Wales more than 4,000,000 of men left out.

I think so much political trepidation—I will say so much political cowardice, if I may be allowed the use of that word— never was exhibited before as in the terror shown by the mover and seconder of this amendment, because 116,000 new voters amongst working-men will be admitted, while more than 4,000,000 will be left out. I am astonished at these alarmist speeches. The right hon. Baronet the Member for Hertfordshire (Sir E. B. Lytton) deals in alarmist speeches. He comes down once or twice during the session, and makes a speech, which gives great satisfaction to the House, provided you do not pay the least attention to what there is in it. I mean that in tone, manner, and imagery we are pleased, but I am grieved when I find the side to which the right hon. Baronet gives his great influence. In the year 1860, the right hon. Gentleman made a speech of a much more alarmist character than the one which he made last week, and therefore we may reckon upon some amendment in his condition. In 1860 he said the Bill that was introduced by Lord John Russell, as a member of Lord Palmerston's Government, was a Bill to admit 'poverty and passion' to the franchise. This is one of his passages :—

'Though we are willing to admit poverty and passion into the franchise, we are not willing to give poverty and passion the lion's share of political power over capital and knowledge.'

That is very much like what the right hon. Gentleman the Member for Cambridge University said of the Bill of the Member for Buckinghamshire. He did not use the words 'poverty and passion,' but he spoke of things that were fatal to the constitution as being likely to be enacted by the Bill.

The right hon. Baronet once held very different opinions from these. Many years ago he published a book called 'England and the English.' This is not a very profound, but a very amusing book, and I should like to read to the House a sentence which the right hon. Gentleman put as a motto to the book, which motto, I think, he took from Ben Jonson. The words are—

> 'I am he
> Have measured all the shires of England over,
> For to these savages I was addicted
> To search their nature and make odd discoveries.'

The discovery which he had made up to 1860 was this : if you introduce artisans and working-men between a 10*l*. and 6*l*. rental, you give the lion's share of the power of representation to the poverty and passion of the country. In his speech last week he did not treat the working-men as if they were made up of poverty and passion, but he used generous words of them, and he told us how there was a tie not only of interest, but of respect and affection, between the rich and the labouring poor ; and doubtless this language far more accurately stated his real opinion than when he said that between 6*l*. and 10*l*. the working-men were represented by 'poverty and passion.' But to give them compliments of this kind, and not votes, seems to me to be a thing which will not be well received by the great body of the people, who are asking that at least some of them may be admitted to a representation in this House. It reminds me very much of that couplet which I am sure the right hon. Gentleman will remember from Shenstone—

> 'He kicked them down stairs with such a sweet grace,
> They may think he was handing them up.'

How is it to be conceived that after a speech full of such noble and generous sympathy the right hon. Gentleman concludes to throw all the weight of his character and influence into the side of a party which says little that is kind and generous of this class?   [Loud Opposition cries of 'No, no.'] I will say, then, of a party which sometimes does say something generous of the working-class, but never shows the slightest disposition to confer upon it any portion of political rights.

I now ask the attention of the right hon. Gentleman and the House to one point which he touched with great force and great beauty of language in referring to some friends and neighbours of mine—the members of the co-operative societies of Rochdale.   When I heard his words I thought he was going back unconsciously to the year 1832, when he was a most enthusiastic supporter of the Reform Bill of that day, and when he was a member of the Parliamentary Candidate Society, with the hon. and learned Member for Sheffield, with Jeremy Bentham, Daniel O'Connell, Francis Place, Charles Buller, and many others.   I thought he was going back to that time, but if not so far, that he was at least going back to 1847 and 1848, in both which years he was in favour of an extension of the franchise.   Now, what did he say of my neighbours and friends?   He said,—

'To artisans of that class, whatever their political creed, I am willing to grant the franchise. Willing, do I say?—that word is much too cold. I wish that, like some old commonwealth of Greece, we could admit them to the franchise by acclamation, to be proud of such fellow-citizens, without asking what rent they pay for their houses.'

I happen to live amongst all these persons of whom the right hon. Gentleman has spoken with so much enthusiasm, and, therefore, if the House will permit me, I will state a little of their case, and I have no objection to rest my case upon theirs.   In 1860, in the discussion of the Bill of the Government, I laid some facts connected with these operative societies before the House.   There are three bodies or companies managed by three committees.   One is called the Rochdale Equitable Pioneers Society, which chiefly concerns

itself in the retail business, and the facts which I am about to
give have been supplied to me by the secretary of the society.
He says that there are 5,500 members, chiefly heads of
families. It has a capital of 85,000*l.*, and it is selling goods
and receiving money at the rate of 230,000*l.* per annum.
Let the House bear in mind that there is not one of these
5,500 members can have one single farthing of credit. The
business is managed by a committee of eleven, of whom two
have a borough vote, and one of them is a book-keeper, and is
treasurer of the society, and therefore, in a certain sense, he is
not exactly what we understand by a working-man. He and
another have borough votes, while the president and secretary
of this great establishment have no votes. We now come to
the Rochdale District Co-operative Corn Mill Society, which
does a large business. It has a capital of 60,000*l.*, and turns
over 164,000*l.* per annum. It has also a committee of eleven;
but neither the president, nor treasurer, nor secretary, nor
any one of this committee has a borough vote. One of the
committee has a county vote, being probably the owner of a
cottage in the neighbourhood. Then there is the Rochdale
Co-operative Manufacturing Society, which has more than
1,500 members, or shareholders, and a capital of 109,000*l.* It
has built two of the largest and handsomest factories in the
neighbourhood, and the meeting in support of this Bill
was held in one of them which has not yet received its
machinery. This society is also managed by a committee of
eleven, of whom three have borough votes, and two have
county votes. But of these five voters only one is 'a working-
man' in the usual sense. The voters are thus described—one
is a manager, one a manufacturer, one a draper, one out of
business, and one only is a mechanic. Now, the total capital
of these societies is 227,246*l.*, the whole of which has been
contributed, or nearly so, by the working-men of Rochdale, of
whom the right hon. Gentleman spoke the other night in such
glowing language. The secretary writes :—

'The present writer has seen members of the Pioneers' Society, who had scarcely any work or income for the family during the famine, come for 5*s.* or 10*s.* from their investments of previous savings, just to help them on with their small earnings. They did not ask or receive relief. This does not show improvidence or want of forethought. Now that the cotton famine is nearly over, the members are again saving money. In June, 1865, their investments were: In the Pioneers' Society, 59,000*l.*; in September, 1865, 63,000*l.*; in December, 1865, 69,000*l.*; and in March, 1866, they reached 76,602*l.*'

I hope the right hon. Member for Calne will forgive me for reading the next line—'This does not agree with the Lowe theory.'

Now, what is taking place in the Rochdale societies is occurring in greater or less degree in all the societies, of which there are five or six hundred throughout the country. What is the answer which anybody has given to these men? Will you give the same answer which the right hon. Baronet the Member for Hertfordshire gave? Will you receive them with open arms and not ask them whether they pay 7*l.* or 6*l.* for their rental? If hon. Gentlemen are in favour of the extension of the franchise—I exclude the hon. and learned Member for Belfast altogether—to those who are so worthy of it, upon the description of one of your own eminent leaders, will you allow these 4,500 men to have the franchise now in Rochdale? I beg to tell them it would be a great mistake to think that the men in Rochdale are better than those in the other manufacturing towns of Lancashire and Yorkshire. They would altogether scout the idea, and I, who know them as well as most men—and I know a good deal of the working-men of Lancashire and Yorkshire—should say that those at Rochdale are a fair sample of the great mass of the industrious, intelligent, and independent population amongst whom we live.

The hon. Member for Wick is terrified at the idea of the votes of these men. Northern breezes and long experience have done nothing for him. He described all the good things which have been done in Parliament during the last twenty years, and he does not seem to be aware that there is not one of those good things which the working-men of Lancashire and Yorkshire did not heartily support. I know not half a dozen Gentlemen opposite who gave any continuous support whatsoever to those good things. The hon. Gentleman puts it to the credit of Parliament that it repealed the Corn-law. If he had consulted my right hon. Friend the President of the Poor Law Board, I think he would have been told that, until Sir Robert Peel abandoned Protection, there never were a hundred Members in the House who gave a vote in favour of the repeal of the Corn-law, and that it was done, as every-body knows now, by an agitation of enormous cost both in money and labour, and by the occurrence of a famine which threw disgrace upon the Government of this country, not because potatoes should have decayed, but that when they did decay a whole population should have run the risk of being destroyed by it. The same men who both out of doors and in Parliament asked for these good measures are the very men who ask for this Bill, and I venture to tell the House that if they do not get this Bill they will get one very much like it.

I shall not ask the attention of the House to more figures, or endeavour to show the inconsistency of any Members on the other side of the House; but I will ask them, if they can, calmly to consider the present position of this question. Look all over the country, and you will find that in a week or a fortnight there have been held more than a hundred public meetings which were unanimous in favour of this Bill. Hon. Gentlemen opposite do not pursue a policy which enables them to hold public meetings. You have had presented many hundred petitions in its favour, with nearly 500,000 signatures appended to them. If the Bill were so destructive, if it struck such terror into the hearts of the people as it seems to have done in the case of the noble Lord the Member for King's Lynn—and I believe there was a petition from Lynn signed by a hundred of his constituents in support of his views—if the people felt that the Government were going on a wrong course, that the middle class were to be swamped, and all kinds of evil to follow the passing of this Bill, is it conceivable that numbers of public meetings would not have been held, and that numbers of petitions would not have been signed, praying that the Bill should not pass?

Look at the moderate and reasonable tone of the meetings that have been held. I appeal particularly to the two right hon. Gentlemen I see before me — they are not so stiff as some in the unteachable prejudices of their party, and the tone of their remarks shows that they have a real conviction, and are desirous of acting upon it. Look, then, at the attitude of the people. Suppose when Lord John Russell, in the years previous to 1830, was bringing forward year after year measures for the reform of Parliament— suppose you had accepted some of those propositions, and that Parliament had been to a certain extent reformed, do you not think that would have been a course as wise as to go on heedlessly step by step until you came to the edge of that terrible abyss over which you could not bear to look in 1832? You may always pass a measure with more honour to yourselves and more good to the country in times of peace and tranquillity than in times of force and compulsion; and times of peace and tranquillity are invariably, if not immediately, followed in matters of this description by times of force and compulsion. The right hon. Member for Oxfordshire told you what must happen if you chose to set up a barrier and thrust the working classes behind it and tell them that that line must for ever separate them from you. You have 1,000,000 electors now, and there are 8,000,000 of grown men in the United Kingdom; can you say that only 1,000,000 shall have votes and that all the rest are to remain excluded? Is the thing possible ? The right hon. Member for Huntingdonshire (Gen. Peel) seems to think it is possible; but he knows it is not possible. He has before him the example of an illustrious member of his own family, who thought it possible to maintain the principle of Protection by the Corn-law, and who, finally, after doing everything he could, after violating his own convictions for years in fighting the battles of his party, was compelled at last to surrender, and to admit to the humblest man in the country, and the poorest weaver, that he, the great Minister of State in this country, had not comprehended the question of the Corn-laws so well as the working-men of England comprehended it.

Are you resolved—and this is the question we are in fact now discussing—that the bolts shall be kept in that door, and that the mass of the people shall be forced to remain on the other side of it ? The hon. and learned Member for Belfast told us that there should be, not a representation of the people, but a representation of classes. If the hon. and learned Gentleman gave opinions in a court of law no sounder than he gives us here on the question of the Constitution, depend upon it he never would have been enabled to reach the high position he now holds in his profession. He knows perfectly well there never was such a thing as a representation of classes in the Commons House of Parliament; we should have been called the House of Classes, or something equally absurd, if anything so absurd ever had existed. He knows perfectly well that in the times previous to the usurpations of the Tudors and the Stuarts, every freeman resident, being a householder in a borough, had a vote for a representative in that House. He knows, also, that the first Parliament of Charles I. declared—and it is now on record in the journals—that the franchise of common right rested with the inhabitant householders of boroughs. Though he contended that the quotation I made from Lord Somers did not bear the meaning I attached to it, yet if we come down to the men of fifty or sixty years ago, he will not deny that all the leading Liberal men of that period were in favour of the extension of the suffrage far beyond that which is proposed in this Bill.

There is much that I think shows you are hurrying to times of difficulty and peril. If you look at what is passing in the United States you will see that there is a question which is causing great difficulties, just as this question is causing them here. It is proposed that the 4,000,000 negroes of the United States shall have these rights granted to them; that they shall no longer be bought and sold; that they may change their employment and their master; that they may sue or be sued in a court of law, and may give evidence in a court of justice. Beyond that their rights are not at present to go, and those who were their masters not two years ago, and who bought and sold them, are not willing, for reasons which they think sufficient, to grant them the franchise, which is universal in that country. The franchise never has been universal in this country. It is not necessary that it should be; but we have a representative constitution, and we are the House of Commons, and if the Throne be sacred in its dignity, and if the Peers be unmolested in their privileges, the House of Commons remains the safeguard of the constitution, and those who are sent here sit by right of free election by the commonalty of this kingdom.

You may defeat this Bill. I am not at all learned in Parliamentary computations, but there are hon. Gentlemen on both sides who can tell exactly what the majority for or against this Bill will be. I will admit fully that you can reject this Bill, defeat the Government, and drive Lord Russell from office. The right hon. Gentleman has no doubt somewhere a Parliamentary Bradshaw—all his lines converge to Downing-street. We have let him in once or twice, indeed, but had very soon afterwards to expel him from that paradise of official men. If the right hon. Gentleman goes to Downing-street, are you prepared to say that there shall be no Reform, or that the right hon. Gentleman and his friends, who in 1859 proposed measures which their most experienced colleagues declared to be fatal to the Constitution, shall again deal with this question? Does not conduct like this always break up a party? When you come to deal with the question of Reform you will find difficulties; if you resolve not to deal with it, your difficulties will not be less. Whatever is said in this House, whether the right hon. Gentleman the Chancellor of the Exchequer carries this Bill or not, there still remains the nation outside this House, and there still remains the great question of Parliamentary Reform.

I believe there never was a Bill submitted to this House by a Government connected with the Liberal party which it was more clearly the duty and the interest of what is called the Conservative party to support. In 1832 the then Tory party opposed the Bill; they went to their constituencies and were mostly destroyed for a time. If this Bill passes, the enlarged constituencies will not look very favourably upon Gentlemen who tried to prevent the Bill from passing. When you see a man like Lord Russell, who was the chief supporter of the Bill of 1832, who promoted it years before it made its appearance, and who proposed it on behalf of the Government— when you see him, knowing certainly as much of this question as any man in this House—when you see him convinced of the necessity of doing something on this question, and offering a Bill so reasonable as this, I cannot help saying, either that hon. Gentlemen are misled by their leaders, or that they have driven their leaders into a course which I think is pernicious to the true interests of their party. Perhaps there never was a Bill which more fairly accommodated itself to the advancing intelligence of the people. There is not a whisper of dissatisfaction with it. [Cries of ' Oh!'] I speak of those persons who are in favour of any improvement of the representation; and so far as I have been able to learn or gather, even those who are called Conservatives throughout the country, are weary of the perpetual discussion of this question, and would be glad that it could be settled on the terms which the Government has proposed.

I did not rise with the expectation that I should convince hon. Gentlemen that they are wrong and that I am right; the most that I can hope for is that some fact or some argument may find a lodgment in some mind, and may moderate hostility to a proposal which I think the country requires, and the country is anxious to receive. I have not spoken in favour of the Government. I have said that I think their figures are wrong and untrue—injurious to their own Bill and their own case. Now, will the House believe for once that I am speaking to them from no party spirit, from no desire to do anything in the country or to the country more than they would wish? My view of the public interest is at least as conscientious and as honest as theirs can be. I have been misrepresented, and condemned, and denounced by hon. Gentlemen opposite, and by not a few writers in their press. My conscience tells me that I have laboured honestly only to destroy that which is evil, and to build up that which is good. The political gains of the last twenty-five years, as they were summed up the other night by the hon. Member for Wick (Mr. Laing), are my political gains, if they can be called the gains in any degree of any living Englishman.

And if now, in all the great centres of our population—in Birmingham with its busy district—in Manchester with its encircling towns—in the population of the West Riding of Yorkshire—in Glasgow and amidst the vast industries of the West of Scotland—and in this great Babylon in which we are assembled—if we do not find ourselves surrounded by hungry and exasperated multitudes—if now, more than at any time during the last hundred years, it may be said, quoting the beautiful words of Mr. Sheridan, that—

'Content sits basking on the cheek of toil '—

if this House, and if its statesmen glory in the change, have

I not as much as any living man some claim to partake of that glory? I know, and every thoughtful man among you knows, and those Gentlemen who sit on that bench and who are leading you to this enterprise, they know that the policy I have urged upon the House and upon the country, so far as it has hitherto been accepted by Parliament, is a policy conservative of the public welfare, strengthening the just authority of Parliament, and adding from day to day fresh lustre and dignity to the Crown. And now, when I speak to you and ask you to pass this Bill—when I plead on behalf of those who are not allowed to speak themselves in this House —if you could raise yourselves for this night, for this hour, above the region of party strife—if you could free yourselves from the pestilent atmosphere of passion and prejudice which so often surrounds us here, I feel confident that at this moment I should not plead in vain before this Imperial Parliament on behalf of the English constitution and the English people.

REFORM.

VIII.

BIRMINGHAM, AUGUST 27, 1866.

[A great open-air meeting was held in Birmingham on the 27th of August, 1866, to pass resolutions in favour of Reform. It was calculated that more than 150,000 men were present at it. In the evening a great meeting was held in the Town Hall of Birmingham, at which an Address of confidence was presented to Mr. Bright, and at which this speech was spoken.]

I ACCEPT the Address which has just been presented to me with feelings which I shall not attempt to express. I accept it as ample compensation for whatsoever labours I have expended in your service, and I shall take it from this meeting, and hold it as a constant stimulus to whatsoever labours may lie in my path in your service for the future. There are times when I feel no little despondency at the small result of many years of public labour; but to look upon a meeting like that assembled here, and to look upon that vast gathering which your town has exhibited to the country and to the world to-day, is enough to dispel every feeling of fear or of despondency, and to fill the heart and nerve the arm to new and greater labours for the future.

During the last session of Parliament, in the debate on

the second reading of the Franchise Bill, I took the opportunity of offering a word of counsel and of warning to the powerful party in the House which opposed that Bill. In those words of warning and of counsel I asked them to remember that if they should succeed in defeating that Bill and overthrowing the Government, there would still remain the people of England to be met, and the claims of the great question of Reform to be considered and settled. We have not had to wait long before that which I foretold has come to pass. In London we have seen assemblies of the people such as for a generation past have not been witnessed. In many other parts of the country there have been meetings greater than have been seen for thirty years, and notably to-day there has been a voice given forth from the very centre and heart of England which will reach at least to the circumference of the three kingdoms. There has been an attempt to measure the numbers that are present in this Hall at this moment. There are probably six thousand persons here. I ask any who were present to-day to reckon how many times this Hall could have been filled from that multitudinous congregation upon which our eyes rested, but to the full extent of which they could scarcely reach. It is highly probable that it might have been filled forty times from that vast number. Yes, and at this moment I am told that outside there is an audience far greater than that I now address; whilst to-morrow morning there will be millions of an audience throughout the whole of the United Kingdom, anxious to know what has been done and what has been said on this 27th day of August in this great town of Birmingham.

We are not here to-night to discuss the question of Reform, because that is a question which we have already settled. What we have to do is to discuss calmly our present position and our future work in reference to this great question. My hon. Colleague has said that the Bill of the late Government was one of singular moderation. It was also a Bill—I speak now only of the Franchise Bill—of a singular and most honest simplicity; and that was the great reason that I felt it my duty, and that you felt it yours, to give it an honest support. I will just tell you how much and how little it proposed to give, or would have given, to the working-classes of this country; and I think it necessary to state this because of the argument which I intend to raise upon it. The Government produced to the House of Commons a Blue Book, most elaborately compiled, and as far as I know, with the exception of one point, correct and trustworthy; but they proposed to inform the House of the number of working-men who are now upon the register, and what addition would be made to that number if the Bill passed. I differed entirely from their estimate, which I believe to have been to a very great extent erroneous, and I think I produced facts in the House of Commons which sustained my opinion.

Mr. Gladstone told us that at present there are on the borough registers in England and Wales working-men to the number of 126,000. He showed, further, that by the abolition of the rate-paying clauses, if there was no alteration in the 10*l.* suffrage, there would be an addition of 60,000 electors, who, he reckoned, would all be working-men; and then he said that if the franchise was reduced from 10*l.* to 7*l.*, there would be a further addition of 144,000, all of whom he estimated as working-men. Therefore he stated that when that Bill passed there would be on the borough registers of England and Wales 330,000 working-men, of whom 204,000 would be new voters added by that Bill. I believe that estimate was made with perfect honesty by Mr. Gladstone, but that it was to a very large extent erroneous. I showed several boroughs, and I believe I might have gone through almost every borough in the United Kingdom, where the number of working-men stated in the

returns was at least double, and in many cases far more
than double, the actual number upon the register. I estimated, also, that although the abolition of the ·rate-paying
clauses might add 60,000 new votes, it would be very unfair
to expect that more than one-third, or 20,000 of them—
being ten-pounders and upwards—would be of the class of
working-men. I said, further, that it was absurd to reckon
that every man between 10*l.* and 7*l.* was of the class of
working-men, and I supposed that at least no more than
two-thirds of them could be placed in that list. My estimate
differed, therefore, from Mr. Gladstone's thus far. I said
that of the 126,000 now upon the register there were. not
more than the half, or 63,000; instead of there being
60,000 admitted by the abolition of the rate-paying clause,
there would not be more than 20,000; and that, instead of
there being 144,000 working-men admitted by the reduction
of the franchise from 10*l.* to 7*l.*, it was a fair estimate to
take two-thirds of that number, or 96,000. My opinion
therefore was, that when that Bill passed, if it should pass,
there would be upon the borough registers of England and
Wales, not 330,000 of working-men, but 179,000, and that
the Bill would not admit 204,000, but only 116,000 of that
class. Take either my estimate of 116,000 or Mr. Gladstone's estimate of 204,000 as the number of working-men
to be added by the late Bill to the register, and I will ask
you what, after all, does it all come to? 204,000 working-
men according to the Government estimate, 116,000 according to mine, and in addition about 200,000 new voters added
to the counties under a 14*l.* franchise, who must of necessity
be almost altogether outside the working-classes. That was
the Bill which my hon. Colleague has described as one of
singular moderation. Out of five or six millions of men in
the United Kingdom who are not now enfranchised, the
whole number of the working-classes to be admitted in the
boroughs of England and Wales was only 200,000.

Now that Bill, so moderate that I confess I had entertained the hope that it would pass through Parliament without any great difficulty, was resisted as if it had been charged with all the dangerous matter which the Tory party actually attributed to it. · It was intrigued against in a manner—I had almost said more base, but I will say more hateful, than any measure I have seen opposed during the twenty-three years that I have sat in the House of Commons; and, finally, under every kind of false pretence, it was rejected by a small majority, and fell, and with it the Government which had proposed it also fell.   The reason I have given you these figures is that I want to show you the desperate resolution of the present Government, and of the party which it represents, to deny to the working-classes of this country any share in its government.   I am not confined to the votes of the House and the destruction of the Bill, but I am able, I think, to show you by the arguments on which the Tory party proceeded that such is their determination, and it may be their unchangeable resolution.

Several of the speakers to-night have referred to the slanders heaped upon the great body of the people during the discussions of the last session; and, no doubt, although his name was not mentioned, the speakers had in their minds one Member of the House who virtually has no constituency—whose sole constituent, at any rate at that time, is now no longer here to partake of the strife or the contests of politics, though I presume another constituent acts and reigns in his stead.   If I quote anything that Mr. Lowe said, understand me that I wish to bring no charge against him whatsoever.   He has spent some years in Australia, and probably has voyaged round the world; and I do not deny him the right to voyage round the world of politics, and to cast anchor in any port that may be pleasant to him.   I merely intend to quote something that he said, because when it was said it was received with rapturous enthusiasm by that great

party in the House who are the supporters of Lord Derby and
of Mr. Disraeli.   This is extracted from the *Times* newspaper,
a paper in which, as is well known, the speaker has been
for many years an eminent writer, and over which, unless
reports speak untruly, he has no small degree of control.
He says —

'I have had opportunities of knowing some of the constituencies of this
country, and I ask if you want venality, ignorance, drunkenness, and the
means of intimidating—if you want impulsive, unreflecting, violent people—
where would you go to look for them ?   To the top or to the bottom ?   It is
ridiculous to blink the fact that since the Reform Act the great corruption has
been among the voters between 20*l.* and 10*l.* rental—the lodging-house and
beerhouse keepers ; . . . but it is said, Only give the franchise to the artisan and
then see the difference.'

He goes on—passing a sentence containing a classical illustration which amused the House, but which it is not necessary to
quote here.   He said :—

'You know what sort of persons live in these small houses' [houses, of
course, between 10*l.* and 7*l.*]   'We have long had experience of them under
the name of freemen, and it would be a good thing if they were disfranchised
altogether.   They were dying out of themselves, but the Government propose
to bring them back again under another name, so that the effect of passing this
Bill would be—first, to increase corruption, intimidation, and all the evils that
happen usually in elections ; and next that the working-men of England, finding themselves in a full majority of the whole constituency, will awake to a
full sense of their power, and say, "We can do better for ourselves.   Don't
let us any longer be cajoled at elections.   Let us set up shop for ourselves.
We have objects to carry as well as our neighbours, and let us unite to carry
those objects.   We have the machinery.   We have our trades' unions.   We
have our leaders ready.   We have the power of combination as we have shown
over and over again, and when we have a prize to fight for we will bring it to
bear with tenfold more force than ever before."'

These are the sentiments which, uttered in my hearing,
were received with enthusiastic approbation by the great
body of the Tory party and by the supporters of the present
Government.   Observe what it really means.   It is that
voters now between 20*l.* rental and 10*l.* are so bad that if
you go lower something like ruin will ensue.   That there
will be more venality, ignorance, and drunkenness ; and then,

speaking to the House of Commons—in which the landed proprietors, or the bulk of them, have always acted as a general
trades' union, where they raised the price of bread and
diminished the size of the loaf as long as the people would let
them—he says there will be combinations of working-men for
their special objects, and therefore—mind, this is his conclusion—shut them out for ever ; bolt the door ; say, loudly and
boldly, you, the Parliament of England, to the 5,000,000 or
6,000,000 men who have now no vote, and whom we pretend
to represent, ' No one of you who cannot pay a rental of
10*l.* shall ever speak by his direct representative within the
walls of this House.' That is the policy which Mr. Lowe
recommends. It is not important at all because Mr. Lowe
recommends it. It is important only because it has been
accepted and approved by the great Tory party in Parliament.
However, I say—I who am charged with designs against the
safety of the institutions of this country—I say it is a
dangerous policy—a policy which enforced in other countries
has done great things. Through it crowns and coronets
have sometimes been lost, and I am not sure that it is a
policy which can be safely maintained with us.

I asked one of the most intelligent and excellent Frenchmen with whom I am acquainted, one of the most confi-
dential friends of the dynasty of Louis Philippe and of the
Orleans family, what it was that drove that family from
France, and I referred to stories of corruption among ministers
and other things which had been circulated in public and in
private. He said : ' None of these things did it. It was the
attempt of the King to govern France by a parliament that
represented an insignificant minority of the people, and which
parliament he thought he could perpetually manage by
a judicious distribution of patronage.' On the principle of
governing this country by a Parliament elected by an insignificant minority of the people, Lord Derby comes into office,
and judging from the speeches and the votes of the last

session of Parliament, his party intends as long as possible
to govern upon that principle and that policy.

Working-men in this hall, I wish my voice had been loud
enough to have said what I am about to say to the vast multitude which we looked on this day; but I say it to them
through the press, and to all the working-men of this kingdom, I say that the accession to office of Lord Derby is
a declaration of war against the working-classes. The course
taken in London the other day by the police, and it had
almost been by the military, is an illustration of the doctrines
and the principles of the Derby administration. They reckon
nothing of the Constitution of their country—a Constitution
which has no more regard to the Crown or to the aristocracy
than it has to the people—a Constitution which regards the
House of Commons, fairly representing all the nation, as
important a part of the governmental system of this kingdom
as either the House of Lords or the Throne itself. If they thus
despise the Constitution they likewise despise the claims of
five or six millions who are unrepresented. You may work, you
may pay taxes, you may serve in the army, and fight; seventy
thousand or more of your brethren are now living under the
burning sun of India, and twice as many more are serving in
the ranks in different parts of the world; and you, the great
body of the people from whom these men are drawn, are not
considered worthy to do so simple an act as to give a vote in
your great town for your present or any future Members.
You are to have no vote, no share in the government; the
country you live in is not to be your country. You are like the
Coolies or the Chinese who are imported into the West Indies
or California. You are to work, but you are not to take root
in the country, or to consider the country as your country;
and, worse than all this, in addition to this refusal of the
commonest right of the Constitution, you are insulted by the
cheers which a great party have given to the language which
I have read to you to-night. You are to be told that you are

so ignorant and so venal, so drunken, so impulsive, so unreflecting, and so disorderly, that it is not even safe to skim off as it were the very cream of you to the number of 116,000, or it may be of 204,000, and to admit them to a vote for Members of the House of Commons.

This is the Tory theory.   This is the faith of Lord Derby and his party, and I maintain that I am not saying a word that is an exaggeration of the truth, for I have heard that party over and over again vociferously cheer sentiments such as I have described.   The Government which has been overturned was a very different Government.   Lord Russell had no fear of freedom.   He could much more easily be persuaded to give up, and he would much more willingly abandon for ever the name of Russell than he would give up his hereditary love of freedom.   The Government, which was led by Earl Russell in one House and by Mr. Gladstone in the other, was founded and acted upon the principle of trust and confidence in the people.   Some said there was not much difference between the Derby Government and the Russell Government. Lord Derby asked Lord Clarendon to take office in his Government.   There was something charming in the very audacity of Lord Derby's effrontery.   Lord Clarendon was an eminent Minister of the Government that brought in a Bill which the Tory party declared to be subversive of the Constitution; and Lord Derby asks Lord Clarendon to keep the Foreign Office in the new Government!

The Government of Lord Derby in the House of Commons sitting all in a row reminds me very much of a number of amusing and ingenious gentlemen whom I dare say some of you have seen and listened to.   I mean the Christy Minstrels. The Christy Minstrels, if I am not misinformed, are, when they are clean-washed, white men; but they come before the audience as black as the blackest negroes, and by this transformation it is expected that their jokes and songs will be more amusing.   The Derby minstrels pretend to be Liberal and white; but the fact is if you come nearer and examine them closely you will find them to be just as black and curly as the Tories have ever been. I do not know, and I will not pretend to say, which of them it is that plays the banjo and which the bones. But I have no doubt that, in their manœuvres to keep in office during the coming session, we shall know something more about them than we do at present; they are in point of fact, when they pretend to be Liberal, mere usurpers and impostors. Their party will not allow them to be Liberal, and they exist only upon the principle upon which they have acted in all their past history, of resisting and rejecting every proposition of a Liberal character that has been submitted to them.

What is this Derby principle of shutting out more than five-sixths of all the people from the exercise of constitutional rights? If any of you take ship to Canada you will find the Derby principle utterly repudiated. But in Canada there is no uprooting of institutions, and no destruction of property, and there is no absence of order or of loyalty. If you go to Australia you will find there that the Derby principle is unknown, and yet there reigns order as in this country, and contentment with the institutions of the colonies, and a regard for law and property. If you go to those greatest and most glorious colonies of this country, the United States of America, there you find a people exhibiting all the virtues which belong to the greatest nations on the face of the earth; there you find a people passing through a great war and a great revolution with a conduct and success, with a generosity and a magnanimity which have attracted and aroused the admiration of the world. And if you go to Europe, you find in the Republic of Switzerland, in the kingdoms of Holland and Belgium, in Norway and Sweden, in France, and now you are about to witness it in Germany, a wide extension of the franchise, hitherto in this country, in our time, unknown; and neither emperor, king, nor noble believes that his authority or his interests, or the greatness or happiness of any one of those countries, will be jeopardised by the free admission of the people to constitutional rights. In Germany, the vote is to be given to every man of twenty-five years of age and upwards. Let them propose to do the same here, and then we shall not be in advance of the great State of North Germany which is now being established. But what is it we are coming to in this country? To this, that the thing which is being rapidly accepted in almost all parts of the world is being persistently and obstinately refused here in England, the home of freedom, the mother of parliaments. For in this England, five millions of grown men, representing more than twenty millions of our population, are to be permanently denied that which makes the only difference between despotism and freedom all the world over.

I venture to say that this cannot last very long. How do we stand at this moment? The noble and illustrious Lady who sits upon the throne—she whose gentle hand wields the sceptre over that wide empire of which we are the heart and centre—she was not afraid of the Franchise Bill which the Government introduced last session. Seven times, I think, by her own lips or by her pen she has recommended to Parliament the admission of a large number of working-men to the Parliamentary franchise. If this proposition was destructive, would not the Queen discover that fact? If the Bill of the last session had been a pernicious Bill, would the thirty millions of people of the United Kingdom not have been able to produce one single public meeting in condemnation of it? The middle class in our towns are by a vast majority in favour of it. All the middle class of Birmingham have sympathised with the great proceedings of this day, and I doubt not that by-and-bye we shall see in the populous districts of Lancashire and Yorkshire assemblies rivalling those which have been held in London and Birmingham. And if we go to the House of Commons—that House elected so much by landlord compulsion

in the counties, and by corruption, intimidation, and tumult in
the boroughs, what do we find? Do not suppose that I am
charging that House of Commons with faults that it does not
itself understand and acknowledge :—have you read the report
of the proceedings at the Commission for Yarmouth? Did you
read that a late Member for that borough is said to have spent
70,000*l.* to maintain his seat? Did you read that one gentleman, an inferior partner in a brewery, contributed 4,000*l.* for
the election of his partner, and that another gentleman, knowing nothing of that borough, went down there and supplied
6,000*l.* to fight a contest spread only over a few days? And
remember that when Yarmouth or any other borough is thus
brought before the public it is only a sample of a very considerable sack—and that for every borough which is thus exposed
there are probably ten or twenty other boroughs which are
to a very large extent liable to the very same condemnation.
Notwithstanding this, if we go to the House of Commons, we
find the Parliament of England at this moment about equally
divided, and that half the House was in favour of the late Bill.
If that be so, what is wanted in this poising and balancing of
the scale? It only wants this, that the working-men of
England should heartily throw their influence into that side
which is for their interests, and that side will prevail.

You know I have preferred that the franchise should be
established upon what I consider to be the ancient practice of
the country. I am not afraid of the principles of the Reform
League. I have no fear of manhood suffrage, and no man is
more a friend of the ballot than I am. It is a great cause
which is offered to your notice to-night. It is a grand and
noble flag under which you are asked to enlist yourselves.
What I would recommend you to do is this—and I imagine
myself at this moment to be speaking in the ear of every
intelligent, sober, and thoughtful working-man in the three
kingdoms—let us try to move on together; let us not split
hairs on this question; let us do as our fathers did thirty-four

years ago; let us have associations everywhere; let every workshop and factory be a Reform Association; let there be in every one of them a correspondent, or a secretary, who shall enrol members and assist this great and noble cause. I would recommend that the passages I have read from that celebrated and unhappy speech should be printed upon cards, and should be hung up in every room in every factory, workshop, and clubhouse, and in every place where working-men are accustomed to assemble. Let us rouse the spirit of the people against these slanderers of a great and noble nation.

There will soon come another election. The working-men may not be able to vote, but they can form themselves into a powerful body, and they can throw their influence in every borough on the side of the candidates who pledge themselves to the question of Reform. If they do this, you may depend upon it they will change many seats, and give a certain majority for Reform in the next Parliament. It may be necessary and desirable to meet Parliament again with petitions from all parts of the country, signed by numberless names. There is no effort which the Constitution, which morality permits us to use, that we should leave unused and unmade for the purpose of furthering this great cause; and let us be sure of this, that we demand only that the question of Reform shall be dealt with by a Government honestly in favour of Reform.

The Address which has been presented to me has referred to 1832. I remember that time well. My young heart then was stirred with the trumpet-blast that sounded ·from your midst. There was no part of this kingdom where your voice was not heard. Let it sound again. Stretch out your hands to your countrymen in every part of the three kingdoms, and ask them to join you in a great and righteous effort on behalf of that freedom which has been so long the boast of Englishmen, but which the majority of Englishmen have never yet possessed. I shall esteem it an honour which my words cannot describe, and which even in thought I cannot measure, if the population which I am permitted to represent should do its full duty in the great struggle which is before us. Remember the great object for which we strive. Care not for calumnies and lies. Our object is this—to restore the British constitution in all its fulness, with all its freedom, to the British people.

REFORM.

IX.

GLASGOW, OCTOBER 16, 1866.

[On the 16th of October, 1866, a procession of many thousands of the friends
of Reform passed through the streets of the city of Glasgow, and formed in
a great meeting on Glasgow Green. The numbers present have been
variously estimated, but it seemed as if nearly all the male population of the
city were there. In the evening a great meeting was held in the City Hall,
and Mr. Bright was presented with an Address, in answer to which this
speech was spoken.]

MR. CHAIRMAN, AND CITIZENS OF NO MEAN CITY,—I accept
this Address which has been read in your hearing and presented to me, with a feeling of deep gratitude to those who
have expressed such friendly feelings towards me, but with
a deep anxiety when I consider the intent and purport of
the document. I am consoled by regarding it as in some
degree a compact or covenant entered into to-night by you
and those whom you represent, with me and those whom
I may be supposed in some degree to represent, and that
we covenant together that whatsoever is moral for us to do
we engage to do in the prosecution of that great cause which
has stirred the heart of Glasgow to-day. I can do but
little—any one man can do but little; but you in your vast
numbers can do much, by uniting with numbers, not smaller,
in other parts of the kingdom.

I have a strong sense that the day is fast approaching which will see the triumph of our cause, and I think he must be blind and foolish indeed who is not willing to admit that it is a great issue which is now submitted to the people of the United Kingdom. Gatherings of scores of thousands of men, extending from south to north, must have some great cause. Men do not leave their daily labour, the necessary occupations of their lives, thus to meet, unless they believe that there is some great question submitted to them in which they have a deep and overpowering interest. And the question is this—Whether in future the government and the legislation of this country shall be conducted by a privileged class in a sham Parliament, or on the principles of the constitution of the nation, through its representatives, fairly and freely chosen ?

There are persons who will think that I am speaking harshly of the existing Parliament. Some probably in this meeting may think that Mr. Beales was indiscriminate in the term which he used when he spoke of our representation as being steeped in corruption ; but I am certain that if the representation of this country existed in any other country, and that its details were explained to Englishmen, there are not five Englishmen within the bounds of England, or five Britons within the bounds of this island, who would not admit that the language he has applied to the Parliament was correct.

What we charge against the Parliament is this—that it is chosen from constituencies not only so small that they do not and cannot adequately represent the nation, but from constituencies so small as to be influenced by corruption, and by all kinds of motives that are neither national nor patriotic. In our boroughs, for example, the numbers for the most part are very small. There are, I think, 254 boroughs in the United Kingdom, but there are only 54 of these that possess a constituency of 2,000 electors and upwards, large and fair constituencies being always the exception. In Scotland, your borough constituencies, though not generally very large, are larger than those in England, and to your honour it must be said that they are far more incorrupt than English consti- tuencies. In the counties the freeholders—those who hold land for cultivation—are constantly diminishing in numbers, and that portion of the constituencies which is not composed of freeholders is composed of tenant-farmers—the most de- pendent class of occupiers, probably, in the nation.

But now, let me point to one or two facts which should sink deep in the minds of all men. Out of every hun- dred grown men in the United Kingdom eighty-four have no votes. Those eighty-four might just as well, for all purposes of constitutional government, so far as they are directly concerned—those eighty-four might as well live in Russia, where there is no electoral system of government, or in those other countries, now very few indeed, in which Parliaments and representations are unknown. If it be the fact that only sixteen men out of every hundred have votes, it is also the fact that those sixteen are so arranged, and so placed, that their representation is in reality almost entirely destroyed. If the electors were fairly divided amongst all the Members, there would be nearly 2,000 electors to every Mem- ber; but what is the state of things? It is this, that one- third of the House of Commons, or 220 Members, are actually elected by 70,000 votes—that is to say, that 220 Members of the House of Commons are chosen by a number of men scattered over the country, who are fewer by almost one-half than the number of grown men in this city of Glasgow alone. And further, one-half of the House of Commons is chosen by about 180,000 electors, being only one-seventh of the whole number of electors, and much below the number of men who are to be found in the cities of Edinburgh and Glasgow. And if we come to that great event which excites so much interest, but which is generally of so little value—a general election—we find, I believe, that not more than 10 in 100, not more than ten per cent. of the whole grown-up male population of the United Kingdom, ever come to the poll and give their vote for the election of a new Parliament.

With regard to a general election, some of you have read, and many of you know something of the cost and corruption of a general election. I will give you one instance and one proof of it. It has been my opinion all along that it was the duty of the Government of Lord Russell, after the defeat of their Reform Bill during the last session, to have dissolved the Parliament. I have no reason to disbelieve what is asserted, that Lord Russell himself was of that opinion. But a general election was a burden which the Members of Parliament did not wish to bear. I was speaking to a Member of the Government on this question about the time when the resignation of the late Government was just about to be submitted to the Queen, and I was telling him that I thought the true policy, the constitutional policy, of the Government was to dissolve the Parliament. A portion of his answer was this:—A Member who sits on our side of the House had spoken to him about it. He said, ' My election has already cost me 9,000*l.*'—and he added, ' I have, besides, 3,000*l.* more to pay.' He said further, what was very reasonable, that this was a heavy burden, that it was grievous to be borne, that it put him to exceeding inconvenience, and, if the Parliament were dissolved, he could not afford to fight his county or his borough, as the case might be, but would be obliged to retire from the field, and leave the contest, if there should be a contest, to some one else. You will believe, then, that the Government were greatly pressed by this consideration; and this consideration, added, it may be, to others, induced them to resign office rather than to dissolve Parliament. Thus you have a proof that whereas general corruption and putridity are the destruction of most bodies which they affect, the corruption of the present Parliament was, and is, the cause of its present existence.

Now bear in mind that this state of things which I have been describing obtains at the present moment, thirty-four years after the passing of the great Reform Bill. What the Government must have been before that Bill was passed it is scarcely possible to describe or to imagine; but I have no doubt of this, that it was one of the worst Governments in civilized countries, and in Europe; and I think this may be fairly argued from the fact of the incessant wars in which the country was engaged for 150 years before that Reform; from the enormous debt that was created; from the crushing taxes that were fixed upon the people; and, worse almost than that, from that most infamous law which ever passed a Parliament of civilized men—the law which limited the supply of bread to the people.

Now, if the Clerk of the House of Commons were placed at Temple Bar, and if he had orders to tap upon the shoulder every well-dressed and apparently cleanly-washed man who passed through that ancient bar, until he had numbered six hundred and fifty-eight; and if the Crown summoned these six hundred and fifty-eight to be the Parliament of the United Kingdom, my honest conviction is that you would have a better Parliament than now exists. This assertion will stagger some timid and some good men; but let me explain myself to you. It would be a Parliament, every member of which would have no direct constituency, but it would be a Parliament that would act as a jury that would take some heed of the facts and arguments laid before it. It would be free, at any rate, from the class prejudices which weigh upon the present House of Commons. It would be free from the overshadowing presence of what are called noble families. It would owe no allegiance to great landowners, and I hope it would have fewer men amongst it seeking their own gains by entering Parliament.

With the Parliament which we have now and have had, facts and arguments go for very little. Take that question to which I have referred, of limiting the supply of bread to the people. The Corn-law was on the Statute-book for thirty-one years—sixteen years before the Reform Bill, and fifteen years after the passing of that Bill—but from the first hour of its enactment until the hour of its destruction the facts and the arguments against it were equally clear and equally conclusive. They would not be convinced though one arose from the dead, and that which convinced them at last was the occurrence of a great famine in Ireland, which destroyed or drove from the country hundreds of thousands of the citizens of the empire. I maintain with the most perfect conviction that the House of Commons, representing as it now does counties and boroughs such as I have described, does not represent the intelligence and the justice of the nation, but the prejudices, the privileges, and the selfishness of a class.

What are the results of this system of legislation? Some of them have been touched upon in that Address which has been so kindly presented to me. You refer to the laws affecting land. Are you aware of a fact which I saw stated the other day in an essay on this subject—that half the land of England is in the possession of fewer than one hundred and fifty men? Are you aware of the fact that half the land in Scotland is in the possession of not more than ten or twelve men? Are you aware of the fact that the monopoly in land in the United Kingdom is growing constantly more and more close? And the result of it is this—the gradual extirpation of the middle-class as owners of land, and the constant degradation of the tillers of the soil. Take a matter about which many Scotch farmers know something — take the perpetual grievance of the game-laws. In the House of Commons that question can scarcely be discussed. The landed interest, as it did in the late cattle-plague debate, tramples down Government and borough Members and everybody and everything that thwarts their inclination. Take the general —I am sorry to say the too general—subserviency of the tenant-farmers in the matter of elections in your country—in Scotland. I entertain the hope that you will lead the way to the deliverance of the farmers from this slavery. In the last elections for Kincardineshire and for Aberdeenshire, the tenant-farmers have taken the politics of those counties into their own hands. I hope, and I believe, that the tenant-farmers of Scotland—the most enlightened agriculturists that live on the face of the earth – I hope they, with perfect justice, and perfect courtesy to their landowners, will still exert their legitimate and right influence in the election of Members for the counties of Scotland.

But take—what some of you cannot comprehend—take the helpless poverty of the farm-labourers in the southern counties of England. Their wages are very low. Their helplessness is extreme. Their power to deliver themselves, their power to combine, seems at the lowest ebb. Look at their ignorance! A friend of mine—a Member of the House of Commons, who lives within six miles of the royal town and castle of Windsor, told me only the other day that he knew the case of a family near his house in which there had grown up eleven children, not one of whom could read or write at all. And he said that he had lately had in his employ upon his property seven men, of whom four could neither read nor write, two of them could read most imperfectly, and one of them could read and write about as well as the other two could read. Bear in mind that all this exists within six miles of the royal castle of Windsor. It exists in a neighbourhood where lords and squires and established clergymen swarm. Such is the state of ignorance of that population at this moment. In the county from which I come, girls of the age of from fifteen to twenty years are earning, many of them, I believe, double the weekly wages of the able-bodied farm-labourer, the head and father of a family, in some of the south-western counties of England. But what must be the ignorance of that population, that when such wages are

offering to them in Lancashire and Yorkshire they scarcely
hear of them! They seem to have no aspiration to better
their condition, and there is no sensible emigration from
these wretched counties to the more prosperous counties of
the north.

Your Address refers to pauperism—the gulf of pauperism.
In the United Kingdom at this moment there are more than
1,200,000 paupers. The pauperism of the United Kingdom
last year—and it will not cost less, I believe, this year—cost
the rate-payers—those who pay taxes for the relief of the poor
—more than seven and a half millions sterling, and this does
not include the cost of many thousands of vagrants who also
come occasionally under the name of paupers. Now look, I
beg of you, to this mass of misery. It is so great a mass that
benevolence cannot reach it. If benevolence could do it,
there would be no pauperism in England, for in no country
do I believe that there is more benevolence than there is in
the United Kingdom. The kindness of the women of England
is beyond all measure and beyond all praise of mine. There
does not exist among created beings, beneath the angelic ranks,
those who are more kind and charitable than the women of
the United Kingdom. But benevolence can touch scarcely
the fringe of this vast disorder. There is another virtue we
could add, and that virtue and that quality is justice. It is
not benevolence but justice that can deal with giant evils. It
was not benevolence that gave the people bread twenty years
ago, but it was justice embodied in the abolition of a cruel
and a guilty law. But justice is impossible from a class.
It is most certain and easy from a nation; and I believe we
can only reach the depths of ignorance and misery and crime
in this country by an appeal to the justice, the intelligence,
and the virtues of the entire people.

That Address has mentioned another question—the question
of your national expenditure, of your army and navy; and
I will state only one fact with regard to the navy. I believe

since the great war, since 1815, that the navy of this country
has cost more than four hundred millions sterling. I believe
that during the last six years it has cost as much as the
United States navy during the same time: we have been in
a condition of profound peace; the United States have had to
build or buy six hundred ships, to man them, to furnish them
with munitions of war, and to fight them during the greatest
struggle that any nation ever waged. And yet at this
moment, after spending so much, we have Sir John Pakington,
the great reconstructor, coming into office, and promising, not
to extend the liberties of the people, but to reconstruct a navy
on which such enormous and countless sums have already
been sunk.

Then, take the taxes. Something has been done to make
the taxes more equal; but take the taxes which are levied
under the name of probate and legacy and succession duties;
and I will give you a case which it is just possible you
have heard before from my lips. A Member of the House of
Commons—at least he was so when he gave me this fact,
though I am sorry to say he is not one now—a Member of the
House of Commons told me he had had left to him by a person
not related to him by blood an estate in land worth 21,000*l.*;
the timber upon it was worth 11,000*l.*; altogether 32,000*l.*
The tax, when the property is left to a person who is not
a relation of the man who leaves it, is ten per cent.; the tax
therefore on 32,000*l.* would be 3,200*l.*; and if any one of
you received a legacy like that in cash, in shares, in ships,
in stock-in-trade, in any of those things which are not lands
and houses, he would pay 3,200*l.* But my friend receiving
his legacy in land, and the timber upon it, paid just 700*l.*
And why? For this reason only, that the law was made by
a landed and propertied Parliament, and the owners and
inheritors of lands and houses were considered specially
worthy of its regard.

But I may be asked—and no doubt some man who, after

this meeting, will take up his pen to write a criticism on my
speech, or upon this meeting, will ask—how comes it, if
Parliament is so bad, that so many good things have been
done by Parliament during the last thirty or forty years?
I acknowledge that good things have been done, and I ought
to know, because I have been concerned in the doing of some
of them. But by whom were they done? Mainly by that
force in Parliament which is sent there by the great and free
borough constituencies of the kingdom. The Members for
the great towns—although but a minority, and not a very
large minority—are the moving force by which these good
things have been done. It has not been the policy of the
Tories to do good things—and I have seen the time when the
Whigs have been much less zealous about them than I could
have wished. They have sprung from the people, and the
people have carried them. What there has been of real
representation in Parliament has urged these measures forward. What there has been of sham representation has
uniformly opposed these measures.

I am of opinion that the rich people of a country, invested
with power, and speaking generally for rich people alone,
cannot sufficiently care for the multitude and the poor. They
are personally kind enough, but they do not care for the
people in the bulk. They have read a passage in Holy Writ
that 'The poor ye have always with you'—and therefore
they imagine that it is a providential arrangement that a
small section of the people should be rich and powerful, and
that the great mass of the people should be hardworking and
poor. It is a long distance from castles, and mansions, and
great houses, and abounding luxuries, to the condition of the
great mass of the people who have no property, and too many
of whom are always on the verge of poverty. We know very
well all of us how much we are influenced by the immediate
circumstances by which we are surrounded. The rich find
everything just as they like. The country needs no reform.

There is no other country in the world so pleasant for rich people as this country. But I deny altogether that the rich alone are qualified to legislate for the poor, any more than that the poor alone would be qualified to legislate for the rich. My honest belief is, that if we could be all called upon to legislate for all, that all would be more justly treated, and would be more happy than we are now. We should have then an average; we should have the influence of wealth and of high culture, and of those qualities that come from leisure, and the influence of those more robust qualities that come from industry and from labour.

Suppose now, without arguing for this or that particular measure of Reform, that we could add another million to the existing constituencies, what would be the result? We should modify the constituencies. Instead of the people coming to the hustings at the nomination and holding up their hands for this candidate or that, and having for the most part no power in the election, the inhabitants of the town would have a much greater power than they have now. The constituency would be less open to management than it . is at present; majorities on one side or the other would be larger and less open to corruption; and we should have Members whose opinions and whose conduct would be modified by this infusion of new and fresh blood into the constituencies which send them to Parliament. We should do this further —we should bring the rich and the great more into contact with the people, and into a better acquaintance with human wants and with the necessities and feelings of their countrymen. What other thing would happen? I dare venture to assert this, that Parliament then would not revile and slander the people as it does now. Nor would it cheer with frantic violence when their countrymen are described in hideous and hateful colours. Probably what I call the Botany Bay view of their countrymen would be got rid of, and we should have a sense of greater justice and generosity in the feeling with which they regard the bulk of the nation. And if there was more knowledge of the people, there would assuredly be more sympathy with them; and I believe the legislation of the House, being more in accordance with the public sentiment, would be wiser and better in every respect. The nation would be changed. There would be amongst us a greater growth of everything that is good.

May I ask if there are any ministers of religion in this audience? I have sometimes thought that I should like to have an audience of four or five thousand of them, to whom I could preach a political sermon, and to whom I could tell something which I fear their theological schools have failed to teach them. An eminent man of your country, the late Dr. Chalmers, in speaking of the question of free-trade, and particularly of the struggle for the abolition of the Corn-laws, uttered some memorable words. He said he thought there was nothing that would tend so much to sweeten the breath of British society as the abolition of the Corn-laws. I believe now that there is nothing which would tend so much to sweeten the breath of British society as the admission of a large and generous number of the working-classes to citizenship and the exercise of the franchise. Now, if my words should reach the ears and reach the heart of any man who is interested in the advancement of religion in this country, I ask him to consider whether there are not great political obstacles to the extension of civilization and morality and religion within the bounds of the United Kingdom. We believe—these ministers, you, and I—we believe in a Supreme Ruler of the Universe. We believe in His omnipotence; we believe and we humbly trust in His mercy. We know that the strongest argument which is used against that belief, by those who reject it, is an argument drawn from the misery, and the helplessness, and the darkness of so many of our race, even in countries which call themselves civilized and Christian. Is not that the fact? If I believed that this misery, and this helplessness, and this darkness could not be touched or transformed, I myself should be driven to admit the almost overwhelming force of that argument; but I am convinced that just laws, and an enlightened administration of them, would change the face of the country. I believe that ignorance and suffering might be lessened to an incalculable extent, and that many an Eden, beauteous in flowers and rich in fruits, might be raised up in the waste wilderness which spreads before us. But no class can do that. The class which has hitherto ruled in this country has failed miserably. It revels in power and wealth, whilst at its feet, a terrible peril for its future, lies the multitude which it has neglected. If a class has failed, let us try the nation. That is our faith, that is our purpose, that is our cry—Let us try the nation. This it is which has called together these count-less numbers of the people to demand a change; and, as I think of it, and of these gatherings, sublime in their vastness and in their resolution, I think I see, as it were, above the hill-tops of time, the glimmerings of the dawn of a better and a nobler day for the country and for the people that I love so well.

—→→→←←←—

REFORM.

X.

MANCHESTER, NOVEMBER 20, 1866.

[The following speech was made in the Free Trade Hall, Manchester, at a
Banquet organized by the National Reform Union. Several Members of
the Liberal Party were invited to the gathering.]

ALTHOUGH, perhaps, this is one of the most striking and
important meetings which have been held in this country
during the last few years, you will, perhaps, be surprised to
learn that I came to it with a sense almost of indifference :
not indifference as to its importance; but with an absence of
that feeling of responsibility which has pressed so much upon
me on some recent occasions. For the committee were kind
enough to send round to their guests a list of the speakers
who were expected to address the meeting. I found them
much more numerous than is common, and I found my name
about half way down the list. I took it, therefore, for granted
that I could come, for once, in some degree as a spectator
and a listener, rather than as a prominent actor at the
meeting. Some gentlemen who were expected to be here
are not here—Mr. Stansfeld, because he is ill; Mr. Layard,
because he has not returned from the Continent. And
Mr. Forster, who seems less able to occupy the time of an
audience when he comes into Lancashire than he is in Yorkshire, has spoken, I may say, uttering the feeling of the

whole meeting, for a very much shorter time than we had a
right to expect. I shall trust, therefore, to those who come
after me to say a good deal which I shall not take up your
time in attempting to say to-night.

During the last memorable session of Parliament you will
probably recollect that it was a very common thing in the
mouths of the opponents of the Government Bill to say that
the working-men—the aggrieved party—felt no grievance;
for they scarcely expressed any favourable opinion on the
Bill, or, indeed, any opinion at all on the question of their
own admission to the franchise. I was repeatedly charged with
being in the position of a leader in a case, in which it was
said that, after all, I had no clients and no following. There
was a general taunt uttered that we were very much exag-
gerating the case of the working-men, and that the condition
of that large class was so comfortable and so prosperous that
they were perfectly content with the Government as it is
carried on by a Parliament so inadequately representing the
whole nation.

I suspect that the argument, so far as it was uttered, and
had any force, has now been fully and satisfactorily answered.
But these gentlemen have turned right round, and have now
another thing to say about our meetings. They say that the
middle class stands entirely aloof, that nobody really cares for
Reform but the working-men, and that no great question can
be carried, or sensibly affected, in this country by the opinions
and action of working-men alone. They point to the great
meetings that have been held, and after dividing the notorious
and proved magnitude of the meetings by four or six, they
then conclude that there were a few thousands of working-
men present; but Members of Parliament, manufacturers,
merchants, and what they call the respectable and influential
classes, were found to be entirely absent. But they forget
that these meetings at which they say working-men only
attended were meetings called expressly by working-men and

for working-men. If they want to know, or wanted to know, how far the main objects of those meetings receive sympathy from a more powerful class, they might have come to those meetings to have learned. In Birmingham, as you know, the Mayor was in the procession, and the Chief Constable of the town took charge of all the arrangements for it; and in the great Town-hall of that city, the Mayor took the chair at the evening meeting, and I venture to say that it would be impossible in any town in this kingdom to assemble upon the platform a greater amount of what these gentlemen call respectability, wealth, and station in the town, than were assembled there and then. If they had come to this hall on the evening of the great meeting in Manchester, and if they had gone to the Town-hall of Leeds, or to the City-hall of Glasgow, they would have found that after the scores of thousands that had attended the great open-air meeting in the daytime, there was a meeting most important, most influential, omnipotent indeed, within that town in which it was held. In the town of Leeds, I was told nearly 1,000 persons paid 5s. each to attend the meeting in the Town-hall, and I think that is some sign of the class of persons who attended.

But if there was any question on this matter, I would ask those gentlemen to come on this platform to-night. Here is the largest and finest hall in Britain, the largest and finest hall in Europe, I believe the largest and finest hall in the world, and yet this hall is crowded with persons to whom our opponents, I think generally, unless they were very fastidious, would admit the term respectable and influential. I doubt if there has ever been held in this kingdom, within our time, a political banquet more numerous, more influential, more unanimous, more grand in every respect, than that which is held here to-night. Just now, it is the fashion to flatter and to court the middle class. The middle class are told that since the Reform Bill of 1832 political power has been in their hands; before 1832 it was with the lords and great landowners, but since 1832 it has been in the hands of the middle class; and now the middle class are asked whether they are willing to surrender that power into the hands of a more numerous, and, as these persons assert, a dangerous class, who would swamp, not the exalted class of lords and great land-owners, the highest in social position, but would swamp also the great middle class with whom power is now said to rest. And they try to teach the middle class that there is an essentially different interest between them and the great body of the people who are not yet admitted into that class. They say the one class is in power, and the other class is outside, and out of power, and they warn the middle class against admitting the outsiders into partnership with them, for fear they should dethrone the middle class and set up an unintelligent, unreasoning, and selfish power of their own.

That is the sort of argument which is used to the middle class to induce them to take no part in any measure that shall admit the working class to a participation in political power. I should be ashamed to stand on any platform and to employ such an argument as this. Is there to be found in the writings or the speaking of any public man connected with the Liberal or the Reform party so dangerous and so out-rageous a policy as that which these men pursue? When separating the great body of the people into the middle and the working class, they set class against class, and ask you to join with the past and present monopolists of power in the miserable and perilous determination to exclude for ever the great body of your countrymen from the common rights of the glorious English constitution. There is no greater fallacy than this—that the middle classes are in possession of power. The real state of the case, if it were put in simple language, would be this—that the working-men are almost universally excluded, roughly and insolently, from political power, and that the middle class, whilst they have the semblance of it, are defrauded of the reality. The difference and the resemblance is this, that the working-men come to the hustings at an election, and when the returning-officer asks for the show of hands, every man can hold up his hand although his name is not upon the register of voters; every working-man can vote at that show of hands, but the show of hands is of no avail. The middle class have votes, but those votes are rendered harmless and nugatory by the unfair distribution of them, and there is placed in the voter's hand a weapon which has neither temper nor edge, by which he can neither fight for further freedom, nor defend that which his ancestors have gained.

On a recent occasion, perhaps it was when I last stood on this platform, I stated certain facts which have not, from that day to this, been contradicted—I stated that out of every 100 men throughout the United Kingdom, grown-up men, liable to taxes, expected to perform all the duties of life, responsible to the laws, 84 were excluded from the franchise, and that 16 only were included. I want to ask whether the 16 out of the 100 may be said to include all the middle class? But there is another fact, if possible more astonishing still, and that is that three men out of every 100 throughout the United Kingdom do apparently by their votes return an actual majority of the present House of Commons. But if a majority of the House of Commons be returned by a number so small as three out of every 100 of the men of the United Kingdom, and if the other House of Parliament asks for no votes at all, I ask you whether it is not a fact of the most transparent character that power, legislative and governing, in this country does not rest with the middle classes? What Mr. Forster says is quite true. You may have suffrage—this or that, but you may have such a distribution of power that even your present representation, bad as it is, may be made something even worse.

Take the case of your boroughs, in which alone may be said to rest everything that exists in the United Kingdom of a free election. Divide the boroughs, 254 in number, into two classes, those under 20,000 inhabitants and those over that number. Under 20,000 there are 145 boroughs; over it 109. But the boroughs under 20,000 return 215 Members, against 181 that are returned by the boroughs over 20,000. But that gives only a very misty idea of the state of the case. Those boroughs over 20,000 inhabitants, having 39 Members fewer than the boroughs under 20,000, still are in this position— their Members represent six times as many electors, seven times as much population, and fourteen times as much payment of income-tax as the larger number of Members represent. It is clear beyond all cavil—for figures, after all, are difficult things to meet and controvert if they are correct— that your representative system, even in the boroughs where alone it exists in any life at all, is a representative system almost wholly delusive, and defrauds the middle classes of the power which the Act of 1832 professed to give them.

Your county representation is almost too sad a subject to dwell upon. Every man who occupies a house or land of an annual value less than 50*l.* is excluded; the number of free-holders on the whole diminishes, and really there remains scarcely anything of independent power and freedom of election within the majority of the counties of the United Kingdom. So, then, I come to this conclusion, that the working classes are excluded and insulted, and that the middle classes are defrauded; and I presume that those who really do wield the power despise the middle classes for their silence under this system. When I look at the great middle class of this country, and see all that it has done, and see the political position in which it has been to some extent content to rest, I cannot help saying that it reminds me very much of the language which the ancient Hebrew patriarch addressed to one of his sons. He said, 'Issachar is a strong ass, couching down between two burdens.' On the one side there is the burden of seven and a half millions per annum, raised by way of tax, to keep from starvation more than 1,200,000 paupers within the United Kingdom — and on the other hand, and higher up in the scale, there is mismanagement the most gross, there is extravagance the most reckless, and there is waste the most appalling and disgraceful which has ever been seen in the government of any country. And this is the grand result of a system which systematically shuts out the millions, and which cajoles the middle class by the hocus-pocus of a Parliamentary Government.

Sir, I am delighted beyond measure, after many years of discussion, of contemplation, of labour — in connection with this great question—I say I am delighted to believe that the great body of the people, call them middle class or call them working class, are resolved that this state of things shall exist no longer. During the last session of Parliament there has been an honest attempt made by an honest Government to tinker the existing system. For, after all, the Bill of the last session, honest and well intended and valuable as it was, was still but a tinkering of a very bad system. But the Tory party refused even to have it tinkered. They remind me of a wealthy but a most penurious old gentleman, who lived some years ago in my neighbourhood, and who objected very much to a tailor's bill; he said that he had found out that a hole would last longer than a patch. I am not sure that this is not the case with Lord Derby and his friends; for it was one of their great arguments that if the Bill of the Government passed it would inevitably follow that something more would almost immediately be demanded. They were so anxious that things should remain as they are that they refused to admit 200,000 more of the middle class by the lowering of the county franchise, and they refused with equal, perhaps with greater pertinacity, to admit 200,000, but, as I believe, not much more than 100,000 working-men, to electoral rights.

They would not suppress, nor allow the suppression of one

single rotten borough, and in fact there was no abuse, however foul, however intolerable, however putrid, to which they would allow the legislative reforming knife to be applied; and they determined to keep everything just as it is. And now these gentlemen, with whom we were obliged, to our great misfortune, to contend so much last session, are in office. They call themselves Her Majesty's servants; but they have not yet dared to proclaim that they are the executive servants of the people. Some of their papers, and some papers which are not theirs, give us to understand—for the papers are often understanding a great many things of which they know nothing—that the Cabinet meetings held during the last fortnight have landed us in this strange position,—that the men who were against all Reform six months ago, are now warmly engaged in concocting a measure which shall be satisfactory to the great body of the Reformers of this country.

My opinion is this:—first of all, that the papers know nothing about it; secondly, that the Government (we are obliged to call them a Government) has not made up its mind at all whether it will bring in a Reform Bill or not. In point of fact, Lord Derby is waiting to see what the weather will be. And I suppose they will postpone their decision perhaps for some few weeks to come. Who knows but that they will wait till this day fortnight—or yesterday fortnight?

Yesterday fortnight, on Monday, the 3rd of December, it is said that, following the example of Birmingham, and the West Riding, and Glasgow, and Manchester, and Edinburgh, the men concerned in the trades in London will make what they call a demonstration, that is, that on behalf of the question of Reform they will assemble and will peacefully walk through some of the main streets of the West End of London, for the purpose of showing that they take an interest in this great question. I know nothing of the arrangements, except what I see in the papers; but it is said that more than 200,000 men have arranged to walk in that procession.

I hear on no mean authority that certain persons at the West End are getting up a little alarm at what may happen on the 3rd of December.

What will happen we all know. If the police do not interfere to break the peace, the peace will not be broken. And, probably, what happened on the last occasion may be of some use in teaching the Home Secretary his duty on this occasion. There are persons, doubtless, so credulous and so willing to wish well of everybody, as to imagine that Lord Derby's Government will bring in a satisfactory Reform Bill. They say that Sir Robert Peel and the Duke of Wellington carried Catholic Emancipation; that Sir Robert Peel and the Duke of Wellington repealed the Corn-law; and why should not Lord Derby pass a Reform Bill? Lord Derby is neither the Duke of Wellington nor Sir Robert Peel. He deserted both those eminent men in 1846, rather than unite with them to repeal the Corn-law; and he has never shown, from that hour to this, one atom of statesmanship or one spark of patriotism, that would lead us to expect that, on this occasion, he would turn round, and, neglecting his party, do something for his country.

It is all very well to say that if the Government bring in a very good Bill, we who want a very good Bill will support it. But it is no use dealing in phraseology and platitudes of that kind. Look at the Cabinet of Lord Derby; look what the members of it have said and done during late years, and during the late Parliamentary session. Lord Derby has told us that it was his mission to stem democracy; his friends in the House of Commons declared last session that the passing of that Bill of the late Government would be to hand over the country to the democracy of the working classes. Mr. Disraeli, in his speeches, was ingenious beyond his fellows, as indeed he generally is, for if he had not been so he would not have reached the position in which we find him. But Mr. Disraeli was anxious to cut off all free election in counties. He is of opinion, so far as I gather from his speeches, that the more entirely the county representation can be made conterminous with the great estates of the peers and the great landowners, the more entirely it will be after his own fashion and his own wishes. No more perilous idea can be entertained by any statesman; if you once get the nominees of the great landowners and the lords on the one side of the House, and the representatives of everybody else on the other side of the House, the beginning of the end will have come. And whilst Mr. Disraeli is tickling the ears and the fancy of the country gentlemen behind him, he is propounding a plan which, if it were carried into effect, would end in the utter extinction of the political power of the country gentlemen and the peerage of England.

Mr. Disraeli and Lord Stanley were the men in the last Derby Government who proposed to disfranchise 70,000 county voters whose property was within the limits of the boroughs, and I cannot believe that men who made such a proposition seven or eight years ago can produce a good honest Reform Bill now. Lord Stanley made a speech during the discussions on the late Bill which his party and their press said was unanswerable. It was a speech leading to this conclusion, that he would give no votes to any of the working class until he saw, by the distribution of seats, that those votes could be made of no use to them. And Lord Stanley lent himself to an unhappy trick, intended, as it appeared to us, to take the Government and the House by surprise, and by which, by gaining a sudden and accidental division, he might have destroyed both the Bill and the Government. Lord Cranborne is a member of this Cabinet—Lord Robert Cecil that was a short time ago. Lord Cranborne quarrelled violently with Mr. Gladstone because Mr. Gladstone said the working-men were of our own flesh and blood. He treated that observation very much in the same way that the Carolinian planter and slaveholder in the Senate of the United

States would have replied to my friend Mr. Sumner if he had said that the black and white were equal in the eye of God, and of one flesh and blood. General Peel is a member of this Government, and he protested violently against any reduction of the franchise, as indeed did Sir Stafford Northcote, who is, I think, now the President of the Board of Trade.

I want to ask you whether from these men you are to expect, you are to wait for, with anxious and hopeful looking forward, any Reform Bill? And, after all these speeches had been made, Lord Derby did his utmost to prevail upon Mr. Lowe to become a member of his Cabinet. If, after all this, they were to attempt to manufacture and introduce a Reform Bill, they would cover themselves and their party with humiliation. I know that in this country politicians change sides; office has a wonderful effect upon men. I suppose there are men here such as were described by our witty friend, Mr. Hosea Bigelow, in painting the character of some politicians in America. He said of them as we perhaps may say of Lord Derby and his party,—

> 'A merciful Providence fashioned them hollow,
> On purpose that they might their principles swallow.'

But, notwithstanding that provision, that merciful provision, for statesmen, I confess that I do not believe that the Government have determined to bring in a Reform Bill, or that they can by any possibility bring in a Bill which the Reformers of this country can accept. They have done everything during the past session by fraudulent statements—by insults to the people—by the most evident baseness of party action—to destroy the moderate and honest attempt of Lord Russell to improve the representation. And I do not believe that in one short year they can turn round; and, capacious as may be the internal cavity of the Tory Government, I think they cannot in one short year swallow all their Conservative principles.

If a man were to tell me that he had a broth composed of half-a-dozen poisonous ingredients, and that he could make of it a wholesome dish, I should not believe him. And if he tells me that Derby, and Disraeli, and Stanley, and Cranborne, and General Peel, and the rest of them, after the speeches to which I listened six months ago, are about to produce a wholesome, and salutary, and liberal Reform Bill, I must ask him not to impose for a moment on my understanding. The enemies of the Bill of 1866 cannot become the honest friends of Reform in 1867— and the conspirators of the session which has just expired cannot become honourable statesmen in the session which is about to open. My opinion may be no better than that of any other man. This, however, may be good advice— that all Reformers should be on the watch, for there are enemies enough to our cause, and false friends enough to convince us that it is by no means out of danger.

But the next Bill—what must it be? One thing I think we have a right to insist upon, that the next Bill which is introduced by a Liberal and Reform Government shall be in its suffrage based upon the ancient borough franchise of the country. Household or rating suffrage has existed for centuries in our parishes. It has existed for many years in our municipal corporations. It has never been found either in parish or corporation to be destructive of the interests of the people of those circumscribed districts of the country. I say, therefore, that we ought to stand by the ancient constitution of England. I believe Lord Russell, speaking of him in his private capacity, would be in favour of extending the borough franchise, at least to the limits of the municipal franchise. There is reason to believe that Mr. Gladstone himself would approve of such a measure. We know that the late Attorney-General, one of the most eminent lawyers and one of the most accomplished Members of the House of Commons, publicly and openly expressed himself in favour of that change. I believe the middle class, as a rule, the Liberal portion of the middle class, would have no objection to see the franchise extended to all householders in boroughs.

I believe that, if it were so extended, we should arrive at a point at which, so long as any of us are permitted to meddle with the politics of our country, no further change would be demanded. I therefore am entirely in favour of it, because I believe it to be wise in itself, and because it is the ancient borough franchise of this kingdom. I am in accord with our ancient constitution. I would stand by it; wherever it afforded support for freedom I would march in its track. That track is so plain that the wayfaring man, though a fool, need not err therein. I would be guided by its lights. They have been kept burning by great men among our forefathers for many generations. Our only safety in this warfare is in adhering to the ancient and noble constitution of our country. And when we have restored it to its bygone strength, and invited the great body of the people to take part in political power, then the House of Commons will be the servant of the nation and not its master, and it will do the bidding, not of a small, a limited, often an ignorant, necessarily a selfish class, but the bidding of a great and noble people.

REFORM.

XI.

LONDON, DECEMBER 4, 1866.

[Mr. Bright was invited to preside over a great meeting of the Members of the various Trades' Unions and Trade Societies in St. James's Hall. The following speech was spoken on that occasion.]

It is about eight years since, in a speech which I delivered on the question ·of Parliamentary Reform, that I took the opportunity of giving what I thought was somewhat whole-some counsel to the unenfranchised working-men of this country. I told them that the monopolists of political power in this country would not willingly surrender that power or any portion of it; and further, that no class which was excluded could rely upon the generosity of any other class for that jus-tice which it could demand, and that, therefore, although large numbers of the middle class were then, and are now, in favour of the enfranchisement of a large number of the working class, yet that they would not make that great effort which is neces-sary to wring political power from those who now hold it, and to extend it to those who are now and were then excluded from it. I said that if the working-men wished for political power they had only to ask for it in a manner to show the universality of their desire, and the union and the power which they were able to bring to bear upon it; and I recollect par-ticularly making a suggestion that involved me in a good

Q 2

deal of unfriendly criticism, namely, that I thought the time
had come, or would soon come, when it would be the duty of
the working class to make use of that great organisation of
theirs which extends over the whole country—the organisation of trades' and friendly societies for the purpose of bringing
to bear upon the Government the entire power of their just
demand. I said, further, that I believed one year only of
the united action of the working class through this existing
organisation would wholly change the aspect of the question
of Reform.

Now it appears that the wholesome counsel which I gave
eight years ago has become the counsel of all those who are
in favour of the enfranchisement of the working-man, and
that counsel has been adopted recently to a large extent, and
every man in the kingdom feels that the aspect of the question has been wholly changed. But, as has been already said
to-night, it is very difficult to please those by whom we are
opposed; and, as was said eight years ago, so it is said now,
that it is very undesirable that associations like these, that
were not formed for political purposes, should be worked for
political ends. That is a matter of which the members of
these societies must be held to be the best judges. We have
known other societies which do not profess to be political, but
which have entered largely into political controversy. I know
that some years ago nearly all the agricultural societies of the
country were converted into political societies, for the purpose
of sustaining an Act of Parliament which denied an honest
and fair supply of food to the people of this country; and
even now, when the agricultural societies and farmers' clubs
meet, we have the opportunity of reading that curious and
confused political discussion which takes place when the
country gentlemen and the county Members make speeches to
their tenantry and county supporters. But these critics of ours
say that this measure—the combination of trades' unions for
political purposes—is one that excites their fears, and is of

a very formidable nature. It was precisely because it would
be of a formidable nature that I first recommended it. The
fact is, that the millions can scarcely move, but the few who
are timid and in some degree ungenerous in this matter, feel
themselves alarmed. You cannot help being numerous;
if you had had better government during the last hundred
years—if the land had been more in the hands of the people
and less in the hands of a small class—if you had had fewer
wars, lighter taxes, better instruction, and a freer trade, one-
half of those in this country who are now called the working
class would have been, in comfort and position, equal to those
whom we call the middle class. But this is your great difficulty now, and it is the great difficulty of our opponents—you
are too numerous, they think, to be let in with safety, and they
are finding out that you are too numerous to be kept out
without danger.

But if these associations and the combinations of these
societies are formidable, who have made them formidable?
These societies took no part in political movements until
they were challenged to it by the speeches, the resolutions,
the divisions, and the acts of a great party in the Parliament
of the kingdom. Did they fail to have fact and argument in
favour of the change proposed last session? No; but fact
and argument had no effect upon whatever there is of reasoning power in the ranks of the Tory party. Did they
think that the working-men of this country—who built this
great city—who have covered this country with great cities—
who have cultivated every acre of its cultivated area—who
have made this country a name of power through all time
and throughout the whole world—did they for one moment
imagine that you would lie down and submit, without raising
your voice against them, to the scandalous and unjust imputations that were heaped upon you? Did they think that you
would be silent for ever, and patient for ever, under a perpetual exclusion from the benefits of the constitution of your

country? If they are dissatisfied with this movement, what would they have? Would they wish that, as men did fifty or sixty years ago, instead of making open demonstration of your opinions, you should conspire with the view of changing the political constitution of your country? Would they like that you should meet in secret societies, that you should administer to each other illegal oaths, that you should undertake the task of midnight drilling, that you should purchase throughout London and the provinces a supply of arms, that you should in this frightful and terrible manner endeavour to menace the Government, and to wring from them a concession of your rights?

But surely one of two modes must be taken. If there be a deep and wide-spread sentiment, that injustice is no longer tolerable, then, judging from all past history of all people, one of two modes will be taken, either that mode so sad and so odious of secret conspiracy, or that mode so grand and so noble which you have adopted. You have at this moment across the Channel, if the reports which the Government sanction are true, an exhibition of a plan which I deplore and condemn. You have there secret societies, and oaths, and drillings, and arms, and menaces of violence and insurrection. Is there any man in England who would like to see the working-men of Great Britain driven to any such course in defence or in maintenance of their rights? Well, I hold, then, that all men in this country, whatever be their abstract opinions on this question of a wide extension of the suffrage, should really rejoice at the noble exhibition, the orderly and grand exhibition of opinion which has been made by the working-men of England and Scotland during the past three months.

I said that if there be a grievance—a deep-seated sentiment that there is a grievance—there must necessarily be a voice to express and to proclaim it. What is the grievance of which you complain? You are the citizens, the native inhabitants of a country which is called constitutional; and what is meant by that is that your government is not the despotic government of a monarch, nor the oligarchical government of an oligarchy; but that it is a government, a large and essential portion of which is conducted by honestly-elected representatives of the people; and the grievance is this—that this constitution, so noble in its outline and so noble in its purpose, is defaced and deformed, and that when you look at it it seems in this respect absolutely worse than any other representative constitution existing in the world. For I believe there is no representation whatsoever at this moment in America or in Europe that is so entirely deformed from its natural, just, and beautiful proportions, as is the representative system of this country. What can be more clear than this—that the aristocracy of land and of wealth usurp the power in both Houses of Parliament? The Lords represent themselves, and generally the great landowners, with great fidelity. But, at the same time, we must admit and deplore that at least one-half of the House of Commons is in fast alliance with the majority of the House of Lords.

Now, I have said before—I repeat it again—that there is no security whatsoever for liberty under any government unless there be an essential power in a fair representation of the nation. An illustrious man, the founder of the great province, and now the great State of Pennsylvania—William Penn—in the preface to his Constitution for that province— a Constitution of the widest and most generous freedom—uses these words :—' Any government is free to the people under it, whatever be the frame, where the laws rule, and the people are a party to the laws; and more than this is tyranny, oligarchy, or confusion.' Now, let us ask ourselves, can it be fairly said, can it be said without the most direct falsehood, that the people of this country, through the House of Commons, are really a party to the laws that are made? It is not at all disputed that only sixteen out of every hundred men are now on the electoral rolls, and are able, all other circumstances favouring, to give their vote at a general election; and it is not disputed that half the House of Commons—that an absolute majority of that House—is elected by a number of electors not exceeding altogether three men out of every hundred in the United Kingdom.

I have taken the trouble to make a little calculation from the facts contained in a very useful book, published by a very old friend of mine, Mr. Acland, called the 'Imperial Poll-Book,' from which a great amount of valuable information may be had upon this question   I have taken out the number of votes given at the last contested election that has been held for every borough and county in the United Kingdom since the passing of the Reform Bill, and I find that there being, so far as I know, at least one contest in every place since that time, the whole number of votes given at the contest in every borough and county is short of the number of 900,000, which is about one in eight of the men in the country; and if you deduct from that number the double votes, that is the men who vote for more than one county, or who vote for a county and a borough, in all probability there would not be registered more than 800,000 votes at a general election in the United Kingdom where there was a contest in every county and in every borough. But I take the election of 1859, which is the last the particulars of which are given in the 'Imperial Poll-Book,' and I find there that the whole number of votes registered, so far as I could make them out, at the general election of 1859, was under 370,000. Now, deduct the double votes from this, and probably there would not be at that general election, or at the general election of last year, more than 300,000 or 320,000 men who recorded their votes. Some other allowances must be made. There are boroughs, and there may be counties, in which the opinion falls so much on one side that there could be no chance of a contest. For example, in the borough which I am permitted to represent there would be no contest, and therefore that borough would not supply any figures to those figures which I am quoting. But there are many boroughs, as we all know, in which there is no contest; in some boroughs there is no contest because there is no freedom of election. And there are many counties in which there is no contest because there is no freedom of election in those counties. But I quote these numbers to show to you that when the Queen orders through her Ministers what is generally called an appeal to the country, it is at the very utmost an appeal to 800,000 electors, and in all probability the appeal is answered by registered voters numbering from 300,000 to 400,000.

After this, then, I undertake to say that the people are not, in the sense of our constitution, a party to the laws, and that the government of the United Kingdom, in the sense indicated in the quotation that I have made from William Penn's preface to his Constitution, is not free to this people. And let me tell you what doubtless many men have not thought of, that there is no form of government much worse than the government of a sham representation. A Parliament like our Parliament has Members enough, and just enough of the semblance of representation, to make it safe for it to do almost anything it likes against the true interests of the nation. There is nothing so safe as a Parliament like this for the commission of what is evil. There is not representation enough to make it truly responsible to the intelligence, and the virtue, and the opinions of the nation.

Take a case which is in the recollection of all of us. Is there any man in the world who believes for a moment that any monarch that ever sat on the English throne would have dared in 1815 to have passed the Corn-law—to have brought into action in this city of London, horse, foot, and artillery—to have surrounded his own palace—and to have beaten off the people who were protesting against the enactment of that law? But the Parliament of England did that, and a

Parliament of landowners, for the express and only purpose
of increasing their own rents by the sacrifice of the comfort,
the plenty, the health, and the life of the great body of
the people.

But to come only to the last session of Parliament. We
will not go back to the time before the Reform Act. We
will only go to the last session of Parliament. Look at
their responsibility then, and their sense of responsibility.
Look at the moderation of that Bill which was brought
in by the late Government. Was it possible to have proposed a more moderate measure than that of the late Government? Well, but what happened? A Parliament of landowners and of rich men, who have wholly despised that
great national opinion which has been exhibited during the
last three or four months, resisted that measure with a
pertinacity never exceeded, and with an amount of intrigue,
and I say of unfairness to the Government, which they
durst not for one single night have attempted if they had
felt any real responsibility to the people of this country.
And now they resist up to this moment, and for aught I
know may resist when they meet at the beginning of
February next, and they may possibly resist until the discontent which is now so general shall become universal,
and that which is now only a great exhibition of opinion
may become necessarily and inevitably a great and menacing
exhibition of force.

These opponents of ours, many of them in Parliament
openly, and many of them secretly in the press, have charged
us with being the promoters of a dangerous excitement.
They say we are the source of the danger which threatens;
they have absolutely the effrontery to charge me with
being the friend of public disorder. I am one of the people.
Surely, if there be one thing in a free country more clear
than another, it is that any one of the people may speak
openly to the people. If I speak to the people of their

rights, and indicate to them the way to secure them—if I speak of their danger to the monopolists of power—am I not a wise counsellor, both to the people and to their rulers? ‖Suppose I stood at the foot of Vesuvius or Etna, and, seeing a hamlet or a homestead planted on its slope, I said to the dwellers in that hamlet or in that homestead, You see that vapour which ascends from the summit of the mountain. That vapour may become a dense, black smoke that will obscure the sky. You see that trickling of lava from the crevices or fissures in the side of the mountain. That trickling of lava may become a river of fire. You hear that muttering in the bowels of the mountain. That muttering may become a bellowing thunder, the voice of a violent convulsion that may shake half a continent. You know that at your feet is the grave of great cities for which there is no resurrection, as history tells us that dynasties and aristocracies have passed away and their name has been known no more for ever. If I say this to the dwellers upon the slope of the mountain, and if there comes hereafter a catastrophe which makes the world to shudder, am I responsible for that catastrophe? I did not build the mountain, or fill it with explosive materials. I merely warned the men that were in danger.

So, now, it is not I who am stimulating men to the violent pursuit of their acknowledged constitutional rights. We are merely about our lawful business—and you are the citizens of a country that calls itself free, yet you are citizens to whom is denied the greatest and the first blessing of the constitution under which you live. ‖If the truth must be told, the Tory party is the turbulent party of this nation. I left the last session of Parliament just about the time when the present Ministers, successful in their intrigues, acceded to office—I left the Parliament with a feeling of sadness, of disgust, and of apprehension. I said to myself, I may as well judge of the future by the past. The

Parliament of England will not do justice to the people until there happens something that will suddenly open their eyes. I remember what took place in the year 1829 when the Duke of Wellington said : 'Either give political power and representation through Catholic Members to the Catholics of the United Kingdom, or encounter the peril and loss of civil war in Ireland.' Up to that moment Parliament had refused to do it. Then Parliament consented and the thing was done. In 1832 you were within twenty-four hours of revolution in this country. This great class which sits omnipotent in one House, and hardly less so in the other, might then, and probably would have been extinguished, and what there would have been left except the people it is difficult to imagine.

In 1846, although every intelligent man in every country throughout the world admitted the justice and force of our arguments against the Corn-law, it still required the occurrence of a crushing and desolating famine in Ireland—a famine which destroyed as many lives in that country as would have been destroyed by a great war, and which drove into exile as many of the people of that island as would have been driven into exile by the most cruel and relentless conquest—it required all that before the Parliament of England, the men amongst whom I sit, and whose faces are as familiar to me as those of any person whom I know in life—I say that it required all that before Parliament would consent to give up that intolerable wrong of taxing the bread of an industrious people. Now, suppose that the Bill which was brought into the House last session as a Franchise Bill only—which was done, as was admitted by Lord Russell, in adoption of advice which I had publicly given to the Government, and which advice I believe was eminently sound, and ought to be followed whenever this question is dealt with again by a Liberal and honest Government— I say, suppose that that Bill, instead of being met with every kind of unfair and ungenerous opposition, had been wisely accepted by the House of Commons and become law, what would have been the state of the country during the present autumn and winter? It would have been one of rejoicing and congratulation everywhere; not because the Bill included everybody and satisfied everybody, but all working-men would have felt that the barrier created at the Reform Bill, if not absolutely broken down, was at least so much lowered that the exclusion was much less general and less offensive. You would have had this result, that we, the people in these islands, would have been no longer two nations. We should have felt more—that henceforth we are one people. Every element of strength in the country would have been immeasurably strengthened, and there would have been given even to the humblest of the unenfranchised a feeling of hope which would have led him to believe in, and to strive after, something higher and better than that to which he had hitherto been able to attain.

Now, who prevented this? Surely we did not prevent it. We who thought we were speaking for the general good of the people, we accepted the measure with an honourable sincerity and fidelity. We said that it is good to the point to which it steps forward. It is perfectly honest; it is no trick or subterfuge. It will give satisfaction to some hundreds of thousands, and it will give that which is as great a boon—it will give hope to millions whom it does not include—and therefore, in perfect honourableness, we accepted that measure. And who opposed it? None other could effectually oppose it than Lord Derby and the party of which he is the acknowledged and trusted leader. They and he opposed and rejected that Bill, and they and he are responsible for what has been done since in the country as a necessary and inevitable consequence of that rejection. Lord Derby now stands nearest to the Throne, and I venture to say that he is not a strength but a weakness to that Throne. By his conduct—and by the conduct of his party, which he adopts—he thwarted at once the benevolent intentions of the Crown and the just expectations of the people.

I confess that I am astonished at the conduct of the Tory party in this matter. When the Bill was introduced into the House of Commons, it appeared to me to be the very last that any statesmen with a spark of sense or honesty could offer any opposition to, and I did not believe that on the other side of the House there was, I will say, if you like, bitter partisanship or stupidity enough to induce them to fight a combined battle with all who would join them for the purpose of rejecting that Bill. One would suppose that the present Government had troubles enough on hand in what is called the sister country without urging the people to excitement here. Ireland, as I have described it before Irishmen, is the favoured field on which all the policy of the Tory party has been exhibited, displayed, and tried. In Ireland the Habeas Corpus Act is suspended. Individual liberty, except by consent of the Executive, is abolished; troops are pouring into the country; iron-clads, it is said, are ordered to the coast to meet some, I hope and believe, imaginary foe; and the country gentlemen and their families are reported to be fleeing from their ancestral homes to find refuge in garrison towns; and all this is the magnificent result of the policy of that party whose head and hope is Lord Derby. And even now, up to this very last session of Parliament, that party has had no remedy for this state of things but that ancient, and rude, and savage remedy, the remedy of military force. But with all this in Ireland, greatly exaggerated, as I hope and believe, by some public writers, yet still with enough to cause pain and anxiety, was it a judicious course for the present party in power to create a great excitement in Great Britain? I say that Lord Derby, as the representative of his party in

Parliament, is himself the fomentor of discord, and that his party, and not our party, is at this moment the turbulent element in English political society.

And let me tell this party—I tell them nothing from this platform that I have not told them upon the floor of the House of Commons — let me tell them that this question will not sleep. Some months ago there was a remarkable convention held in Switzerland composed of men of eminence and character, by which an address or memorial was prepared and forwarded to the Government of the United States, congratulating them upon the close of their gigantic struggle, and upon the establishment of universal freedom throughout the wide bounds of the republic. There was a passage in that memorial, an expression of true philosophy and true statesmanship, to this effect: ' Unfinished questions have no pity for the repose of nations.' That referred to the great question of negro slavery; but it is just as true when it is applied to the question before us, where from five to six millions of grown men in this United Kingdom, under a Constitutional Government and with a representative system, are shut out directly and purposely from that Constitution and Representation. This great question which we are debating to-night is an unfinished question, and, as the Swiss express it, it will have no pity for the repose of this nation until it is a finished question.

I observed to-day, in a newspaper considered by some to be of great authority, that the working-men are supposed by what are called our betters—for that paper only writes for our betters—they are supposed to have now done enough, and they are exhorted—by the very hand, probably, which during the whole of the last session of Parliament was doing all it could against them — to stand still and wait for the action of Parliament. But it is the same Parliament, it is the same House of Commons which I left with sadness and apprehension in July last. There are in it yet the men who, on our side of the House, betrayed the cause which they were supposed to sit there to defend, and the only change that we know of is, that the men who threw out with all terms of ignominy the Bill which we wished to pass last session, are now and will be in February next—if they do not break in pieces before—they will be then on the Treasury bench, and will take that leading and authoritative position in the House which belongs to the Ministers of the Crown.

I differ from this writer altogether; I would not put any confidence in the course to be taken by this House of Commons if I were a man unenfranchised and asking for a vote. I should like them to tell me that they had wholly repented of the cheers with which they met all those vile and violent imputations upon your character. My opinion is this: that your duty, your obvious duty—a duty from which you cannot escape—is to go on as you have begun, to perfect in every part of the country your organisation in favour of your enfranchisement. It is to bring every society with which you are connected, to give itself for a time—it will only be a short time—to the working out of your political redemption. I should advise you, whether you are supporters of the Reform League in London, or are connected in any way with the Reform Union of Manchester or any similar association, to establish a system of small, but weekly or monthly contributions. Do not allow my friend Mr. Beales — or my ancient friend and political brother, Mr. George Wilson of Manchester — do not allow them to want the means to carry on and direct the great societies of which they are chiefs. And let me beg of you, more than all else, to have no jealousies amongst each other. Give our Chairman his due; give Mr. Beales and the council their due; give every man who, with a single eye to this great question, is working zealously in your cause, his due, and help in every way you can every honest endeavour to bring this great national question to such a solid and final issue, that it shall no longer disturb the repose of this nation.

And lastly, I beg of you to rise to something like a just contemplation of what the great issue is for which you are contending. It is to make you citizens of one of the noblest nations on the face of the earth—of a nation which has a grand history in the past, and which I trust, partly through your help, will have a still grander history in the future. Let me beg of you, then, and it is the last word I may speak to you to-night, that, in all you do, you may be animated by a great and noble spirit, for you have set your hands and hearts to a great and noble work.

REFORM.

XII.

VOTING-PAPERS.

HOUSE OF COMMONS, JUNE 20, 1867.

From Hansard.

[The Government Reform Bill proposed to permit the vote to be given by 'Voting-papers,' and not to require personal attendance at the Poll. This was objected to by the Opposition on the ground that it would afford opportunity for fraud and for practices inconsistent with freedom of election. The Government proposition was rejected.]

I THINK the right hon. Gentleman the Chancellor of the Exchequer has concluded his speech with perfect fairness, and left the decision to the House in a way worthy of the position he occupies. The debate has been one of considerable satisfaction to me, for whatever I may think of the proposition as it now stands, I cannot conceal from myself the fact that the arguments both on this and on that side of the House lead us a great deal further than the proposition itself; and should end, after this wide extension of the suffrage, in a change which in almost every other country has been made—namely, in establishing the vote by ballot. There are two divisions of this question, and to one of them the right hon. Gentleman applied himself; and other Members also touched upon the same—that is, with regard to out-voters.

R 2

I believe, if we were establishing a system of representation for the first time, that we should do in counties what we do in boroughs—we should take care that all the electors of the counties should be resident in the counties. A different system prevails, and I do not recommend that it should be interfered with; but I suggest that you should not, for the purpose of aiding the extension of the present system by adding to the non-resident voters, make a substantial change for which no substantial reason has been given.

The hon. Member for the Tower Hamlets has made a speech—one of the best and the most convincing that I have heard on the subject. He referred to what might be done by certain persons at certain Clubs. The Reform Club is very near the Carlton. If a man wants to go to one he is driven, not invariably, but occasionally, to the other. What the hon. Gentleman says might be done at the Reform Club might also be done at the Carlton. But what has been done? Take the case of a small Scotch county in which there was a contest at the last election. The losing candidate had a decided majority of the resident voters in the county, and yet he did not take his seat in this House, and this through the influence of large proprietors—and of strangers whose votes might be called in question as contrary, if not to the letter, to the spirit of the law. These voters over-ruled the votes of the resident constituency, and the candidate who had the majority of the resident votes was defeated, and his opponent is, I presume, at this moment sitting somewhere in this House. [Cries of ' Name.'] Let any Gentleman who wants to know the name ask the Scotch Member who sits nearest him.

I trust that the decision of the House this session, and the passage of this Bill, will lead to a more satisfactory representation of the country. I therefore hope that there is no Member of the House who would wish to see the system I have just described indefinitely extended. And I am not speaking as against the influence of landed proprietors alone; there are other influences that can play this game. I recollect some years ago, during the discussion on the Corn-laws, that the friends of the Anti-Corn-law League resolved to purchase freeholds in some counties, and threatened to change the representation of those counties. In a case like that it would be a great bar to such a movement, that every voter, at the time of an election, should travel to the county where his freehold was situate. It is not the true policy of the country—it is contrary to the interests of the country—it is opposed to the purity and reality of the electoral system, that you should give even to an eminent lawyer like the hon. and learned Gentleman on the front bench, or to any landlord or club, any greater inducement than now exists to obtain votes in counties where people do not reside, for the purpose of interfering with the real and honest representation of the residents of the county.

There are many small counties—some in England, some in Wales, and several in Scotland—in which there would be no difficulty, under this system, of placing as many persons on the register as would defeat the honest rights of the electors of those counties. The right hon. Gentleman dwelt on the success of the system as tried in the Universities; and some Gentlemen smiled because they thought he meant—what I am sure he did not mean—that it had proved successful in dislodging a late Member for the University of Oxford. But that is a small matter; and, if England were appealed to, England would say that it is of great advantage to the country that that dislodgement has taken place. But while the right hon. Gentleman defends the measure on account of its success at Oxford University, the right hon. Baronet the Member for Droitwich admitted that the case was so entirely different that he would not base his argument in favour of the Bill on anything that had happened, or could happen, in connection with the learned Universities of the country. The Committee on which the hon. Member for the Tower Hamlets sat, had the whole of the matter before it; and that Committee saw the great difference between the circumstances of the Universities and of the great constituencies of the country; and they distinctly—I know not if they were unanimous—rejected the proposition in regard to the country at large, and decided on special grounds that the plan might only be safely adopted in regard to the Universities.

I now pass to the other branch of the subject. My own belief is that it is bad. It seems to me that it has not the good effect —and I have never denied that there is some good in the system—of open voting. It escapes from that which you have always claimed as the great advantage of open voting, that is, the general publicity and influence of public opinion, and what you call the salutary effect of a man performing a great public duty in the face of his fellow-men. It is clear that the whole of that is got rid of by his system. [Cheers and cries of 'No.'] It is clearly got rid of so far as this system will work.

The right hon. Gentleman calls it a permissive Bill. Of course, to individuals it is permissive, but on the whole country it can hardly be so styled. Wherever, being permissive, it is employed, it will entirely secure the voter from that public opinion under which every man in some degree acts when he goes to the poll and gives his vote in the face of his fellow-electors and townsmen. On the other hand, I complain of it very much, on this ground: that whilst it altogether shelters him from public opinion, it does not in the least give him the advantages of secret voting. The advantages of the really secret vote are these. You may estimate them at less than I do, but I think they are these—that when a man votes there is no power on earth to interfere with him but his own conviction as to what he ought to do, and he has a perfect freedom to carry out these convictions in his vote.

Now, a proposition which is so great a change that it

repudiates all which you have said to be good in open voting, and does not accept a single particle of the good which we have said belongs to secret voting, at least is not a proposition which should be accepted hastily by the House. The right hon. Gentleman, following the example of many hon. Members, dwelt upon the expenses of county elections. I think those expenses are most deplorable. I was speaking to a Gentleman in this House the other day who said he was a candidate for ten days in a county which is neither very large nor very populous, and in those ten days his expenses were 4,000*l.* I know another candidate—I think I am not mis-stating the facts—who polled 2,000 votes, and they cost him 8,000*l.* But that expense is by no means all connected with the carriage of voters; a very large portion is connected with that hateful and intolerable system of legal agency, which is, I believe, all but universal in the counties, and which unfortunately prevails to a very large extent in a great number of boroughs. But there cannot be the smallest doubt that it is possible to cure that evil without this clause. With regard to the resident voters of a county, you might establish — and establish cheaply—polling-booths in so many districts that no man will have to go further than he has to go every week to market, and very often he would have to go no further than he goes on Sunday to church.

The noble Lord the Member for Stamford (Lord Cranborne), who made as good a speech as could be made in favour of this clause, spoke of persons who could not get to the poll—sick people and nervous people. I am not speaking of the sick, because we ought not to make special laws for a comparatively small portion of the people, and those who are sick are much better in their rooms and in bed, than taking any part whatever in the excitement of a contested election at a time when they are suffering mental and bodily depression. The noble Lord said there are many who do not go to the poll. I think he is entirely mistaken. I have had several contests in the course of my political career. Two contests in the city of Durham, two or three in the city of Manchester, and one at least in the town of Birmingham. I do not believe that any appreciable number—I cannot say that I ever heard of ten, nor even five, in the whole of these three constituencies—who could not go to the poll for any of the reasons stated by the noble Lord.

There is not the slightest doubt that his argument does not apply to the metropolitan boroughs, because if there are any boroughs which are free from confusion and riot it is those boroughs. Therefore, I hold that as regards this safeguard there is nothing in it. But there is this in it. The noble Lord appears to be wishful—I will not impute that, but I will say that it will be understood that he would establish a system which would very nearly give the security of the Ballot to the rich people, and that it is for them that this system is mainly devised. I must leave hon. Gentlemen opposite to imagine how long it will be, if this class is adopted, before the Ballot itself will be established amongst all other classes. Now, as regards the poorer electors. My hon. Friend (Mr. Ayrton) described what would take place with agents. There is a wonderful fertility of invention at election times, and clever agents would busy themselves in the streets of our boroughs, and in some parts of the counties, with a view of obtaining these polling-papers.

And what happens when they have been signed and sent in? You establish one of the most hateful and most unheard-of things that can be imagined, which is the giving of votes by proxy. I understand that lately there has been a discussion in another place on the subject of voting by proxy, and there is a general impression that this system—which no man defends upon any principle—will not last long. Therefore, I hope the House of Commons will not now attempt to establish in any shape anything so unprincipled and hateful

with regard to our parliamentary elections as this would prove
to be. Because, when any person has received a number of
voting-papers from any borough or part of a county, it is
quite clear that he can either poll them or not, as he thinks
fit. He can hold them back, or make a traffic of them. They
are not exactly bank notes; but as he holds them in his hand,
he may traffic with them as if they were bank notes. Now,
I think it

> ' Better to bear the ills we have
> Than fly to others that we know not of.'

I think the noble Lord, or at all events some hon. Members,
have spoken of the character of magistrates. I am not a
magistrate myself, and I should be sorry to depreciate or
lower their character in this House or in the country; but
there is nothing that stands, as I can see, between the present
system of voting for Poor-law guardians, and this, but the
magistrates. The magistrates are not infallible. I have
known many magistrates who were not at all too acute to
be taken in. And I think the security is not sufficient to
justify the House in making the great change proposed.

The noble Lord made another observation, which was very
unfortunate for him, and I am surprised that it should have
escaped his lips. He went so far as to say that the drawing-
room of the magistrate would be the place of the polling-
booth. If I am not very much mistaken in the opinion of
my countrymen, I think that observation will sink very deep
into their minds and hearts; and if they thought such a
thing were possible—and we have the authority of the noble
Lord that it is advisable, and that he admires it—I say that
is enough to condemn the Bill. The question is this—
whether our whole system of polling should be changed to
what is right, or whether it should be a general system of
voting through the Post Office. My own impression is, that
every man who gives a vote should appear before the recognised authority by whom that vote shall be recorded—

whether he gives it openly, by saying, 'I am So-and-so, and I have voted for A, B, C, or D,' or whether he should vote as Englishmen do in the Australian colonies, by depositing a card or ticket.

I saw one hon. Member anticipating what I was going to say by the radiant smile which came over his countenance. But I am not now asking for the Ballot. What I say is this. I prefer what now exists to what you propose. Either let us have the open voting which we have, and which we all understand, and which we have had from time immemorial, so that we understand the good and evil of it, or let us go to that more excellent way of polling by the Ballot. At least, do not let us make a change, the results of which would, in my opinion, lead to very great danger in the corrupt exercise of the franchise throughout the country.

The hon. Gentleman the Member for Middlesex has to-night made a curious speech—and he treated very lightly the argument which had been used, that if a man had given his voting-paper seven days before an election in the county, and three days before in the borough, he should not be at liberty to change his mind. No doubt in the borough he could try to outwit his proxy, by being at the poll when it opened at eight o'clock in the morning, and then it would be a scuffle between him and his proxy as to the vote to be given; but generally speaking, there are many persons who honestly change their minds between the time when the election is proclaimed and the time that it takes place. ['Oh!'] Hon. Members do not appear to believe that there is any honest change of opinion. I differ from them very much, and if Members of the House of Commons by vast bodies can change their opinions at once on a question, there can be no doubt whatever that electors are equally open to proper arguments. Take a case. Between the time when an election is proclaimed and the day fixed for the polling, very often a new candidate comes into the field. Then, there is often something found out about a candidate in the field which makes him unsatisfactory to the constituency; or some person comes into the field, and by a speech of great power affects the votes of many electors. Yet by this system a man may have within seven days of the election in the county, and three days of the election in the borough, signed this fatal voting-paper; he is committed to it, and he is not even open to the discussion for which I understand your hustings are erected and maintained. I say hon. Gentlemen opposite ought by reason of their ancient principles not to support this proposition.

The Chancellor of the Exchequer concluded his speech by saying that he would take the decision of the House on this matter, and I thought that I observed on the countenance of his supporters a feeling of satisfaction, as if probably they would be glad to relieve the Government of the clause altogether. Hon. Gentlemen have often said that they do not like anything un-English. I shall not use that phrase, because if I were to reiterate it, I might say with great force that hardly anything can be more un-English than to have a system of this kind which is to be permissive. Some have argued in favour of the permissive Ballot. I must say that I have always been opposed to the permissive Ballot. Let a question of this kind work in the public and parliamentary mind, and do not change until you are determined to do the thing honestly and well. Then let it be made legal and imperative—and do not let us have anything like permissive action on a great and solemn question like this.

The noble Lord below me (Lord Elcho) made a suggestion to the right hon. Gentleman; I should be very glad to see the clause negatived, and I should not be opposed at any future time to the appointment of a committee to consider the whole question of our electoral system. There are many alterations which might be made in that system, and to which I think the House might agree with very great advantage. At present, however, it seems to me quite clear, and beyond all doubt, that in this Bill we ought not, and I believe we shall not, insert a clause which will make this great change, on which there has been no inquiry except that in 1860, which inquiry resulted in an emphatic condemnation of the system. I say that the country has not asked for this. The right hon. Gentleman says he thinks that it will be received with very great favour. He is so fond of his own children that he supposes everybody will admire the political offspring he introduces into this House. I think I have met a good many persons during the past four or five months who know something about Reform; but I declare that I never met with a single person outside this House who did not speak of this proposal—I am afraid to use the term, because I do not wish to deny that the clause has been very fairly introduced—who have not spoken of the proposition with contempt; and I believe if it were adopted, that it would create amazement and consternation throughout the country.

I shall say no more. I admit that the right hon. Gentleman has argued the question fairly from his point of view, and has put it before the committee in a manner that became him. The matter is one of very grave importance. The only result will be, if we reject the clause, that the question will stand where it is, and it will be open to the Government, or to any Member of the House who differs from me, to propose, either this session or next session, a select committee to inquire into the whole question. In conclusion, therefore, I beg the committee not to commit itself to a thing which nobody asks for, which is entirely novel with regard to the great constituencies of the country, and which I, from no party-view whatsoever ['Oh, Oh!']—I do not think there has been a single argument or fact used to-night to show that it would be advantageous to hon. Gentlemen opposite more than it would be to this side of the House ; therefore, I declare solemnly I have no feeling of that kind ;—but I believe it would introduce a very evil system into a system which is now, in some respects, very good ; and therefore I entreat the House to reject the clause which the right hon. Gentleman has submitted to them.

REFORM.

XIII.

HOUSE OF COMMONS, AUGUST 8, 1867.

From Hansard.

[An attempt was made during the passing of the Reform Bill through the
House of Commons to insert in it a clause interfering with the ancient
rights of majorities in the constituencies. It was rejected by a large
majority, Mr. Disraeli and the Government party opposing it. A somewhat
similar clause was inserted by the House of Lords, and was agreed to by
the Commons, Mr. Disraeli and his friends now supporting what they had
before strenuously opposed. This speech was delivered in the debate on the
Lords' amendments.]

I was rather surprised at the speech of the right hon.
Gentleman the Chancellor of the Exchequer upon this point,
when I recollected the speech which he delivered when the
same matter was before the House some few weeks ago. He
concluded his speech by admitting that his views had not
changed. That I knew without his saying it. It would
be impossible for any person holding the view he held on
a former occasion, and seeing the subject so clearly, to have
changed his mind upon the matter.

If the House will permit me—though, perhaps, I am
leading a forlorn hope after the desertion of the Chancellor

of the Exchequer—I will recall for a moment to the House
what has taken place on this point. The right hon. Gentleman the Member for Calne (Mr. Lowe) proposed a mode of
giving Members in these large boroughs to that minority
which is alleged now to be unrepresented. The proposal
of the right hon. Gentleman was different from that which
has come down from the House of Lords; but although it
was different it really had the same object, and, doing it in
a different way, would have brought about the same result.
[Mr. Lowe: 'No!'] The right hon. Gentleman says 'No.'
I do not say it would bring about the same result with the
same amount of minority in any borough. But the general
result would have been the same. Whether you take Liverpool,
Manchester, Birmingham, or Leeds, the scheme of the right
hon. Gentleman would have given to minorities a representation in this House, which is precisely what in all probability
will be done by the clause which has come down from the
House of Lords.

The right hon. Gentleman—and I ask hon. Members on
this side of the House to bear this in mind—acting in precise
accordance with the noble and learned Lord in the Upper
House by whom this change was proposed, suggested his
change as a corrective of the liberal, or probably he would
have said democratic, character of the Bill before the House.
He did not propose it as a portion of a grand scheme to give
to every person in the country, whether one of a minority or
one of a majority, a representative in this House, but as a
proposal made necessary by the extravagant and perilous
character of the Bill which the Chancellor of the Exchequer has
introduced, and which has been supported with so much
good-will by hon. Gentlemen on that as well as on this
side of the House. That proposal was supported by the
noble Lord the Member for Stamford (Viscount Cranborne),—
who has been perfectly consistent in everything he has
done on this question,—and by all those Gentlemen opposite

who differ from the Government with regard to the question of Parliamentary Reform. It was also supported by certain Members on this side who are in favour of representing minorities—not because it is the corrective of a democratic measure, but because they think that everybody should be represented. I understood that the hon. Member for Westminster (Mr. Mill) took that view. He, in a long and very able, though I must say, arising probably from the nature of the subject, in a somewhat intricate speech, explained it as the plan proposed by Mr. Hare. But that plan is by no means a plan of representing minorities. It is a plan for representing everybody, in a peculiar way, and probably could not be accomplished by any other plan offered to the country.

I think we have a right to complain of the hon. Member for Westminster and his friends, not that they are in favour of representing everybody, but that they are in favour of a proposal like this, which really does not represent every-·body, but strikes off a large portion of the representative power which the population of this country enjoys; and does not effect in any degree that which my hon. Friend and his friends wish to be done by the establishment of Mr. Hare's system. It appears to me that they have been taken—I want a suitable word to express my contempt for the proposal without expressing in the slightest degree anything offensive to hon. Members on this side; no man can conceive for a single moment that the hon. Member for Westminster, in the view he has held on this question, has been actuated by any but the most honourable motives, perfectly consistent with everything he has written or said on the subject—but I say they have been taken by the phrase that in these four great boroughs you are about to give to the minorities a power which they do not now possess. They therefore see in it, in some small degree, an approach to, or the admission of, a principle or of a plan which my hon. Friend and his friends support, in which everybody would be represented, and such things as majorities and minorities no longer known.

I think those Gentlemen who are in favour of Mr. Hare's plan are not in the slightest degree bound to support this plan. There is no intention at present on the part of the Government, or on the part of this House, or of the House of Lords, or of any one in the country, to establish 'Mr. Hare's plan in this country. Carrying therefore this proposal only, or anything likely to follow this, is an unmixed injustice to the boroughs thus treated, is not likely to lead to the plan of Mr. Hare being adopted, and in all probability will create so much ill-will in a large borough to which it may be applied, that we may be farther than ever from taking Mr. Hare's plan into consideration. When this question was formerly before the House of Commons the division was one of a very remarkable character. There were some Members on this side voted with some Members on the other side. There was a majority of 140 against the proposal. The Chancellor of the Exchequer made a speech on that occasion more earnest and full of feeling than any other speech he has made during the protracted discussion on this Bill. But the right hon. Gentleman now says the proposal was carried by a great majority in the House of Lords. The majority there was but 90—here it was 140. A majority so large on a question which so particularly affects us and our constituencies—a majority of 140—is much more important in a matter of this kind than a majority of 90 in the other House.

I do not recollect the precise words of the Chancellor of the Exchequer, but I think he said it was a scheme to introduce into the House all sorts of crotchety people. I have no objection to crotchety people. I believe there must be all sorts of people in this House. I have never been in any Parliament in which there has not been at least one Member generally believed by the rest of the Members to be not quite strong—

and excuses were made for his eccentric conduct because he was not as responsible as others. That, probably, will always be the case in the House of Commons. The Chancellor of the Exchequer said he did not want the introduction of crotchety people, but he condemned the proposal on stronger grounds, on grounds of the highest policy and constitutional principles. The Gentlemen I see opposite, and those not before convinced—as the right hon. Gentleman the Member for Oxfordshire (Mr. Henley) was—accepted the arguments of the Chancellor of the Exchequer. I cannot presume to say that they were influenced by my arguments, although I offered them with as much force as I could. I think the arguments of the Chancellor of the Exchequer were unanswerable.

Then what did Lord Derby say in the House of Lords? I presume we can speak of exalted persons who send Amendments down here from an exalted place. Lord Derby said the principle was entirely unconstitutional, and that 'Its mischief would only be bounded by the extent or the narrowness of its operation.' I shall not pretend to have a greater reverence for Lord Derby than hon. Gentlemen opposite have; I have often thought him rash; I have often thought him unwise; and I have often had occasion during twenty-four years of political life to be in opposition to his views. But I think when he, as Prime Minister, having considered this question of Reform minutely since last session, expresses so strong an opinion on a point of this nature, is backed by the opinion of the Chancellor of the Exchequer and of his friends, and is backed by a vote of more than 300—I forget how many voted, but the majority was 140—I have a right to state that his opinion as Prime Minister on a matter of this nature is one we should not lightly pass by. I think hon. Gentlemen opposite, if they will bear in mind the tone of the Chancellor of the Exchequer, will feel that he adhered to his original opinion, and would have preferred that the House of Lords had not made the alteration. I think they may feel that they will only be carrying out what is for the true interest of the country, and what is the true wish of the Government, if they adhere to the vote they gave when the question was before us on a former occasion.

I said I thought our vote of more importance than that of the House of Lords. I do not pretend to say the House of Lords has not full power to consider this Bill and pass amendments upon it. They have the legal and the constitutional power to do that, and we have no right to call it in question. But in a matter affecting the fundamental principles of our representation, affecting the power of our representatives—of a considerable number of the Members of this House—affecting the status of Members of this House—the opinion and vote of the House of Commons is necessarily and must be of more weight than the vote of the House of Lords. It is a question of delicacy. It is possible that the House of Lords would not enter into any contest with regard to this, and that whatever the House of Commons may decide to do will be accepted with that moderation and dignity to which the right hon. Gentleman has paid—as he believes, and as I hope—so just a tribute. What is the change you are about to make? It is a fundamental change. There is no precedent for it in our Parliamentary history. You affect by it the very foundation of what I may call the constitution of your constituencies.

I have said elsewhere that the alteration proposed has never been asked for. The hon. Member for North Warwickshire (Mr. Newdegate), I understand, presented a petition in favour of it from Birmingham. I am sorry it should come from Birmingham—that there should be a petition from Birmingham signed by a number of persons in favour of the change. [Mr. Newdegate: ' 4,000!'] Well, I will not dispute about numbers in regard to a town of 400,000 inhabitants. That is not an overwhelming consideration, especially as the 4,000 have just smarted from a defeat—I will not say an ignominious one, for it was not ignominious. At all events they have not been able to seat a Member for the minority, having been outvoted by their fellow-townsmen. I am sorry that men who were unable to return their candidate for Birmingham by a fair majority should come and ask this House, in obedience to the mandate of the House of Lords, to allow him to take his seat by the votes of the minority. With the exception of that case this proposal has never been asked for from the House of Commons, by any constituency, by petition, or at any public meeting. Never has there been a minority defeated fairly—I speak not of drink, or coercion, or bribery, and corruption—who did not accept that defeat in a fair spirit, and look forward to the time when, by the growth of their opinions and of their numbers, that minority would ultimately become a majority.

For six hundred years—as far as our Parliamentary annals go back, and one of the learned Clerks at the table can tell us how far they go back—the principle of Parliamentary election has been this, that the majority of the voices of a constituency to which the writ of the Crown has issued should elect a Member or Members to sit in this House, and no others. Bear this in mind. You are urged to accept a proposal of a most important character, which the Chancellor of the Exchequer has denounced in the strongest language, of which Lord Derby says the mischief can only be bounded by the narrowness of its operation—when it has never come before the public for discussion. In all the discussions which have taken place this year or last year, at all the meetings which have been held, under roof or the open sky, there has been no debate, discussion, or consideration of the principle now offered to us in this clause as it has come down to this House. I would suggest, without unfairly urging my views, that the House of Commons should at least suspend its judgment in favour of this proposal until it has been a longer period before the country, and the constituencies have had an opportunity of considering it and making up their minds upon it.

It is often said that we are not delegates; but if we are not delegates, we are not rulers. We are sent here to represent the general views of our constituents. We have morally no power to cut off the influence of those constituents—to make fundamental changes in the constitution, and to vary, alter, and overthrow the practice of six hundred years. This House is not in favour of it; a majority of 140 voted against it. You have no moral right, therefore, to agree to such a proposal, because a House which is not representative, which has no direct influence in the matter, and no Member of which can vote for a Member of this House, or without the infringement of our rules influence a vote at his election, chooses to suggest it. It is an unintelligible and unbelievable thing that this House should under these circumstances agree to a proposal which makes this fundamental change in our constitution, which alters and cripples the power of four of the largest constituencies in the kingdom. What are these four constituencies you are asked thus to treat? I appeal to the Chancellor of the Exchequer; I know some of the difficulties of his position. Still he is accessible to reason, and he has been disposed to take the House very much into his confidence. If a census were taken, those four boroughs would be found to contain a population of nearly, if not quite, 1,500,000. What was done when the Bill was passing through Committee? It was proposed that an additional Member should be given to several boroughs. First of all, six boroughs were proposed for this honour. The number was afterwards limited to four. The hon. Member for Liverpool proposed that three should have an additional Member. The Chancellor of the Exchequer, in a moment of very good-humour, got up at the table and said, ' Not three, but four additional Members shall be given.' He not only received the proposal handsomely, but he dealt with it generously, and gave four Members to four of the largest boroughs.

Look at those four boroughs. There is Liverpool, with its commercial interests, and with perhaps the largest port in the world. Look at Manchester, with its 400,000 population, and vast manufacturing interests. Look at Birmingham, the very centre and heart of the island, also with a population of 400,000, and with interests which I need not describe, because they are well known to the House. Look at Leeds, the centre and capital of the county of York. [Mr. Leeman: 'No, no!'] My hon. Friend the Member for York is quite at liberty to dispute that; still the House will not say that I have overcharged the picture in describing these four boroughs. They asked the House to grant them additional representation. They wanted more than one new Member. They said that their population was great, their interests beyond arithmetical computation, and their influence in the country large. They asked the House for greater representation. The House unanimously consented, for I will undertake to say there was as much satisfaction on that side as there was on this, when the Chancellor of the Exchequer said that he would give these additional Members to the four boroughs I have named. If it were a question of minorities, I might say to my hon. Friend behind me and to others, There are these 1,500,000 in those four boroughs who are now represented by eight Members only, and if this Bill passes they will have twelve Members only—I am not speaking whether they sit on that side of the House or this—I believe my opinion would be exactly the same, and just as strong, if I represented any other of the boroughs, as it is representing Birmingham.

As the Bill comes from the Upper House these four boroughs would have twelve representatives, and when there was a great question before the country—as for example the question of the character of the administration, or the question of

a further change in Parliamentary representation, or the condition of Ireland—and I might mention many other questions
in which the case would arise—these twelve Members would
be eight on one side of the House and four on the other, and
the four on the one side would, of course, neutralize four out
of the eight sitting on the other. So that, assuming party
ties to be adhered to, these four boroughs with a million and
a half of population would be so entirely emasculated and
crippled by the proposal now submitted to the House, that
really only four names would be found affecting any of those
great questions to which I have referred. I do not think
anybody is prepared to deny that statement.

I put it the other day at Manchester in this way—that the
borough of Salford, which is only part of Manchester, is to
return two Members under this Bill, and that Manchester
itself is to return three Members. But nothing can be more
clear than this—that in all great divisions in this House
henceforth, if this proposal be admitted, the voice of Manchester will be less potent than the voice of Salford. I say
that is utterly at variance with all the principles of representation, and with the whole practice of the Constitution of this
country. But what can the House say to these boroughs?
When the Chancellor of the Exchequer accepted the proposal
of the hon. Member for Liverpool, and when the House
entirely agreed with him, and when these boroughs expressed
the great satisfaction which they felt at the mode in which
they had been treated, there was not a single syllable said
that in giving these new Members you were to give them in
such a manner as should not increase, but should actually
diminish their power in this House. There is no case on
record in the annals of Parliament in which a borough, however small in point of Members and contemptible in influence
in comparison with these I have mentioned, has ever been
treated in a manner so unfair, so ungenerous, and so unjust.
I can speak for Manchester, and I can speak for Birmingham,

and I say that the great majority of the present, and the proposed future constituents—nay, a great majority of the population of these two great towns, would have rejected, as I certainly should have voted against, the proposal that additional Members were to be given to them—if I had believed the House would only consent to give more Members under this crippling and injurious clause.

There is one other point before I have done, and I put this to hon. Members. We have a preliminary election which is called the nomination. We have the hustings, the candidates, the electors, and the population all gathered round. The name of every candidate is submitted to the electors, and every elector who is present is called upon by the returning officer to hold up his hand in favour of the candidate of his choice. If there be no contest, and nobody demands a poll, the lifting up of the hand is made the actual and conclusive election of the Members. How are you to reconcile that constitutional practice with this unconstitutional innovation? Here is a man who can vote in Birmingham, Manchester, Liverpool, or Leeds at the hustings for three candidates—three Liberals or three Conservatives—I have nothing to do with party in this matter, and I should think it contemptible to introduce a question of party into it. That man at the hustings will hold up his hand for the three candidates he wishes to be elected. When he goes to the poll, should one be demanded, following out the constitutional process already began, he ought to be able to vote for all the Members to be elected, but under this system he is only to vote for two. Therefore, you establish an extraordinary and entirely novel and unconstitutional difference and discrepancy between the preliminary election at the hustings, and the subsequent and final election at the poll.

What you are wanting to do is a thing which is absurd upon the face of it. You take a constituency which has always hitherto been held to be a united and compact body, and you propose that it should return two voices at one election, and that by an arrangement ordered, not by this House, but recommended by the other House of Parliament, this constituency is to speak in two voices—one end of the constituency shall be allowed to say this, and the other end shall be allowed to·say that. There are jugglers whom we have seen exhibiting their clever tricks—pouring out port, champagne, milk, and water from one and the same bottle. The proposal resembles this. The scheme is, that an electoral body, by a peculiar contrivance hitherto unknown, and I will undertake to say, if ever heard of, only despised, shall not be asked, but shall be made to do this—to return two Members to sit on this side and one on the other, or *vice versá*.

We are told that the result will be admirable, because we shall put an end to animosities, contests, and the expenditure of elections—in fact, nothing is to be so charming as the tranquillity and good-humour to prevail in all these boroughs. But look at Huntingdon. There has been the greatest tranquillity in that borough for the last thirty years. Ever since the right hon. Gentleman (General Peel) went there, I believe there has been hardly a single contest. In all that time nothing can be more admirable than the way things have been managed. But Huntingdon is not a centre of political life. If all the boroughs of England were like Huntingdon, the political life of the country would be extinguished—its freedom would be extinguished—and when once England's freedom has gone, I wonder what there would be left in the country worth preserving.

One word of caution, if the House will permit me, before I close. You are about to give to many hundred thousands of your countrymen, not hitherto possessing it, a vote for a representative in Parliament. Lord Derby said last night, or a night or two ago, in the House of Lords, that you were taking a leap in the dark, and he trusts somehow or other that the ground upon which you are about to alight will be soft, and that you will not be much injured. But you are admitting this number of persons who have never hitherto had a vote in boroughs, and you ought to be guided by the ancient principles of the Constitution, by those principles which have been laid down for us by our ancestors and forefathers. You want those you are admitting to the franchise to be guided by the ancient principles of the Constitution in all that they do when they have power, in order that they may not depart from that great chart which I hope in some degree they have studied, and which was laid down by our forefathers in this House. Suppose you depart from it in this matter that we are now discussing, and introduce something entirely novel, something that cannot be defended by argument—for nobody in my opinion has ever attempted to defend it—the Chancellor of the Exchequer never heard of an argument about it which he thought worth answering—if you introduce something so entirely novel and so offensive, is it not possible that those who will have the power after this Bill passes may think also that there are many fantastic things which they might do, and doing them would be as much justified as the House is now in doing this?

When I have addressed great meetings of my countrymen I have always advised them to adhere strongly to that which is constitutionally and morally right. If they at any future time, whilst I am in Parliament or in any degree of prominence before the country, attempt to do things with regard to your class or order which I believe to be morally or constitutionally wrong, I shall be as firm in opposing them as I have been in supporting the rights which they have demanded. And I lament over the possibility of such a proposal as this being acceded to, because I am certain that it will afford an example hereafter to those who may wish to follow, not in this precise direction, but in some other direction which they may equally justify, but which may be very perilous and injurious to the country. I enter my protest against this proposal on all grounds. I enter it as one of the Members for a great constituency to which the other day you offered an additional Member, and from which you are now about to take one-half of their present political power. I say that constituency would prefer that the Member you are about to give it had been given to Keighley, St. Helen's, Barnsley, or Luton, as first proposed, than that it should be given under such conditions as you now wish to impose.

I saw 5,000 men only two nights ago in the Free Trade Hall in Manchester. It was not a packed meeting. Everybody in Manchester had a right to go. · I believe about 1,000 paid to do so, and 4.000 or 5,000 went in free. They unanimously passed a Petition that has been presented to-night by my hon. Friend the Member for Manchester, and in it they prayed the House to do one of three things. They asked that either the borough might be divided as in the case of Glasgow—and why should Glasgow be in a better position as to its third Member than Liverpool, or Birmingham, or Manchester, or Leeds?—or that the majority should decide the election as at present, or, failing either of these courses, that the House should withdraw the fatal gift of an additional Member who is merely to be paired off against one of their present Members. Will you refuse that Petition? Has there ever been a case like this in the annals of the English Parliament, where a great constituency besought you not to confer upon them additional representation because you were going to give it in a manner notoriously destructive of their existing political power?

I say, then, as one of the Members for Birmingham, I wholly protest against this proposal. What will you do with my Colleague if I should be humiliated to sit for a borough in which I cannot say that I have been elected by the majority of the voices of the constituency? What will you say to the Member for the minority of Birmingham? Suppose we

had had within the last few months three Members for
Birmingham, and suppose, which is an impossible supposition,
that my lamented Friend and late Colleague had been the
Member for the minority. At his death there must have
been a new writ issued for a Member for Birmingham. Would
you, by any clause in this Bill, or in any future Bill, prevent
the majority of that constituency from voting for his successor? What could you do in such a case? Or suppose
that my hon. Colleague the Member for the minority in a
future Parliament, if I should be unfortunate enough to be
associated with such an one, proved serviceable to the right
hon. Gentleman the Chancellor of the Exchequer, and Lord
Derby invited him to take a seat in his Government. Under
this very Bill you have enacted that those who take certain
offices shall be re-elected. But if he went down as Member
for the minority of Birmingham, who is to elect him? Do
you think the two-thirds who support myself and Colleague
would be so condescending as to return your minority
Member to sit as a part of a Government to which they are
opposed?

The whole matter is so monstrous and so unconstitutional,
that I feel that I am humiliating you and myself in discussing
it. No, I am not humiliating you, because you do not believe
in it—you believe in the Chancellor of the Exchequer. Well,
the Chancellor of the Exchequer, in one of the most impressive speeches ever made in this House—and no man speaks
more impressively than he does when he speaks from his
heart—opposed this scheme. You believed him, and voted
with him. He thinks now as he thought then. He has
followed my speech from beginning to end, and there is not a
single word which he is prepared at this moment to contradict. This is not a question of mere convenience to the
Government or of acquiescence with the House of Lords.
The House of Lords has done what it thought was right, and
if you should disagree, the House of Lords will consult, not

only the interests of the country and the dignity of the
House of Commons, but its own dignity, in acquiescing in
the view you take.

You are a responsible and representative body. You have
powers—though they cannot be written exactly; and though
you cannot take a clause from the Constitution which shall
strictly define them, you have powers that are far above the
powers of the Monarchy or of the aristocracy in the House of
Peers. Of those powers you cannot divest yourself. They
spring from the very source of your existence, for you come
from the people throughout the length and breadth of the
country. You cannot and you dare not—I say you dare not
—betray their rights and desert their interests. I am afraid
the right hon. Gentleman will say I am speaking strongly
and passionately, because I am one of the Members whose
constituents are interested specially in this matter. I do not
deny it. I should be ashamed of myself if I did not admit
that it made some difference in the earnestness and warmth
of my feelings with regard to it. But if I went out of the
House to-night—and I would rather go out of it to-night
than vote for this proposal or sit for a constituency as the
representative of the minority—if I were to leave the House
to-night and never to return to it, I should entertain the
same feeling, and should express it with the same warmth
and earnestness with which I submit my views at this
moment to the House.

May I ask the House to lift themselves just for a moment
from any narrow view of party? It is not a question of
party; let us put that aside altogether. Let us not suppose
for a moment that we are going to injure or aid the Government—there is nothing of that kind in it. It will be greatly
to the credit of Lord Derby and of the right hon. Gentleman
in regard to the historic character of their measure that it
should not be defaced by a great evil like this. I am speaking
in their interest as much as any can do who have supported

this Bill. Let us, therefore, get rid of the feeling of party—of the feeling that we are going to vote for or against the Government. Let us get rid of all feeling except that this change has been recommended to us by the House of Lords, in which there cannot be either the same knowledge or the same interest in the matter which exists in this House. Let us look at this simply as it refers to the great body in whose names we sit and speak here. Let us look at it in reference to that grand old freedom which our forefathers struggled for and secured, and maintained, and the advantages of which, from the day of our birth till this hour, we have been constantly enjoying. If this proposal had come before this House at the time when the great men, the giants of the English Constitution, sat in this House, they would have treated it in a manner far less decorous than we shall treat it. There is no name that appears among the great men of that day, parents of English freedom, which would not have been found among the names of those who shall this day say 'No!' to the mischievous proposition sent down to us by the House of Lords.

SPEECHES

ON

VARIOUS SUBJECTS.

FREE TRADE.

COVENT GARDEN THEATRE, DECEMBER 19, 1845.

[During the agitation for the repeal of the Corn-laws, the Anti-Corn-law
League held many great meetings in Covent Garden Theatre, at which
Mr. Cobden, Mr. Bright, Mr. C. P. Villiers, and other prominent advocates
of Free Trade, spoke on the great question of the day. The following
speech was delivered at one of these celebrated Covent Garden meetings,
held immediately after the temporary resignation of Sir Robert Peel.]

DURING the last month, I have visited, as one of a deputation from the Council of the League, many towns in this
country. I have been present at meetings in Lancashire,
Cheshire, Yorkshire, Nottinghamshire, Derbyshire, Gloucester-
shire, Staffordshire, Somersetshire, and now in Middlesex;
and I am forced to the conclusion that the agitation now
in progress throughout this kingdom is one of no common
or trivial character. Notwithstanding the hope that my
Friend who has just addressed you has expressed, that it
may not become a strife of classes, I am not sure that it
has not already become such, and I doubt whether it can
have any other character. I believe this to be a movement
of the commercial and industrious classes against the lords
and great proprietors of the soil.

Within the last fifty years trade has done much for the people of England. Our population has greatly increased; our villages have become towns, and our small towns large cities. The contemned class of manufacturers and traders has assumed another and a very different position, and the great proprietors of the soil now find that there are other men and interests to be consulted in this kingdom besides those of whom they have taken such great care through the legislation which they have controlled. In the varying fortunes of this contest we have already seen one feeble and attenuated Administration overthrown, and now we see another, which every man thought powerful and robust, prostrate in the dust. It is worth while that the people, and that statesmen, should regard this result, and learn from it a lesson. What was it that brought the Whig Government down in 1841, and what is it that has brought down Sir Robert Peel now? Have not we good grounds for asserting that the Corn-law makes it impossible for any party longer to govern England during its continuance? No statesman dare now take office upon the understanding that he is to maintain the system which the Protectionists have asserted to be a fundamental principle in the constitution of the kingdom.

We have heard that the Whig Government left the country in great distress, and its financial affairs in much embarrassment. But no one has ever pointed out the particular acts of that Government which made the revenue deficient. It was not the taking off of taxes injudiciously—it was not a more than ordinarily extravagant expenditure of the public funds which produced that effect; but it was the collapse of the national industry—it was the failure of the sources whence flow the prosperity of our trade, a calamity which arose from deficient harvests, those deficient harvests being destructive to our trade and industry, because the Corn-law denied to us the power of repairing the mischief by means of foreign supplies.

Great landed proprietors may fancy that trade is of small importance; but of this we are at present assured, that no Government can maintain its popularity or keep up its power so long as we have deficient harvests and restriction on the importation of foreign food.

Under such a state of things, how is social order to be preserved? When prices are high the revenue invariably declines, and higher taxes must be imposed; general discontent prevails, because there is general suffering; and the Government, whatever be its party name, or however numerous may be its supporters in either House of Parliament, must, under these circumstances, first become unpopular, and then, finally, become extinct. We are now brought to this conclusion, that the continuous government of this country by any administration is totally incompatible with the maintenance of the Corn-laws. Lord John Russell acknowledges it, and Sir Robert Peel, by his sudden retirement from office, has given his testimony to the fact. But there are men who deny it; such men, for example, as Sir John Tyrrell and Mr. Bramston, the latter celebrated, I believe, as the leader in the great lard debate. These men, down in Essex, speak of Sir Robert Peel in the most opprobrious language. They say they are glad that the ' organised hypocrisy' is at an end—that they are delighted that ' the reign of humbug is over;' that they are astounded at the perfidy and treachery of the men whom they lifted into office. It is neither perfidy nor treachery of which they have to complain. Sir Robert Peel cannot, any more than other men, do impossibilities; and it is an impossibility to govern this country with the Corn-law in existence. Sir John Tyrrell, and the like of him, do not shrink from the heavy responsibility of attempting this impossible task; but Sir Robert Peel does shrink from it. Sir Robert Peel is in a very different position from that which they occupy. The country has a hold upon him; he is responsible, and as Prime Minister he knows that he must be held responsible. But, further, he is responsible also to posterity, and no man more than Sir Robert Peel wishes to stand well upon the page of his country's history. But as for the squires, the country has no hold upon them; it expects nothing from them, and will make them responsible for nothing. The Tyrrells and the Bramstons are lost amid the herd of squires, and nobody can lay hold of them to make them atone for national calamities. And if the country has no hold upon them, certainly posterity has none. No man who records the history of this period will ever write long paragraphs about the Tyrrells and the Bramstons. All that posterity will know of these, and of such as these, will be communicated to them upon a marble tablet in some obscure parish church.

This contest has now been waged for seven years; it was a serious one when commenced, but it is a far more serious one now. Since the time when we first came to London to ask the attention of Parliament to the question of the Corn-law, two millions of human beings have been added to the population of the United Kingdom. The table is here as before; the food is spread in about the same quantity as before; but two millions of fresh guests have arrived, and that circumstance makes the question a serious one, both for the Government and for us. These two millions are so many arguments for the Anti-Corn-law League—so many emphatic condemnations of the policy of this iniquitous law. I see them now in my mind's eye ranged before me, old men and young children, all looking to the Government for bread; some endeavouring to resist the stroke of famine, clamorous and turbulent, but still arguing with us; some dying mute and uncomplaining. Multitudes have died of hunger in the United Kingdom since we first asked the Government to repeal the Corn-law, and although the great and powerful may not regard those who suffer mutely and die in silence, yet the recording angel will note down their patient endurance and the heavy guilt of those by whom they have been sacrificed.

We have had a succession of skirmishes; we now approach the final conflict. It may be worth while to inquire who and what are the combatants in this great battle? Looking in the columns of the newspapers, and attending, as I have attended, hundreds of meetings held to support the principles of Free Trade, we must conclude, that on the face of it the struggle is that of the many against the few. It is a struggle between the numbers, wealth, comforts, the all in fact, of the middle and industrious classes, and the wealth, the union, and sordidness of a large section of the aristocracy of this empire; and we have to decide,—for it may be that this meeting itself may to no little extent be the arbiter in this great contest,—we have to decide now in this great struggle, whether in this land in which we live, we will longer bear the wicked legislation to which we have been subjected, or whether we will make one effort to right the vessel, to keep her in her true course, and, if possible, to bring her safely to a secure haven. Our object, as the people, can only be, that we should have good and impartial government for everybody. As the whole people, we can by no possibility have the smallest interest in any partial or unjust legislation: we do not wish to sacrifice any right of the richest or most powerful class, but we are resolved that that class shall not sacrifice the rights of a whole people.

We have had landlord rule longer, far longer than the life of the oldest man in this vast assembly, and I would ask you to look at the results of that rule, and then decide whether it be not necessary to interpose some check to the extravagance of such legislation. The landowners have had unlimited sway in Parliament and in the provinces. Abroad, the history of our country is the history of war and rapine: at home, of debt, taxes, and rapine too. In all the great contests in which we have been engaged we have found that this ruling class have taken all the honours, while the people have taken all the scars. No sooner was the country freed from the horrible contest which was so long carried on with the powers of Europe, than this law, by their partial legislation, was enacted —far more hostile to British interests than any combination of foreign powers has ever proved. We find them legislating corruptly : they pray daily that in their legislation they may discard all private ends and partial affections, and after prayers they sit down to make a law for the purpose of extorting from all the consumers of food a higher price than it is worth, that the extra price may find its way into the pockets of the proprietors of land, these proprietors being the very men by whom this infamous law is sustained.

In their other legislation we find great inequality. For example, they deal very leniently with high gaming on the turf, and very severely with chuck-farthing and pitch and toss. We find them enacting a merciless code for the preservation of wild animals and vermin kept for their own sport; and, as if to make this law still more odious, we find them entrusting its administration, for the most part, to sporting gentlemen and game preservers. We find throughout England and Wales, that the proportion of one in eleven of our whole population consists of paupers; and that in the south and south-western counties of England, where squiredom has never been much interfered with, the pauperism is as one to seven of the whole population. We find, moreover, that in Scotland there is an amount of suffering no less, perhaps, though not so accurately set down in figures. We find the cottages of the peasantry pulled down in thousands of cases, that the population on the landed estates may be thinned, and the unfortunate wretches driven into the towns to procure a precarious support, or beyond the ocean, to find a refuge in a foreign land. But in that country across the Channel, whence we now hear the wail of lamentation, where trade is almost unknown, where landowners are predominant and omnipotent, we find not one in seven, but at least half the population reduced to a state which may be termed a condition of pauperism.

The men who write for Protectionist newspapers sometimes heap their scorn upon the inhabitants of the American republic. New York is that State of the Union in which there is the most pauperism, for to that State the stream of emigration from this country and from Ireland flows; and yet in that State, the most pauperised in the whole republic, there is only one pauper to every 184 of the population. It is true that they have not an hereditary peerage to trust to. They know nothing there of a House of Lords, seventy or eighty Members of which deposit their legislative power in the hands of one old man. It is not a wise thing for the hereditary peerage and the Protectionist party to direct the attention of the people of this country to the condition of the American republic. We do not expect perfection either in the New World or in the Old; all we ask is, that when an abuse is pointed out, it may be fairly and openly inquired into, and, if it be proved to be an abuse, honestly abated.

I am always fearful of entering upon the question of the condition of that portion of our working population amongst whom these squires and lords principally live; but I find that those newspapers which stand in a very ambiguous character before the public, which sometimes are, and sometimes are not, the organs of the Government, but are always organs which play a tune that jars upon the nerves of the people —I find those papers are now endeavouring to play the old game of raising hostile feelings in the manufacturing districts between the employers and the employed. Let them write; bread has risen too much within the last six months, and within the last two months trade has suffered too sad a reverse, for their writing to have any effect now. There is the most cordial, complete, and, I believe I may add, lasting union amongst all classes in the manufacturing districts in reference to this cause. But how stands the case in the rural districts? Can the Protectionists call a meeting in any town or village in the kingdom, giving a week's notice of their intention to call their tenants together, and imagine that they will have a vote in favour of Protection?

They sometimes think we are hard upon the aristocracy. They think that the vast population of Lancashire and Yorkshire are democratic and turbulent. But there are no elements there, except that of great numbers, which are to be compared in their dangerous character with the elements of disaffection and insubordination which exist round about the halls and castles of this proud and arrogant aristocracy. You have seen in the papers, within the last fortnight, that the foul and frightful crime of incendiarism has again appeared. It always shows itself when we have had for some short time a high price of bread. The Corn-law is as great a robbery of the man who follows the plough as it is of him who minds the loom, with this difference, that the man who follows the plough is, of the two, nearest the earth, and it takes less power to press him into it. Mr. Benett, one of the Members for Wiltshire, at an agricultural meeting held not long since, made a very long speech, in which he said some remarkable things—the most remarkable being, that if he had again to come into the world, and had the option of choosing the particular rank or class in society to which he would belong, after reviewing, I believe, a period of about seventy years, he confessed that he would choose to be an agricultural labourer. Now, this sentiment is certainly of a very novel character; and it is one worth examining, coming, as it did, from a man who had at one time, I am told, a property of eight or ten thousand a-year in land.

Now, what is the condition of this agricultural labourer, for whom they tell us Protection is necessary? He lives in a parish whose owner, it may be, has deeply mortgaged it.

The estate is let to farmers without capital, whose land grows almost as much rushes as wheat. The bad cultivation of the land provides scarcely any employment for the labourers, who become more and more numerous in the parish; the competition which there is amongst these labourers for the little employment to be had, bringing down the wages to the very lowest point at which their lives can be kept in them. They are heart-broken, spirit-broken, despairing men. They have been accustomed to this from their youth, and they see nothing in the future which affords a single ray of hope. We have attended meetings in those districts, and have been received with the utmost enthusiasm by these round-frocked labourers. They would have carried us from the carriage which we had travelled in, to the hustings; and if a silly squire or a foolish farmer attempted any disturbance or improper interference, these round-frocked men were all around us in an instant, ready to defend us; and I have seen them hustle many a powerful man from the field in which the meeting was being held.

If there be one view of this question which stimulates me to harder work in this cause than another, it is the fearful sufferings which I know to exist amongst the rural labourers in almost every part of this kingdom. How can they be men under the circumstances in which they live? During the period of their growing up to manhood, they are employed at odd jobs about the farm or the farm-yard, for wages which are merely those of little children in Lancashire. Every man who marries is considered an enemy to the parish; every child who is born into the world, instead of being a subject of rejoicing to its parents and to the community, is considered as an intruder come to compete for the little work and the small quantity of food which is left to the population. And then comes toil, year after year, long years of labour, with little remuneration; but perhaps at sixty or seventy, a gift of 20s. and a coat, or of 2l., from the Agricultural Society, because they have brought up a large family, and have not committed that worst of all sins, taken money from the parochial rates.   One of their own poets has well expressed their condition :—

> ' A blessed prospect—
> To slave while there is strength—in age the workhouse,
> A parish shell at last, and the little bell
> Toll'd hastily for a pauper's funeral !'

But the crowning offence of the system of legislation under which we have been living is, that a law has been enacted, in which it is altogether unavoidable that these industrious and deserving men should be brought down to so helpless and despairing a condition.   By withdrawing the stimulus of competition, the law prevents the good cultivation of the land of our country, and therefore diminishes the supply of food which we might derive from it.   It prevents, at the same time, the importation of foreign food from abroad, and it also prevents the growth of supplies abroad, so that when we are forced to go there for them they are not to be found.   The law is, in fact, a law of the most ingeniously malignant character.   It is fenced about in every possible way.   The most demoniacal ingenuity could not have invented a scheme more calculated to bring millions of the working classes of this country to a state of pauperism, suffering, discontent, and insubordination than the Corn-law which we are now opposing.

And then a fat and sleek dean, a dignitary of the church and a great philosopher, recommends for the consumption of the people—he did not read a paper about the supplies that were to be had in the great valley of the Mississippi, but he said that there were Swede turnips and mangel-wurzel ;—and the Hereditary Earl Marshal of England, as if to out-herod Herod himself, recommends hot water and a pinch of curry-powder. I was rejoiced, not for the sake of the Duke of Norfolk, for I pitied him, but still I was in my heart rejoiced when I saw the speech which he had made in Sussex. The people of England have not, even under thirty years of Corn-law influence, been sunk so low as to submit tamely to this insult and wrong. It is enough that a law should have been passed to make your toil valueless, to make your skill and labour unavailing to procure for you a fair supply of the common necessaries of life—but when to this grievous iniquity they add the insult of telling you to go, like beasts that perish, to mangel-wurzel, or to something which even the beasts themselves cannot eat, then I believe the people of England will rise, and with one voice proclaim the downfall of this odious system.

This law is the parent of many of those grievous fluctuations in trade under which so much suffering is created in this commercial kingdom. There is a period coming—it may be as bad or worse than the last—when many a man, now feeling himself independent and comfortable in his circumstances, will find himself swept away by the torrent, and his goodly ship made a complete wreck. Capital avails almost nothing; fluctuations in trade we have, such as no prudence can guard against. We are in despair one year, and in a state of great excitement in the next. At one time ruin stares us in the face, at another we fancy that we are getting rich in a moment. Not only is trade sacrificed, but the moral character of the country is injured by the violent fluctuations created by this law. And now have we a scarcity coming or not? They say that to be forewarned is to be forearmed, and that a famine foretold never comes. And so this famine could not have come if the moment we saw it to be coming we had had power to relieve ourselves by supplies of food from abroad. The reason why a famine foretold never comes, is because when it is foreseen and foretold, men prepare for it, and thus it never comes. But here, though it has been both foreseen and foretold, there is a law passed by a paternal legislature, remaining on the statute-book, which says to twenty-seven millions of people, 'Scramble for what there is, and if the poorest and the weakest starve, foreign supplies shall not come in for fear some injury should be done to the mortgaged landowners.'

Well, if this class of whom I have spoken have maintained this law for thirty years—if they continued it from 1838 to 1842—be assured that no feeling of mercy, no relenting, no sympathy for the sufferings of the people, will weigh one atom in the scale in making them give up the law now. They have no one to whom they can look for a promise to maintain it; but we have some one to whom to look for a promise to repeal it. But the promises of Lord John Russell, or any other minister, are entirely conditional. He knows that he alone cannot repeal the Corn-law. I had almost said that the overturning of the monarchy would be a trifle compared with the touching of the pockets of the squires. Lord John Russell himself has said that it can only be done by the unequivocal expression of the public will. How is this expression to be made? By meetings such as this, and by the meetings which myself and others have seen in all parts of the kingdom; and also by preparations of the most active character for that general election which, in all human probability, is near upon us.

I believe you have heard that we had a meeting in Manchester the other day, which was attended by more of the wealth and influence of that district than I have ever seen assembled at a meeting of the same numbers before. It was resolved on Tuesday to have a general meeting of all those who are wishful to support the League in this great and final struggle. It has been announced that the Council of the League are calling upon their friends throughout the country to raise a fund of 250,000*l.* for the purpose of being ready in any emergency, and for the sake of maintaining before the ranks of the Protectionists, at least, as bold and resolute a character as we have maintained for the past seven years.

Now, that money will be subscribed as it is required, and that large sum will be paid, and I can promise this meeting and the country that it will be honestly and judiciously applied to carry out the great national object for which the League has been established. If the Protectionists like to defer the settlement of this question till the warm weather comes, we will not trouble our friends to tear themselves half to pieces in getting within the walls of this theatre, but we will ask them to meet here, in Manchester, Leeds, Glasgow, Sheffield, Birmingham, and other towns, in numbers so great, in unanimity so remarkable, and in resolution so undaunted, that the aristocracy of this country, with all their pride of ancestry and their boasted valour, will quail before the demonstration that will then be made.

Two centuries ago the people of this country were engaged in a fearful conflict with the Crown. A despotic and treacherous monarch assumed to himself the right to levy taxes without the consent of Parliament and the people. That assumption was resisted. This fair island became a battle-field, the kingdom was convulsed, and an ancient throne overturned. And, if our forefathers two hundred years ago resisted that attempt—if they refused to be the bondmen of a king, shall we be the born thralls of an aristocracy like ours? Shall we, who struck the lion down, shall we pay the wolf homage? or shall we not, by a manly and united expression of public opinion, at once, and for ever, put an end to this giant wrong?

Our cause is at least as good as theirs. We stand on higher vantage-ground; we have large numbers at our back; we have more of wealth, intelligence, union, and knowledge of the political rights and the true interests of the country; and, what is more than all this—we have a weapon, a power, and machinery, which is a thousand times better than that of force, were it employed — I refer to the registration, and especially to the 40*s*. freehold, for that is the great constitutional weapon which we intend to wield, and by means of which we are sure to conquer, our laurels being gained, not in bloody fields, but upon the hustings and in the registration courts. Now, I do hope, that if this law be repealed within the next six months, and if it should then be necessary that this League should disperse, I do trust that the people of England will bear in mind how great a panic has been created among the monopolist rulers by this small weapon, which we have discovered hid in the Reform Act, and in the Constitution of the country. I would implore the middle and working classes to regard it as the portal of their deliverance, as the strong and irresistible weapon before which the domination of this hereditary peerage must at length be laid in the dust.

BURDENS ON LAND.

HOUSE OF COMMONS, MARCH 15, 1849.

From Hansard.

[On March 8, 1849, Mr. Disraeli submitted a resolution to the effect that the whole of the local taxation of the country falls mainly, and presses with undue severity, on real property. He suggested that one-half of these local rates should be paid out of the Consolidated Fund. The debate was adjourned to March 15, when the resolution was negatived by 280 votes to 189.]

IT seems to me that a great deal of misapprehension exists among hon. Gentlemen on the benches opposite with regard to the proposition of the hon. Member for Buckinghamshire. We were originally given to understand, if I mistake not, that the basis or groundwork of that proposition was the prevalence of great distress among all classes of the community connected with agriculture in this country. But the speech of the hon. Mover of the proposition described a case of a very different description, whilst the speech of the hon. Member for Somersetshire, who has just sat down, has apprised you that none of the distress resulting from the burdens on land complained of falls on that class whom the hon. Mover would induce you to relieve by adopting his proposition.

The hon. Member for Buckinghamshire, in his speech on introducing this question, quoted something which I am said to have stated on a former occasion, admitting the great distress prevailing among the agricultural classes. He misquoted what I then said; very unintentionally, I am quite sure, but very strangely. I never expressed myself to the effect—and, if I had done so, I should have betrayed great ignorance of that which must be within the cognisance or experience of almost every man—that, generally speaking, the distress of the times has been very severely felt by the agricultural community. I said that little had been said about the pressure of agricultural distress further northwards than Cambridge or Suffolk, and that in the south of England the cry of agricultural distress had scarcely been heard of. And I say further, that hardly anything has been ever asserted of late in the north as to the depression of agricultural prices.

Well, Sir, I can only assure the House that I met but a few days ago with some gentlemen who had lately come up from the southern counties of Scotland, and who told me that they had been selling their wheat in the markets there at from 47*s.* to 48*s.* per quarter on an average. They had a fair crop last year of good quality, and they are satisfied with the prices they have received. They must be subject to the same vicissitudes, for example, as men are in every other trade. Farmers, no more than any other traders, can expect to be always lucky. Just prior to the harvest of last year, the rain fell exactly at the critical moment for the farmers of the south, and just before the critical moment for the farmers of the north. What has been the consequence? The farmers of the northern counties have harvested their produce in good condition, and obtain good prices; those of the south have been less fortunate, and realise less encouraging returns. This is simply the reason why we have great complaints from the one, and few or none from the other class of tenant-farmers. If any of these parties, however, seek a ground upon which to found his appeal to. Parliament for legislative relief, he must look for it in the speech of the hon. Member for Somersetshire, whose fortune it has been to make such an appeal in vain.

I shall not enter into those questions connected with the general condition of the trade and finances, and of the agricultural classes of this country, which have been already, in my opinion, disposed of by the speech of the right hon. Baronet the Chancellor of the Exchequer. But the hon. Gentleman who has just sat down made one statement upon which I must be allowed to offer a word or two. That hon. Member told us that he had lately been selling some wheat. He told us that his wheat was only of inferior quality, yet that he realised, I think, 42*s*. per quarter for it. Now, I think if he could get such prices for an inferior wheat, wheat of ordinary average goodness must be fetching very fair prices just now. There are other Gentlemen, Sir, in this House who are themselves manufacturers of other articles. I should like to ask the hon. Member for Somersetshire what he thinks is the scale of prices they obtain when they carry into the market that which they admit to be a damaged or an inferior article. They will obtain, of course, only the lowest scale of prices for such goods. They will not get after the rate of 42*s*., which the hon. Member who complains of unremunerating prices can obtain for his inferior article— a wheat of inferior quality. But as for better wheats, I met with a gentleman a few days since who told me that Dantzic wheat was worth now, in London, from 53*s*. to 54*s*. per quarter. He added, that other foreign wheats of fair quality were obtaining, on an average, about 48*s*. per quarter. I tell the hon. Gentlemen opposite to' me, that their home-grown wheat, of the same quality, will now fetch the same prices.

I say, then, that the pretences on which this motion has been brought forward have totally failed—that no ground has been laid for any change in the existing burdens upon

the land, which can be justified, either by the present condition of the tenant-farmer, or by the prices of agricultural
produce in our markets.   I do not intend to enter into
any elaborate array of figures in following the statements
which have been made by the hon. Gentleman the Member
for Buckinghamshire, in the speech with which he introduced
his motion; because, all that could be said in reference to
them was said, last night, by the right hon. Gentleman the
Chancellor of the Exchequer, certainly in the best speech
which I have ever heard from these benches since the accession of the right hon. Gentleman and of his Colleagues to
power.   But the right hon. Gentleman did not, as it appeared
to me, notice some points in the case or plea on which the
hon. Member for Buckinghamshire rested his case for our
adoption of such a proposal as he has brought forward, or at
least did not regard them in all the lights under which they
might have been viewed.

The hon. Gentleman seems to adopt for his principle the
notion that all classes of the community ought to bear, col-
lectively, certain burdens which he assumes to be, at present,
borne exclusively by the landed proprietary and real property
of this country.   Is this so?   If such be really the proposition of the hon. Member for Buckinghamshire—and that it
is, I must presume from the statement of the hon. Member
for Somersetshire—how does the speech we have just heard
support it?   The hon. Member for Buckinghamshire admits
that he is opposed to, and would not vote for, a national
rate of this kind.   And I think he is very wise in coming to
this conclusion.   The arguments against a national rate are,
in my mind, of insuperable force.   I am firmly persuaded that
the various expenses connected with it would run up these
rates, of which the burden is already said to be oppressive, at
least five-fold within five years.

But I think the original objects and working of these
local rates have been a good deal misunderstood.   A Report of

the Poor Law Commissioners on Local Taxation was printed in 1843. I will read one remarkable passage from this Report; a passage which clearly defines the period at and the circumstances under which the practice of rating stock in trade for the relief of the poor was first resorted to in this country :—

'The practice of rating stock in trade never prevailed in the greater part of England and Wales. It was, with comparatively few exceptions, confined to the old clothing district of the south and west of England. It gained ground just as the stock of the woolstaplers and clothiers increased, so as to make it an object with the farmers and other ratepayers, who still constituted a majority in their parishes, to bring so considerable a property within the rate. They succeeded by degrees, and there followed upon their success a more improvident practice in giving relief than had ever prevailed before in England. It was in this district, and at this time, that relief by head-money had its origin, and produced its most conspicuous effects in deteriorating the habits and depreciating the wages of the agricultural labourer. When the practice of rating stock in trade was fully established in this district, the staple trade rapidly declined there, and withdrew itself still more rapidly into the northern clothing districts, where no such burden was ever cast upon the trade.'

Now, the hon. Gentleman appears to contend that these burdens should be imposed on all classes of the community, instead of one particular class, and that by such a redistribution a great good would be effected, so far as the landlord and tenant-farmer are concerned. But, unless he could devise some means for getting at the same principle of rating all property equally, he would accomplish nothing towards effecting his own purpose. I happen to be connected with the local administration of a township in which the proportion of local rating actually expended on the relief of the poor does not exceed, perhaps, 7*d.* in the pound. There are townships and districts in its immediate neighbourhood in which the rate for the same purpose is not less than 7*s.* or 8*s.* in the pound. Now, it is quite clear that any manufacturer or capitalist who is largely engaged in trade, and has built a mill or a factory in such a district, would be anxious, under a general rate, to come within such a township, and thus so much enhance the charge for the relief of the poor, under any pressure of trade that should throw labour largely out of employment, as to drive away particular trades, as well as capitalists, from the locality. All rates would, under such a state of things, be enormously increased, and you would thus, by supporting the proposition before the House, be accessory to the ruin of both the landed and the commercial interests of the kingdom.

It has been said that the proposition of the hon. Gentleman the Member for Buckinghamshire is enveloped in a great deal of mystery and confusion. I have endeavoured to penetrate the veil by which it is surrounded; and I will endeavour to explain the conclusions at which I have arrived upon it. It appears, then, to me that it is a proposition intended to withdraw burdens to the amount of some 6,000,000*l.* per annum from certain shoulders on which they are now saddled, and to impose them upon others—to relieve, in short, those who now carry them, by transferring them to those who hitherto have not borne them. The hon. Gentleman's scheme of redistribution would probably reimpose 3,000,000*l.* on those from whom he would take the present aggregate of 6,000,000*l.*, and apportion the other 3,000,000*l.* to other classes of the community. Well; but the 3,000,000*l.* that he would so withdraw from those who at present pay 6,000,000*l.*, would by no means represent the real proportion in which hon. Gentlemen opposite desire to relieve the land from its present liabilities, or of the enhanced value which their scheme would practically confer upon the land generally. Assuming the whole aggregate of land in this kingdom capable of cultivation to represent an increase equal to what it has been stated at by Gentlemen opposite, a rise in the value of the fee-simple of an acre, consequent on the remission of three millions of taxation on that aggregate, would be equivalent to 2 per cent., or 60,000,000*l.* sterling. An increased value of 2*l.* per cent. would represent 120,000,000*l.* as the increased value of the land, supposing it to be brought for sale into the market, or that the Legislature sanctioned such a proposition as that which is now before it.

I, for one, do not think that these are times in which the Legislature could be brought to listen to any such proposition. It is not likely, I trust, to meet with much favour from this House. The hon. Member for Buckinghamshire and his friends seem altogether to forget the ultimate effect if Parliament entertains so exclusive a proposition as he has brought before it with a view of benefiting the landlord. If I am not mistaken, the whole cultivable lands of all England and Wales amount to more than twenty-five—perhaps, indeed, to thirty—millions of acres. Every acre you would thus relieve, I must repeat, would rise in value in the proportion of from 5*l.* to 10*l.* ['No.'] Well, I will be content to say 5*l.* only. This increase would represent an extension of capital invested in the lands held by tenant-farmers and others of not less than 150,000,000*l.* sterling. Would not this be to perpetrate a great injustice to all other descriptions of property for the sake of an exclusive benefit to the land? I ask hon. Gentlemen opposite whether or not they themselves consider that this would be right or proper?

I do think, however, that the proposition now before the House is not less extraordinary than it is unjust. It has for its ostensible object to relieve the present pressure of that which I believe to be the temporary distress of the landed interest. But then the hon. Member for Buckinghamshire is so very discriminating in his views of that question, that the case of the agriculturists of Scotland did not elicit even a single word in his speech. And as for the agriculturists, or any other classes of the unhappy community of the sister island, he turned the cold shoulder to the Irish, and all his sympathy for them extended to that which is proverbially said to be the alms of those who have no money in their pockets wherewith to afford more substantial relief. He gave them—advice. Sir, the hon. Gentleman said that many schemes had been brought forward for the amelioration of the condition of Ireland, but that nothing effectual had been done for her for some sessions past. And here his admission left her. I do not think that Ireland will derive any great benefit from the advocacy of the hon. Gentleman. She will have little to thank him for, if he is prepared to tender her no other consolation for her sufferings but—his advice.

It has been contended that the proposition of the hon. Member would, if carried into effect, remove a great cause of dissatisfaction among the tenant-farmers. But I am convinced that it would create very great discontent among the people. [Laughter.] I repeat this is my conviction—notwithstanding the laughter which it has occasioned. The hon. Member who spoke last has quoted largely from a paper well known to most of those who hear me—a print of great authority in all agricultural society, and of great respectability—I mean the *Mark Lane Express*. The article from which the hon. Gentleman read, indulges in stronger language, perhaps, than I should desire to employ: it stigmatises certain official documents, the authenticity of which it challenges, as the most deceiving statements ever concocted by the duplicity of man. It also expresses great dissatisfaction at the proposition of the hon. Member for Buckinghamshire. I really think that the proposition of the hon. Member for Buckinghamshire is founded on fallacies which are intended to beguile the House into its adoption, but which are amenable to a censure scarcely less severe. That proposition, indeed, reminds me of a story which many hon. Gentlemen have perhaps heard before, yet which I will venture to tell the House in very few words. It happened once, in a country town, and an agricultural district, that a company of strolling players proposed to get up a performance 'for the benefit of the poor' of the neighbourhood. It was calculated by those who announced this intention that the object of contributing towards the relief of the poor would certainly induce the gentry to come forward generously in supporting the performance; and the event proved the soundness of this anticipation. But when it came to a question as to how the proceeds were to be appropriated, the strolling company claimed them all for themselves, on the principle that they themselves were 'the poor' intended.

This is just the case with the proposal of the hon. Member, if you look at its real tendencies. He would procure this boon for the tenant-farmers—of relief from local rates; but he does not go—nor any of his hon. friends near him—for the repeal of the Malt-tax. 'We,' he says, 'do not ask for that at present. It is not the time to ask this relief for you; for we don't go for a revision of the whole scheme of existing taxation.' As to the Malt-tax, I am not altogether prepared to embrace all the views entertained by some of my hon. friends on that subject. I am not one of those who think that the people at large will be much the happier for being relieved from the Malt-tax. As little do I think you will make the people generally more satisfied by taxing malt; or that you will ever succeed in getting rid of drunkenness, or any other vice, simply by rendering its indulgence dear. But I do think that if by repealing the duty on malt, you leave more money in the poor man's pocket for the purchase of other articles of more profit, or value, or convenience to him than that into the cost of which this tax enters, you do well; and notwithstanding what an hon. Baronet has said in the course of this debate, I believe what has fallen from the hon. Member for Lincolnshire, that the Malt-tax is one injurious to agriculture, and oppressive upon the working labourer and consumer. I own that I am astonished at the conduct of hon. Gentlemen opposite on this question, after hearing them both in this House and at public meetings out of doors advocate the repeal of the Malt-tax. The same parties who on this side of the House were its most strenuous advocates, have ceased to mention it now that they have crossed to the benches opposite.

> 'Their lips are now forbid to speak
> That once familiar word.'

Not one voice now calls for that favourite act of justice, but we are told to wait till the proper time shall arrive.

The hon. Member for Buckinghamshire holds this language, but he has not indicated when the time will come. I wish the hon. Gentleman would look a little into the real state of the country; if he would consult the feelings of the people, he would find that nothing more displeases them than to have their representatives hold one language here, and another before their constituents. Sir, hon. Gentlemen know, that at meetings in the country, even tithes are permitted in their presence to be spoken of in the most violent and intemperate language. They encourage, by their own conduct, the people to expect remissions of burdens which must diminish the public revenues, and leave it to Parliament to provide the substitute as best it may. I am astonished at the conduct of hon. Gentlemen. If I were myself an owner of land, I should say this to my tenant-farmers: 'Men, you have got the land, and it must be your object to work it to the best of your ability with the capital you have. Parliament, like the landlord, must deal with those on whose behalf this proposition is said to be made, on the same principles on which it would deal with trades of all other descriptions. You must exert the same virtues of perseverance, industry, and frugality, which others possess, and in which you are not wanting; you must look to the exercise of these means for your profit and success, not to external aid or exclusive assistance, which can only be rendered at the cost of gross injustice to others.'

But the speech of the hon. Member for Buckinghamshire was so purely agricultural, that he did not enter into any such considerations. He recognised no such principle of dealing with the interests of all classes, instead of addressing ourselves to the benefit of one only. He himself quoted from the *Standard*, a newspaper of high authority with his party, and so exclusively agricultural in its predilections, that in one of its leaders a few years ago it contended that if the whole of the manufactures of England were destroyed to-morrow, England would not be a less great country by one iota, or the English a less happy people. But the *Standard* now takes up different ground. It announced in a recent number that unions were now formed in most of the southern counties of England, the object of which was carefully to exclude all the products of the mills of the north, so that the cloths of Cheshire and Yorkshire would not be allowed to come into competition with the productions of Wiltshire. If this is to be the spirit in which hon. Gentlemen are disposed to make common cause against the manufacturing interest, I wonder they do not carry out their principle to its full extent, and, as their ancestors once wandered over the country clothed in skins and with their bodies painted, that they do not come down here in that way. They might come at last to clothe themselves in thatch, by which means I trust the farmers will obtain a remunerative price for their straw.

I am not at all disposed to dispute the meritorious and industrious character of the tenant-farmers; on the contrary, I believe them well entitled to the praise of possessing those qualities in a high degree. But I protest against a proposition on their behalf which would certainly prejudice the interests of all other classes, for the doubtful benefit of one. I am opposed to all these partial experiments. I would willingly support any proposition which went to the reduction of those taxes on raw material which stand in the way of manufacturing labour and close the market on the industry of our artisans. This proposition was recommended to our sympathy on behalf of farmers who have small or no capital; but what would be said of any similar proposition by which it should be proposed to mulct the manufacturers of the north for the benefit of manufacturers without capital in the south? You ought to endeavour to secure to your farms men who have capital and great spirit in agriculture. But you do not do this. If a farmer comes to you, and asks for a farm, wishing to make stipulations—which may be called stipulations of a commercial character—such as that he shall plough and grow as he likes, that he shall have every creature that lives upon the land, and that he must not have it infested with game; if such a man comes to you, you do not like him as a tenant : but it is the consequence of free trade that you must introduce such principles in your future arrangements between landlord and tenant. It is impossible that this great country, with its large and increasing interests, and its dense population, should stand still or rest under the baneful influence of protection to agriculture, simply because you are unwilling to adopt those principles with relation to your tenants which are adopted in every other branch of industry throughout this country.

Now our proposition is admitted on all hands, I believe, to be more distinct and intelligible than that of the hon. Member for Buckinghamshire. He has come forward as a Chancellor of the Exchequer—as the framer of a budget— but it is clear that he is only a novice in his new work, because he has not shown where he is going to obtain the money which he is wishing to remit in the shape of taxation. I suppose, judging from what slight hints fell from the hon. Gentleman, that he means to increase the income-tax; or the hon. Baronet the Member for Lincolnshire (Sir M. Cholmeley) says that a fixed duty upon corn will serve the purpose as well. But let hon. Gentlemen beware how they turn their attention to the question of the reimposition of the duties upon corn. If you do so, you are attempting that which, I believe, is as impossible as the repeal of any

Act which has passed this House in former times. You might probably effect the repeal of the Reform Bill or the Catholic Emancipation Act in the same session as that in which you reimpose the duty upon corn. Take care what you are about. Hon. Gentlemen fancy that there is a lull in the public mind; that events abroad have frightened people at home. Bear in mind that in all , the European capitals a system is being established which will have a strange effect upon the minds of people in this country, who are looking, and wisely looking, to great and permanent changes in the constitution of Parliament; and that whilst your conduct is encouraging such ideas, you are leading the farmers of England in the pursuit of that false and uncertain light which must land them hereafter in the midst of difficulties much greater than those which encompass them at present.

You talk of the experiment of Free Trade as though it had failed, or was but an experiment. I ask, have you not legislated, since the oldest amongst you first came here, in favour of Protection, and with the view of keeping up the price of corn; and do you not recollect that under protective laws in 1836 the whole average price of the year for good wheat—not sprouted wheat—was but 39*s.* 4*d.* per quarter? whilst now, as we are told, sprouted wheat is sold at 42*s.* a quarter. Because that system was abolished, you have wreaked your vengeance upon a Minister. You have scattered a powerful party—you have shown an anger which political parties in this country have scarcely ever exhibited, because through the power, and I will say the patriotism, of the Minister whom you discarded, the industry of this great and growing population has escaped from the pressure of that screw which, through the medium of the Corn-laws, you had laid upon the necessaries of life.

I fear that hon. Gentlemen opposite are not aware of what is passing in this country. Throughout the great towns, that question of the reduction of expenditure which we have placed before you is exciting the intensest interest; whilst in every meeting of farmers the same cry is echoed. The men who thought us their greatest enemies, are now ready to shake hands with my hon. Friend the Member for the West Riding. They are anxious that the great justice which we advocate should be done to this country, and that you should force upon the Executive Government the greatest possible economy, compatible with the public exigencies. You say, tauntingly, that the Government is about to follow the advice of my hon. Friend. The fact is, that you will make my hon. Friend a most extraordinary man. The right hon. Gentleman the Member for Tamworth followed the advice of my hon. Friend; and now you say the present Government are about to do so too. And why is this? It is because we live amongst the people—because we have travelled in every county amongst them, and know their feelings and wishes—because we are identified with their desires, and have been returned to this House by great and free constituencies. It is on this account you find that the measures which my hon. Friend proposes have the sympathy of millions in this country; and I warn you that not many sessions will pass, before you, powerful as you are, will vote for the measure which he recommends.

AGRICULTURAL DISTRESS.

HOUSE OF COMMONS, APRIL 11, 1851.

From Hansard.

[On this day, Mr. Disraeli brought forward an amendment on the motion that the Speaker do leave the Chair, to the effect that in any relief to be granted by the omission or adjustment of taxation, due regard should be paid to the distressed condition of the owners and occupiers of land in the United Kingdom. The amendment was negatived by 263 to 250.]

I SHALL endeavour, in the observations I intend to offer to the House, to address myself closely to the question brought before us by the hon. Member for Buckinghamshire. I do not think the hon. Gentleman intends by his motion to lead us into a discussion on the various parts of the Budget brought forward by the Chancellor of the Exchequer; on the contrary, he seems to agree for the most part that this Budget is acceptable to the country, and that it must pass the House. I shall not be tempted to go into the question of the Corn-law to an extent which might be justified by the speeches of the hon. Member for Northamptonshire (Mr. Stafford), and the noble Lord the Member for Colchester (Lord J. Manners).

I must say that those hon. Gentlemen and others do their leaders great damage by the course they take in this and

similar discussions. If I understand the object of the hon.
Member for Buckinghamshire—taking it from his speeches in
this House—I come to the conclusion that the hon. Gentleman is convinced that any project of returning to Protection
is the merest delusion; and that he (Mr. Disraeli) knows
perfectly well—every man who considers the subject must
know—that so long as hon. Gentlemen opposite will have
this question of Protection as the main part of their policy,
their leaders are destined to sit on the shady side of the
House, and could never cross the table and sit on the Ministerial benches. I therefore will advise all those who support
the hon. Member for Buckinghamshire to avoid the question
of Protection altogether, as one which has been finally and
irrevocably settled.

The hon. Gentleman has made this proposition to the
House, that the agricultural interest (the labourers, who were
once a part of the agricultural interest, are now left out)—
that the agricultural interest, consisting of the owners and
occupiers of land, have some special claim to some special
relief. He has assumed that they are suffering generally, if
not universally, throughout the United Kingdom; but he has
not brought anything like proof, first of all, that the owners
and occupiers of land are suffering much, or, indeed, that they
are suffering at all; and, secondly, the hon. Gentleman has
failed, I think, to show that they have any special claim to
relief, even if they are suffering.

I admit that the hon. Member has a right to assume
the fact of the alleged distress, when arguing with the noble
Lord at the head of the Government, because the noble Lord,
with that want of caution which not unfrequently dis-
tinguishes him, has admitted into the Queen's Speech a
paragraph which was a direct invitation to the hon. Member
for Buckingham to get up a discussion on this topic in the
first week of the session; and then the Chancellor of the
Exchequer, committing another blunder, has brought forward

a proposition in his first Budget which he ought not to have made, but to which, if he has brought it forward, hon. Gentlemen opposite have a right to expect he will adhere. That paragraph and proposition have caused the hon. Member for Buckinghamshire to get up this interesting discussion on a subject which I had hoped was worn threadbare. Now, I am prepared at once to dispute half their case—that is, that the owners of land are suffering distress, or that they have any claim on such a ground to come to this House for relief.

The hon. Member for Herefordshire (Mr. Booker) said the other night that there had been a fall of rent to the amount of 25 per cent.; but though that hon. Gentleman's oratory may be applauded in Herefordshire, yet I believe that he durst not assert that to be a fact in the face of the farmers of that county. Again, the hon. Member for Buckinghamshire has admitted this night, or rather he has assumed, that the reduction of rent may be taken to be 10 per cent. I do not believe it is 10 per cent. I have never seen a single authenticated case which went beyond 15 per cent. I have found many cases in which no reduction has been made; and where there has been a reduction, it is very often made not by permanent agreement with the landlord, but is merely a temporary remission, precisely such as I have known to be given by landlords on several distinct occasions. I take it for granted, therefore, that the fall of rent is to a very small extent; and that, in point of fact, it is not worth comparing with the losses which those who have property invested in other ways, except in land, are constantly liable to in all parts of the kingdom.

There may be, and I believe there are, cases of difficulty among landowners, and particularly among the landowners in Ireland. There are landowners who have small net incomes and large rent-rolls, and from extravagance and other causes have engaged to give to their creditors, or to annuitants of one kind or another, nine-tenths of their actual rent-roll.

Of course a fall of 10 per cent. in such cases is equal to the destruction of the whole income.   But this is no fault of free trade or of the free-traders; the Manchester school are not to be blamed for anything of this kind.   We have never admired settlements and entails.   On the contrary, we should prefer to see landed property free.   We have never recommended gentlemen, who cannot afford it, to keep a great house in the country and a great house in town, or that so many packs of hounds and other sources of enjoyment should be maintained. I confess that if I were a landed proprietor—and I am very sorry that I am not—I should feel humiliated if my advocate in this House made such a speech as the hon. Member for Buckinghamshire has made to-night and on former occasions.

Now, let me ask if there is any class that passes so triumphantly through every commercial hurricane and disaster as the class of landed proprietors does?   I see that the candidate at Aylesbury has stated, as a proof of the distressed condition of the landed proprietors, that money invested in land only returns $2\frac{1}{2}$ per cent.   But that in itself is a proof of the security of the return from land, and that it is not subjected to the vicissitudes to which other property is liable.   There are some in this House who could tell a different tale respecting investments of another character—investments, for instance, in the manufacture of iron during the last four years.   They could tell of the extraordinary revulsion which has taken place in that time, consequent on the demand for iron for railway purposes having declined.   I can speak of my own trade, although I cannot confirm the view taken of it by the noble Lord the Member for Colchester.   Yet I can state that a very large portion of that trade during the last five years, when there were three failures in the American cotton crop—that during these years all the coarse departments of the trade have been of the most unprofitable character.

The noble Lord (Lord J. Manners) has read from Mr. Littledale's circular the parts which suited him—not the parts which suited another view of the question—not the statement which that circular contained that the trade appeared to be settled on a solid and sound basis. The noble Lord ought to know that trade has been so good in Yorkshire for the last two years, and the increase in the consumption of wool so great, that the price of wool has become extremely high, and that it is the price of the raw material at this moment which is interfering with profits in Yorkshire. It was only yesterday that I came from the Hatfield station on the Great Northern railway to London in company with a buyer of wool, who told me that his trade was bad at present; that wool was so dear, and so little of it to be had, that, as a buyer of wool from the farmers, and a seller of it to the Yorkshire manufacturers, he found his trade entirely unprofitable. I gathered from that fact, that the farmers were enjoying a considerable profit on their wool, and that it had been a prosperous article for a very long period.

But the hon. Member for Buckinghamshire has made an admission which is worth something. He said he calculated that the landowners, losing ten per cent. of rental, were losing 6,000,000l. per annum; but he added that the fall of rent gave them no claim whatever to come to that House for relief. I was very glad to hear that fact asserted by the hon. Member. But then a great number of his followers hold a very different opinion, and I have heard even from the Ministerial benches in former times that it was necessary to keep up the price of corn in order to keep up the rent. But if the hon. Member for Buckinghamshire would now look at this fact, that the labouring population are comfortably off, and generally in a state of prosperity—if that prosperity has been caused by the transfer of the 6,000,000l. of rent from the landed proprietors, who never ought to have possessed it if given to them by the Corn-law—if labourers are prosperous by the transfer of that 6,000,000*l.* to them, they are enjoying that of which they have been deprived for thirty-five years by the operation of a law, the repeal of which is so much regretted by some hon. Gentlemen opposite. I deny altogether that the landowners are suffering, or that they are suffering to an extent which requires that they should be pointed out as an ill-used class.

I now come to the question of the occupiers. Now, it is affirmed broadly that the occupiers of land are suffering great distress. I believe that some distress must necessarily arise from the circumstance that the prices of farm produce are temporarily depressed. But this distress is not a rare malady with the occupiers of land. Violent speeches have been made in this House from 1815 onwards, in favour of relief to the distressed occupiers of land. Mr. Preston, a distinguished gentleman connected with the law, wrote a pamphlet two or three years after the Corn-law was enacted, in which he showed that the distress of the occupiers was most agonising, and that they had lost 100,000,000*l.* of their capital, which was transferred to other classes. There is nothing to show that any considerable portion of what they suffered now, arose directly or indirectly from the legislation of that House. But, if it did, what is the remedy proposed, stripped of anything like delusion? The hon. Member for Buckinghamshire does not propose to remedy the grievance by raising the price of corn; but his proposition is this—the making some small transfer of a certain rate, now paid by a certain description of property, to the Consolidated Fund, by which that description of property now paying the rate should henceforth only pay a portion of it, and the rest might be distributed over the tax-payers of the United Kingdom generally.

In connection with the poor-rate there are some facts to which I wish to call the attention of hon. Gentlemen opposite. I will refer to and quote from a return moved for by the

AGRICULTURAL *DISTRESS.* 309

right hon. Baronet the Member for Ripon (Sir J. Graham)
in 1846, showing the proportions in which this rate has been
levied on land, houses, and other property. I am sorry
that there is no return down to the present year, because I
believe the facts proved by it will be found to be the most
conclusive argument against any proposition based upon the
assumption that the landed interest suffers unduly from the
incidence of the poor-rate. In 1826, it appears the land alone
paid 69 per cent. of all the poor-rate. In 1833 the land paid
63 per cent. only. In 1841 it paid 52 per cent. only. Thus,
it will be observed, that in the period from 1826 to 1841,
being a period of fifteen years, the share which the land alone
paid of the whole poor-rate of the country, fell from 69 per
cent. to 52 per cent., that is to say, from two-thirds to about
one-half of the whole amount. And I think we may fairly
take for granted, seeing the fall in those fifteen years, that
a return made out to the last year would show that the land
is not now paying more than forty per cent. of the whole
amount. [Mr. Wilson: 'Forty-five per cent.'] The hon.
Member for Westbury suggests that forty-five per cent. will
be the correct estimate. Well, let us look at the whole poor-
rate levied. In 1833 the whole amount was 8,600,000*l.*;
in 1842 the amount had fallen to 6,500,000*l.*; in 1850, last
year, it had fallen to 5,395,000*l.* Now, here we have the
broad fact, that, within the eight years during which we
have had that legislation of which hon. Gentlemen opposite
complain, the poor-rate of England and Wales has fallen in
amount more than a million sterling. The calculations which
I have made in reference to these figures are upon the assumption that the land now paid only 40 per cent., and not 45 per
cent., and of course the House will make all allowance for that
circumstance. I take the year 1833, and find the land paying
63 per cent., that is to say, 5,434,000*l.*; and then, taking
1850, and assuming the land pays 40 per cent., you will find
that in amount the land now pays only 2,158,000*l.* In other

words, the land of England and Wales paid, in 1833, double the poor-rate which it paid in 1850.

This is an important element in the question we are now considering. The right hon. Gentleman opposite (Mr. Herries) shakes his head; but I do not mind that, for the right hon. Gentleman has been in the habit of shaking his head at everything from this side ever since he has entered this House. Does the right hon. Gentleman mean to say, for example, that the condition of the landed proprietary has not been affected by the hundreds of millions expended on railways in this country, and which now pay 300,000*l.* per annum to the poor-rate on parishes to which they have never contributed a pauper? Does he mean to assert that manufacturing towns and villages could be springing up in every direction, and the moment they spring up be taxed for the poor-rate, without to that extent relieving the land from the burdens to which it has been subjected? If the right hon. Gentleman means this, he certainly could never have been fit for the post of Chancellor of the Exchequer. At any rate, these are facts to which I think it not inappropriate to call the attention of the House. But the argument is, that, notwithstanding this diminution in the poor-rates, the farmers are still distressed. That, after all, is an argument in favour of that view of the question which I and my friends take; our conviction being, that the transference of the rate from the occupying farmer to the occupying householder, by means of taxing his tea or his sugar, will not prove permanently beneficial to the tenant-farmers. For all the reductions in the poor-rate to which I have alluded have not in the slightest degree affected the interest of the tenant-farmers, those cases of course excepted in which the farm has been held continuously at the same rent during those years over which the reductions have extended; and any transference which the hon. Gentleman (Mr. Disraeli) can make, in the event of his obtaining a majority, will have no effect whatever on the tenant-farmer—for if there is any truth in economical science, the tenant-farmer will be compelled in the end to pay an increased rent for the land he holds. ·

Undoubtedly, however, at this moment the condition of the tenant-farmer is one which every man must regard with sympathy. I defy any one to say, looking to the course which I and my friends have pursued as free-traders in this House, that we have ever manifested any want of sympathy for any one class of the tax-payers of this country. At least there can be no denial of the assertion that we have always advocated diminished expenditure and diminished taxation; and that we have urged a diminution of taxation in that particular direction which would have alike affected all classes, inasmuch as our object has been to remove taxes from articles of general and universal consumption, where the farmer would have obviously benefited not less than the weaver. But the farmers are in an unfortunate position; they are the victims of a vicious system. That, however, is not our system. It is the system of hon. Gentlemen opposite. They created it for their own purposes in 1815, and they maintained it for their own purposes up to 1846. They led the farmers to believe that there could be no path to prosperity but through the county Members and the House of Commons. I, for one, should be very sorry to be connected with any trade or manufacture if I had no reliance but on the Members for Manchester. I should be extremely sorry to entrust my interests either to the impartiality of political parties in this House, or to its intelligence on commercial subjects. The unfortunate · position of those among the tenant-farmers who suffer most, consists in this—that they notoriously hold more land than they have capital to cultivate. Their case is precisely the same as that of many landowners, who own extents of land on which they cannot pay all that is due. All this is very sad. If landowners buy land only to obtain political influence, they are on the road to ruin. If a tenant-farmer takes more land than he can properly cultivate in reference to his capital, he is also on the road to ruin.

There are, no doubt, other questions which ought to be considered in speaking of the condition of the tenant-farmer. There is, in particular, one question, in which I took great interest in former years, but the advocacy of which I have been compelled to relinquish in consequence of my not having received that aid from the farmers which their private representations had induced me to expect. I allude to the question of the Game-laws. [Ironical cheers from the Protectionists.] Surely that question is as pertinent to this discussion as the question of lunatic asylums. I mentioned the fact before, and I will again call attention to it, as a most important circumstance, that every witness examined by the Game-laws Committee (and no Member of that Committee would be found to dispute the respectability or credibility of these witnesses) declared that, whenever game was even moderately preserved, greater injury was done to the farmer occupying the land than was inflicted by the whole amount of his general and local taxes. I am satisfied that hon. Gentlemen who preserve game, who indulge in sporting, have no conception of the evils which their tastes inflict on the community. I should, however, be ashamed of myself if, while advocating the cause of the tenant-farmers in this House, I did not appeal to hon. Gentlemen opposite, supposing them to be the true friends of the occupiers of the land, either to alter the Game-laws, which they certainly ought to do, or, if they will not do that, at least to alter their practices, and to discontinue that system which is abhorrent to the civilization of our day, and which, at all events, is most cruelly injurious to those whom hon. Gentlemen opposite profess to represent. [Cries of 'Question!'] I am sorry some hon. Gentlemen do not think that this is speaking to the question. There are those out of doors who do think that it is very near the question.

But what are the remedies for the difficulties of the tenant-farmers? You have your set of remedies. We have our set of remedies. I am free at once to admit that I have no expectation, in passing from the system of the last forty years to that sound system which now prevails, and must henceforth prevail, that we shall find the tenant-farmers, one and all, and immediately, by any kind of contrivance on the part of this House, jumping into a state of unequivocal prosperity. As they now are, they have been before. I heard but yesterday of a farm in Hertfordshire which has had six tenants in eighteen years. Their prosperity was not universal in past years, and it is not now. But if they do get into a better position, it can only be by paths which are very evident; in some cases, by reductions in the rents; in other cases, by increase of produce; and in most cases, by a more successful adaptation of the powers of their farms to the production of those articles which the markets would be most willing to take from them.

There is no doubt whatever that there are great numbers of tenant-farmers who are not complaining, and who have no reason for complaint. And I firmly believe that if all were like the few, and possessed the same energy, the same skill in the adaptation of the resources of their land to the requirements of the markets—above all, if they asserted their independence in making terms with their landlords, they would all overcome their difficulties, and overcome them more speedily, more certainly, and more permanently, than can be looked for from any assistance likely to be extended to them by the House of Commons.

The noble Lord the Member for Colchester (Lord J. Manners) has adverted at some length to the present state of crime. In reference to this, I wish to state to the House some facts to which I desired to call attention the other night, in the discussion on the income-tax, but which are quite applicable on this occasion. Probably these statistics

will be consolatory to the noble Lord, who is not wanting
in benevolence. I hold in my hand a return of the number
of persons taken into custody in Manchester since 1842, the
return being for every two years. In 1842, the number was
13,801; and I believe the number was 12,000 in the two
years preceding. In 1844, the number fell to 10,700; in
1846, to 7,600; in 1848, to 6,200; in 1849, to 4,600; and
in 1850, the number was only 4,578. Thus, in 1850, not
one-third of the number of persons were taken into custody
in Manchester who were found to have been taken into
custody in the year 1842. If we take the general facts as
to England and Wales (not taking last year into account,
as to which there is no return), we shall find a great reduction of committals from 1842 down to 1849. The
diminution was from 31,000 to 27,000; and thus, although
the population has increased ten per cent., the committals
have decreased not less than 12½ per cent.

I have now stated, in detail, what I regard as the reasons
why the proposition of the hon. Gentleman (Mr. Disraeli)
would be of no value if it were agreed to. It can only serve
to delude—not the owners of the land, for they understand
all these tricks—but the occupying farmers throughout the
country. It will serve but to delude these men into a belief
that the thing which is really intended as a measure to cement
a party in Parliament, is intended to do something for their
benefit. One great result of the alteration in our commercial
system with regard to corn is, I hope, this—it has not come
yet, but it is in process of coming about—that the farmers
will no longer conceive themselves to be a class having special
privileges, special rights, and special claims upon the House
of Commons. They will now know that their only chance
is precisely that chance which all the rest of the community
enjoy—a good education for their children for the next generation, and for themselves, their intelligence, such as they
have, and their industry, such as they can employ. And

I will add, especially, the more they make themselves independent of their landlords as respects the old retainer
and chieftain theory, the more they enable themselves to
make bargains with their landlords, just as they would with
other persons with whom they do business, the sooner will
they find themselves out of their present undoubted difficulties. And I believe in my conscience that if you talk
here for ever of agricultural distress, you will still find that
there is no remedy which it is in the power of Parliament
to give. The only possible chance for the farmers is in the
exercise of those virtues and those talents by which the rest
of their countrymen thrive; and if they exercise their own
energies, and cultivate the quality of self-reliance, I am
convinced that this country, with the finest roads, with the
best markets, and with a favourable climate, will be found
to triumph not only in her manufactures, but also in her
agriculture.

GAME LAWS.

ST. ALBAN'S, MARCH 26, 1845.

[A public dinner was given to Mr. Horncastle, a respectable farmer in Hertfordshire, as a testimony of the approbation felt by his brother farmers at
his courage in exposing the grievance of the Game-laws. Mr. Bright
was invited to the dinner, and delivered the following speech on the
occasion.]

I NEED scarcely say that when I received the invitation
to be present at this meeting I felt it as an exceedingly
gratifying proof that the trouble I have recently taken in
connection with the question of game-preserving had not
passed unnoticed by the farmers of this district of the
country. But, whatever pleasure I felt at receiving the invitation, I may acknowledge with the utmost sincerity, that it
has been far surpassed by the gratification I have had in being
present here to-night. I have been delighted to see so many
of the farmers from this part of the country assembled for the
purpose of expressing their opinion upon the conduct of one of
their brother farmers in connection with one of the most
important questions which can bear upon the prosperity of
the agricultural portion of the community.

I was delighted to see, from the public papers, the spirited manner in which Mr. Horncastle came forward for the purpose of speaking what was known to be the opinions of nineteen out of every twenty farmers in the kingdom; and not to the public only, but in direct opposition, and with personal application, to the very man upon whom a farmer is generally supposed to be most dependent. But it must now be a matter of satisfaction of the very highest kind that the effort which he then made—and which hundreds of farmers ought to have made, and which, I believe, hundreds will soon be prepared to follow—that the efforts which he has made have been so highly appreciated by his brother farmers. I think a farmer ought not so much to cultivate the good opinion of landowners as that of farmers; and though I have no wish that there should be that class spirit amongst us which would lead to the supposition that we hold together for peculiar privileges or party interests of our own class, yet I do think that a man is craven-hearted and mean-spirited who, when his own class is attacked, as the farmers have been through the operation of this system of game-preserving, would not come forward and speak on behalf of his own class and of that vast body of men with whom he is constantly associated, and whose interests are so bound up with his own. It is well that you should testify your high estimation of such men as your brother farmer whom you have met to-night to honour. Independent farmers, men who dare speak and dare come out, are not so abundant in this country as that you can afford to think lightly of any of them. Probably under no conceivable circumstances can it be expected that there should not be somewhat more dependence between the occupiers and the owners of land than there is between some other classes in society; but it is of the utmost consequence that a system like this—which wars against the prosperity of the farmers, which blights all their hopes, and makes it utterly impossible that their industry should procure its reward—it is, I say, of the utmost possible consequence that there should be men who dare speak out, and that when such individuals are found they should receive honour, and be repaid with the gratitude of their brother farmers in every part of the kingdom.

We have heard a good deal within the last year or two of farmers' friends; but I take it that Mr. Horncastle is a true farmers' friend, and, if it were not that fortunate circumstances have made him in some degree independent of those who would be likely to injure him, he would not only be the farmers' friend, but he would be likely to become a martyr for farmers. I am delighted to see this meeting, because I take it to be a sign of the times, and a sign of better times—an evidence that farmers are about to think, act, and do something for themselves. I conceive there is no delusion so great as that of believing that the great and the mighty of the earth will ever be the true, sincere, and disinterested friends of the middle classes, either in this or any other kingdom.

I have heard men say that there is no spirit amongst farmers. I never believed that statement. I have felt that there has always been spirit, but that it has been slumbering. It has not been dead, but it has been less active on account of many circumstances; but circumstances may arise, and now I believe have arisen, to make that spirit appear not only existent, but to show it active, resolute, and determined.

The real object of this meeting is to give an expression to the opinions of the farmers in this district with respect to what is now commonly called the game nuisance. It is a protest against a mischievous and unjust system. The time will come, and that too before the children of some now present are as old as we are, when people will look back with astonishment at what farmers have suffered in connection with this question of game. Look at the position in which you now stand. The landowner lets his land, and the farmer, a capitalist to some amount, takes it. Well, everybody who is not acquainted with the circumstances of this country, and who is not puzzled with the extraordinary things he sees round him, would suppose that, when the landowner lets his land, he gave up its ownership during the term for which it was let. That is, he lets the land to the tenant, the tenant having the right to possess fully all the produce of the land, and the whole of the animals and stock which live upon it. Now, look at the position of the farmer when he takes his farm. It is said he himself makes half his bargain; he is uncommonly fortunate if he does so. Is it not notorious that in every county of Great Britain there is, and has been for years past, a competition for land so fierce that nearly all the bargain is in the hands of the landlord? The effect of this competition is to bid up rent to the very highest point at which it can be hoped to be paid, and to bear down every covenant and right which, under other circumstances, the farmer might reasonably expect to be granted to him for the preservation of his interests.

Now, the farmer gets possession of his land; it becomes the centre of the hopes of himself and his family; his capital is more or less invested in it—some sunk in permanent improvements, and some in the stock, implements, and materials upon the surface of the farm. He hopes that it may turn out well for him; he gets up early, works hard and late—thousands of farmers with their hands, and thousands more with their heads. He gives his skill, industry, and perseverance to the soil; he is subject to the vicissitudes of seasons, against which no human foresight can altogether prevail, and he stands the chance and hazard of the markets. He has to contend also against the effect of the ignorance of landowning legislators, in which ignorance, unfortunately for him, there are no vicissitudes. The result is but a very moderate compensation for his expenditure and labour, and that compensation is in many cases altogether destroyed, and in very many more cases much lessened, by a system which does no good to any human being whatever, which exists solely for the amusement of the rich and powerful class at the expense of the interests of the tenantry and peasantry, and at a very great and enormous sacrifice to the whole community. There can be no success to the farmer under a system of game-preserving.

In moving for a committee in the House of Commons, two or three weeks ago, I brought forward cases which were laughed at in that assembly, and which I was told were not true. I did not bring before them my worst cases, for I was afraid that had I done so they would not have believed them; but, now we have obtained that committee, I will produce cases infinitely worse than the very worst of those I then cited. I shall call before them farmers, who will prove, on oath were it necessary—which it is not before a committee of the House of Commons—that they had sacrificed at least 500*l*. a-year for a succession of years. I can bring forward a tenant who can show that for a number of years he has expended 1,000*l*. annually in the purchase of artificial manure, and yet so completely was his farm ravaged by game that he found it useless to toil and sacrifice his capital and to farm in this manner, and he therefore discontinued this large purchase of artificial manure, and thus to a very great extent diminished the employment of labourers, and consequently lessened their chance of a fair remuneration in the parish in which that farm was situate.

By this system of game-preserving the landlords are made the greatest enemies of a class in whose real well-being they have the truest and greatest interest; for of all men in the world the landlord is the most interested in having his tenants contented and prosperous: not only because he lives among them, occasionally meets them, and hears from and about them, but because his own pocket interest is involved in it, if he could but see it in its true light; for where you find the tenants most prosperous, enlightened, and satisfied, there you find the soil best cultivated, the amount of its produce the greatest, poor-rates the lowest, and rent invariably highest, and paid with the greatest certainty and security. But the landlords take extraordinary means to make their farmers suspect them. I maintain that there is not, and never has been since the time when man first peopled this earth, if history may be relied on, any race of beings so unsuspecting and confiding as the tenantry of this country. During the last year the landlords have been asking the farmers—nay, in some cases threatening to compel them — to employ more labourers. A landed proprietor, a Member of the House of Commons, told me only a week ago, when discussing this very question, that he *forced* all his tenants to employ a certain amount of labour upon each of his farms. If a man preserves game, refuses security of tenure, talks all sorts of nonsense to his tenants if he ever gets them round him, and discourses about everything but their real grievances and the true way by which a man can become prosperous, and then, when he finds that some labourers are not employed, and that there are not sufficient means for the farmer whereby he can pay a high rent and a high rate of wages also—if he comes and forces them by covenants in their leases, that they shall employ an amount of labour over and above that which they would otherwise be willing to employ—I say that all this introduces a system which is most destructive to the interests of the landowners themselves, and most degrading and ruinous to the independence and interests of the tenantry. Capital must yield profit, or labour will not thrive. Men do not take farms merely for the pleasure of paying rents or employing labourers. I am a manufacturer in a considerable way of business, but I never professed to keep on my manufactory for the benefit of my work-people, or for the sake of clothing my customers. My object is, by the expenditure of capital and by giving labour to a business, to procure for myself and family a comfortable income, with a hope of realising some-

thing like a competency at a late period of my life. I appre-
hend that the tenant-farmer takes his farm with a precisely
similar view; and yet I am convinced that there is no class
of capitalists in this country who, for the last thirty years,
have obtained so small a return for the amount of capital and
labour they have employed as have the cultivators of the
soil.

If the landowners are interested in the well-being of their
tenantry, the tenantry are also interested in the prosperity of
the labourers. I have been in some of the northern parts of
this kingdom, where I have seen a very different condition
of the agricultural labourers from that which is to be noticed
in the southern counties: a state in which the labourers seem
to be interested in the success of the farmer and the prosperity
of the soil. The same condition might exist all over the
kingdom. Get rid of this infamous trifling with the interests
of the farmer; do not let the amusements of a small class be
put in competition not only with the prosperity, but with
the very existence of a much larger class. Let us, if possible
—I say ' *us,*' for, although I am not a farmer, I am deeply
interested, as every man must be, in the prosperity of agriculture—I say, let us get a system of farming, of agreements,
of management, from one end of it to the other, placed on
some intelligible, rational, business-like footing, and then
we shall have landowners respected because they are just,
and tenants independent because they are prosperous.

I have said that by this system the amusements of the rich
are put in the balance, and actually weigh down considerations of much greater importance—the prosperity of farmers,
the well-being of the labourers, and the true interests of the
community. Who does not know that from 1838 to 1842
we had, for nearly five years, harvests which were under
the average; that the consequence was great scarcity of provisions with very high prices? Some men may think that
this is a very desirable state of things. I will not argue for

a moment with any individual who maintains that scarcity can be beneficial either for individuals or nations. During that period we had an importation from abroad to a considerable extent, such as the law allowed; but we had at the same time millions of heads of game of every description— game which, in a country densely peopled like this, must soon come to be considered as vermin; and yet there they were throughout the whole of that period devouring probably as large a quantity of the produce of the soil of England as the whole amount that we imported from abroad.

The community, then, have a claim upon the landowners, if not upon the tenant-farmers. They have made themselves by law, though we are not here to discuss that law, and we should very likely greatly differ, and you might not agree with us, on that question; but they have made themselves the purveyors-general — that is, they supply the food, or profess to do so—for the 27,000,000 of people who inhabit Great Britain and Ireland. If they do thus think it desirable for State purposes that the population should be restricted to the food they are willing to supply them with, they are not to deem it unreasonable if some portion of the population, who sometimes do not get enough, should ask them why it is that while they maintain this system of restriction they also maintain a practice by which a large portion of the produce is devoured by game kept solely for their own amusement? I believe—indeed I know—that at the end of last session, when I gave notice of my intention to bring forward this question of the Game-laws in Parliament, it was thought to be rather an odd and somewhat impertinent meddling with a matter not precisely within my province.

I remember, when I read the notice that I should move the House upon the subject at the commencement of the present session, that there was a little titter, a little derisive laughter from the opposite side of the House. The land-owners were not well acquainted with the condition of the farmers, or the state of the country in which they live. I believe they do not know much about the mischief which game does to their tenants and themselves. I think I may venture to say that I know more about the state of the tenantry of this country than the majority of those to whom the tenants pay their rents. When this case was brought forward, unless my statements could have been altogether denied, it was utterly impossible for the House to refuse the committee. There were the cases of damage well authenticated—injury to the tenant, destruction to the allotments of the labourers, the insolence, depredations, and irritation caused by gamekeepers, the demoralization of the labourers, the thousands in gaol, the hundreds transported, and the scores murdered—the House of Commons would have been infinitely worse than its greatest calumniator or enemy has ever dared to brand it, had it refused the investigation which I demanded, founded upon the cases which I was then able to submit to it.

The committee which has been appointed, I believe, will be a tolerably fair one. I chose seven of its members myself, and the Government selected the remaining eight. I am bound to acknowledge that throughout the whole of this matter Ministers have behaved in the most honourable and handsome manner; that there was not the slightest objection to any one person proposed by me as a member of that committee; and I believe that, if the Government had dared to have done it, they would have put upon it from their side of the House men more favourable to the interests of the tenantry than those who were eventually placed there. We are about to meet next week, for the first time, for evidence. I have had an amount of correspondence which it is almost impossible to get through. I have written for the last fortnight or three weeks not unfrequently from thirty to fifty letters a-day, nearly all of which have been to persons connected, more or less, with the cultivation of the soil, and having reference to the question of game. I have here a large number of names of persons who will come up and give evidence before the committee. I do not think the other party will call many witnesses; for he would be a very bold man who would come up and say that game-preserving was advantageous, or not positively injurious, to agriculture. They will probably content themselves by cross-examining the witnesses that we shall bring up. But what we want is specific and accurate statements of damage, and opinions formed upon experience of the past, by men who have had the best possible opportunities of judging.

I do hope, when this evidence is brought out to the public, as it will be before or about the close of this session, that we shall then have this grievous abuse fairly exposed; and when that is once done we may be certain that there is no man out of Bedlam, no individual who does not wish to bring down upon himself the ridicule or, what is worse, the execration of the public, will ever say another word in favour of this grievance of preserving game, which has been practised for so many years past by a great portion of the landed proprietors in most parts of the kingdom. But what I want is, that farmers everywhere should seriously consider their position. There are farmers who yet believe that I am their enemy, inasmuch as I have been prominently connected with the agitation of another question. It may be that those farmers are right, and that I am wrong. I believe they are honest; I am quite sure that I am. Upon that question we must agree to differ until one or the other be converted. I trust that all discussion upon it may be carried on in a rational and kindly spirit, such as becomes men who wish only for the truth, and then I believe the time cannot be far distant when that which is true will be discovered, and not only discovered, but established.

But upon this question of game ninety-nine farmers out of every hundred would shake hands and agree with me entirely.

I had a letter from Wiltshire the other day, from a gentleman connected very closely with farmers, and whose family are all similarly situated. He says, ' Your name is a household word with the farmers in this district; and they literally swear by you!' If we agree upon this point we will work harmoniously; we will go together as far as we can, and do all the good we can in company. I wish the farmers in this county—and there are some who are well able to do it—would put themselves still more in communication with me upon this question. Let us have from every county where game-preserving has been carried to any serious extent, a body of witnesses who shall for ever settle the question, as respects the particular county. It is not sufficient that I should prove that game-preserving has done alarming mischief in Suffolk or in Wiltshire, for to prove that there is a local malady would not perhaps justify Parliament in applying that which may be termed a general remedy; but what I want is to bring out as much as possible the truth from every county where this nuisance has been oppressive. They should come up now before the committee, and that will be infinitely better than petitioning Parliament. Let them come up now and state before the committee what they know and what they have seen, and you may rely upon it, such is the intelligence and determination in the public mind of England, that when an abuse is fairly exposed and brought out to demonstration so that nobody can deny that it is an abuse, the time is near at hand when Parliament will be forced to abate it.

It will be a fine thing for this country when farmers lose a little bit of that overweening confidence they have in the farmers' friends. I would not to-night say a syllable against any landed proprietor—I believe in my conscience that many of their errors are errors of judgment and not of heart. I believe that they have been living amongst circumstances the most unfavourable to a discovery of what is their true interests; and their ignorance of their own affairs has made them most officious in offering advice, which was wholly valueless to their tenants when assembled at dinners and meetings of various kinds. What I want farmers to do henceforth is this, to take nothing upon credit. I would not take anything for granted. Do not believe anything that I say, or which my friend Mr. Cobden may utter; do not, for a moment, think it worth anything, until you have reasoned it out and examined the facts, and made yourselves sure. But apply the same rule to the landowners. I want you to apply it to all. Candidates come before you at the hustings, and they pledge themselves to all sorts of impossible things. It is notorious that half the things which men say they will do when they go to Parliament, that assembly has no more power to perform than it has to prevent the sun rising to-morrow. These men come, and they promise a variety of impossible things; they go to Parliament and cannot perform them, and then those who sent them there are disappointed, and fancy they are betrayed.

If the tenantry of this country, powerful as they are now in numbers on the county registers, would look a little to their own rank, and not quite so much to another rank and order, they would find more real attention to their true interests on behalf of county representatives than they do at present. I bought the *Times* newspaper at the station as I was coming down, and I find a paragraph in it which may be worth reading. It is extracted from the *Western Times*, a Devonshire paper. It states—

'A requisition is actually determined on, to invite three eminent renting farmers to stand as candidates for the next Parliamentary election. The farmers of Devon are determined to have men who pay rent to look after their interests in the House of Commons. We do not anticipate much immediate success from such a step, but it will teach the aristocracy a lesson, and open the eyes of the tenant-farmers to their power, if they choose to act in concert.'

How would it be if a tenant-farmer were to put up for some county? In my neighbourhood there used to be a little jealousy about manufacturers. They had a notion that nobody should go to Parliament but a man who had no other occupatiou to fill up his time, and who had moreover a great deal of money to bear the expense of a life in London, which was supposed to be enormous. But now they have found out their mistake, and they take a man here and another there, who is not a lord, and whose ancestors we do not know exactly what they were, but a man who has common sense and common honesty—which two things I suppose are called ' common' for the very reason that they are so rarely to be met with.

We have heard frequently—I have read repeatedly, at the proceedings of agricultural meetings of various kinds—that the toast has been proposed of ' agriculture and commerce' by men who despise commerce but yet sell game—they have had the audacity to toast commerce and agriculture together. There is and ought ever to be a real union between these two great branches, by which nations subsist, but heretofore it has been only nominal, and never real : legislation has prevented its being so, for legislation has been foolish in commerce as it has been in agriculture. Speeches made at meetings such as I have referred to have also had the effect of making this union unreal. I hope that to-night is the beginning of a new era. No man here will believe for a moment that I can have personally the smallest interest in injuring any individual in this country who is the possessor or the cultivator of a single acre of its soil. There never can be prosperity in any country while all the numerous cultivators of the soil are permanently depressed and injured ; there can be no doubt that under all circumstances the vast bulk of the subsistence of our people must be derived from our own soil, and from the direct labour, as cultivators, of a vast portion of our own countrymen.

There can be no doubt whatever that any law passed in Parliament for any particular benefit of commerce, unless it be a just law,—and being just, which can be permanent,—

must be injurious to the prosperity of agriculture itself. In
the county from which I come, Lancashire, the most prominent in the world for manufactures and commerce, there
is at this time a condition of prosperity, when contrasted
with what we saw three years ago, so remarkable that it
appears to be nothing less than a miracle. I say it is that
miracle which we see every day, and yet are unobservant of
it: the miracle that the sun shines, and that the showers
fall in due season, the earth is prolific, and the great and
bountiful Benefactor of our species gives abundance to the
people; and that abundance having come for two or three
years in succession, the prostrate millions of working-men who
were idle and pauperised are now standing erect, and are
employed, and well paid, and independent, as much so as
I have ever seen them at any former period. Whilst I see
that with this abundance there is that prosperity in the most
numerous classes of the people, I cannot for a moment suppose
that the prosperity of a nation can in any degree depend
upon the foolish fallacies which ignorant men of all parties
have spread in connection with these subjects.

But with reference to this game movement I must ask
this meeting to bear in mind that when a man connected
with the district which I come from—having no claim by
long standing in the House of Commons, nor by lengthened
service anywhere—when he comes forward upon a question
like this, you must be certain that to carry it to a successful
issue it needs far more than my own individual efforts: it
requires the assistance of intelligent, independent, and experienced men in all parts of the country. There are some
in this meeting who within the next month will give evidence
on your behalf before the Game Committee, and I trust that
the names I already have down here will be increased before
that time, so that—at least—half a dozen good witnesses may
go from this district, I mean from this particular county. So
far with respect to this Game Committee.

There is one more topic to which I would call your attention.
An attempt was made only a fortnight ago to procure a
committee to inquire into other complaints of the agricultural
portion of the community; that committee was refused; but
from the altered tone which I have seen in the House, even
within the very short time that I have been a Member of
it, I am persuaded that the time is hastening on when all
parties in that House—the highest Protectionist and the
most active and prominent Free-trader, with all that are
between those points—will be anxious to come to a real and
honest investigation into the circumstances which do affect
the prosperity of the cultivators of the soil.   When once
there comes that spirit over the minds of men,—a spirit which
repudiates party—which seeks not to gain advantage here
by the spoliation of somebody there—but a spirit which
wishes the truth to be fully discovered and established,—
when once that spirit prevails upon both sides of the House,
as I believe it will before long with reference to some of these
matters, then the farmers of this country, and every class,
may look upon that day as the dawning of a better era,
when the cultivators of the soil, the honourable, ancient,
numerous, and most necessary of all classes of the community,
shall no longer be made the shuttlecock of political parties,
but be treated as rational men, and their interests considered
in a rational manner.

I will say, in conclusion, that I am delighted with this
meeting. I have met now, for two years past, with large
bodies of farmers in different parts of the country; many
have been friendly and others hostile to my views; I have
always gone from them with this conviction, that wherever
they have erred, as I believe they have often done, it has
been from mistaking their way, and because either they have
followed blind leaders, or are themselves unsuspectingly blind.
But I come more and more to this conviction, that there is
no class of men in this country who, if they know what is

right, and have the power to follow their convictions, will make a more unanimous and determined effort for the attainment of that right than will the tenant-farmers of this kingdom.   When I see what my friend Mr. Horncastle has done, and the manner in which you have received his services, and expressed your approbation of his conduct, I cannot but think that, as there are thousands who can applaud his conduct, there must be great numbers ready to imitate it.

THE DISTRIBUTION OF LAND.

BIRMINGHAM, JANUARY 26, 1864.

[In November, 1863, Mr. Cobden and Mr. Bright spoke at a meeting at
Rochdale, on the subject of the English laws affecting Land and Labourers.
These speeches were grossly misrepresented by the *Times* newspaper,
and Mr. Cobden charged Mr. Delane, the Editor of that Journal, with
intentional and scandalous misrepresentation in his comments upon them.
The correspondence between the Statesman and the Editor was instructive,
and created much interest at the time. The following speech was delivered
as a comment on the conduct of Mr. Delane, and as a defence of the opinions
expressed at the meeting at Rochdale.]

ALTHOUGH I have often stood before you on this platform,
yet I can assure you that on no former occasion have I felt
it necessary so much to ask your forbearance and your silent
attention as on this occasion. I had no hope a week ago
that I should be able to attend here to-night, and to address
this large audience, but being here in the performance of my
duty as one of your representatives, I shall endeavour to lay
before you the thoughts which are uppermost in my mind,
and which bear upon the questions in which we are all deeply
interested.

There are two subjects which have been treated upon by
my hon. Colleague, about which I would say a few words
before I come to that which I had intended to speak about.

The first is the question which now keeps Europe in suspense, which may end in a war, or may end in some diplomatic accommodation of a long-standing quarrel. I will not go into the history of the Danish and German dispute. I have received since I came here a long and most able letter from a German Professor resident in this country on behalf of the German view of that question—probably he is now within the sound of my voice. I can only tell him, in telling you, that I agree entirely, and from my heart, with every word that my hon. Colleague spoke upon that question; and I will say further, that if there be a Government possible in our day that will plunge this country into war under the pretence of maintaining the balance of power in Europe and sustaining any kingdom there, be it little or great, I say that Government not only is not worthy of the confidence of the people of England, but deserves our execration and abhorrence.

There is one other question to which my hon. Colleague has devoted a considerable portion of his speech. He said, and I believe it, that a year ago he felt it a painful thing to stand here and to avow opinions contrary to those of many of his friends, and contrary to those which I had avowed before. I told you then how painful a thing it was for me to stand up and to controvert on this platform any of the statements which he had made. I came here to-night intending to say no single word as to the question between North and South in the United States. My opinion is that the unanimous judgment of the people of England, so far as that is ever shown upon any public question, is in favour of the course which her Majesty's Government have publicly declared it to be their intention to pursue. I believe that my hon. Friend is mistaken in the view he takes of the meaning of the result of what he calls a recognition of the South. I have seen it stated by authority, North as well as South, and by authority which I may term English, and

by authority from France, that in the present condition of
that quarrel, recognition, by all the usages of nations, must
necessarily lead to something more. And, therefore, although
there were no question of slavery, even though it were simply
a political revolt, and though there were no special moral
question connected with it, I believe, looking to the past
usage of this country with regard to the rebellion of the
Greeks against Turkey, and with regard to the revolt of
the colonies of South America against Spain, that it can be
demonstrated that this case affords no support whatever to
the argument that we are permitted now to recognise the
South, and that if such recognition did take place now, it
could only exasperate still more the terrible strife which exists
on the North American continent, and would spread that
strife even to Europe itself.

I am myself of opinion, as I have been from the first,
that the people of America—so numerous, so powerful, so
instructed, so capable in every way—will settle the difficulties of that continent without asking the old countries
of Europe to take any share in them. I believe that in
the providence of the Supreme, the slaveholder—untaught,
unteachable by fact or argument, or Christian precept—
has been permitted to commit—I will not call it the
crime—but the act of suicide. Whether President Lincoln
be in favour of abolition; whether the Northerners are
unanimous against slavery; whatever may be said or
thought with regard to the transactions on that continent,
he must be deaf and blind—and worse than deaf and blind—
who does not perceive that, through the instrumentality of
this strife, that most odious and most indescribable offence
against man and against heaven—the slavery of man, the
bondage of four millions of our fellow-creatures—is coming to
a certain and rapid end.

Sir, I will say of this question that I look forward to the
time when I shall stand on this platform with my honourable

Colleague, and when he will join with me—for he is honest enough and frank enough to do that—when he will join with me in rejoicing that there does not breathe a slave on the North American Continent, and that the Union has been completely restored. And not only so, but he will rejoice that England did not in the remotest manner, by a word or a breath, or the raising of a finger, or the setting of a type, do one single thing to promote the atrocious object of the leaders of this accursed insurrection.

Now, Sir, I must ask you to listen to me for a little on matters less exciting—and our friends down below here who are enduring a sort of purgatory,—I must ask them to be as compassionate to me as they can, and I will commiserate them as much as possible. About two months ago, on the twenty-fourth of November, I had the opportunity of making a speech in the town of Rochdale, where I live. The meeting was, I suppose, nearly as large as this. It was called for the purpose of affording an opportunity to our distinguished representative, Mr. Cobden, to address his constituents. There are very few meetings of that kind at Rochdale to which I am not invited, and in which I am not expected to take part. On that occasion I took the opportunity of objecting to those persons who think that everything is done in this country that needs to be done—that everybody is so happy that politics are at an end. I spoke particularly of the question of the million or million and a-half of our labouring population who are employed in cultivating the soil. I need not tell you that from that time to this there has been rather a lively discussion in the newspapers about what was said at that meeting.

I have had no opportunity of speaking since, and I have not thought it necessary to write anything on the matter, but if you will give me your attention for a short time I should like to say a little about it. What I said at that meeting on the subject of the land was this :—

' I should say, if we were fairly represented, that feudalism, with regard to the land of England, would perish, and that the agricultural labourer throughout the United Kingdom would be redeemed from that poverty and serfdom which, up to this time, have been his lot. It would take a night, it would take a long speech, to go into the question of the condition of that unfortunate class ; but with laws such as we have, which are intended to bring vast tracks of land into the possession of one man, that one man may exercise great political power, that system is a curse to the country, and dooms the agricultural labourer, I say, to perpetual poverty and degradation.'

There were comments on that speech, but I will only refer to the comments of one paper, the *Times*. The *Times*, in an article upon foreign politics, and speaking of small States in Europe who may have something to gain by change, said that they might look upon these changes with something of that satisfaction with which the poor might regard Mr. Bright's proposition for the division among them of the lands of the rich. Well, you know that a correspondence took place almost immediately, and in consequence of that passage, between my friend Mr. Cobden and Mr. John Delane, the editor of the *Times*. Now, this is what the *Times* had said, that I am now about to read, two days after the speech :—

' This language'—

that is the language of Mr. Cobden, and yet my language, I am free to say, was more strong upon the general question, I think, than Mr. Cobden's—

' so often repeated and so often calculated to excite discontent among the poor and half-informed, has really only one intelligible meaning. " Reduce the electoral franchise ; for when you have done so you will obtain an assembly which will seize on the estates of proprietors of land and divide them gratuitously among the poor." '

Well, Sir, when this notable newspaper editor was brought to book, what did he say ? On the same day he wrote a letter to Mr. Cobden, the 18th December, and also published an article in his newspaper. In his letter he says : ' You seem to assume that I charged you with proposing that this division should be accomplished by violence.' Does anybody believe that any one without violence can seize upon the lands of the rich, and distribute them gratuitously, that is, for nothing, amongst the poor? On the same day, in an article, he made this statement :—

'Nobody was likely to charge those two gentlemen with recommending "agrarian" outrages, for their interest is as much bound up with social order, the rights of property, and the Queen's peace as that of the whole peerage.'

Which is true; but why did not he find that out before he had made that charge? He says,—

'Nobody who read the single line which Mr. Cobden has seized for a peg to hang his defence upon could imagine for a moment that it pointed to violence.'

This is the gentleman who professes to counsel and lead the nation. Now, suppose he had charged Adam Smith, the great apostle of political economy, with approving piracy, or if he had charged John Wesley with being an encourager of drunkenness and profanity, would it have been more extraordinary than that he should charge Mr. Cobden and myself with instigating agrarian outrages and the seizure of the estates of those who now hold them, for the purpose of dividing them among the people, of course taking nothing from the people for them, and therefore giving nothing to the rich for them? If there be two men in England, I will undertake to say, who have more conscientiously and more faithfully preached for twenty-five years the doctrines of absolute honesty with regard to political questions in England, those two men are Mr. Cobden and myself. But Mr. Cobden came forward to assail Mr. Delane when he made this charge against me. He found a man in a mask endeavouring to stab me in the back,—for he had not seen that the same man had been, in a previous article, also stabbing him,—and he came forward, and dragged his mask from him, and he showed him to the gaze of the whole nation and of the world. And at last, after denial and equivocation of every kind, this unmasked editor of this great journal was obliged to retire from the personal part of this controversy, and to skulk back into his anonymous hiding-place, which suits him better.

I will tell you how it was. Neither Mr. Cobden nor I have ever said anything to show that we thought it desirable to abolish by force of law anonymous writing in our newspapers; but Mr. Cobden laments, as I do, and as you all do, that the anonymous system is inevitably a shelter for a man who has no sense of honour. I recollect a description which I am sure will suit Mr. Delane admirably. It was published some time ago in the city of New York, and described a notorious politician there who, if I am not mistaken, has been at the elbow of the New York correspondent of the *Times* for the last twelve months—with what happy success to the forecast and the honesty of that paper we all know. It was said of him that 'he was a just man and a righteous man, and that he walked uprightly *before the world*, but when he was *not* before the world his walk was slantindicular.' Sir, the *Times* newspaper, notwithstanding all this, is a power in this country, and a power in Europe. No man laments more than I do that so much power should be associated with what I will call a godless intellect and a practical atheism. No one laments more than I do that a paper which was once great in its independence has become now—what shall I say? —domesticated, for the editor of the *Times* is now domesticated in the houses of Cabinet Ministers and members of high families in London. He has learned now,—in this day, when that paper might have been more useful than ever,—to fetch and carry for Cambridge House. And, Sir, for aught I know, looking at what is said in the clubs in London about the dispensation of patronage to men who have been writers for that journal, I am not sure, unless what I say now may make it difficult, that some day or other some proprietor (or chief proprietor) of that paper may not find himself placed in the House of Peers as compensation for the services offered to the present Prime Minister of England.

But now, passing from that subject, you will remember that my argument at Rochdale was that the agricultural

labouring population of this country were in a deplorable
condition, and that I believed that to a large extent it was
to be attributed to the unsound and unjust laws which regu-
late the possession and distribution of land.   Now you know,
of course, living in Birmingham, as well as we know, that,
contrary to what exists in some countries, we have three great
classes connected with land.   We have the landowner first,
who is always becoming richer—that is if he does not spend
too much.   His land is always becoming more valuable.   You
find him living in a better house, with more gorgeous fittings,
with a more splendid equipage, and following more expensive
amusements.   [A Voice : 'I thought the cotton lords did that.']
No doubt.   If you pursue it further, you find the tenant-
farmers occupying larger farms, and in connection with the
tenant-farmers there is a much greater apparent wealth.   But
if you come to the labourers, who cultivate the land, by whose
toil and whose sweat your tables are furnished with bread and
with beef, and with many other things that they produce, you
find these labourers at this moment, I believe, at a comparatively greater distance from the landlord, and from the tenant
probably, than they were at any former period.   [' No, no.']
There is a gentleman present who differs from me; I am
glad he is in the meeting.

   I will ask you whether, during past years, you have read
any letters in the *Times* newspaper signed by the initials
'S. G. O.'   These letters were written by a gentleman of rare
intelligence and of great benevolence.   His descriptions I
believe may be entirely relied upon.   If any of you have
read some letters written three or four months ago from
parts of Buckinghamshire and published in the *Star* newspaper, with regard to the condition of that population,—
you will know what it is that I mean,—but if you are unwilling to take their evidence, let us take the evidence of
a witness that nobody here will call in question, and that
is the evidence of the *Saturday Review*.   On the 26th of

September last there was an article in that journal on 'Agricultural Labourers,' in which it said—and I beg you to listen to it, for, in point of fact, it is the great part of my speech. The extract from the article reads thus :—

'When the dull season of the year comes round [it is between October and the meeting of Parliament] all sorts of odd persons and things have their share of public attention, and even agricultural labourers are pitied and discussed. At other times they live on with no one much to care for them—the farmer looking on them as his natural enemies, the parson's kindly soul getting weary of his long combat with their helpless stolid ignorance, and the squire not knowing what he can do for them further than build two or three Elizabethan cottages, covered with honeysuckle, close to his gates.'

And then the writer of the article proceeds to say that when foreigners come here and read of the condition of agricultural labourers they must be much shocked, for he adds:—

'We are moved to a languid shame and sadness by thinking how true the picture is, and what *wretched, uncared-for, untaught brutes* the people are who raise the crops on which we live.'

And then :—

'There is a wailing over the dirt and vice and misery that must prevail in houses where seven or eight persons, of both sexes and all ages, are penned up together for the night in the one rickety, foul, vermin-haunted bedroom. The picture of agricultural life unrolls itself before us as it is painted by those who know it best. We see the dull clouded mind, the bovine gaze, the brutality and recklessness, the simple audacity of vice, the confused hatred of his betters,. which mark the English peasant, unless some happy fortune has saved him from the general lot, and persuaded him that life " has something besides beer that the poor man may have and may relish."'

He then goes on to declare that ' the old feudalism'—feudalism is precisely the thing I mentioned—

'The old feudalism of England—the state of things when there yet were serfs, and when the lords of the soil were almost a different order of beings— still colours the relations of the rich and the poor.'

And perhaps you would like to know what he says an agricultural labourer should be. The writer states :—

'It is looked on as the duty and place of the poor man to stay in his native village for ever ; to work hard for ten or twelve shillings a-week, and bring up a large family respectably on the money ; to touch his hat to the gentry, to go to church regularly, and to make out as much as he can of the service ; to hate the public-house, and feel no longing for company and a bright fire or gossip, and to be guided towards heaven by the curate and the young ladies. This is the poor man which modern feudalism actually produces, and who may be seen by any one who stands opposite the door of the village beershop on a Saturday evening.'

Now this is the testimony of the *Saturday Review*, and what do you think the writer of the article from which I have just quoted proposes?—he proposes that instead of a man receiving parochial relief from the parish, he shall be allowed to receive it from that larger area, namely, from the Union ; and that a law which he says is hardly ever put in practice should be repealed, by which a working-man breaking a contract to work is treated as a felon. I do not believe those remedies would be sufficient for the terrible malady which he has described in such powerful language. May I ask you this question? Is it the unchangeable law of Heaven that the agricultural population of this country shall continue in that condition? Writers tell you, that your agriculture is far better than any other agriculture, that you produce a larger quantity of wheat or any other produce over a given surface. We know that there is the greatest market in the world close at their doors, and the means of conveyance to every part of the kingdom. Then I want to know why it is that the labouring population upon the farms of this country are in the condition I have just described. Is it so in the most civilized parts of Europe; is it so in the United States of America? No. I could give you, if it were not that reading evidence from books is not suited to a speech, and to a great meeting like this—I could read you evidence from every kind of man—from the highest in rank—from the most cultivated in mind—from the most extensively known in public affairs—I could prove to you, beyond all doubt, that in all these countries in Europe where the land is divided and the people have a chance of having some of it—those in fact who are industrious and frugal—that the condition of the agricultural and peasant population is infinitely superior to anything that is to be seen in Great Britain and Ireland.

Well, then, you may ask me very reasonably,—what is the difference between the laws of these countries and the laws of ours, and what changes do you propose? I will tell you in as few words as I can. In the greatest portion of the Continent of Europe—in France, in Germany, in Belgium, in Holland and in Norway, and in point of fact it is likely to become general throughout Europe, the law follows what is believed to be the natural law of affection and justice between parent and children. The large portion of the property of the parent must be by will (or if not by will the law will so order it) divided amongst the children; not land alone, but all the property of the parent, according to the number of his children. And you are to be frightened by this law of bequests as if it were something very dreadful. It only follows the rule which the majority of your merchants, your manufacturers, and of all the people in the world have followed in these later days, of treating their children with equal affection and with equal justice. On going to the United States, you find a very different state of the law. There a man may leave his property as he likes amongst his children, because the United States' law believes that natural affection and justice are of themselves a sufficient law in the majority of cases, and therefore that it is not necessary to enforce these moral duties by any statute. But if a man dies without leaving a will, the law of the United States takes his property, and looking upon his children with equal affection and equal justice, makes that distribution which it believes the just and living parent would have made.

But if you come to this country what do you find? You find this, that with regard to all kinds of property, except what is called real property, (meaning the land of the country and the houses upon it,) the law does exactly the same thing. It divides it equally amongst the children, because it knows that this is what the parent should have done, and would have done, if he had been a just parent. But when it comes to the question of the land, our law is contrary to the European law which makes a statute according to natural justice, contrary to the United States' law, which, when there is no will, makes a distribution also in accordance with natural justice. Thus our law steps in and does that which natural justice would forbid. Now I should like to know if anybody is prepared to deny this. Personalty, that is, property which is not land, is divided equally; the property which is land is not divided equally, but is given to the eldest son in one lump. Now, tell me whether the principle which the law of Europe for the most part wishes to enforce, that which the law of America enforces when there is no will, that which we enforce when land is not in question—whether that is not a more just law, does not approve itself more to the hearts of men, and before the eye of Heaven, than a law by which we send beggars into the world,—it may be half-a-dozen children,—that we may make one rich in the possession of unnecessary abundance?

What are the reasons—these things are not done without reasons—ask anybody what are the reasons, and you are told, perhaps, that they are high political reasons. These high political reasons are often very curious. In some countries—in Turkey, for example—it has been the custom for a long time, and is hardly abandoned yet, that the wielder of the sceptre should destroy his younger brothers, lest they should become competitors with him for the throne. What would you think if the law of this country doomed all the younger children to a want of freedom and to a total want of education,—if it conferred all the freedom and all the education on the eldest sons, and left the others to go to the streets? It would be as reasonable to cut off all the younger boys and girls from all education and all freedom, as it is to cut them off from their share of their father's property. But you will find to-morrow morning, in all probability, that the editor in this town,—who does not generally, as I have noticed, serve you up very strong meat,—will say, if he comments on this part of my speech, what use would it be to make a law that the property shall be divided in cases where there is no will, when men die so seldom without making a will, and will argue that the difference will be very small. I will tell you what difference it would make. It would take the tremendous sanction of the law from the side of evil, and put it on the side of good.

There is a case—it is the only one which occurs to me—bearing upon this point. About the time when the American colonies were severed from this country, the laws of primogeniture and entail were enforced in the State of Virginia in the most rigid manner. Mr. Jefferson, who was afterwards President of the Republic, considered it one of the greatest acts of his life that he prevailed upon the Legislature of Virginia to abolish these laws. You will find this statement in his Life,—'The class which thus provided for the perpetuation of its wealth also monopolized the civil honours of the colony.' You will be able to judge whether that is not very much the case in this country. Amongst the reasons which he gave for abolishing the law of entails was that he wished ' to make an opening for the aristocracy of virtue and talent, which nature has wisely provided for the direction of the interests of society, and scattered with equal hand throughout all its conditions.' And when he came to the abolition of the law and custom of primogeniture, that is, by the enactment of a law that property should be equally divided whenever the parents did not leave a will, it is said by his biographer that these laws—

'Have not merely altered the distribution of that part of the landed property which is transmitted to surviving relatives by the silent operation of law, but they have also operated on public opinion so as to influence the testamentary disposition of it by the proprietors, without which last effect the purpose of the Legislature might have been readily defeated.　The cases are now very rare in which a parent makes, by his will, a much more unequal distribution of his property among his children than the law itself would make.　It is thus that laws, themselves the creatures of public opinion, often powerfully re-act on it.'

And he goes on to show that the effect of the distribution was to lessen the chances of a man being so enormously rich, and to give an opportunity to a large number to become moderately so.　He said further, that if there were fewer coaches and six in the State of Virginia, there were twenty times as many carriages and pairs.

I have thus briefly touched upon the question of primogeniture.　The question of entails is much of the same kind, and with regard to its effect upon the public I shall only say a sentence or two.　The object of entailing land is to keep great estates together, and to keep them in one family.　Upon this system land in this country is sometimes tied up for fifty, or eighty, or a hundred years, no person having power to sell it, however advantageous it might be to the proprietors that the land should be sold.　And then, if you come to the question of the difficulties of transfer, I might ask gentlemen near me connected with the law—and they will tell you that it always takes months, and it sometimes takes years, to prove a title; and the cost of this in money comes to no inconsiderable portion of the purchase money of the property.

Now, may I ask you what is the political reason for which this state of things is maintained?　It is for the very reason for which this system was established eight hundred years ago—that there may be in this country a handful of persons, three or four times as many as there are here— twice as many perhaps—who are the owners of nearly all the land, in whose hand is concentrated nearly all the power, by whom the Government of the country is mainly conducted, and amongst whom the patronage of the Government is mainly distributed.　In every country in the world, as far as I know, the possessors of land are the possessors of power. In France, at this moment, we all know perfectly well that, notwithstanding there may be a revolution now and then in the streets of Paris, if you come to the question of voting, the majority of the voting population at this moment are found in the number of the proprietors of the land. Ten or twelve years ago it was their suffrages which conferred the supreme power on the present Emperor of the French. If you go across the Atlantic, and study the political system of the United States, where almost all the farmers are owners of their farms, you will find that they are the holders of political power. The city of New York may denounce the policy of the Government at Washington; but it is the land-owning farmers—the cultivators of the great States in the interior of the country—who are the real holders of political power, and by whose will alone the President of the United States is able to carry on the great matters which belong to his exalted station. It is the same in the Southern States, for the great planting population—the owners of immense plantations—are the life and soul of Southern politics. And if you come to our own country— to your own county, Warwickshire, or any county you choose to walk into—you will find that two or three great landowners can sit down together and determine who shall or who shall not go to Parliament, as the pretended representative of the population in that county.

I believe that with these vast properties, which are of no real advantage to those who hold them—for 100,000*l.* a-year, or 200,000*l.* a-year, can give no man greater real happiness than 10,000*l.* or 5,000*l.* a-year,—I say these great properties, with great political power, form what we call our great territorial system—a system which prevails to an extent in this country which is probably unknown in any other, but which leaves the cultivator of the soil ignorant, and hopeless, and dependent, and degraded. There is, as you know, a great tendency to increase the size of farms throughout the country, a practice which makes it still more difficult for the labourer ever to become a tenant, or to rise from the condition in which he is. You see a ladder—the social ladder—upon which you wish to see the poor, and depressed, and unfortunate nine-or-ten-shillings-a-week-labourer ascend gradually. You would rejoice to see him get up a few steps and become a farmer, although but in a small way; or the owner of a small piece of land. But you find that for six or eight, or ten feet up the ladder, the steps are broken out; and, in his low position, he has not a chance of beginning the ascent. Let there be steps in the shape of small farms and small estates, and land freely bought and sold, and then he will have something to hope for, something to save even his small earnings for, that he may be enabled to purchase or to occupy one of these small farms and get away from the humble and melancholy position in which he is now, to one which I wish, from my soul, every labourer in this country could find himself placed in.

Now, Sir, for fear that the Man in the Mask—he has got his mask on again for a time—for fear that the Man in the Mask should misrepresent me to-morrow, let me tell you that I am not against great estates, or great farms, or great factories, but I have a very great liking for small estates, small farms, and small factories. In this country, where there is such a rapid creation of wealth, there is always a great power urging to the accumulation of land. I know the case of a nobleman now, in a southern county, from report, who is stated to have an income of 120,000*l.* a-year; and being a wise man, as regards his expenditure compared with his income, he only spends—though it is a mystery to me how he spends it—he only spends 40,000*l.* a-year, and he has 80,000*l.* a-year left. What does he do with this? He buys up every farm, every estate, big or little, all over the district, and the consequence is that his immense estate is constantly becoming larger. I do not blame him for that. I applaud him so far, that he is a man who does not waste his property, and I have heard that among those with whom he lives he is a man of excellent character. There are persons who come from Manchester, from Leeds, and there are some in Birmingham who are able to purchase large estates. There is a tendency to this in this country, where we have so much manufacturing and commercial industry, and wealth to buy estates with. In addition to this, their possession gives great social position and great political influence. I am not complaining of this. It is a natural, and advantageous, and healthy thing; for it is desirable that farmers should have the stimulus of ambition to have a larger farm, and that the men who have an estate should have an ambition —if they can entertain it honestly—to have a larger estate. The stimulus by which men strive at something honourable is useful to the country; but at the same time, to add to this the force of a most intricate and complicated system of law, to give to this force greater force, is, in my opinion, contrary to all the true interests of England; and I believe if it goes on for another half-century, as it has for the last half-century, it will cause great discontent and great embarrassment within this now peaceful kingdom.

What I propose is this—it is nothing that I have not stated before—it is the most moderate thing that can be proposed. If you want to see an admirable description of what I think it would be wise to do, you will find it in a paper which certainly is not very Radical—is rather, in my opinion, though conducted with considerable ability, conceited in some of its criticisms upon us—I mean the *Spectator*. There was an article on Saturday last in this paper on the subject of land laws in New York, and although there are only three or four lines about New York in the article, that does not matter, for it is admirably written. In one place it reads as follows:—'No doubt Mr. Bright would consider this not sufficient change for the purposes he wishes.' He is quite mistaken. The changes which he proposes are more extensive than any changes I have ever proposed, either in public or in private. What are these changes? First of all, that the law shall declare that when any person owning property dies without making a distribution of it by will, the law shall distribute it upon the same principle that it now adopts when it divides—I am now speaking of landed property—any other kind of property. For example: Suppose a man has got money in the bank—I wish everybody had—suppose he has machinery in his mill, merchandise in his warehouse, ships upon the ocean, or that he has shares, or the parchments for them in his safe — if he dies, the Government by the law, or rather the law itself, makes a distribution of all that property amongst all his children, in accordance with the great universal law of natural parental affection and justice. Then, I say, let that principle be extended to all the property which a man may die possessed of; and, so far as that goes, I want no further change. Then, with regard to the question of entails, I would say this: the *Spectator* proposes that a man, by entailing his property— so far as I can understand—shall only prevent himself and his next heir from disposing of it—that there shall be, in point of fact, only two persons in the entail. Now, what I propose is, that a man may leave his property to as many persons as he likes, to A, B, C, D, and E and F, and so on all through the alphabet, if they are all alive at the time he makes his will, and he can put all their names into it. But at present he can leave it to these people, and to a child then unborn, and who shall not be born, it may be, till twenty years after he has made his will. I would cut that off. I contend that it should be left to persons who are in existence, and whose names are in the will, and you will find that as A, B, and C died it would finally come into the hands of a man who would have the absolute disposal of it, and who could keep, or sell, or give, or waste it as he pleased.

And. I believe it will be much better for the public when that freedom of transfer is given to the possessors of land which is given to the possessors of every other kind of property. If I were to sit down for ten minutes and a lawyer were to take my place, he could tell you what a trouble our law is; and—although I am sorry that some of them think that they make a good thing out of it—what a curse it is to a man who buys landed property or who sells it. Everything which I am proposing is carried out, I believe, through most of the States in the American Union, and to a greater extent on the Continent of Europe, and is being adopted in the Australian colonies. It is the most curious thing in the world that whenever an Englishman leaves these shores— whether it is the effect of the salt air, or of sea-sickness, or the result of that prolonged meditation which a voyage of some weeks' duration invites, I do not know—but whenever an Englishman leaves these shores, the effect is to peel off, not the rags of his body, but the verminous rags from his intellect and soul. He leaves behind him in England all the stupidity which some of us cherish, and he lands in Australia with his vision so clear, that he can see things in a common-sense manner.

I want to ask you as reasonable men, as men of business —there is not a man who cannot understand this question moderately well—is this spoliation? Is this agrarian outrage? Is this stimulating the working-man and the agricultural labourer to—what shall I say?—to, it may be, incendiarism or to something worse? It is nothing of the kind; it is but laying before them those just principles of law and practice which are admitted to be just in every other country in the world than this, and which we admit to be just with regard to everything else, except the single article of land.

We are charged with all sorts of dreadful things by that gentleman in the Mask. On the 27th of November he wrote this of Mr. Cobden. He said :—

'He [Mr. Cobden] stoops down and picks up a weapon which has never yet been used but for anarchy and revolution. Is it not in fact to tell the labourer and the workman to look over the fence of the neighbouring proprietor, and learn to think that they have a natural right to a slice of the soil ?'

Surely, if they are industrious and frugal, and can save the means to purchase, and there be anybody who would wish to sell, and the law steps in and makes it difficult to sell and to buy, then, I say, that labourer has a right to look over the hedge, and to feel that the law deals a grievous injustice to him.

And it is this gentleman in the Mask that frightens the landed proprietors. I met the other day with a gentleman connected with one of the largest properties in the kingdom. He said to me,—and he is a very liberal and thoughtful man,—he said to me, 'You have no idea of the terror which your speeches create amongst landed gentlemen.' Now, I never frighten any of my neighbours. I do not know why I should be so alarming to those gentlemen who live in their great houses and castles. But the fact is the landed gentlemen are not a wise class. There are brilliant exceptions. There are men amongst them, many of whom cannot be surpassed by any of their own class, or of any other class in the world. But as a class, and, perhaps, one might say it of nearly every class—I believe it is true of that to which I belong in Lancashire— they are not a wise class. They know something of agriculture—county Members have to get it up for agricultural dinners—and they know something of horses—and they know all that can be known on the subject of game. But on the principles of law and of government, speaking of them as a whole, and judging of them by their past course, they are dark as night itself. Would you believe it—young men here do not recollect it—that the landed proprietors could never find out, till Mr. Cobden and a few others told them, that the Corn-law was a great injury to them? They did not know that it actually lowered the value of their land, and diminished the security of their rents, and that it loaded them with an inconceivable amount of public odium; whilst, at the same time, it beggared hundreds and thousands of the people, and it menaced this nation with rebellion.

Mr. Cobden and I, and others who acted with us, but we chiefly, because perhaps we were the most prominent, were slandered then by the gentleman in the Mask, just as we have been now. The *Times* was as foul-mouthed upon us twenty years ago as it is at this moment. It said that we went about the country setting class against class. It said that our views led to the confiscation of landed property. It said everything that was spiteful and untrue, as it says now. And yet, is there any man in this country who will not admit that property is more secure in consequence of the abolition of that law, which landowners believed to be the anchor of their safety, and that animosities between class and class have been allayed? And who shall tell how much it is owing to this reform that our Queen at this moment wields an unchallenged sceptre over a tranquil realm? A landowner in the House of Commons, an old Member of the House, a representative of a south-western county, a man of excellent character, for whom I have always had the greatest respect, even when he was most in the wrong,—he told me not long ago, speaking about the Corn-law, that they did not then know the good we were doing to his class. I smiled and said to him, 'If you would only have faith I could tell you one or two other things that would do you just as much good if you would let us try them.' But he had no faith.

Now, I will just say to the landowners that I was never more their friend than when discussing this question which I am occupied with to-night, without the least animosity to them, and with a belief as firm as I ever had on the question of the Corn-law, that their interests are bound up with the interests of the people in the right solution of this question. I would ask, then, to what are they tending under the operation of these laws? They are becoming every year smaller and smaller in number. The large owners are rapidly eating up the smaller ones. The census returns show that the number of landed proprietors is but a handful in the nation, and every day becoming fewer and fewer. Their labourers remain at the 9s. or 10s. a-week. Somebody will write to the paper to-morrow and say they get 12s.; but bear in mind that they do not always receive wages on wet days, and I believe the average money-income of the agricultural labourer throughout the United Kingdom will not exceed—and many persons will say it will not reach—10s. a-week. Now the smaller in number these landed proprietors become, the more, it may be, these labourers will become discontented. There may arise some political accident, and political accidents are almost as unlooked-for as other accidents. You do not hear the tread of the earthquake which topples down your firmest architecture, and you do not see—the country gentlemen do not see—the tread of that danger, it may be that catastrophe, which inevitably follows upon prolonged unjust legislation. There may come a time, and I dare prophesy that it will come if there be an obstinate retention of our present system, when there will be a movement in this country to establish here, not what I believe to be the just and moderate and sufficient plan which I recommend, but a plan which shall be in accordance with that which is established by the Code Napoleon in France, and which is spreading rapidly over the whole of the Continent of Europe. And I would ask them again how do they purpose to keep their population if this system is to be maintained?

And now, addressing you working-men who are here, I beg your attention to two or three observations on this point. America, though three thousand miles off, is not so far off but that people may go there in about twelve days, and may go there for a sum varying from 2l. to 5l. You know that in this very year—I mean the year which is just passed—150,000 or

160,000 persons have sailed from this country to New York. Every man who settles there is not blinded by the mystifications and the falsities uttered by the New York correspondent of the *Times*. He is there and can see what the working-man earns, and how he is treated, and what he is, and he writes over to his friends in this country—as has been the case for years in Ireland—and the result is that Ireland is being drained, not of its surplus population, but of the population absolutely necessary to the proper cultivation of the soil.

Let me tell you a fact, and if you do not treasure it up in your minds, I hope some of those gentlemen, the landowners, who think I am very hostile to them, will just consider it, if they have time, as they eat their breakfast and read the paper to-morrow, or the next day. In America there are 140,000,000 of acres of land, surveyed, mapped out, set apart for those who are ready to settle upon them. In the year 1861 (that was the first year before the war attained its present proportions), there were not less than 40,000 new farms, averaging eighty acres each, occupied in the Western States. But the Government of the United States, not content with that measure of progress, framed an Act which came into operation on the 1st of January, 1863, called the Homestead Act. I have a copy of the Act here, and the circular which was issued from the Department of State, giving directions as to how this Act should be worked throughout the Union. What is the Homestead Act? It is this. It says that any man of twenty-one years of age, or younger, if he has been for a fortnight or a little more in the service of the United States, whether in the army or navy—any man of twenty-one years of age may come into these territories, may choose what is called a section, which is 160 acres of land, being one-fourth of a square mile, and on payment of a fee of ten dollars, which is equal to two pounds English, may apply to have this land conveyed to him for no other payment for a term of five years. It cannot be alienated, he is not allowed to sell it, it remains in his possession. At the end of five years, he having done to it what the Government requires, that is, settled upon it and begun cultivation and so forth, the law gives him what is called a patent, but what we should call a Parliamentary title, and the land is his own absolute freehold for ever. Now it would not take more than 15*l.* for a man to go from Birmingham to the territory where this land is to be disposed of. If he had not got any money by which he could take up 160 acres, he might engage himself to a neighbouring farmer, and would get, I believe, now, about twenty shillings a-week wages, besides his board and lodgings, and if he worked as a labourer for two or three years he would be able to save a sum sufficient for him to commence the cultivation of a portion of his farm, and would be settled down there as a farmer and freeholder on his own estate.

Do not let me leave you with the idea that there is no rough and rugged career in this. There is much that is rough and much that is rugged, but there is a good deal of that sort in this country now. And when a man looks upon those children that create even in the poorest house, sometimes, a gleam of joy,—when he thinks what those boys and girls must be in this country,—that they can never rise one step higher than that which he occupies now as an agricultural labourer, and when he looks abroad and he sees them, not labourers in the sense in which we speak here, not tenants even, but freeholders, and landowners, and farmers of their own property—then, I say, that the temptation held out to men here to emigrate, if men knew all the facts, would be irresistible to hundreds of thousands who have now no thought of moving to another country. But the agricultural labourer is not as he once was, in one respect. There are some feeble efforts made to give him some little instruction. There are newspapers published at a price which at one time was deemed impossible, and these find their way into agricultural villages. And the labourers will gradually begin to open their eyes, and to see that a change of their position is not so impossible as once they thought it was. What is it the United States offer more? They offer social equality—they offer political equality—they offer to every child of every man in whose face I am now looking, education—from the learning of his alphabet to, if he has the capacity to travel so far, the highest knowledge of classics and mathematics which are offered to the best students in the colleges of this country. And all this without the payment of one single farthing, except that general payment in which all the people participate in the school-rate of the various States of the Union.

I ask you if I am wrong in saying to the rich and the great, that I believe, if they knew their own interests, that it would be worth their while to try to make this country a more desirable country for the labourer to live in. If they disregard this great question, we, who are of the middle, and not absolutely powerless class, shall have to decide between the claims of territorial magnates and the just rights of millions of our countrymen. Some men I meet with—and now and then I wonder where they were born, and why they came into the world—regard these territorial magnates as idols before whom we are all to bow down in humble submission. Travellers tell us there is a tribe in Africa so entirely given up to superstition that they fill their huts and hovels with so many idols that they do not even leave room for their families. It may be so in this country. We build up a system which is injurious to our political freedom, and is destructive of the intelligence, and the comfort, and the morality, and the best interests of our producing and working classes. Now, am I the enemy of any class, when I come forward to state facts like these, and to explain principles such as these? Shall we go on groping continually in the dark, and make no effort to strengthen our position? Do not suppose because I stand here oftener to find fault with the laws of my country than to praise them, that I am less English or less patriotic, or that I have less sympathy for my country or my countrymen than other men have. I want our country to be populous, to be powerful, and to be happy. But this can only be done —it never has been done in any country—but by just laws justly administered. I plead only for what I believe to be just. I wish to do wrong to no man. For twenty-five years I have stood before audiences—great meetings of my countrymen—pleading only for justice. During that time, as you know, I have endured measureless insult, and have passed through hurricanes of abuse. I need not tell you that my clients have not been generally the rich and the great, but rather the poor and the lowly. They cannot give me place and dignities and wealth; but honourable service in their cause yields me that which is of far higher and more lasting value —the consciousness that I have laboured to expound and uphold laws, which, though they were not given amid the thunders of Sinai, are not less the commandments of God, and not less intended to promote and secure the happiness of men.

PEACE.

EDINBURGH, OCTOBER 13, 1853.

[This speech was spoken at the Conference of the Peace Society, held at Edinburgh in the autumn of 1853. The relation of this meeting to the Russian war, then impending, made the gathering more than ordinarily important.]

IT is a great advantage in this country, I think, that we have no want of ample criticism. Whatever we may have said yesterday and to-day will form the subject of criticism, not of the most friendly character, in very many newspapers throughout the United Kingdom. I recollect when we met in Manchester, that papers disposed to be friendly, warned us as to the course we were taking, and that the time was ill-chosen for a peace meeting. It was said that the people were excited against France, and were alarmed at their almost total defencelessness, and that there was no use in endeavouring to place before them the facts which the peace men offered to their audience. The result showed that they were mistaken, for you will recollect that, while up to that meeting there was a constantly swelling tide of alarm and hostility with regard to France, from the day the Conference was held there was a gradual receding of the tide, that the alarm and apprehension rapidly diminished, and that by the time the House of Commons met in February we were willing to receive from Lord John Russell and other statesmen the most positive assurances that France was not increasing her force, and that there was not the slightest reason to believe that the Government of France entertained anything but the most friendly feeling towards the Government of this country.

The right time to oppose the errors and prejudices of the people never comes to the eyes of those writers in the public press who pander to these prejudices. They say, We must not do so and so, we shall embarrass the Government. But rumour says the Government has been pretty well embarrassed already. They say that we shall complicate the question if we interfere; but it cannot well be more complicated than it is; for hardly anybody but the peace men can tell how to unravel it. Next, they tell us that we shall impair the harmony of opinion which there appears to be in the country, from the fact of there having been three or four insignificant meetings, by which the Government is to be impelled to more active and energetic measures. Now, what is it that we really want here? We wish to protest against the maintenance of great armaments in time of peace; we wish to protest against the spirit which is not only willing for war, but eager for war; and we wish to protest, with all the emphasis of which we are capable, against the mischievous policy pursued so long by this country, of interfering with the internal affairs of other countries, and thereby leading to disputes, and often to disastrous wars.

I mentioned last night what it was we were annually spending on our armaments. Admiral Napier says that the hon. Member for the West Riding, who can do everything, had persuaded a feeble Government to reduce the armaments of this country to 'nothing.' What is 'nothing' in the

Admiral's estimation? Fifteen millions a-year! Was all
that money thrown away? We have it in the estimates,
we pay it out of the taxes—it is appropriated by Parliament,
it sustains your dockyards, pays the wages of your men,
and maintains your ships. Fifteen millions sterling paid in
the very year when the Admiral says that my hon. Friend
reduced the armaments of the country to nothing! But take
the sums which we spent for the past year in warlike
preparation—seventeen millions, and the interest on debt
caused by war—twenty-eight millions sterling; and it
amounts to 45,000,000*l.* What are our whole exports? Even
this year, far the largest year of exports we have ever known,
they may amount to 80,000,000*l.* Well, then, plant some
one at the mouth of every port and harbour in the United
Kingdom, and let him take every alternate ship that leaves
your rivers and your harbours with all its valuable cargo
on board, and let him carry it off as tribute, and it will
not amount to the cost that you pay every year for a
war, that fifty years ago was justified as much as it is
attempted to justify this impending war, and for the preparations which you now make after a peace which has
lasted for thirty-eight years.

Every twenty years—in a nation's life nothing, in a person's life something—every twenty years a thousand millions
sterling out of the industry of the hard-working people of this
United Kingdom, are extorted, appropriated, and expended to
pay for that unnecessary and unjust war, and for the absurd
and ruinous expenditure which you now incur. A thousand
millions every twenty years! Apply a thousand millions,
not every twenty years, but for one period of twenty years, to
objects of good in this country, and it would be rendered more
like a paradise than anything that history records of man's
condition, and would make so great a change in these islands,
that a man having seen them as they are now, and seeing
them as they might then be, would not recognise them as

the same country, nor our population as the same people.
But what do we expend all this for? Bear in mind that
admirals, and generals, and statesmen defended that great
war, and that your newspapers, with scarcely an exception,
were in favour of it, and denounced and ostracised hundreds
of good men who dared, as we dare now, to denounce the
spirit which would again lead this country into war. We
went to war that France should not choose its own Government; the grand conclusion was that no Bonaparte should
sit on the throne of France; yet France has all along been
changing its Government from that time to this, and now
we find ourselves with a Bonaparte on the throne of France,
and, for anything I know to the contrary, likely to remain
there a good while. So far, therefore, for the calculations
of our forefathers, and for the results of that enormous expenditure which they have saddled upon us.

We object to these great armaments as provoking a war
spirit. I should like to ask, what was the object of the
Chobham exhibition? There were special trains at the
disposal of Members of Parliament, to go down to Chobham
the one day, and to Spithead the other. What was the
use of our pointing to the President of the French Republic two years ago, who is the Emperor now, and saying
that he was spending his time at playing at soldiers in
his great camp at Satory, and in making great circuses
for the amusement of his soldiers? We, too, are getting into
the way of playing at soldiers, and camps, and fleets, and
the object of this is to raise up in the spirit of the people
a feeling antagonistic to peace, and to render the people—
the deluded, hard-working, toiling people—satisfied with
the extortion of 17,000,000l. annually, when, upon the very
principles of the men who take it, it might be demonstrated
that one-half of the money would be amply sufficient for
the purpose to which it is devoted. What observation has
been more common during the discussion upon Turkey

than this—' Why are we to keep up these great fleets if
we are not to use them? Why have we our Mediterranean
fleet lying at Besika Bay, when it might be earning glory,
and adding to the warlike renown of the country?' This
is just what comes from the maintenance of great fleets and
armies. There grows up an *esprit de corps*—there grows a
passion for these things, a powerful opinion in their favour,
that smothers the immorality of the whole thing, and leads
the people to tolerate, under those excited feelings, that
which, under feelings of greater temperance and moderation,
they would know was hostile to their country, as it is
opposed to everything which we recognise as the spirit of
the Christian religion.

Then, we are against intervention. Now, this question
of intervention is a most important one, for this reason,
that it comes before us sometimes in a form so attractive
that it invites us to embrace it, and asks us by all our love
of freedom, by all our respect for men struggling for their
rights, to interfere in the affairs of some other country. And
we find now in this country that a great number of those
who are calling out loudest for interference are those who,
being very liberal in their politics, are bitterly hostile to the
despotism and exclusiveness of the Russian Government. But
I should like to ask this meeting what sort of intervention
we are to have? There are three kinds—one for despotism,
one for liberty; and you may have an intervention like that
now proposed, from a vague sense of danger which cannot
be accurately described. What have our interventions been
up to this time? I will come to that of which Admiral
Napier spoke by-and-by. It is not long since we inter-
vened in the case of Spain. The foreign enlistment laws
were suspended; and English soldiers went to join the Spanish
legion, and the Government of Spain was fixed in the present
Queen of that country; and yet Spain has the most exclusive tariff against this country in the world, and a dead

Englishman is there reckoned little better than a dead dog. Then take the case of Portugal. We interfered, and Admiral Napier was one of those employed in that interference, to place the Queen of Portugal on the throne, and yet she has violated every clause of the charter which she had sworn to the people; and in 1849, under the Government of Lord John Russell, and with Lord Palmerston in the Foreign Office, our fleet entered the Tagus and destroyed the Liberal party, by allowing the Queen to escape from their hands, when they would have driven her to give additional guarantees for liberty; and from that time to this she has still continued to violate every clause of the charter of the country. Now, let us come to Syria; what has Admiral Napier said about the Syrian war? He told us that the English fleet was scattered all about the Mediterranean, and that if the French fleet had come to Cherbourg, and had taken on board 50,000 men and landed them on our coasts, all sorts of things would have befallen us. But how happened it that Admiral Napier and his friends got up the quarrel with the French? Because we interfered in the Syrian question when we had no business to interfere whatever. The Egyptian Pasha, the vassal of the Sultan, became more powerful than the Sultan, and threatened to depose him and place himself as monarch upon the throne of Constantinople; and but for England, he would assuredly have done it. Why did we interfere? What advantage was it to us to have a feeble monarch in Constantinople, when you might have had an energetic and powerful one in Mehemet Ali? We interfered, however, and quarrelled with France, although she neither declared war nor landed men upon our coast. France is not a country of savages and banditti. The Admiral's whole theory goes upon this, that there is a total want of public morality in France, and that something which no nation in Europe would dare to do, or think of doing, which even Russia would scorn to do, would be done without any warning by the polished, civilised, and intelligent nation across the Channel.

But if they are the friends of freedom who think we ought to go to war with Russia because Russia is a despotic country, what do you say to the interference with the Roman Republic three or four years ago? What do you say to Lord John Russell's Government,—Lord Palmerston with his own hand writing the despatch, declaring that the Government of her Majesty, the Queen of England, entirely concurred with the Government of the French Republic in believing that it was desirable and necessary to re-establish the Pope upon his throne? The French army, with the full concurrence of the English Government, crossed over to Italy, invaded Rome, destroyed the Republic, banished its leading men, and restored the Pope; and on that throne he sits still, maintained only by the army of France.

My hon. Friend has referred to the time when Russia crossed through the very Principalities we hear so much about, and entered Hungary. I myself heard Lord Palmerston in the House of Commons go out of his way needlessly, but intentionally, to express a sort of approbation of the intervention of Russia in the case of Hungary. I heard him say, in a most unnecessary parenthesis, that it was not contrary to international law, or to the law of Europe, for Russia to send an army into Hungary to assist Austria in putting down the Hungarian insurrection. I should like to know whether Hungary had not constitutional rights as sacred as ever any country had—as sacred, surely, as the Sovereign of Turkey can have upon his throne. If it were not contrary to international law and to the law of Europe for a Russian army to invade Hungary, to suppress there a struggle which called for, and obtained too, the sympathy of every man in favour of freedom in every part of the world, I say, how can it be contrary to international law and the law of Europe for Russia to threaten the Sultan

of Turkey, and to endeavour to annex Turkey to the Russian
Empire?

I want our policy to be consistent. Do not let us interfere now, or concur in or encourage the interference of
anybody else, and then get up a hypocritical pretence on
some other occasion that we are against interference. If
you want war, let it be for something that has at least
the features of grandeur and of nobility about it, but not
for the miserable, decrepit, moribund Government which is
now enthroned, but which cannot long last, in the city of
Constantinople. But Admiral Napier is alarmed lest, if
Russia was possessed of Turkey, she would, somehow or
other, embrace all Europe—that we all should be in the
embrace of the Bear—and we know very well what that is.
I believe that is all a vague and imaginary danger; and
I am not for going to war for imaginary dangers. War is
much too serious a matter. I recollect when France endeavoured to lay hold on Algeria, it was said that the Mediterranean was about to become a French lake. I do not
believe that France is a bit more powerful in possessing it.
It requires 100,000 French soldiers to maintain Algeria; and
if a balance-sheet could be shown of what Algeria has cost
France, and what France has gained from it, I believe you
would have no difficulty whatever in discovering the reason
why the French finances show a deficit, and why there is
a rumour that another French loan is about to be created.

But they tell us that if Russia gets to Constantinople,
Englishmen will not be able to get to India by the overland journey. Mehemet Ali, even when Admiral Napier
was battering down his towns, did not interfere with the
carriage of our mails through his territory. We bring
our overland mails at present partly through Austria, and
partly through France, and the mails from Canada pass
through the United States; and though I do not think there
is the remotest possibility or probability of anything of the

kind happening, yet I do not think that, in the event of war with these countries, we should have our mails stopped or our persons arrested in passing through these countries. At any rate it would be a much more definite danger that would drive me to incur the ruin, guilt, and suffering of war.

But they tell us, further, that the Emperor of Russia would get India. That is a still more remote contingency. If I were asked as to the probabilities of it, I should say that, judging from our past and present policy in Asia, we are more likely to invade Russia from India than Russia is to invade us in India. The policy we pursue in Asia is much more aggressive, aggrandising, and warlike than any that Russia has pursued or threatened during our time. But it is just possible that Russia may be more powerful by acquiring Turkey. I give the Admiral the benefit of that admission. But I should like to ask whether, even if that be true, it is a sufficient reason for our going to war, and entering on what perhaps may be a long, ruinous, and sanguinary struggle, with a powerful empire like Russia?

What is war? I believe that half the people that talk about war have not the slightest idea of what it is. In a short sentence it may be summed up to be the combination and concentration of all the horrors, atrocities, crimes, and sufferings of which human nature on this globe is capable. But what is even a rumour of war? Is there anybody here who has anything in the funds, or who is the owner of any railway stock, or anybody who has a large stock of raw material or manufactured goods? The funds have recently gone down 10 per cent. I do not say that the fall is all on account of this danger of war, but a great proportion of it undoubtedly is. A fall of 10 per cent. in the funds is nearly 80,000,000*l.* sterling of value, and railway stock having gone down 20 per cent. makes a difference of 60,000,000*l.* in the value of the railway property of this country. Add the two — 140,000,000*l.* —and take the diminished prosperity and value of manufactures of all kinds during the last few months, and you will understate the actual loss to the country now if you put it down at 200,000,000*l.* sterling. But that is merely a rumour of war. That is war a long way off—the small cloud, no bigger than a man's hand—what will it be if it comes nearer and becomes a fact? And surely sane men ought to consider whether the case is a good one, the ground fair, the necessity clear, before they drag a nation of nearly 30,000,000 of people into a long and bloody struggle, for a decrepit and tottering empire, which all the nations in Europe cannot long sustain. And, mind, war now would take a different aspect from what it did formerly. It is not only that you send out men who submit to be slaughtered, and that you pay a large amount of taxes—the amount of taxes would be but a feeble indication of what you would suffer. Our trade is now much more extensive than it was; our commerce is more expanded, our undertakings are more vast, and war will find you all out at home by withering up the resources of the prosperity enjoyed by the middle and working classes of the country. You would find that war in 1853 would be infinitely more perilous and destructive to our country than it has ever yet been at any former period of our history. There is another question which comes home to my mind with a gravity and seriousness which I can scarcely hope to communicate to you. You who lived during the period from 1815 to 1822 may remember that this country was probably never in a more uneasy position. The sufferings of the working classes were beyond description, and the difficulties, and struggles, and bankruptcies of the middle classes were such as few persons have a just idea of. There was scarcely a year in which there was not an incipient insurrection in some parts of the country, arising from the sufferings which the working classes endured. You know very well that the Government of the day employed spies to create plots, and to get ignorant men to combine to take unlawful oaths; and you know that in the town of Stirling, two men who, but for this diabolical agency, might have lived good and honest citizens, paid the penalty of their lives for their connection with unlawful combinations of this kind.

Well, if you go into war now you will have more banners to decorate your cathedrals and churches. Englishmen will fight now as well as they ever did, and there is ample power to back them if the country can be but sufficiently excited and deluded. You may raise up great generals. You may have another Wellington, and another Nelson too ; for this country can grow men capable for every enterprise. Then there may be titles, and pensions, and marble monuments to eternise the men who have thus become great; but what becomes of you and your country, and your children? For there is more than this in store. That seven years to which I have referred was a period dangerous to the existence of Government in this country, for the whole substratum, the whole foundations of society were discontented, suffering intolerable evils, and hostile in the bitterest degree to the institutions and the Government of the country.

Precisely the same things will come again. Rely on it, that injustice of any kind, be it bad laws, or be it a bloody, unjust, and unnecessary war, of necessity creates perils to every institution in the country. If the Corn-law had continued, if it had been impossible, by peaceful agitation, to abolish it, the monarchy itself would not have survived the ruin and disaster that it must have wrought. And if you go into a war now, with a doubled population, with a vast commerce, with extended credit, and a wider diffusion of partial education among the people, let there ever come a time like the period between 1815 and 1822, when the whole basis of society is upheaving with a sense of intolerable suffering, I ask you, how many years' purchase would you give even for the venerable and mild monarchy under which you have the happiness to live? I confess when I think of the tremendous

perils into which unthinking men—men who do not intend
to fight themselves—are willing to drag or to hurry this
country, I am amazed how they can trifle with interests so
vast, and consequences so much beyond their calculation.

But, speaking here in Edinburgh to such an audience—an
audience probably for its numbers as intelligent and as
influential as ever was assembled within the walls of any
hall in this kingdom—I think I may put before you higher
considerations even than those of property and the institutions of your country. I may remind you of duties more
solemn, and of obligations more imperative. You profess to
be a Christian nation. You make it your boast even—though
boasting is somewhat out of place in such questions—you
make it your boast that you are a Protestant people, and that
you draw your rule of doctrine and practice, as from a well
pure and undefiled, from the living oracles of God, and from
the direct revelation of the Omnipotent. You have even conceived the magnificent project of illuminating the whole earth,
even to its remotest and darkest recesses, by the dissemination
of the volume of the New Testament, in whose every page are
written for ever the words of peace. Within the limits of
this island alone, on every Sabbath, 20,000, yes, far more than
20,000 temples are thrown open, in which devout men and
women assemble that they may worship Him who is the
'Prince of Peace.'

Is this a reality? or is your Christianity a romance? is your
profession a dream? No, I am sure that your Christianity
is not a romance, and I am equally sure that your profession
is not a dream. It is because I believe this that I appeal
to you with confidence, and that I have hope and faith in
the future. I believe that we shall see, and at no very distant
time, sound economic principles spreading much more widely
amongst the people; a sense of justice growing up in a soil
which hitherto has been deemed unfruitful; and, which will
be better than all—the churches of the United Kingdom—

the churches of Britain awaking, as it were, from their slumbers, and girding up their loins to more glorious work, when they shall not only accept and believe in the prophecy, but labour earnestly for its fulfilment, that there shall come a time —a blessed time—a time which shall last for ever—when 'nation shall not lift up sword against nation, neither shall they learn war any more.'

FOREIGN POLICY.

BIRMINGHAM, OCTOBER 29, 1858.

[This speech was spoken at a banquet given to Mr. Bright in the Town Hall of Birmingham, on the occasion of his first visit to his constituents there. It treats of the Foreign Policy of the country since the Revolution of 1688, and defends the Foreign Policy advocated by Mr. Cobden and himself.]

THE frequent and far too complimentary manner in which my name has been mentioned to-night, and the most kind way in which you have received me, have placed me in a position somewhat humiliating, and really painful; for to receive laudation which one feels one cannot possibly have merited, is much more painful than to be passed by in a distribution of commendation to which possibly one might lay some claim. If one-twentieth part of what has been said is true, if I am entitled to any measure of your approbation, I may begin to think that my public career and my opinions are not so un-English and so anti-national as some of those who profess to be the best of our public instructors have sometimes assumed. How, indeed, can I, any more than any of you, be un-English and anti-national? Was I not born upon the same soil? Do I not come of the same English stock? Are not my family committed irrevocably to the fortunes of this country? Is not whatever property I may have depending as much as yours is depending upon the good government of our common fatherland? Then how shall any man dare to say to any one of his countrymen, because he happens to hold a different opinion on questions of great public policy, that therefore he is un-English, and is to be condemned as anti-national? There are those who would assume that between my countrymen and me, and between my constituents and me, there has been, and there is now, a great gulf fixed, and that if I cannot pass over to them and to you, they and you can by no possibility pass over to me.

Now, I take the liberty here, in the presence of an audience as intelligent as can be collected within the limits of this island, and of those who have the strongest claims to know what opinions I do entertain relative to certain great questions of public policy, to assert that I hold no views, that I have never promulgated any views on those controverted questions with respect to which I cannot bring as witnesses in my favour, and as fellow-believers with myself, some of the best and most revered names in the history of English statesmanship. About 120 years ago, the Government of this country was directed by Sir Robert Walpole, a great Minister, who for a long period preserved the country in peace, and whose pride it was that during those years he had done so. Unfortunately, towards the close of his career, he was driven by faction into a policy which was the ruin of his political position. Sir Robert Walpole declared, when speaking of the question of war as affecting this country, that nothing could be so foolish, nothing so mad as a policy of war for a trading nation. And he went so far as to say, that any peace was better than the most successful war. I do not give you the precise language made use of by the Minister, for I speak only from memory; but I am satisfied I am not misrepresenting him in what I have now stated.

Come down fifty years nearer to our own time, and you

find a statesman, not long in office, but still strong in the affections of all persons of Liberal principles in this country, and in his time representing fully the sentiments of the Liberal party—Charles James Fox. Mr. Fox, referring to the policy of the Government of his time, which was one of constant interference in the affairs of Europe, and by which the country was continually involved in the calamities of war, said that although he would not assert or maintain the principle, that under no circumstances could England have any cause of interference with the affairs of the continent of Europe, yet he would prefer the policy of positive non-interference and of perfect isolation rather than the constant intermeddling to which our recent policy had subjected us, and which brought so much trouble and suffering upon the country. In this case also I am not prepared to give you his exact words, but I am sure that I fairly describe the sentiments which he expressed.

Come down fifty years later, and to a time within the recollection of most of us, and you find another statesman, once the most popular man in England, and still remembered in this town and elsewhere with respect and affection. I allude to Earl Grey. When Earl Grey came into office for the purpose of carrying the question of Parliamentary Reform, he unfurled the banner of ' Peace, retrenchment, and reform,' and that sentiment was received in every part of the United Kingdom, by every man who was or had been in favour of Liberal principles, as predicting the advent of a new era which should save his country from many of the calamities of the past.

Come down still nearer, and to a time that seems but the other day, and you find another Minister, second to none of those whom I have mentioned—the late Sir Robert Peel. I had the opportunity of observing the conduct of Sir Robert Peel, from the time when he took office in 1841; I watched his proceedings particularly from the year 1843, when I entered Parliament, up to the time of his

lamented death; and during the whole of that period, I
venture to say, his principles, if they were to be discovered
from his conduct and his speeches, were precisely those which
I have held, and which I have always endeavoured to press
upon the attention of my countrymen. If you have any
doubt upon that point I would refer you to that last, that
beautiful, that most solemn speech, which he delivered with
an earnestness and a sense of responsibility as if he had
known he was leaving a legacy to his country. If you refer
to that speech, delivered on the morning of the very day
on which occurred the accident which terminated his life, you
will find that its whole tenor is in conformity with all the
doctrines that I have urged upon my countrymen for years
past with respect to our policy in foreign affairs. When
Sir Robert Peel went home just before the dawn of day,
upon the last occasion that he passed from the House of
Commons, the scene of so many of his triumphs, I have
heard, from what I think a good authority, that after he
entered his own house, he expressed the exceeding relief
which he experienced at having delivered himself of a speech
which he had been reluctantly obliged to make against a
Ministry which he was anxious to support, and he added,
if I am not mistaken, ' I have made a speech of peace.'

Well, if this be so, if I can give you four names like
these,—if there were time I could make a longer list of still
eminent, if inferior men,—I should like to know why I, as
one of a small party, am to be set down as teaching some
new doctrine which it is not fit for my countrymen to hear,
and why I am to be assailed in every form of language, as
if there was one great department of governmental affairs
on which I was incompetent to offer any opinion to my
countrymen. But leaving the opinions of individuals, I
appeal to this audience, to every man who knows anything
of the views and policy of the Liberal party in past years,
whether it is not the fact that up to 1832, and indeed to

a much later period, probably to the year 1850, those sentiments of Sir Robert Walpole, of Mr. Fox, of Earl Grey, and of Sir Robert Peel, the sentiments which I in humbler mode have propounded, were not received unanimously by the Liberal party as their fixed and unchangeable creed? And why should they not? Are they not founded upon reason? Do not all statesmen know, as you know, that upon peace, and peace alone, can be based the successful industry of a nation, and that by successful industry alone can be created that wealth which, permeating all classes of the people, not confined to great proprietors, great merchants, and great speculators, not running in a stream merely down your principal streets, but turning fertilizing rivulets into every bye-lane and every alley, tends so powerfully to promote the comfort, happiness, and contentment of a nation? Do you not know that all progress comes from successful and peaceful industry, and that upon it is based your superstructure of education, of morals, of self-respect among your people, as well as every measure for extending and consolidating freedom in your public institutions? I am not afraid to acknowledge that I do oppose—that I do utterly condemn and denounce—a great part of the foreign policy which is practised and adhered to by the Government of this country.

You know, of course, that about 170 years ago there happened in this country what we have always been accustomed to call 'a Glorious Revolution'—a Revolution which had this effect: that it put a bit into the mouth of the monarch, so that he was not able of his own free-will to do, and he dared no longer attempt to do, the things which his predecessors had done without fear. But if at the Revolution the monarchy of England was bridled and bitted, at the same time the great territorial families of England were enthroned; and from that period, until the year 1831 or 1832—until the time when Birmingham politically became famous—those territorial families reigned with an almost undisputed sway over the destinies and the industry of the people of these kingdoms. If you turn to the history of England, from the period of the Revolution to the present, you will find that an entirely new policy was adopted, and that while we had endeavoured in former times to keep ourselves free from European complications, we now began to act upon a system of constant entanglement in the affairs of foreign countries, as if there was neither property nor honours, nor anything worth striving for, to be acquired in any other field. The language coined and used then, has continued to our day. Lord Somers, in writing for William III, speaks of the endless and sanguinary wars of that period as wars 'to maintain the liberties of Europe.' There were wars ' to support the Protestant interest,' and there were many wars to preserve our old friend ' the balance of power.'

We have been at war since that time, I believe, with, for, and against every considerable nation in Europe. We fought to put down a pretended French supremacy under Louis XIV. We fought to prevent France and Spain coming under the sceptre of one monarch, although, if we had not fought, it would have been impossible in the course of things that they should have become so united. We fought to maintain the Italian provinces in connection with the House of Austria. We fought to put down the supremacy of Napoleon Bonaparte; and the Minister who was employed by this country at Vienna, after the great war, when it was determined that no Bonaparte should ever again sit on the throne of France, was the very man to make an alliance with another Bonaparte for the purpose of carrying on a war to prevent the supremacy of the late Emperor of Russia. So that we have been all round Europe, and across it over and over again, and after a policy so distinguished, so pre-eminent, so long-continued, and so costly, I think we have a fair right—I have, at least—to ask those who are in favour of it to show us its visible result. Europe is not at this moment, so far as I know, speaking of it broadly, and making allowance for certain improvements in its general civilisation, more free politically than it was before. The balance of power is like perpetual motion, or any of those impossible things which some men are always racking their brains and spending their time and money to accomplish.

We all know and deplore that at the present moment a larger number of the grown men of Europe are employed, and a larger portion of the industry of Europe is absorbed, to provide for, and maintain, the enormous armaments which are now on foot in every considerable Continental State. Assuming, then, that Europe is not much better in consequence of the sacrifices we have made, let us inquire what has been the result in England, because, after all, that is the question which it becomes us most to consider. I believe that I understate the sum when I say that, in pursuit of this Will-o'-the-wisp, (the liberties of Europe and the balance of power,) there has been extracted from the industry of the people of this small island no less an amount than 2,000,000,000*l*. sterling. I cannot imagine how much 2,000,000,000*l*. is, and therefore I shall not attempt to make you comprehend it. I presume it is something like those vast and incomprehensible astronomical distances with which we have been lately made familiar ; but, however familiar, we feel that we do not know one bit more about them than we did before. When I try to think of that sum of 2,000,000,000*l*., there is a sort of vision passes before my mind's eye. I see your peasant labourer delve and plough, sow and reap, sweat beneath the summer's sun, or grow prematurely old before the winter's blast. I see your noble mechanic, with his manly countenance and his matchless skill, toiling at his bench or his forge. I see one of the workers in our factories in the north, a woman—a girl, it may be—gentle and good, as many of them are, as your sisters and daughters are—I see her intent upon the spindle, whose revolutions are so rapid that the eye fails altogether to detect them, or watching the alternating flight of the unresting shuttle. I turn again to another portion of your population, which, 'plunged in mines, forgets a sun was made,' and I see the man who brings up from the secret chambers of the earth the elements of the riches and greatness of his country. When I see all this I have before me a mass of produce and of wealth which I am no more able to comprehend than I am that 2,000,000,000*l.* of which I have spoken, but I behold in its full proportions the hideous error of your Governments, whose fatal policy consumes in some cases a half, never less than a third, of all the results of that industry which God intended should fertilise and bless every home in England, but the fruits of which are squandered in every part of the surface of the globe, without producing the smallest good to the people of England.

We have, it is true, some visible results that are of a more positive character. We have that which some people call a great advantage—the National Debt—a debt which is now so large that the most prudent, the most economical, and the most honest have given up all hope, not of its being paid off, but of its being diminished in amount. We have, too, taxes which have been during many years so onerous that there have been times when the patient beasts of burden threatened to revolt—so onerous that it has been utterly impossible to levy them with any kind of honest equality, according to the means of the people to pay them. We have that, moreover, which is a standing wonder to all foreigners who consider our condition—an amount of apparently immovable pauperism, which to strangers is wholly irreconcilable with the fact that we, as a nation, produce more of what should make us all comfortable, than is produced by any other nation of similar numbers on the face of the globe. Let us likewise remember that during the period of those great and so-called glorious contests on the continent of Europe, every description of home reform was not only delayed, but actually crushed out of the minds of the great bulk of the people. There can be no doubt whatever that in 1793 England was about to realise political changes and reforms, such as did not appear again until 1830; and during the period of that war, which now almost all men agree to have been wholly unnecessary, we were passing through a period which may be described as the dark age of English politics ; when there was no more freedom to write or speak, or politically to act, than there is now in the most despotic country of Europe.

But, it may be asked, did nobody gain ? If Europe is no better, and the people of England have been so much worse, who has benefited by the new system of foreign policy ? What has been the fate of those who were enthroned at the Revolution, and whose supremacy has been for so long a period undisputed among us ? Mr. Kinglake, the author of an interesting book on Eastern Travel, describing the habits of some acquaintances that he made in the Syrian Deserts, says, that the jackals of the Desert follow their prey in families like the place-hunters of Europe. I will reverse, if you like, the comparison, and say that the great territorial families of England, which were enthroned at the Revolution, have followed their prey like the jackals of the Desert. Do you not observe at a glance, that, from the time of William III, by reason of the foreign policy which I denounce, wars have been multiplied, taxes increased, loans made, and the sums of money which every year the Government has to expend augmented, and that so the patronage at the disposal of Ministers must have increased also, and the families who were enthroned and made powerful in the legislation and administration of the country must have had the first pull at, and the largest profit out of, that patronage ? There is no actuary in existence who can calculate how much of the wealth, of the strength, of the supremacy of the territorial families of England has been derived from an unholy participation in the fruits of the industry of the people, which have been wrested from them by every device of taxation, and squandered in every conceivable crime of which a Government could possibly be guilty.

The more you examine this matter the more you will come to the conclusion which I have arrived at, that this foreign policy, this regard for 'the liberties of Europe,' this care at one time for 'the Protestant interests,' this excessive love for 'the balance of power,' is neither more nor less than a gigantic system of out-door relief for the aristocracy of Great Britain. [Great laughter.] I observe that you receive that declaration as if it were some new and important discovery. In 1815, when the great war with France was ended, every Liberal in England, whose politics, whose hopes, and whose faith had not been crushed out of him by the tyranny of the time of that war, was fully aware of this, and openly admitted it, and up to 1832, and for some years afterwards, it was the fixed and undoubted creed of the great Liberal party. But somehow all is changed. We who stand upon the old landmarks, who walk in the old paths, who would conserve what is wise and prudent, are hustled and shoved about as if we were come to turn the world upside down. The change which has taken place seems to confirm the opinion of a lamented friend of mine, who, not having succeeded in all his hopes, thought that men made no progress whatever, but went round and round like a squirrel in a cage. The idea is now so general that it is our duty to meddle everywhere, that it really seems as if we had pushed the Tories from the field, expelling them by our competition.

I should like to lay before you a list of the treaties which we have made, and of the responsibilities under which we have laid ourselves with respect to the various countries of Europe. I do not know where such an enumeration is to be found, but I suppose it would be possible for antiquaries and men of investigating minds to dig them out from the recesses of the Foreign Office, and perhaps to make some of them intelligible to the country. I believe, however, that if we go to the Baltic we shall find that we have a treaty to defend Sweden, and the only thing which Sweden agrees to do in return is not to give up any portion of her territories to Russia. Coming down a little south, we have a treaty which invites us, enables us, and perhaps, if we acted fully up to our duty with regard to it, would compel us to interfere in the question between Denmark and the Duchies. If I mistake not, we have a treaty which binds us down to the maintenance of the little kingdom of Belgium, as established after its separation from Holland. We have numerous treaties with France. We are understood to be bound by treaty to maintain constitutional government in Spain and Portugal. If we go round into the Mediterranean, we find the little kingdom of Sardinia, to which we have lent some millions of money, and with which we have entered into important treaties for preserving the balance of power in Europe. If we go beyond the kingdoms of Italy, and cross the Adriatic, we come to the small kingdom of Greece, against which we have a nice account that will never be settled; while we have engagements to maintain that respectable but diminutive country under its present constitutional government. Then, leaving the kingdom of Greece, we pass up the eastern end of the Mediterranean, and from Greece to the Red Sea, wherever the authority of the Sultan is more or less admitted, the blood and the industry of England are pledged to the permanent sustentation of the 'independence and integrity' of the Ottoman Empire.

I confess that as a citizen of this country, wishing to live peaceably among my fellow-countrymen, and wishing to see my countrymen free, and able to enjoy the fruits of their labour, I protest against a system which binds us in all these networks and complications, from which it is impossible that

we can gain one single atom of advantage for this country.
It is not all glory, after all.   Glory may be worth something,
but it is not always glory.   We have had within the last
few years despatches from Vienna and from St. Petersburg,
which, if we had not deserved them, would have been very
offensive and not a little insolent.   We have had the Ambassador of the Queen expelled summarily from Madrid, and we
have had an Ambassador driven almost with ignominy from
Washington.   We have blockaded Athens for a claim which
was known to be false.   We have quarrelled with Naples, for
we chose to give advice to Naples, which was not received in
the submissive spirit expected from her, and our Minister was
therefore withdrawn.   Not three years ago, too, we seized
a considerable kingdom in India, with which our Government
had but recently entered into the most solemn treaty, which
every lawyer in England and in Europe, I believe, would
consider binding before God and the world.   We deposed its
monarch; we committed a great immorality and a great
crime, and we have reaped an almost instantaneous retribu-
tion in the most gigantic and sanguinary revolt which probably any nation ever made against its conquerors.   Within
the last few years we have had two wars with a great Empire,
which we are told contains at least one-third of the whole
human race.   The first war was called, and appropriately
called, the Opium War.   No man, I believe, with a spark of
morality in his composition, no man who cares anything for
the opinion of his fellow-countrymen, has dared to justify
that war.   The war which has just been concluded, if it has
been concluded, had its origin in the first war; for the
enormities committed in the first war are the foundation of
the implacable hostility which it is said the inhabitants of
Canton bear to all persons connected with the English name.
Yet, though we have these troubles in India—a vast country
which we do not know how to govern—and a war with China
—a country with which, though everybody else can remain at

peace, we cannot—such is the inveterate habit of conquest, such is the insatiable lust of territory, such is, in my view, the depraved, unhappy state of opinion of the country on this subject, that there are not a few persons, Chambers of Commerce to wit, in different parts of the kingdom (though I am glad to say it has not been so with the Chamber of Commerce. at Birmingham), who have been urging our Government to take possession of a province of the greatest island in the Eastern seas; a possession which must at once necessitate increased estimates and increased taxation, and which would probably lead us into merciless and disgraceful wars with the half-savage tribes who inhabit that island.

I will not dwell upon that question. The gentleman who is principally concerned in it is at this moment, as you know, stricken down with affliction, and I am unwilling to enter here into any considerable discussion of the case which he is urging upon the public; but I say that we have territory enough in India; and if we have not troubles enough there, if we have not difficulties enough in China, if we have not taxation enough, by all means gratify your wishes for more; but I hope that whatever may be the shortcomings of the Government with regard to any other questions in which we are all interested—and may they be few!—they will shut their eyes, they will turn their backs obstinately from adding in this mode, or in any mode, to the English possessions in the East. I suppose that if any ingenious person were to prepare a large map of the world, as far as it is known, and were to mark upon it, in any colour that he liked, the spots where Englishmen have fought and English blood has been poured forth, and the treasure of England squandered, scarcely a country, scarcely a province of the vast expanse of the habitable globe would be thus undistinguished.

Perhaps there are in this room, I am sure there are in the country, many persons who hold a superstitious traditionary

belief that, somehow or other, our vast trade is to be attributed
to what we have done in this way, that it is thus we have
opened markets and advanced commerce, that English greatness depends upon the extent of English conquests and
English military renown.   But I am inclined to think that,
with the exception of Australia, there is not a single depen-
dency of the Crown which, if we come to reckon what it has
cost in war and protection, would not be found to be a positive
loss to the people of this country.   Take the United States,
with which we have such an enormous and constantly increasing trade.   The wise statesmen of the last generation,
men whom your school histories tell you were statesmen,
serving under a monarch who they tell you was a patriotic
monarch, spent 130,000,000*l.* of the fruits of the industry of
the people in a vain—happily a vain—endeavour to retain the
colonies of the United States in subjection to the Monarchy
of England.   Add up the interest of that 130,000,000*l.* for
all this time, and how long do you think it will be before
there will be a profit on the trade with the United States which
will repay the enormous sum we invested in a war to retain
those States as colonies of this Empire?   It never will be
paid off.   Wherever you turn, you will find that the opening
of markets, developing of new countries, introducing cotton
cloth with cannon balls, are vain, foolish, and wretched
excuses for wars, and ought not to be listened to for a
moment by any man who understands the multiplication table
or who can do the simplest sum in arithmetic.

Since the 'Glorious Revolution,' since the enthronisation of
the great Norman territorial families, they have spent in wars,
and we have worked for, about 2,000,000,000*l.*   The interest
on that is 100,000,000*l.* per annum, which alone, to say
nothing of the principal sum, is three or four times as much
as the whole amount of your annual export trade from that
time to this.   Therefore, if war has provided you with a
trade, it has been at an enormous cost; but I think it

is by no means doubtful that your trade would have been no less in amount and no less profitable had peace and justice been inscribed on your flag instead of conquest and the love of military renown. But even in this year, 1858—we have got a long way into the century—we find that within the last seven years our public debt has greatly increased. Whatever be the increase of our population, of our machinery, of our industry, of our wealth, still our national debt goes on increasing. Although we have not a foot more territory to conserve, or an enemy in the world who dreams of attacking us, we find that our annual military expenses during the last twenty years have risen from 12,000,000l. to 22,000,000l.

Some people believe that it is a good thing to pay a great revenue to the State. Even so eminent a man as Lord John Russell is not without a delusion of this sort. Lord John Russell as you have heard, while speaking of me in flattering and friendly terms, says he is unfortunately obliged to differ from me frequently; therefore, I suppose, there is no particular harm in my saying that I am sometimes obliged to differ from him. Some time ago he was a great star in the northern hemisphere, shining, not with unaccustomed, but with his usual brilliancy at Liverpool. He made a speech, in which there was a great deal to be admired, to a meeting composed, it was said, to a great extent of working-men; and in it he stimulated them to a feeling of pride in the greatness of their country and in being citizens of a State which enjoyed a revenue of 100,000,000l. a-year, which included the revenues of the United Kingdom and of British India. But I think it would have been far more to the purpose if he could have congratulated the working-men of Liverpool on this vast Empire being conducted in an orderly manner, on its laws being well administered and well obeyed, its shores sufficiently defended, its people prosperous and happy, on a revenue of 20,000,000l. The State indeed, of which Lord John Russell is a part, may enjoy a revenue of

100,000,000*l*., but I am afraid the working-men can only be said to enjoy it in the sense in which men not very choice in their expressions say that for a long time they have enjoyed ' very bad health.'

I am prepared to admit that it is a subject of congratulation that there is a people so great, so free, and so industrious, that it can produce a sufficient income out of which 100,000,000*l*. a-year, if need absolutely were, could be spared for some great and noble object; but it is not a thing to be proud of that our Government should require us to pay that enormous sum for the simple purposes of government and defence. Nothing can by any possibility tend more to the corruption of a Government than enormous revenues. We have heard lately of instances of certain joint-stock institutions with very great capital collapsing suddenly, bringing disgrace upon their managers, and ruin upon hundreds of families. A great deal of that has arisen, not so much from intentional fraud, as from the fact that weak and incapable men have found themselves tumbling about in an ocean of bank-notes and gold, and they appear to have lost all sight of where it came from, to whom it belonged, and whether it was possible by any maladministration ever to come to an end of it. That is absolutely what is done by Governments. You have read in the papers lately some accounts of the proceedings before a Commission appointed to inquire into alleged maladministration with reference to the supply of clothing to the army, but if anybody had said anything in the time of the late Government about any such maladministration, there is not one of those great statesmen, of whom we are told we ought always to speak with so much reverence, who would not have got up and declared that nothing could be more admirable than the system of book-keeping at Weedon, nothing more economical than the manner in which the War Department spent the money provided by public taxation. But we know that it is not so. I have heard a gentleman—one who is as

competent as any man in England to give an opinion about it
—a man of business, and not surpassed by any one as a man
of business, declare, after a long examination of the details of
the question, that he would undertake to do everything that
is done not only for the defence of the country, but for many
other things which are done by your navy, and which are not
necessary for that purpose, for half the annual cost that is
voted in the estimates !

I think the expenditure of these vast sums, and especially
of those which we spend for military purposes, leads us to
adopt a defiant and insolent tone towards foreign countries.
We have the freest press in Europe, and the freest platform
in Europe, but every man who writes an article in a newspaper, and every man who stands on a platform, ought to do
it under a solemn sense of responsibility. Every word he
writes, every word I utter, passes with a rapidity, of which
our forefathers were utterly ignorant, to the very ends of the
earth ; the words become things and acts, and they produce
on the minds of other nations effects which a man may never
have intended. Take a recent case ; take the case of France.
I am not expected to defend, and I shall certainly not attack,
the present Government of France. The instant that it
appeared in its present shape, the Minister of England
conducting your foreign affairs, speaking ostensibly for the
Cabinet, for his Sovereign, and for the English nation,
offered his congratulations, and the support of England
was at once accorded to the re-created French Empire.
Soon after this an intimate alliance was entered into
between the Queen of England, through her Ministers,
and the Emperor of the French. I am not about to
defend the policy which flowed from that alliance, nor shall
I take up your time by making any attack upon it. An
alliance was entered into, and a war was entered into.
English and French soldiers fought on the same field, and
they suffered, I fear, from the same neglect. They now lie

buried on the bleak heights of the Crimea, and except
by their mothers, who do not soon forget their children, I
suppose they are mostly forgotten. I have never heard it suggested that the French Government did not behave with the
most perfect honour to this Government and this country all
through these grave transactions; but I have heard it stated by
those who most know, that nothing could be more honourable,
nothing more just, than the conduct of the French Emperor to
this Government throughout the whole of that struggle. More
recently, when the war in China was begun by a Government
which I have condemned and denounced in the House of
Commons, the Emperor of the French sent his ships and
troops to co-operate with us, but I never heard that anything
was done there to create a suspicion of a feeling of hostility
on his part towards us. The Emperor of the French came to
London, and some of those powerful organs of the press who
have since taken the line of which I am complaining, did all
but invite the people of London to prostrate themselves under
the wheels of the chariot which conveyed along our streets
the revived monarchy of France. The Queen of England went
to Paris, and was she not received there with as much affection
and as much respect as her high position and her honourable
character entitled her to?

What has occurred since? If there was a momentary
unpleasantness, I am quite sure that every impartial man
will agree that, under the peculiarly irritating circumstances
of the time there was at least as much forbearance shown
on one side of the Channel as on the other. Then we have
had much said lately 'about a naval fortification recently com-
pleted in France, which has been more than one hundred years
in progress, which was not devised by the present Emperor
of the French. For one hundred years great sums had
been spent on it, and at last, like every other great work,
it was brought to an end. The English Queen and others
were invited over, and many went who were not invited.

And yet in all this we are told that there is something to create extreme alarm and suspicion; we, who have never fortified any places; we, who have not a greater than Sebastopol at Gibraltar; we, who have not an impregnable fortress at Malta, who have not spent the fortune of a nation almost in the Ionian Islands; we, who are doing nothing at Alderney; we are to take offence at the fortifications of Cherbourg! There are few persons who at some time or other have not been brought into contact with a poor unhappy fellow-creature who has some peculiar delusion or suspicion pressing on his mind. I recollect a friend of mine going down from Derby to Leeds in the train with a very quiet and respectable-looking gentleman sitting opposite to him. They had both been staying at the Midland Hotel, and they began talking about it. All at once the gentleman said, 'Did you notice anything particular about the bread at breakfast?' 'No,' said my friend, 'I did not.' 'Oh! but I did,' said the poor gentleman, 'and I am convinced there was an attempt made to poison me, and it is a very curious thing that I never go to an hotel without I discover some attempt to do me mischief.' The unfortunate man was labouring under one of the greatest calamities which can befall a human creature. But what are we to say of a nation which lives under a perpetual delusion that it is about to be attacked—a nation which is the most combined on the face of the earth, with little less than 30,000,000 of people all united under a Government which, though we intend to reform it, we do not the less respect it, and which has mechanical power and wealth to which no other country offers any parallel? There is no causeway to Britain; the free waves of the sea flow day and night for ever round her shores, and yet there are people going about with whom this hallucination is so strong that they do not merely discover it quietly to their friends, but they write it down in double-leaded columns, in leading articles,—nay, some of them actually get up on platforms and proclaim it to hundreds and thousands of their fellow-countrymen. I should like to ask you whether these delusions are to last for ever, whether this policy is to be the perpetual policy of England, whether these results are to go on gathering and gathering until there come, as come there must inevitably, some dreadful catastrophe on our country?

I should like to-night, if I could, to inaugurate one of the best and holiest revolutions that ever took place in this country. We have had a dozen revolutions since some of us were children. We have had one revolution in which you had a great share, a great revolution of opinion on the question of the suffrage. Does it not read like madness that men, thirty years ago, were frantic at the idea of the people of Birmingham having a 10*l.* franchise? Does it not seem something like idiotcy to be told that a banker in Leeds, when it was proposed to transfer the seats of one rotten borough to the town of Leeds, should say (and it was repeated in the House of Commons on his authority) that if the people of Leeds had the franchise conferred upon them it would not be possible to keep the bank doors open with safety, and that he should remove his business to some quiet place out of danger from the savage race that peopled that town? But now all confess that the people are perfectly competent to have votes, and nobody dreams of arguing that the privilege will make them less orderly.

Take the question of colonial government. Twenty years ago the government of our colonies was a huge job. A small family party in each, in connection with the Colonial Office, ruled our colonies. We had then discontent, and, now and then, a little wholesome insurrection, especially in Canada. The result was that we have given up the colonial policy which had hitherto been held sacred, and since that time not only have our colonies greatly advanced in wealth and material resources, but no parts of the Empire are more tranquil and loyal.

Take also the question of Protection. Not thirty years ago, but twelve years ago, there was a great party in Parliament, led by a Duke in one House, and by the son and brother of a Duke in the other, which declared that utter ruin must come, not only on the agricultural interest, but upon the manufactures and commerce of England, if we departed from our old theories upon this subject of Protection. They told us that the labourer—the unhappy labourer—of whom it may be said in this country,—

> 'Here landless labourers hopeless toil and strive,
> But taste no portion of the sweets they hive,'

— that the labourer was to be ruined; that is, that the paupers were to be pauperised. These gentlemen were overthrown. The plain, honest, common sense of the country swept away their cobweb theories, and they are gone. What is the result? From 1846 to 1857 we have received into this country of grain of all kinds, including flour, maize, or India corn—all objects heretofore not of absolute prohibition, but which were intended to be prohibited until it was not safe for people to be starved any more—not less than an amount equal in value to 224,000,000*l*. That is equal to 18,700,000*l*. per annum on the average of twelve years. During that period, too, your home growth has been stimulated to an enormous extent. You have imported annually 200,000 tons of guano, and the result has been a proportionate increase in the productions of the soil, for 200,000 tons of guano will grow an equal weight and value of wheat. With all this, agriculture was never more prosperous, while manufactures were never, at the same time, more extensively exported; and with all this the labourers, for whom the tears of the Protectionist were shed, have, according to the admission of the most violent of the class, never been in a better state since the beginning of the great French war.

One other revolution of opinion has been in regard to our criminal law. I have lately been reading a book which I would advise every man to read — the *Life of Sir Samuel Romilly.* He tells us in simple language of the almost insuperable difficulties he had to contend with to persuade the Legislature of this country to abolish the punishment of death for·stealing from a dwelling-house to the value of 5s., an offence which now is punished by a few weeks' imprisonment. Lords, bishops, and statesmen opposed these efforts year after year, and there have been some thousands of persons put to death publicly for offences which are not now punishable with death. Now, every man and woman in the kingdom would feel a thrill of horror if told that a fellow-creature was to be put to death for such a cause.

These are revolutions in opinion, and let me tell you that when you accomplish a revolution in opinion upon a great question, when you alter it from bad to good, it is not like charitably giving a beggar 6d. and seeing him no more, but it is a great beneficent act, which affects not merely the rich and the powerful, but penetrates every lane, every cottage in the land, and wherever it goes brings blessings and happiness. It is not from statesmen that these things come. It is not from them that have proceeded these great revolutions of opinion·on the questions of Reform, Protection, Colonial Government, and Criminal Law—it was from public meetings such as this, from the intelligence and conscience of the great body of the people who have no interest in wrong, and who never go from the right but by temporary error and under momentary passion.

It is for you to decide whether our greatness shall be only temporary or whether it shall be enduring. When I am told that the greatness of our country is shown by the 100,000,000l. of revenue produced, may I not also ask how it is that we have 1,100,000 paupers in this kingdom, and why it is that 7,000,000l. should be taken from the industry chiefly of the labouring classes to support a small nation, as it were, of paupers? Since your legislation upon the Corn-laws you have not only had nearly 20,000,000*l.* of food brought into the country annually, but such an extraordinary increase of trade that your exports are about doubled, and yet I understand that in the year 1856, for I have no later return, there were no less than 1,100,000 paupers in the United Kingdom, and the sum raised in poor-rates was not less than 7,200,000*l.* And that cost of pauperism is not the full amount; for there is a vast amount of temporary, casual, and vagrant pauperism that does not come in to swell that sum.

Then do·not you well know—I know it, because I live among the population of Lancashire, and I doubt not the same may be said of the population of this city and county— that just above the level of the 1,100,000 there is at least an equal number who are ever oscillating between independence and pauperism, who, with a heroism which is not the less heroic because it is secret and unrecorded, are doing their very utmost to maintain an honourable and independent position before their fellow-men? While Irish labour, notwithstanding the improvement which has taken place in Ireland, is only paid at the rate of about 1*s.* a-day; while in the straths and glens of Scotland there are hundreds of shepherd families whose whole food almost consists of oatmeal porridge from day to day, and from week to week; while these things continue, I say that we have no reason to be self-satisfied and contented with our position; but that we who are in Parliament and are more directly responsible for affairs, and you who are also responsible though in a lower degree, are bound by the sacred duty which we owe our country to examine why it is that with all this trade, all this industry, and all this personal freedom, there is still so much that is unsound at the base of our social fabric?

Let me direct your attention now to another point which I never think of without feelings which words would altogether fail to express. You hear constantly, that woman, the help-mate of man, who adorns, dignifies, and blesses our lives, that

woman in this country is cheap; that vast numbers whose
names ought to be synonyms for purity and virtue are
plunged into profligacy and infamy. But do you not know
that you sent 40,000 men to perish on the bleak heights of
the Crimea, and that the revolt in India, caused, in part at
least, by the grievous iniquity of the seizure of Oude, may
tax your country to the extent of 100,000 lives before it is
extinguished; and do you not know that for the 140,000
men thus draughted off and consigned to premature graves,
nature provided in your country 140,000 women? If you
have taken the men who should have been the husbands of
these women, and if you have sacrificed 100,000,000*l.*, which
as capital reserved in the country would have been an ample
fund for their employment and for the sustentation of their
families, are you not guilty of a great sin in involving yourselves in such a loss of life and of money in war, except on
grounds and under circumstances which, according to the
opinions of every man in the country, should leave no kind of
option whatever for your choice?

I know perfectly well the kind of observations which a
certain class of critics will make upon this speech. I have
been already told by a very eminent newspaper publisher in
Calcutta, who, commenting on a speech I made at the close
of the session with regard to the condition of India and our
future policy in that country, said, that the policy I recommended was intended to strike at the root of the advancement
of the British Empire, and that its advancement did not
necessarily involve the calamities which I pointed out as
likely to occur. My Calcutta critic assured me that Rome
pursued a similar policy for a period of eight centuries, and
that for those eight centuries she remained great. Now, I do
not think that examples taken from pagan, sanguinary Rome,
are proper models for the imitation of a Christian country, nor
would I limit my hopes of the greatness of England even to
the long duration of 800 years. But what is Rome now?

The great city is dead. A poet has described her as ' the lone mother of dead empires.'   Her language even is dead.   Her very tombs are empty; the ashes of her most illustrious citizens are dispersed—

' The Scipios' tomb contains no ashes now.'

Yet I am asked, I, who am one of the legislators of a Christian country, to measure my policy by the policy of ancient and pagan Rome !

I believe there is no permanent greatness to a nation except it be based upon morality.   I do not care for military greatness or military renown.   I care for the condition of the people among whom I live.   There is no man in England who is less likely to speak irreverently of the Crown and Monarchy of England than I am; but crowns, coronets, mitres, military display, the pomp of war, wide colonies, and a huge empire, are, in my view, all trifles light as air, and not worth considering, unless with them you can have a fair share of comfort, contentment, and happiness among the great body of the people.   Palaces, baronial castles, great halls, stately mansions, do not make a nation.   The nation in every country dwells in the cottage; and unless the light of your constitution can shine there, unless the beauty of your legislation and the excellence of your statesmanship are impressed there on the feelings and condition of the people, rely upon it you have yet to learn the duties of government.

I have not, as you have observed, pleaded that this country should remain without adequate and scientific means of defence.   I acknowledge it to be the duty of your statesmen, acting upon the known opinions and principles of ninety-nine out of every hundred persons in the country, at all times, with all possible moderation, but with all possible efficiency, to take steps which shall preserve order within and on the confines of your kingdom.   But I shall repudiate and denounce the expenditure of every shilling, the engagement of every man, the employment of every ship which has no object but intermeddling in the affairs of other countries, and endeavouring to extend the boundaries of an Empire which is already large enough to satisfy the greatest ambition, and I fear is much too large for the highest statesmanship to which any man has yet attained.

The most ancient of profane historians has told us that the Scythians of his time were a very warlike people, and that they elevated an old cimeter upon a platform as a symbol of Mars, for to Mars alone, I believe, they built altars and offered sacrifices. To this cimeter they offered sacrifices of horses and cattle, the main wealth of the country, and more costly sacrifices than to all the rest of their gods. I often ask myself whether we are at all advanced in one respect beyond those Scythians. What are our contributions to charity, to education, to morality, to religion, to justice, and to civil government, when compared with the wealth we expend in sacrifices to the old cimeter? Two nights ago I addressed in this hall a vast assembly composed to a great extent of your countrymen who have no political power, who are at work from the dawn of the day to the evening, and who have therefore limited means of informing themselves on these great subjects. Now I am privileged to speak to a somewhat different audience. You represent those of your great community who have a more complete education, who have on some points greater intelligence, and in whose hands reside the power and influence of the district. I am speaking, too, within the hearing of those whose gentle nature, whose finer instincts, whose purer minds, have not suffered as some of us have suffered in the turmoil and strife of life. You can mould opinion, you can create political power,—you cannot think a good thought on this subject and communicate it to your neighbours,—you cannot make these points topics of discussion in your social circles and more general meetings, without affecting sensibly and speedily the course which the Government of your country will pursue. May I ask you, then, to believe, as I do most devoutly believe, that the moral law was not written for men alone in their individual character, but that it was written as well for nations, and for nations great as this of which we are citizens. If nations reject and deride that moral law, there is a penalty which will inevitably follow. It may not come at once, it may not come in our lifetime; but, rely upon it, the great Italian is not a poet only, but a prophet, when he says,—

> ' The sword of heaven is not in haste to smite,
> Nor yet doth linger.'

We have experience, we have beacons, we have landmarks enough. We know what the past has cost us, we know how much and how far we have wandered, but we are not left without a guide. It is true we have not, as an ancient people had, Urim and Thummim—those oraculous gems on Aaron's breast—from which to take counsel, but we have the unchangeable and eternal principles of the moral law to guide us, and only so far as we walk by that guidance can we be permanently a great nation, or our people a happy people.

FINANCIAL POLICY.

THE FINANCIAL POLICY OF THE LATE GOVERNMENT.

HOUSE OF COMMONS, JULY 21, 1859.

From Hansard.

[Mr. Disraeli took occasion to give an elaborate defence of the financial policy
of the late Government, and to criticise the position which the income-tax
assumed in the scheme of the existing Administration. He recommended
that the additional income-tax, instead of being collected in six months,
should be extended over a year. But he assumed that the public expenditure of the country could not be diminished. It was to this point especially
that Mr. Bright directed himself. When the report of this speech arrived
in Paris, it attracted the attention of M. Chevalier, the distinguished French
Economist. He wrote at once to Mr. Cobden, expressing his belief that a
Commercial Treaty between England and France might be negotiated, and
urged him to come to Paris during the autumn to make the attempt.
Mr. Cobden went to Paris during the autumn, having received the sanction
of the leading Members of the Government, and sought an interview with
the Emperor of the French. Negotiations were at once entered into, and
the Treaty of Commerce with France was the result. This was the crowning
labour of the public life of Mr. Cobden, and with it his name and fame will
be for ever associated.]

I AM not sorry that I had the opportunity of hearing the
speech of the Chancellor of the Exchequer before I was permitted to address the House. I am sure the House will
understand me when I say that I have listened to large
portions of his speech, and of that of his predecessor in office,
with great satisfaction. As far as the right hon. Gentleman

opposite (Mr. Disraeli) is concerned, I think that my hon. Friend the Member for Rochdale (Mr. Cobden), myself, and others who have generally acted with us, may consider him a convert to the views which we have very often expressed in this House. I recollect that Sir Robert Peel on one occasion made a speech of very much the same tenor, and hon. Gentlemen opposite charged him with being a convert to our views. I believe that any man of intellect and genius who may lead that party to which the right hon. Gentleman belongs, and none other can lead it with any success, will, as time rolls on, more and more adopt those principles of political economy and of foreign policy which we have felt it our duty to propound to the House and the country.

The speech of the right hon. Gentleman the Member for Bucks (and, in fact, also that of the Chancellor of the Exchequer), was a speech upon two subjects, the first part being devoted to finance, and the second to the question of foreign policy; and perhaps the House will allow me to make a few observations in the same order. The budget of the Chancellor of the Exchequer has, I think, met with general satisfaction—at least with as much satisfaction as generally falls to the lot of unpleasant propositions of this nature; but I may say for myself that whatever approbation of it I have to express arises from the fact that it is a proposition confined to a single year, and that the right hon. Gentleman himself has suggested to the House that next year it will be necessary to take a general and more comprehensive review of the whole question of our finances and taxation.

I shall, if the House will permit me, state one or two reasons why I feel particular satisfaction at the temporary nature of the plan which the right hon. Gentleman has proposed. I believe that, notwithstanding all that Chancellors of the Exchequer may say with regard to the advantages of the income-tax, it is as hateful as ever it has been to the people, and I believe it to be hateful chiefly because it is unjust. I shall not now enter into the question which has been so often debated, whether the tax ought to continue to be levied at the same rate upon fixed and precarious incomes, because I think that, whatever we may say, every one feels that there is a fixed injustice and a fixed wrong which it is utterly impossible that you should ever work out of the minds of the people of this country by whom the tax is paid. Just before coming into the House I had in the lobby an interview with some gentlemen who have come up to town to protest against the continuance of this injustice. I made this answer to their representations: 'I agree with you entirely. I think the tax odious beyond all others that I know of, and odious beyond all others because it is unjust beyond all others; and I will never consent that in its present shape it should be made a permanent tax. But the Chancellor of the Exchequer proposes it for one year, under an emergency which some people suppose to have arisen. Therefore, I am obliged to consent to it this year; but if I am here next year, and any proposition is made for its continuance in its present shape, it shall receive no countenance from me.'

But there is another ground on which I should have to object to this tax, and at which I will now only just hint. It is not a pleasant view of the case for hon. Gentlemen opposite or for those whom they chiefly represent. When the time comes I am prepared to show that the income-tax presses upon all capital employed in shops or manufactures with double the weight that it does upon that which is employed strictly in the cultivation of the land. I am sure that hon. Gentlemen opposite will see the injustice in one particular— namely, that farmers in England, if I am not mistaken, pay on a rate of income calculated upon half their rent, while farmers in Scotland pay only upon an income calculated upon one-third of their rent. I know no reason for differences of that kind. I do not think they should exist. You may tolerate them for a single year—we can tolerate a great deal if we think it necessary to maintain the honour or interests of the country, or even for the convenience of Parliament at times—but you cannot tolerate them as representing the permanent settlement of a question in taxation.

There is another ground upon which I should wholly object to the course which the Chancellor of the Exchequer is taking if he was making his arrangement for more than a year, and in adverting to this I must call his attention to measures of great importance, which were much boasted of at the time, and to which he prevailed upon Parliament to assent in the year 1853. I hold that, whatever be our taxes—let us have 50,000,000*l.*, or 70,000,000*l.*, or 100,000,000*l.* a-year—and I know not but we may live to see taxation grow up to 100,000,000*l.* a-year as heedlessly as we have seen it grow up to 70,000,000*l.*—whatever be the amount of our taxes, let us endeavour to do honestly by our countrymen; not pressing the poor, whether our taxes be heavy or light in the main; laying them on with a stronger and more resolute hand upon property, but in dealing with property, dealing just as honestly with its owners as we should deal with the poorest subjects of the realm. I take the taxes on successions of every kind—probate-duty, legacy-duty, and the tax levied under the Act of 1853—to be strictly in their nature property taxes. They are taxes which are collected or intended to be collected as part of every man's possessions and property which change hands on the death of their owner. Those who are poor—those whose means are nothing—of whom there are unfortunately many in this country—who make no wills, for whom no one takes out letters of adminis-tration, who have nothing to leave as a fortune or a little property to their children, are not directly interested in this matter; but all other classes of society are directly interested in it; and I say that, whether a man be employed in manu-factures, or have property in land, in the Funds, or in Stocks and shares of any kind, he has a fair right to appeal to this

House that in the imposition of taxes of this nature there should be the most just regard that is possible for the interests of all those whom the law is intended to affect.

I shall tell the House in a few words of what I complain, and what I shall move next year before anything be done to re-impose the income-tax. The Chancellor of the Exchequer in his budget speech of 1853, where he introduced that not very welcome guest to hon. Members opposite, the succession-tax, adverted to the probate-duty, which he said ought fairly to be levied upon all kinds of property, and not confined to one description alone. The hon. Member for Lambeth (Mr. W. Williams) has brought that duty repeatedly before the House, and has shown that 40,000,000*l.* or 50,000,000*l.*, if not more, have been paid into the Exchequer by taxes upon probates and legacies, all of which has been collected by taxes on personal property, but from which real and freehold property has been entirely exempted. I do not believe that any hon. Gentleman on the opposite side of the House feels that there ought to be this gross inequality. The probate-duty in 1858 raised to the Exchequer a sum of 1,338,000*l.*, and next session I shall ask the Chancellor of the Exchequer why it is not extended, as it ought to be, to all property which passes by death from one owner to another.

It was curious to observe that the right hon. Gentleman in his speech the other night—it was not quite so long as one he made before, but it was none the worse for that— did not refer to what was said to be the greatest effort of his financial genius. In 1853 everybody said there never was such a Chancellor of the Exchequer. He persuaded the country gentlemen to pass a Bill which inflicted upon them, as they allege, the very same succession-duty as the law imposed upon personal property. What did the right hon. Gentleman say upon that occasion? He calculated that in the following year, 1854, the succession-tax would produce 500,000*l.* to the Exchequer; in 1855 an additional 700,000*l.*;

in 1856 an additional 400,000*l.*; and in 1857 an additional
400,000*l.* It will thus be seen that he anticipated the annual
produce of this tax to amount in 1857 to 2,000,000*l.* If
his calculation had turned out to be correct, the succession-
duty would have yielded up to the present time no less a
sum than 9,300,000*l.* What has been the actual result?
I cannot give the exact figures, because the Board of Inland
Revenue say they cannot separate that which has been
received from the succession-tax of 1853 from that which has
been received from the old legacy-duty. But, adopting the
mode which was pursued by the Chancellor of the Exchequer
the other night, I can inform the House that the legacy-duty
in 1852, before the succession-tax came into existence, produced 1,380,000*l.*, whereas the legacy and succession duties
combined yielded in 1859 the sum of 2,211,000*l.*, being an
increase of 831,000*l.* From that sum, however, I must
deduct the increase of the ancient legacy-duty in the interval
between 1853 and 1859, and I ought also to deduct something, but unfortunately I have no means of ascertaining
what, for that description of property which the Chancellor
of the Exchequer in 1853 called rateable property, and which
he withdrew from the legacy-duty, and put under the succession-tax at a much smaller amount. Passing that by,
however, and deducting only 50,000*l.* for the increase of the
old legacy-duty, I find that the succession-tax, from which
the Chancellor of the Exchequer expected two years ago to
receive 2,000,000*l.* a-year, brought in last year no more
than 781,000*l.*

How came the Chancellor of the Exchequer, he that understands his business so well, to make so grievous a mistake as
this? I shall tell the House how it was. It is an odd thing
that he could make such a mistake, but it is still more odd
how any one could be taken in by such a mistake when made.
The tax was not what it pretended to be; it was not a succession-tax upon the value of property passing from one person

to another, but something very different; and the Chancellor of the Exchequer, while he undertook to adjust a great inequality, established another just as great and as offensive. I do not blame him for what he did; perhaps it was all he could do at the time; but surely he was deficient in acuteness when he supposed that his new tax would in 1857 produce 2,000,000*l.*, whereas in 1859 it yielded only 781,000*l.* How the tax has been so unproductive is easily explained. If a man dies and leaves 10,000*l.*, which is in the Funds, or in the North-Western Railway, or in ships, or in machinery, or employed in trade—what is done in reference to that 10,000*l.*? I will take the case of the 10 per cent. duty—that is where there is no kindred; 10,000*l.* left by one man to another, where there is no relationship, would have to pay a tax of 1000*l.* to the Exchequer. But, supposing the 10,000*l.* were invested in land, or in that rateable property which is the new distinction that the right hon. Gentleman establishes, what would be the result? Take two men, one twenty-two and the other eighty years of age. You would find that the Inland Revenue Board would turn to a table, which would say the man of eighty has a life worth three or four years only, and the man of twenty-two has a life worth twenty or twenty-five years; and they would then take the income from the 10,000*l.* and multiply it by the number of years supposed to remain to the young man and to the old man, and thus come to the sum on which each would have to pay.

I was fortunate enough to have a small property left to me by a person of whom I had no knowledge. I never saw him. He was an old gentleman, a great friend of peace, and opposed to the Russian war, and seeing that my hon. Friend the Member for Rochdale and myself were very strenuous in our opposition to that war, he did what was in his power to mark his opinion of the course we had taken. I sold the property for 1400*l.* or 1500*l.*; and when I came to pay my legacy-duty—that is, the succession-tax—I was greatly astonished at the small sum I had to pay. My age was taken; an estimate of the annual value of the property was made; and I was told that I had to pay something like 40*l.* or 50*l.* If the property had been in the Funds, or invested in any other of the modes to which I have referred, I should have had to pay 140*l.* at least. Take the case of an hon. Gentleman on this side of the House who has been more fortunate than myself. A property worth 32,000*l.* was left to him by a person who was not a blood relation. If it had been in the Funds, or in ships, or in railways, or employed in trade, the succession-duty would have amounted to 3200*l.* What did he pay? - He is not an old man—younger probably than the average of Members in this House—and yet, upon the property being valued and a calculation made of the number of years he might live, he found that he had to pay, not 3200*l.*, but 700*l.* Is it consistent with fairness—with our personal honour—for, after all, that is a quality which enters into these questions—with our duty to the public, that we, sitting here as a representative body, should take one class of property, the most solid and durable, attracting to it the largest social and political advantages, having in it the greatest certainty of accumulation and improvement from the general improvement in the condition of the people, and charge it to the extent of 700*l.*, while at the same time we impose 3200*l.* upon another class of property not more valuable and far more fleeting in its character?

I think the reason why I should object to a permanent re-imposition of the income-tax will now be obvious to the House. I should object to it with all the force I am capable of until the taxes which now exist are put on a satisfactory and honest footing, so that every man and every description of property may be called upon by the State in its just proportion to support the burdens and the necessities of the State. I do not intend beyond this to refer to the proposition which the Chancellor of the Exchequer has made. I have only now referred to it that I may lay the ground for the course which I shall take in another session of Parliament, if this question comes before the House again; and I believe that this course will be sanctioned by a large number of Members here, and will meet with almost unanimous approval from all the honest men who are taxpayers in the kingdom.

But this question of the mode of levying taxes is apart from a very serious question referred to by the right hon. Gentleman—that of our growing and frightful expenditure. The Chancellor of the Exchequer said, and very justly, that up to 1853 in the great departments of the expenditure there had been no great increase for many years. I confess that, although I have been protesting session after session against this growing expenditure, I was not fully aware of the enormous increase which has taken place until I compared the present year with 1853 and some preceding years. I find that in 1853, on the estimate of the right hon. Gentleman, the expenditure was only 50,782,000*l.*, while the expenditure in the current year is 69,207,000*l.* The House must bear in mind that this is somewhat of an unfair picture, because since 1853 there has been a sum of money charged to the expenditure which formerly went in the collection of the revenue. Making every allowance, however, for the 4,740,000*l.* which is disposed of in this way, the expenditure has positively increased in the interval by 13,685,000*l.* The right hon. Gentleman opposite (Mr. Disraeli) was not, I think, quite correct in his statement respecting the Miscellaneous Estimates; but there can be no doubt that the great and serious item in our outgoings is that of armaments, for I find that the military and naval expenditure of the country has risen from 17,000,000*l.* in 1853 to upwards of 26,000,000*l.* in 1860.

Now, I should like to ask the House two or three quiet, serious questions, on this matter. The hon. Member sitting

here just now (Sir Charles Napier), who commanded the
Baltic fleet, and who represents the borough of Southwark, has
left his place, and I am very sorry for it, because I should
have liked to ask him two or three questions. Does the
House believe that we are now more or less safe from a foreign
war, and particularly from an invasion of this country, than
we were in 1853? We have men—the right hon. Gentleman
has referred to them—who are afflicted with a periodical
panic. There is no complaint, I believe, so incurable as that.
One fit begets another, and every fit seems so to enfeeble the
constitution of the patient that each succeeding attack becomes more alarming than the last. We have two or three
newspapers in this city, which appear to suffer in this way.
One, which is supposed to represent a particular trading
interest, pours forth from day to day, from week to week,
from month to month—I know not at whose instigation, I
know not if at the instigation of any man save the editor—
the most foolish but the most bitter invectives against the
French Government, and by that means against the French
nation. I say against the French nation, because I hold that,
no matter whether we approve the Government now existing
in France or not, if we had such a Government, and some
foreign nation through its press were constantly insulting
that Government, we should take not a small portion of those
insults to ourselves, and we should become proportionately
irritated against that nation.

Take another paper, the *Times*, which, unfortunately and
untruly, is believed on the Continent to represent the opinions
of the English people. Who is there on that paper—let him
stand forward if there be such a man—who has a bitter personal animosity against the Emperor of the French? Day
after day, every form into which the English language can
be pressed is made use of for the purpose of stirring up the
bitterest animosity between two of the greatest nations on the
face of the earth. Have these men published letters from

Italy in vain? Have they told us of acres of bloody and mangled human bodies over which guns have been dragged and cavalry have galloped—have they told us of such scenes until a shudder has passed, I may almost say, through universal human nature—and yet have they learnt for one single moment to restrain that animosity which, if it continues many months longer, will place it beyond the power of this or any Government to prevent our being embroiled in a war with France?

And it is not only the Member for Southwark and such as he, it is not only the editors of newspapers, who suffer from and create these panics; but go into another and what is generally supposed to be a higher place, and what do you find there? Why, you hear some aged Peer turning back as it were to the convictions and the facts of his early youth, and delivering speeches which might have been somewhat in character with the barbarism of sixty years ago, but which are very unfit for our time and for our opinions. We find another Peer ['Order!']—another Gentleman, then, making a speech. I believe I am transgressing by the mention of certain things which are too sacred for allusion here; but really I do not wish to go into detail and point to particular persons in connection with this matter. What I say is, that throughout Europe every intelligent man who reads speeches of that character, whether made in this House or in another place, can only arrive at one conclusion, thoroughly false as I believe in my conscience it would be—namely, that these persons represent a very large amount of public opinion in this country, and that we have forgotten the disasters and the ruin entailed by the great Revolutionary War of which the Chancellor of the Exchequer has spoken, and are ready to engage in another conflict of equal duration and equal cost in blood and treasure, with a result as utterly bootless to England and to Europe.

Look at our position with regard to France at this moment.

One of our wars is just over. I do not know that I use the exact words of the right hon. Gentleman opposite, but I agree with him that there can be no peace in Italy between those two great Powers which can compare for evil with the war which that peace has terminated. When I read of peace being concluded, I felt as if I could breathe more freely since the species to which I belong is no longer engaged in the fiend-like destruction of its fellow-creatures. What do we now find in the Manifesto of the Emperor of the French just received in this country? He said he discovered—I am not now using his exact words—that he was making war against the mind of Europe. That is a most important and valuable admission, and I only wish the Emperor had found this out three or six months ago. He says, further, that the war was assuming dimensions with which the interests which France had in the struggle were not commensurate. I am surprised that a man reputed to be so acute did not perceive that he would be exposed to this great danger before he entered upon the war. But the two admissions made in this remarkable and memorable address prove to me that the suspicious which have been so studiously raised in this country as to the future objects of the Emperor of the French are altogether unfounded. I do not believe it possible for either the Emperor of the French or the Emperor of Austria to have returned home with all those scenes of horror, such as we have read of, flitting before their eyes, and I hope before their consciences, and to be now prepared to enter into another struggle—least of all a struggle with a nation like ours, containing 30,000,000 of united people, the most powerful, the richest, and, all things considered, perhaps the best satisfied with their Government of any nation in Europe.

Besides this, have they not learnt something from the improvements effected in weapons of warfare, and the increased destructiveness of life of which those weapons are now capable? They see now how costly war is in money, how destructive in human life. Success in war no longer depends on those circumstances that formerly decided it. Soldiers used to look down on trade, and machine-making was, with them, a despised craft. No stars or garters, no ribbons or baubles bedecked the makers and workers of machinery. But what is war becoming now? It depends, not as heretofore, on individual bravery, on the power of a man's nerves, the keenness of his eye, the strength of his body, or the power of his soul, if one may so speak; but it is a mere mechanical mode of slaughtering your fellow-men. This sort of thing cannot last. It will break down by its own weight. Its costliness, its destructiveness, its savagery will break it down; and it remains but for some Government—I pray that it may be ours!—to set the great example to Europe of proposing a mutual reduction of armaments. Our policy in past times—and the right hon. Gentleman did not go so far into this question as I could have wished—has been one of perpetual meddling, with perpetually no result except that which is evil. We have maintained great armaments, not, I sincerely believe, because we wanted to conquer or to annex any territory in Europe, but in order that whenever anything happens in Europe we may negotiate, intervene, advise, do something or other becoming what is called the dignity of this great country.

Do not you suppose this is precisely the language of the French Emperor at this moment? The Emperor of the French builds great fleets because you build great fleets; and then you build greater fleets because he builds great fleets. What does France want with great fleets? Precisely that which you have always wanted with yours. If there be any disturbance between any countries in Europe, do you not think it would be beneath the dignity of France not to take a part in it, and, taking a part in it, not to take a part with that influence and success which becomes a great country like France? And, therefore, without wishing any more than England

wishes to make conquests or to annex territory, France wishes
to have great influence in Europe because it suits its dignity,
and will add to the glory and historical renown of its
Emperor. Well, now, that is exactly the position in which
we are, and we have no more right to blame the Emperor of
the French than he has a right to blame us. We are both very
silly, and I hope, from what I have heard to-night, that at
last we on our side the water are beginning to find this out.

I shall not go into the question whether we are really about
to be invaded. I am told that so much has been said about it
that the French really believe we are making this outcry to
cover our designs of invading them. I saw a letter in one of
their newspapers this morning in which it is stated that from
Dunkirk to some other town there are mounds and fortifications and guns all ready, though concealed from the eye by
grassy banks, to repress and to frustrate our designs. Recollect that the French Government went into the Russian war
because they were anxious to associate themselves with the
foreign policy of England. Subsequently they went into
another war with us with a more distant nation—they went
into the war with China. They took part with the noble
Viscount now at the head of the Government in the interference which he promoted in Italy with regard to Naples
some two or three years ago. It appears to me that looking
at it from every point of view, reading the newspapers, and
hearing what everybody has to say, if there be one thing
which is more distinctly marked in the policy of the Emperor
of the French since his accession to the throne of France
than another, it is his perpetual anxiety, by every means
consistent with his own safety, and with the interests as he
believes of France, to ally himself with England and with the
foreign policy of England. Well, if that be so, why should
we perpetually create these suspicions, and generate in the
minds of the people, nine-tenths of whom have small opportunity of ascertaining the facts, alarms which give colour and

justification to this enormous increase of our armaments, of which we have heard such loud complaints from both sides of that table to-night?

I shall not go into the question of this Conference. At the first view my opinion would go very much with the right hon. Gentleman (Mr. Disraeli). I doubt very much—indeed, I ought to say, I do not doubt, but I feel sure—that if England is to go into the Conference merely to put its name to documents which are of no advantage to Italy, which do not engage the sympathies of this nation, England had much better have nothing to do with it. But there is another course which I should like to recommend to the noble Lord who now holds the seals of the Foreign Office. I cannot believe that Frenchmen in matters of this nature are so very different from ourselves as some people wish to teach us. I do believe that the 36,000,000 Frenchmen engaged in all the honest occupations of their country, as our people are engaged here, are as anxious for perpetual peace with England as the most intelligent and Christian Englishmen can be for a perpetual peace with France. I believe, too, because I am convinced that it is his wisest course and his truest interest, that the Emperor of the French is also anxious to remain at peace with us, and the people in France are utterly amazed and lost in bewilderment when they see the course taken by the press, and by certain Statesmen in this country.

With that belief what would I do if I were in that responsible position?—for which, however, I know that I am thought to be altogether unfit—but if I were sitting on that bench and were in the position of the noble Lord, I would try to emancipate myself from those old, ragged, worthless, and bloody traditions which are found in every pigeon-hole and almost on every document in the Foreign Office. I would emancipate myself from all that, and I would approach the French nation and the French Government in what I would

call a sensible, a moral, and a Christian spirit. I do not say
that I would send a special envoy to Paris to sue for peace.
I would not commission Lord Cowley to make a great
demonstration of what he was about to do; but I would make
this offer to the French Government, and I would make it
with a frankness that could not be misunderstood; if it were
accepted on the other side it would be received with enthusiasm in England, and would be marked as the commencement of a new era in Europe. I would say to the French
Government, 'We are but twenty miles apart, the trade
between us is nothing like what it ought to be, considering
the population of the two countries, their vast increase of
productive power, and their great wealth. We have certain
things on this side, which now bar the intercourse between
the two nations. We have some remaining duties which are
of no consequence either to the Revenue or to Protection,
which everybody has given up here, but they still interrupt
the trade between you and us. We will reconsider these and
remove them. We have also an extraordinarily heavy duty
upon one of the greatest products of the soil of France—upon
the light wines of your country.' The Chancellor of the Exchequer, and perhaps the right hon. Gentleman opposite, may
start at once, and say that involves a revenue of 1,500,000*l.*, or
at least of 1,200,000*l.* The right hon. Gentleman talked of
the national debt being a flea-bite. What is 1,200,000*l.*—
what is 1,500,000*l.*, if it be so much as that—what is
2,000,000*l.* for the abolition of the wine duties or their reduction to a very low scale, if by such an offer as this we should
enable the Emperor of the French to do that which he is most
anxious to do? The only persons whom the French Emperor
cannot cope with are the monopolists of his own country. If
he could offer to his nation 30,000,000 of the English people
as customers, would not that give him an irresistible power
to make changes in the French tariff which would be as
advantageous to us as they would be to his own country?

I do believe that if that were honestly done, done without any diplomatic finesse, and without obstacles being attached to it that would make its acceptance impossible, it would bring about a state of things which history would pronounce to be glorious.

The tone taken to-night by the right hon. Gentleman the Member for Buckinghamshire and by the right hon. Gentleman the Chancellor of the Exchequer will find a response in the country. I am not accustomed to compliment the noble Lord at the head of the Government. I have always condemned the policy which I thought wrong, but which, I have no doubt, the noble Lord thought was best calculated to promote the interests of the country. I believe he was mistaken, and that he was importing into this century the politics of the last; but I do not think it would be possible to select a Minister who could better carry out a policy which would be just to France, and beneficial to ourselves, than the noble Lord. Blood shines more, and attracts the vision of man more than beneficent measures. But the glory of such measures is far more lasting, and that glory the noble Lord can achieve. I live among the people. I know their toils and their sorrows, and I see their pauperism—for little better than pauperism is the lot of vast numbers of our countrymen from their cradles to their graves. It is for them I speak; for them I give my time in this assembly; and in heartfelt sorrow for their sufferings I pray that some statesman may take the steps which I have indicated. He who can establish such a state of things between France and England will do much to promote the future prosperity of two great nations, and will show that eighteen hundred years of Christian professions are at length to be followed by something like Christian practice.

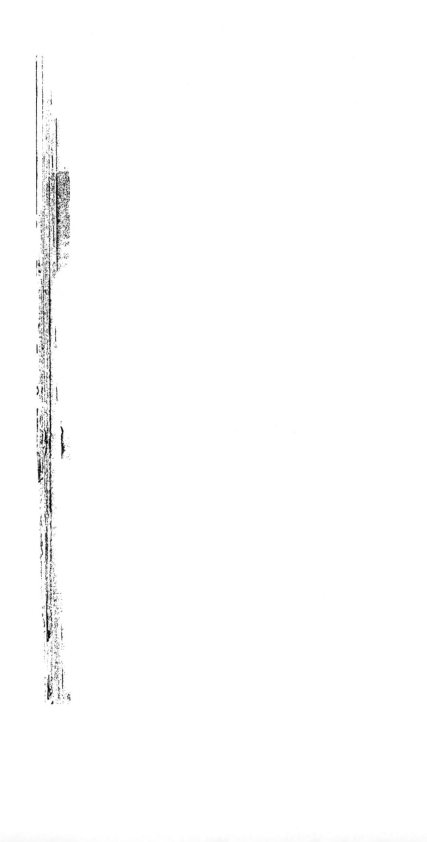

TAX BILLS.

POWER OF HOUSE OF LORDS.

HOUSE OF COMMONS, JULY 6, 1860.

From Hansard.

[Mr. Gladstone's Budget of 1860 provided for the repeal of the Paper-duty. This portion of the Budget was rejected by the House of Lords. Subsequently, a Committee of the House of Commons was appointed to inquire for precedents as to the power of the Lords to deal with Money Bills. Mr. Bright served on that Committee, and drew up a report. The following speech was spoken on the Resolutions which were submitted to the House in pursuance of the report ultimately adopted by the Committee.]

I CANNOT help being struck with an inconsistency in the right hon. Gentleman (Mr. Horsman) who has just resumed his seat. I am surprised that he has not concluded by moving that certain words in the first Resolution should be omitted, and in point of fact that the declaration which the House is about to make should be reversed. That would be in accordance with the speech of the right hon. Gentleman, and with the sentiments which many Members opposite have most vociferously cheered. I confess I do not know what a number of hon. Gentlemen opposite thought of the statements of the right hon. Gentleman about the headlong, precipitate, and reckless Budget of the Chancellor of the Exchequer, because I think there were some fifty of them

who were more enthusiastic supporters of that Budget than a
great number of the Members on this side of the House.

I shall not follow the right hon. Gentleman in his endea-
vours to support his theories with regard to the extreme value
of the House of Lords, nor shall I attempt to controvert
them, because, in reality, that is not the question which is
before the House.   But, if the House will permit me, I will
endeavour to keep as close to the question as I can, and
I will state the grounds on which I am not satisfied with
the course which this House is invited to take.   I will not
attack the Resolutions of the noble Lord, and I will not
defend them, for I am not responsible for them.   They appear
to me unworthy of the occasion which is before us.   I
think they bear marks of having been prepared by more than
one hand, and if they pass, and constitute the sole expression
of our mind on this occasion, posterity will hardly fail to
pronounce them the Resolutions of a somewhat degenerate
House of Commons.   The first Resolution is a very good one,
but it is very old.   It is none the worse for that; and I am
glad the noble Viscount did not think it necessary to endeavour to amend it.   The other two Resolutions are, to my
mind, somewhat ambiguous and feeble, and are not in their
expression of what I believe is constitutional usage, any more
than as examples of composition in the English language, to
be compared to the first and oldest.

Last night we had two speeches from that side of the
House after long silence—speeches which, I confess, I heard
with some surprise and with some pain.   They appeared to
me marked—to use a favourite phrase of the right hon.
Gentleman below me—by great recklessness, and, if I may so
speak, with great levity.   Whatever may be the opinion of
hon. Members on this question, it is not one to be treated in .
that manner.   It is a serious question—whether the powers of
this House have been infringed or not, and whether the other
House of Parliament shall hereafter exercise powers which

it has never heretofore exercised. I confess I was compelled to think of the truth we learn from history, that there is no greater sign of the decadence of a people than when we find the leaders of parties and eminent statesmen treating great questions as if they were not great, and solemn realities as if they were not real at all. I think I could observe in those speeches the triumph of men who had found an advocate in the Prime Minister, whom they expected to meet as an opponent, and who were delighted that, acting with their confederates in the other House of Parliament, they were likely to obtain a signal party advantage.

Is there anybody who has denied in point blank terms, except the right hon. Gentleman, that the House of Lords, in the course it has taken, has violated—I will not say the privileges of this House, for privilege is a word not easily defined—but has broken in upon the usages of many centuries old—usages which our predecessors in this House have acknowledged to be of the utmost importance to our own powers and to the liberties of those whom we represent? If there was nothing wrong, then why was there a committee? The right hon. Gentleman the Member for Bucks neglected to answer that question. He made no opposition at the time; but three weeks afterwards he thinks that it would have been better if the committee had not been appointed. I will, however, undertake to affirm that, when the noble Viscount proposed that committee, every Member of this House thought the proposition a reasonable one. Why did we ransack the journals unless something had happened which jarred upon every man's sense of the rights and privileges of this House and the usages of the House of Lords? And why, having this committee, and instituting these researches, have we these Resolutions moved, not by a young, inexperienced, and unknown Member—if any such there be in the House of Commons—but by one of the oldest Members of this House, one of the ablest statesmen of the day, and at

this moment the chief Minister of the Crown ?   Surely every
one will admit that the circumstances were such as to justify
the course that was taken in appointing the committee.

Then I have another reason to give to hon. Gentlemen
opposite, notwithstanding their spasmodic cheering—I do not
intend the word offensively—why we should have these very
Resolutions which you are about to agree to, which the right
hon. Gentleman the Member for Bucks, as far as I could
understand, entirely approves, and which you all feel delighted
should be proposed by the noble Viscount, because they relieve
you from a considerable difficulty.   I say that these Resolutions are a proof that the course which has been taken by
the other House has been unusual, if not wrong; because the
Resolutions by implication condemn what the Lords have
done, and although they do not revoke the Act, or pledge
this House to any particular course, yet, when those Resolutions come to be considered, it will never be denied that the
House of Commons does by them express a unanimous
opinion that the course which has been taken by the other
House is contrary to usage, and is calculated to excite the
jealousy and alarm of the Members of this House.

I have been a member of that committee, and the right
hon. Gentleman the Member for the University of Cambridge
knows my opinion of the committee and its labours.   I think
that committee fell wonderfully below its duties—that the
course which it pursued was poor and spiritless; and at a
future time when the course it has taken is contrasted with
the course taken by the House of Commons on previous occasions, it will be justly said that there has been a real and
melancholy declension in the spirit of this House.   That
which I complain of in the proceedings of the committee, I
also complain of in respect to the manner in which some hon.
Members have discussed this question.   Half of the committee
appeared to me to go into that committee as much the advocates of the House of Lords as of the House of Commons, and

I find that some Members of this House are of the same character. Speeches have been delivered here that very few Members of the House of Lords would make on this question, and I will undertake to say that not one Member of that House, who is known to the public by his political influence, legal knowledge, high character, or extensive learning, would dare to make the speech that has been made to-night by the right hon. Gentleman the Member for Stroud. I went into the committee with the utmost frankness in order that I might ascertain, not altogether in what manner the Lords had asserted their privileges, but what our predecessors had done with regard to theirs. We have no right to let go one single particle of the privileges and powers which the House of Commons have gained in past times; and I took it for granted that if I examined for some centuries back the course which the House of Commons had pursued—if I read their Resolutions, if I read the reasons adduced at their conferences, if I observed the Acts which they passed, and the result of the discussions between the two Houses—we should be justified in concluding that we have rights to maintain for which our predecessors have contended.

Now, several Members, following the example of the committee, have taken the House back for a long period of time. I will not go into those precedents with the view of contending whether they do or do not refer to this particular case; but the House will permit me to mention two or three facts which I brought out of the Journals, and which convinced me that we should not take a sufficiently bold or decided course if we merely agree to the Resolutions of the noble Viscount. I will first refer to that very case which the right hon. Gentleman the Member for the University of Cambridge and myself fixed upon as the starting-point of our precedents—the precedents of the year 1407; and I trust every hon. Member has read it, either in the translation, or in the old Norman-French. It is worth reading, for it is a very curious

case, and there is no other so like the recent action of the
House of Lords as that which took place 453 years ago;
for the House of Lords then proposed to continue a tax to
which the Commons had not assented, and the House of
Commons were greatly disturbed at the House of Lords pro-
longing a tax to which the House of Commons had not given
its assent. We then made a great leap, and from the
year 1407 came down to the year 1628. We then found the
House of Commons insisting upon the initiation of Bills of
Supply. They would not permit the name of the Lords to be
inserted in the preamble of a Bill of Supply, neither would
they agree to the compromise that neither the Lords nor the
Commons should be introduced, but that the High Court of
Parliament should be mentioned. The House of Commons
refused to pass the Bill in that shape, and submitted that the
Commons should be named alone in the grant. This was
done, and that has been the practice ever since in the preamble
of Supply Bills.

Then we come to 1640, when the House of Lords were
much more modest than they ought to have been, according
to the right hon. Gentleman, who maintains that they ought
to check, alter, amend, improve, and if necessary overthrow,
all the financial arrangements of the year that this House may
agree to. The Declaration of 1640 set forth that the Lords
stated at the Conference that—

'My Lords would not meddle with matters of subsidy, which belong naturally and properly to you—no, not to give you advice therein, but have utterly
declined it.'

Then the House of Lords in 1640, we are asked to suppose,
knew nothing of their constitutional rights, and the House of
Commons of that day were less able than they are at present to
judge of what is necessary for the performance of their proper
functions in the State, and for the liberties of those whom they
represent. Mr. Pym told their Lordships that they had not
only meddled with matters of Supply, but that they had

'Both concluded the matter and order of proceeding, which the House of Commons takes to be a breach of their privilege, for which I was commanded to desire reparation from your Lordships.'

The Lords made reparation by declaring that they did not know they were breaking a right of the Commons in merely suggesting that Supply should have precedence over the consideration of grievances. I am not sure that even now, notwithstanding what has been said, the House of Lords have ever admitted by any Resolution that they have not the power to originate Supplies. They have not the power, of course, to carry such a Bill, because if it came to this House it would fall down dead, unless that unhappy time should come when the theories of the right hon. Gentleman the Member for Stroud are carried out.

Then comes the question of Amendments. The Lords endeavoured to amend a Bill of Supply. I do not wonder that they did so, because the theories of the right hon. Gentleman must have been palatable to a good many of them. In 1671 it was proposed not to continue a tax, but to reduce a tax—the duty on white sugar. The Lords proposed to reduce the duty from one penny per pound to five-eighths of a penny, and the House of Commons came to a Resolution that 'in all aids given to the King by the Commons the rate or tax ought not to be altered by the Lords.' A conference was held with the House of Lords, and the House of Commons then declared that the right which they claimed 'was a fundamental right, both as to the matter, the measure, and the time.' Then, what followed in the House of Lords? They replied by the very same Resolution which the House of Commons had passed in its own favour. The Resolution they passed asserting their power to make Amendments was just as strong, and in the same words as the Resolution which had been passed in a contrary sense by this House. They said, with reason, 'for if they cannot amend, or abate, or revise a Bill in Parliament'—they said this, mind, in answer to the Commons, who declared that they could not amend, but might negative the whole—they said, 'if we cannot amend, or abate, or alter in part, by what consequence of reason can we enjoy the liberty to reject the whole?'

The right hon. Gentleman the Member for the University of Dublin last night showed himself a most unhappy critic. He called our attention to the condition of things in the United States. In fact, he proved himself—only he did not exactly understand what he was saying—he showed himself to be strongly in favour of Americanizing our institutions in one respect. He said the Senate of the United States has the power not only of rejecting but of amending—which is quite true. When the founders of the American Republic were binding together the thirteen sovereign States in one great —and to be still greater—combination, they looked back naturally to the practice of the country from which they were separating, to determine, or at least to learn, something from our Parliamentary practice. They found that in England the Lords could not begin Money Bills, could not alter or amend them ; but that theoretically—because the matter had never been decided—theoretically they had power to reject. But, then, what was the conclusion which they came to? They said the very same thing that the House of Lords had said in the year 1671—'It is perfectly childish to say that the House of Lords cannot alter, abate, or increase, but yet shall be able to reject.' They knew well that, although there was that theoretical right in England, yet, practically, it had never been enforced, and they came to the conclusion that if they should give to their own Senate power to reject, it would be necessary also to give them the power to amend; and at this very moment the Senate of the United States might, not with that sort of responsibility of which the right hon. Gentleman is so fond, but with a real responsibility, every two members being the representatives of a particular sovereign

State—that elected Senate does amend, and does reject, and does deal with finance in a manner which has never been permitted, nor even proposed in this country, except in the extraordinary speech to which we have just listened.

Seven years after the last date to which I have referred there arose another contest, in the course of which a Resolution was passed. It is the strongest and most comprehensive Resolution that the House of Commons has ever passed in relation to this subject. I will not go into any elaborate argument upon it, but I will just read it, because it makes the argument I am about to bring before the House more continuous and clear. The House of Commons declared this; and it was not one of those sudden acts which the House of Commons is now alleged to continually commit; but it was a Resolution drawn up by a committee specially appointed for that purpose—a Resolution specially considered and solemnly entered in the Journals of the House. It was in these words,—

'All Aids and Supplies, and Aids to His Majesty from Parliament, are the sole gifts of the Commons, and all Bills for granting such Aids and Supplies are to begin with the Commons ; and it is the undoubted and sole right of the Commons to direct, limit, and appoint in such Bills the ends, purposes, considerations, conditions, limitations, and qualifications of such grants, which ought not to be changed or altered by the House of Lords.'

At this time, when the Lords had never pretended to reject a Bill, it is probable that such a proposition was a thing that never entered into the head of any Member of the House of Peers. I will undertake to say it would be difficult for any Member of this House to draw up a Resolution more comprehensive and conclusive as to the absolute control of the House of Commons than that of the year 1678, which I have just now read.

Shortly afterwards, in the year 1691, there is another Resolution which goes minutely to the case before the House, and I beg the right hon. Gentleman's attention to it. In that year a Bill was passed for appointing Commissioners to

Examine the Public Accounts of the Kingdom.   The House
of Lords amended, the House of Commons dissented; and
among the reasons which the House of Commons gave was
this—'That in aids, and supplies, and grants, the Commons
only do judge of the necessities of the Crown.'   What are we
asked now?   We are asked to take into partnership another
judge of the necessities of the Crown.   The House of Commons which for five hundred years, which, since the Revolution at least, has never withheld adequate Supplies from the
Crown, is now to be depreciated and defamed, as if it had
been guilty of scantily supplying the wants of the Crown, and
the House of Lords is to be asked to do that which the House
of Commons alone did in 1691, namely, to judge of the
necessities of the Crown, and to make the Supply greater
than that which the House of Commons have believed to be
sufficient.   And, referring to that famous record of Henry the
Fourth, we find it stated there that 'all grants and aids are
made by the Commons, and are only assented to by the
Lords.'

A few years afterwards, our forefathers were concerned in
a question about the paper duties, just as we are at this time;
only they managed it better than we are doing now.   In the
year 1699 they declared:—

'It is an undoubted right and privilege of the Commons, that such aids are
to be given by such methods, and with such provisions, as the Commons only
shall think proper.'

But now we are told that aids and provisions for the Crown
are to be raised by methods, not which the Commons think
proper, but which the Lords think proper in opposition to the
Commons.

The House will perceive that I am very hoarse, and I am
sorry to trouble them with other cases.   In the year 1700
there was another question raised between the two Houses:
and the Commons told the Lords that they could not agree
with their Amendment, and they again affirmed that

' All the Aids and Supplies granted to His Majesty in Parliament are the sole and entire gift of the Commons ; and that it is the sole and undoubted right of the Commons to direct, limit, and appoint the ends, purposes, considerations, limitations, and qualifications of such grants.'

And in 1702 there was another statement that ' the granting and disposing of all public moneys is the undoubted right of the Commons alone.'

In the year 1719 they objected to a clause which the Lords had introduced; on the ground that it levied a new subsidy not granted by the Commons, ' which is the undoubted and sole right of the Commons to grant, and from which they will never depart.' I want to ask the House, or any reasonable man, if we were discussing this question between the American Senate and the House of Representatives, or between the two Chambers of any foreign country, to what conclusion would each one of us necessarily come as to the purpose and object of all these declarations, to which I have referred, and which are only a portion of those which are to be found in the Journals of this House for the last five hundred years? Would you say that they lead to the conclusion that the House of Lords could throw out a Bill repealing a tax of the value and magnitude of 1,300,000*l.* a-year? Would you say that if they could not abate a tax, or continue a tax, or limit a tax, or dispose of a tax, or control in any way a tax, or even give advice to the Commons in respect of a tax—could you say that notwithstanding all that which is clear and undeniable, they could, in the face of this House, reject a Bill which repealed a tax of 1,300,000*l.* a-year, without violating Parliamentary usage, and running contrary to all the declarations of this House for many centuries? I think—and I put it before the Committee—and if any hon. Gentleman has done me the honour to read the draft Report which I prepared, he will see that I put before the Committee this long string of Cases and Resolutions, and Declarations, couched in language not ambiguous, not feeble, but in language clear and forcible, which could not be mistaken; and then I wished to ask the Committee— as I now ask the House—what was the end and object which the House of Commons had in view in these repeated declarations of their rights and opinions touching the granting of Supplies, and the imposition of taxes upon the people? I should say that it was this—they confirm and consecrate a practice of five hundred years, the principle which, till within the last hour, I thought every man in England admitted—the fundamental and unchangeable principle of the Government and Constitution of the English people, that taxation and representation are inseparable in this kingdom.

Let us look and see how these Declarations and Resolutions apply to this case. We are now in the year 1860, and for a long period we have had no question of importance of this nature; and we begin to fancy that, after all, there is no great importance in such a question. We have long had our personal liberties in this country; longer almost, in some classes of society, than history can tell; but people perhaps fancy that their personal liberty cannot be endangered by this matter. No; in this case we were so confident of our right and our power that we could not comprehend any infringement of our rights. These paper-duties, I believe, were granted in the reign of Queen Anne; partly for revenue, and partly for other purposes; which purposes, I presume, had some effect in procuring the rejection of this Bill by the Lords. It was a tax to prevent the publication and spread of political information. I see an hon. Gentleman up there in the gallery who is very much astonished at this; but he is not aware, probably, that all which I have stated is, if I am not misinformed, in the Preamble of the Bill. Public opinion in those days allowed of very bad reasons being given. They can be acted on now even when they are not given. From the time of Queen Anne, to the present time, this paper-duty has crippled a very important industry. It has taxed all the trades which required large quantities of paper—such as those of Manchester, of Sheffield, of Nottingham, of Birmingham, and elsewhere; but more than that, it has very successfully done what Queen Anne's Ministers wanted; it has threatened, and, to a large extent, it has strangled the press of this country. Within the last thirty years—and hon. Members on the opposite side of the House I presume by this time are becoming conscious of it—new principles have become established in this country with regard to taxation on industry. New and wiser principles have been adopted, and not only adopted but established; and there are some very powerful defenders of these new principles, whom I have the pleasure to see opposite me to-night.

The right hon. Gentleman the Member for Stroud has proceeded on the old mode of discussion when arguments are not plentiful and facts are entirely wanting. He has raised his old friend, the hobgoblin argument, and has tried to show us that some frightful calamity must come upon us if this paper-duty be repealed : it is but a million-and-a-quarter. Does any hon. Gentleman believe that our prosperity or success—or that any vast interest of this country—can possibly depend on a million, more or less, in the general revenue of the empire ? A million is a million. ['Hear.'] I am glad to have said something in which the hon. Gentleman the Member for Leicestershire can coincide. There is no Member who has laid more stress on the importance of a million in the taxation of the people than I have done ; it is the tax of many villages, of many towns ; and it makes the difference sometimes between comfort and desolation ; and therefore I am the last person who would undervalue the amount of a million of the public revenue. But still I should be only making myself foolish, if I were to say that a million sterling—whether our taxation be 50,000,000*l.* as it was twenty years ago, or 70,000,000*l.* as it is now—was of the gigantic importance attributed to it by the right hon. Gentleman : for on this million, which we had

provided a substitute for, before we relieved the people of
that million, he founds his argument as to our recklessness,
precipitancy, and madness, and drunkenness — I think he
added—at least it was to be inferred from what he said; for
he made use of the converse, and spoke of sobriety.

The noble Lord the Member for the City of London in his
speech last night reviewed the course of events, and told us
what we all knew, that within the recollection, I suppose, of
almost the youngest Member of the House, there have been
Excise duties on many other articles; I think, at one time, on
candles; certainly at a later period on leather; I believe,
since I came into this House, on glass; and, still more
recently, on soap.   Well, all these Excise duties have been
abolished.   Can you find a man, from John O'Groat's to the
Land's End, who will not tell you that these reckless principles, applied to the repeal of these Excise duties, were not
of essential benefit, not only to the particular trades most
interested, but to the great mass of the people, and to the
industry by which your people live?

Well, then, having followed for many years a course so
beneficial, we come at length, in the year 1860, to the repeal
of the paper-duty, which was promised by the House; which
was recommended by the Government officers; which was
called for by innumerable petitions; which was hoped for,
I believe, by every person in the country who took an intelligent view of what was essential to aid the efforts which
Government are making, by liberal grants every year, to
promote the instruction of the people.   This tax was
1,300,000*l*.   It was a question whether sugar should be
relieved to the extent of a million, tea of a million, or paper
of a million: I am speaking in round numbers.   The hon.
Gentleman, not caring in the least about this reckless deficit,
would evidently have preferred sugar or tea; but surely, as
regards the question of the Supplies for the year, it was
equally a matter of indifference to the Chancellor of the

Exchequer whether the duty were taken off tea, or sugar, or paper. But the conclusion to which he necessarily came was, that while in the cases of tea and sugar the relief was to the extent of a million of taxation, in the case of paper it was not only a relief to that amount in money, but it was a relief to a great industry, and to several other industries, whose prosperity must depend on an abundant and cheap supply of paper. I speak with some knowledge of the subject, and I have not the least doubt that the abolition of the paper-duty was a positive relief to the whole people of the country equal to double the relief which would have been afforded by a reduction equal in amount to the duty on the articles of tea and sugar.

But the question may be still more narrowed; and I beg the right hon. Gentleman's particular attention—for it appears now that his hostility to the Chancellor of the Exchequer renders him unable to understand the multiplication table, or anything else that is plain. If the paper-duty expired on the 15th of August, the reduction of revenue between that time and the end of the financial year would probably not be more than 600,000*l.*, but certainly would not exceed 700,000*l.* I am sorry the House did not take more economical advice in past years. But we are now come, according to the right hon. Gentleman, to this extremity of our resources, that you cannot take 700,000*l.* this year from an Excise which is strangling a great trade, and put an additional halfpenny or penny on the income-tax, without bringing about such a frightful state of things, that the Constitution itself and the usage of Parliament must be violated, and we must bring in a foreign power to check us in our precipitous, reckless, and headlong career.

It may be very far from the modesty which becomes a Member of this House, but I confess I am of opinion that the House of Commons is the best judge in this country of what is necessary for the trade, and also what is required by the financial condition of the country. First of all, there are among us a good many sagacious men of all sorts. There are, as I know, some very sagacious landowners; we found it very hard to beat them even when they had a very bad case. We have a very sagacious Gentleman down here who spoke to-night, and who, whatever be the question which comes before us, always finds some very fitting object for his merciless and unscrupulous vituperation. We know, many of us intimately, all the details connected with these questions; in fact, I suppose, there is not a trade in this country of any importance or note that cannot find its representatives in this House. For many years past we have had the absolute control of questions of finance, and I undertake to declare, notwithstanding what the right hon. Gentleman has stated, that there is not a representative body in the world which during the last twenty years has done more in the way of financial and fiscal reforms with greater advantage to the people. And yet, at the end of that period, when the triumphs of this House are to be found not in granite and bronze monuments, but in the added comforts of the population, and in the increased and undoubted loyalty of the people, you are now, forsooth, asked by the right hon. Gentleman to abdicate your functions, and to invite 400 gentlemen, who are not traders, who have never been financiers, who do not possess means in any degree equalling your own of understanding the question—you are to ask them to join your councils, and not only to advise, but to check, and even to control.

It is one of the points which gave me most grief in regard to this question, that I have seen the House of Lords taking, of all cases, perhaps the worst that could possibly come before them, and inflicting suddenly, unexpectedly, and, in my opinion, groundlessly, most harsh and cruel treatment on all the persons who were interested directly in this question of the paper-excise. We are asked now, in terms not ambiguous, to overthrow the fabric which has grown up in this country, which has existed, and existed without damage, for at least 500 years. By the Report of the right hon. Gentleman we find that as far back as the year 1640 the House of Commons made this declaration, to which I ask the particular attention of Members of the present House. They said :—

> 'We have had uninterrupted possession of this privilege' [the privilege of the undisputed control over the taxation and finances of the country] 'ever since the year 1407, confirmed by a multitude of precedents both before and after, not shaken by one precedent for these 300 years.'

If that be so, it carries us back for a period of 520 years ; and yet we are asked to-night in the most unblushing and audacious manner, to overthrow this magnificent and time-honoured fabric, and admit to powers, to which they have hitherto been unaccustomed, the hereditary branch of the Legislature..

Now, I say that the House of Lords in the course they have taken have committed two offences, which I had much rather they had not committed, because I am not anxious that they should depreciate themselves in the eyes of the people of this country. [A laugh.] If hon. Gentlemen opposite were as anxious that they should continue limited to their proper functions, doing all the good that it is possible for them to do, and as little harm as possible, they would not laugh with an apparent unbelief in what I have just stated. I say the House of Lords have not behaved even with fair honour towards the House of Commons in this matter. Every man of them who knew anything about what he was voting for knew that the House of Commons repealed the paper-excise, not merely because it wished to remit a million of taxes, but because it thought that to strangle a great industry was an injurious mode of raising revenue, and, therefore, it transferred that amount of taxation from the paper-excise to the income-tax. Then, I say if that were known in the House of Lords, although they might have disapproved the change, and might have thought it better if it had not been made, it was not an honourable treatment of this House ; and further, if they had the power which the American Senate has, and which the right hon. and learned Gentleman wishes them to have, still it would not have been fair to this House to enact the additional penny on income, and to refuse to repeal the tax on paper. That is a question which every man can understand; and I cannot believe that there is any Member of this House who does not comprehend it when put in that shape.

But there is another thing in which the House of Lords have done wrong. They have trampled on the confidence and taken advantage of the faith of the House of Commons. The right hon. Gentleman last night made a very curious state-ment on this subject, which, if I were a Member of the House of Lords, I should be disposed to find fault with. He said :— ' Why, what can you expect ? It was the *láches* of the House of Commons that gave the House of Lords the opportunity of doing what they have done.' But, surely, if for 500 years the House of Lords has never done this,—if since the Revo-lution, even with the search into precedents made by the Committee, not a single case which approaches this can be discovered,—is the House of Commons blameable for think-ing that it was at least dealing with a House which would abide by the usages of the Constitution, and would not take advantage of the change which the House of Commons made for the public interest in the mode of imposing taxation ? Instead of certain taxes being imposed annually, or for short periods, by which the House held a constant control over them, they were made permanent. The West India interest said they did not want their trade to be troubled and disturbed every year; and the sugar duties were made perpetual. But then are we always to treat the Lords as political burglars, and invent bolts, bars, locks, everything which may keep them from a possible encroachment on our rights? Must we treat them as men who, if you give them the smallest opportunity, will come down upon you and do that which you wish them not to do? If that be so, you must assuredly take certain precautions to prevent them from continuing such a course.

It is said that the Paper Duty Abolition Bill was thrown out in the Upper House by a great majority. That is a fact with which we are all well acquainted. I was talking recently to a Peer who gave an explanation of this, which I will venture to repeat. 'If,' he said, 'the regular House of Lords, that is to say, the hundred Members who during the session really do transact the business, if they only had been in the House, the Paper Duties Repeal Bill would certainly have passed.' That, however, happened which we all understand, and I have no objection to repeat the exact words used to me. 'About two hundred Members, who hardly ever come there, were let loose for the occasion.' Most of them are unknown to the country as politicians, and they voted out this Bill by a large majority, with a chuckle, thinking that by doing so they were making a violent attack on the Ministry, and especially on the Chancellor of the Exchequer. That is a House, recollect, in which three Members form a quorum. I sometimes hear complaints in this House that Ministers pass measures very late at night, when, perhaps, only fifty Members are present, of whom thirty are connected with the Government; but in the House of Lords three form a quorum. Proxies may be used too; and these three Peers forming a quorum, with proxies in their pockets, are to dispose of great questions involving 70,000,000*l.* of taxes raised from the industry of the people of this country. At all events, if the two hundred Peers who voted that night choose to come down on other occasions, there is no single measure of finance, however liberal or however much for the advantage of the people, that they would not reject, and thus frustrate the beneficial intentions of this House.

But after all I have said I am going to make this admission, that the Lords of course can reject a Bill, and can also initiate a Bill if they like. If it were not so late (and the Lords like to get away about seven)—if it were not so late, the Lords might to-night bring in a Bill levying a tax or voting money for the service of the year, and they can also reject any Bill you may send up to them. They are omnipotent within the four walls of their House, just as we are within the four walls of this House. But if they take their course, one contrary to the general practice of that House and of Parliament, it becomes us to consider what course we will take. We cannot compel them to make any change; but we may ourselves take any course that we please, and we may at least offer them the opportunity of altering the course they have taken.

My opinion is that it would have been consonant with the dignity of this House, wholly apart from the question of 1,300,000*l.* a-year, or of 700,000*l.* the sum for this year, to have passed another Bill to repeal the paper-duty. If that had been a duty which I considered not the best to repeal, I still should have laid aside all partiality for a particular tax. The question before us is of far more importance than the maintenance or abolition of any particular tax. There can be nothing more perilous to the country, or more fatal to the future character of this House, than that we should do anything to impair and lessen the powers we have received from our predecessors. I understand there are other sums amounting to about 1,500,000*l.* or 2,000,000*l.* which have yet to go up to the House of Lords. Now, if the noble Lord at the head of the Government, acting up to his position, which I think he has failed to do in this matter, had asked us, not on the ground (for that is a low ground) that the paper-duty was the best duty to repeal, but on the ground that as the House of Commons have come to that decision they should abide by it; but if he had asked us to pass another Bill, with an altered date, perhaps, and sent it up again to the House of Lords, he would have given them the opportunity of reconsidering their decision; and my full belief is that a course like this, taken without passion and without collision, would have been met in a proper temper by that House; this difficulty would have been got over, and in all probability both Houses for the future would have proceeded more regularly and easily than they are likely to do under the plan proposed by the noble Lord.

Having stated that I shall leave the questions of these Resolutions, I say there is no reason whatever in the arguments which have been used why this duty should have been maintained, or why it was perilous to remit it. Its repeal was consistent with the policy of the Whigs before Sir Robert Peel came into power, with the policy of Sir Robert Peel's Government, of Lord Derby's Government, of Lord John Russell's Government, of Lord Aberdeen's Government, of Lord Palmerston's Government, of Lord Derby's last Government, and of the existing Government. The policy of the repeal of the paper-duty is the recognized policy of this House, and it is the admitted interest of this country. Then, why, unless it be for a party triumph, unless it be to attack a particular Minister, why is this question of 700,000*l.* this year, and less than double that sum in future years, raised to an importance which does not belong to it? and why, for the sake of a party triumph, are the great interests connected with it to be damaged and tortured, as they now are, by the action of one House of Parliament? I am told there are Members of this House who would not support the Government in this course, and I should certainly hardly expect that all the Gentlemen on the benches opposite would lend it their sanction. Yet I doubt whether if the noble Lord at the head of the Government were to act in the manner I have indicated, the great majority of them would be induced, upon reflection, to adopt the policy which they have pursued with respect to these

Resolutions, and whether the House of Commons would not have passed a second Bill even by a larger majority than that by which we passed the last.

There is a rumour that some Gentlemen on this side of the House object to such a course of proceeding, and hon. Gentlemen opposite have, perhaps, on that account been led to take up a line of action upon this question in which they otherwise could not hope to succeed. An hon. Gentleman behind me, from whom I should have expected something better, said only last night, in speaking of the Chancellor of the Exchequer, that he was a reckless and unsafe Finance Minister. That observation he no doubt confined to the question of the repeal of the paper-duty ; but I cannot forget that in 1853 we had the same Chancellor of the Exchequer as to-day, and that it was asserted then also that he had committed great errors. [Cheers from the Opposition.] Yes ; but your Chancellor of the Exchequer was not in office long enough to perpetrate any great mistakes. Not long after that right hon. Gentleman acceded to office, he brought in a Budget which the House of Commons rejected ; and upon the next occasion on which he proposed one, he found it necessary to shift the burden of responsibility to the shoulders of his successor. But in 1853, when the right hon. Gentleman the Member for the University of Oxford was Chancellor of the Exchequer, I put it to those among us who were then Members of this House, whether it is not the fact that the strength of the Government of Lord Aberdeen, of which he was a Member, was not mainly to be attributed to his dealing with the taxation of the country in a manner which met with universal approbation out of doors ?

We come now to the present year, and while I do not wish to depreciate the popularity, or the character, or the ability of the noble Lord at the head of the Government, or any of his colleagues, still I undertake to say that the power and authority which his Administration has acquired during the present session, it has gained mainly as the consequence of the beneficial propositions which the Chancellor of the Exchequer has made. I heard somebody last night—I am not quite sure it was not the right hon. Gentleman below me to-night—talk of the House of Commons having been partly charmed and partly coerced into the acceptance of these propositions. But if that be so, and if we have proved ourselves to be soft-headed children who could be so swayed, I must say it appears to me very strange that such should be the case; for I think the House of Commons has upon the contrary shown wonderful independence, and has proved itself to be extremely free from all those ties, the acting in accordance with which usually enables a Government to conduct the business of a session with success. Be that, however, as it may, I repeat that the Budget of the right hon. Gentleman the Chancellor of the Exchequer, when it was laid before the country, was received throughout all the great seats of industry, and among the farmers too—for it tended to benefit them as well as the inhabitants of towns—with universal approbation.

The right hon. Gentleman below me has been indulging himself to-night, in accordance with his custom, in condemning the French Treaty, and I must say we have heard a great deal upon that subject since it was first mooted in this House. We have had it commented upon by a great journal in this country, whose motives I will not attempt to divine, but whose motto must, I think, be that which Pascal said ought to have been adopted by one of the ancients—' Omnia pro tempore, sed nihil pro veritate,'—which being translated, may be rendered—' Everything for the *Times*, but nothing for truth.' We have had, in short, every description of falsehood propounded with respect to this Treaty. The right hon. Gentleman below me has not hesitated to-night to give currency to representations with respect to it which are wholly inaccurate, and to which, if I were not here, I would apply a still stronger term. Did not the right hon. Gentleman say our manufacturers were—I forget the word—plaintiffs—no, suppliants in the antechamber of the Emperor of the French? The statement is one, I can tell him, which is wholly untrue; nay, more,—and I may say that with the exception of some right hon. Gentlemen sitting on the Treasury bench, there is no one more competent to give an opinion on the subject than myself, for reasons with which the House is of course acquainted,—I tell the right hon. Gentleman that nothing can exceed the good faith and the liberality with which that whole question is being treated by the Commissioners of the French Government. I would have him know that they are as anxious as our Commissioners that a great trade between England and France should spring up; and I will add that in the case of nations and Governments in amity one with the other, whose representatives are endeavouring in all fairness and frankness to extend the commerce between both, he is neither a statesman nor a patriot who seeks to depreciate in the eyes of his countrymen the instrument by which it is hoped these results will be accomplished, and who thus does his utmost to prevent its success.

I come now to ask the House what is this reform in the tariff introduced by the right hon. Gentleman the Chancellor of the Exchequer, by which you are so frightened? Is it something novel? The right hon. Gentleman below me says it is a scheme both new and gigantic in its proportions, and fatal in its principle. I was speaking last week to an hon. Member for a south-western county who sits on the benches opposite, and he spoke in terms of exultation to me of the success of late years of that branch of industry in which you are peculiarly interested. Is it honest, then, that you should make such acknowledgments and not consent to extend further the principles which the whole country has pronounced to be sound and beneficial? We boast of the freedom of our commerce. That commerce has more than doubled since I had first the honour of a seat in this House. When, therefore, you now attack, through the Chancellor of the Exchequer, principles, the adoption of which has wrought this great good, you are not, in my opinion, pursuing a course which will enhance your reputation with the country which you profess to represent. There is not, I contend, a man who labours and sweats for his daily bread; there is not a woman living in a cottage, who strives to make her humble home happy and comfortable for her husband and her children, to whom the words of the Chancellor of the Exchequer have not brought hope, and to whom his measures, which have been defended with an eloquence few can equal, and with a logic none can contest, have not administered consolation. I appeal to the past and present condition of the country, and I ask you, solemnly, to oppose no obstacle to the realization of those great and good principles of legislation.

I will not enter further into this question. I am unable from physical causes to speak with clearness, and I am afraid I must have somewhat pained those who have heard me. I must, however, repeat my regret that the noble Viscount at the head of the Government has not shown more courage in this matter than he appears to me to have exhibited, and that the House of Commons has not evinced more self-respect. I fear this session may as a consequence become memorable as that in which, for the first time, the Commons of England has surrendered a right which for 500 years they had maintained unimpaired. I, at least, and those who act with me, will be clear from any participation in this; we shall be free from the shame which must indelibly attach to the chief actors in these proceedings. I protested against the order of reference which the noble Lord proposed, though I sat and laboured on the Committee with earnest fidelity on behalf of the House of Commons. I have felt it an honour to sit in this House up to this time, and I hope that hereafter the character of this House will not be impaired by the course

which is about to be taken.   I have endeavoured to show
to my countrymen what I consider to be almost the treason
which is about to be committed against them.   I have refused
to dishonour the memory of such Members as Coke and
Selden, and Glanville and Pym ; and, if defeated in this
struggle, I shall have this consolation, that I have done all
I can to maintain the honour of this House, and that I have
not sacrificed the interests which my constituents committed
to my care.

PUNISHMENT OF DEATH.

HOUSE OF COMMONS, MAY 3, 1864.

From Hansard.

[Spoken on Mr. Ewart's Motion for the Abolition of the Punishment of Death.]

I SHALL not, after the discussion which has taken place, and which has been, I think, almost all on one side, take up the time of the House by making a speech. But the right hon. Gentleman (Sir George Grey) has said something which I am obliged to contest to some extent. He has quoted the opinions of Judges upon this question, and he has laid, I think, more stress upon those opinions than they generally deserve. I think, if there is one thing more certain than another, it is this—that every amelioration of the criminal code of this country has been carried against the opinion of the majority of the Judges. And I may on this point quote the opinion of an eminent Irish Judge, who, I believe, is still living, and with whom I had some conversation in Ireland about fifteen years ago. The conversation turned on this very question. He said, ' Beware of the Judges. If Parliament had acted on the opinion of the Judges, we should have been hanging now for forgery, for horse-stealing, and for I know

not how many other offences for which capital punishment
has long been abolished.'

Now the right hon. Gentleman proposes to have a Commission, as I understand, instead of a Committee.   There was
an inconsistency in his speech, I thought, on that point; for
at first he seemed to say that the question, whether capital
punishment should be continued or be abolished, was not one
which a Committee of this House was fitted to consider; but
towards the close of his speech he moderated that by admitting that some of the points referred to in the Amendment,
which is, I suppose, to be agreed to, might be considered by
a Commission.   I will undertake to say that if he were to
inquire in every civilized country in the world where there is
a representative legislative assembly, he would find that the
changes which had been made in their laws have been made
invariably in consequence of inquiries instituted by those
Chambers and carried on by means of Committees formed
amongst their members.

I admit that the bulk of the Committees of this House are
not fairly constituted.   I served very assiduously on Committees for the first ten or fifteen years after I became a
Member of this House, and I did not find out till about the
year 1850 or 1853 that a Committee was generally of no use;
and from that time to this I have avoided, in nine cases out
of ten, when I have been applied to, sitting upon a Committee.
But that observation refers principally to questions where
political interests are concerned.   When, however, you come
to a question of this nature, where we should necessarily take
the opinion of Judges, to whom the right hon. Gentleman
pays so much attention, and of those men of whose great
authority he has spoken, and of a great many other men who
are not wedded to existing systems, and of men who could
give us the facts with regard to other countries, I say that
a Committee of this House, so far at any rate as obtaining
evidence is concerned, I think would be equal to any tribunal,

or any court of inquiry, which the right hon. Gentleman could establish.

The right hon. Gentleman has led the House away a little from the main question. The main question proposed by my hon. Friend the Member for Dumfries is whether capital punishment should be retained or abolished. The right hon. Gentleman has led the House into a discussion of a question somewhat personal to himself—in connection with recent cases. I know the right hon. Gentleman was justified in what he said in reference to the position which he holds in the performance of his painful duties with regard to the execution of the criminal law. But that is not exactly what is wanted—this Motion was not brought forward for that purpose.

I think the House would agree with great unanimity if the right hon. Gentleman would introduce a Bill proposing certain changes at which he has hinted. This country has always been the most barbarous of all civilized nations in its punishments; and at this moment is the most barbarous still, notwithstanding what the right hon. Gentleman said about the punishment of death being inflicted only for the crime of murder. But did he not afterwards tell the House that this crime of murder is a net which includes cases as different in their quality as in their guilt and in their consequences to society, as the difference between the lowest class of murder which the law now includes and the pettiest larceny which is punishable before a single magistrate. Yet all these are part of the same list of crimes, and if a jury does its duty—that is what is always said, as if a jury had no other duty but inexorably to send a man to the scaffold—if a jury will find a verdict of guilty, the punishment is death, unless the right hon. Gentleman, importuned by a number of persons, or having examined into the case himself, will interfere to save the unfortunate wretch from the gallows.

There can be no doubt whatever that if capital punishment

be retained, and if it be absolutely necessary that there should be a crime called murder to which capital punishment attaches, it is no less necessary that there should be, as there are in some other countries, three or four degrees of manslaughter, and that for the highest degree of manslaughter there should be the highest kind of secondary punishment, and that the power should be placed in the hands of the jury of determining what should be the particular class in which the criminal should be placed. There is no doubt that this is necessary to be done. I think Voltaire—who said a good many things that were worth remembering—remarked that the English were the only people who murdered by law. And Mirabeau, when in this country, hearing of a number of persons who had been hanged on a certain morning, said, 'The English nation is the most merciless of any that I have heard or read of.' And at this very moment, when we have struck off within the last fifty years at least a hundred offences which were then capital, we remain still in this matter the most merciless of Christian countries.

If anybody wishes to satisfy himself upon this point let him take those late cases in which the right hon. Gentleman has had so much trouble. Take the case of Townley; take the case of Wright; take the case of Hall at Warwick; and I will take the liberty of repeating—what I said to the right hon. Gentleman when I was permitted to see him on the case of the convict Hall—that there is not a country in Europe, nor a State among the Free States of America, in which either of those criminals would have been punished with death. Yet we have gone on leaving the law as it is; and the right hon. Gentleman, to my utter astonishment, every time this question has been discussed, has given us very much the same speech as he has addressed to us to-night: he has repeated the same arguments for continuing a law which drives him to distraction almost every time he has to administer it.

I am surprised that the right hon. Gentleman, who has had to face the suffering which has been brought on him by this law, has never had the courage to come to this House and ask it fairly to consider, in the light of the evidence which all other Governments and the laws of all other countries afford, whether the time has not come when this fearful punishment may be abolished. The right hon. Gentleman says the punishment is so terrible that it will deter offenders from the commission of crime. Of course it is terrible to one just standing upon the verge of the grave; but months before, when the crime is committed, when the passion is upon the criminal, the punishment is of no avail whatsoever. I do not think it is possible to say too much against the argument that because this is a dreadful punishment, it is very efficient to deter a criminal from the commission of crime.

As the right hon. Gentleman proposes to give a Commission, I shall not trouble the House with some observations that I had intended to make. There are, however, two or three cases which have not been mentioned, and which I should like to bring under the notice of the House. My hon. Friend the Member for Dumfries referred to Russia. Russia is a country in which capital punishments have for almost a hundred years been unknown. I was reading yesterday a very remarkable Report of a Committee of the Legislature of the State of New York, written in the year 1841. It states that the Empress Elizabeth determined that for twenty years there should be no capital punishments in Russia. The Empress Catherine, in giving her instructions for the new Grand Code, stated her opinion upon the subject in these words:—

'Experience shows that the frequent repetition of capital punishment has never yet made men better. If, therefore, I can show that in the ordinary state of society the death of a citizen is neither useful nor necessary, I shall have pleaded the cause of humanity with success.'

She then says what I think is worthy of hearing :—

'When the laws bear quiet and peaceful sway, and under a form of government approved by the united voices of the nation, in such a state there can be no necessity for taking away the life of a citizen.'

The exception is in the case of some great political offender whose incarceration might not destroy his power of doing mischief; and I believe that since the enactment of this law there have been only two cases of persons who have been put to death by law in Russia, and that these have been cases arising out of circumstances of a political and insurrectionary character. Count Ségur, the French Ambassador at St. Petersburgh, states that the Empress Catherine said to him—

'We must punish crime without imitating it. The punishment of death is rarely anything but a useless barbarity.'

In reporting this to the French Government, Count Ségur stated that under the mildness of the law murders were very rare in Russia.

My hon. Friend the Member for Dumfries referred to the case of Tuscany, where it is well known that for a lifetime capital punishment has never been inflicted. In the case of Belgium, to which reference was made by the learned Member for Tiverton, as one of the most remarkable, I think the right hon. Gentleman was not successful in getting rid of his figures. It happens, as I understand, that the law in Belgium does not prohibit capital punishments; but the result of omitting to inflict capital punishment has been so satisfactory that now the law is literally obsolete, and that capital punishment is never inflicted. Take then the case of Bombay, which is of a very striking character. We have the evidence from the pen of Sir James Mackintosh, who says,—

'It will appear that the capital crimes committed during the last seven years (1804 to 1811) with no capital executions, have in proportion to the population not been much more than a third of those committed in the first seven years (1756 to 1763) when forty-seven persons suffered death.'

He adds,—

'The intermediate periods lead to the same results.'

The House ought to bear in mind, that to us who have

examined this question for many years, no fact is more clearly demonstrated than this—there is no country in the world, be it a great empire or be it a small state, where the law has been made milder and capital punishment has been abolished, in which there is any proof that murders have been more frequent, and the security of life in the slightest degree endangered. If that be so — if I could convince every Member of this House that the abolition of capital punishment would not cause more murders than the average of the last ten years—if all that would be left would be that those ten or twelve wretches who are publicly strangled every year would be living in some prison, or engaged in some labour with a chance of penitence, and with life not suddenly cut off by law—is there a man in this House—I speak not of party, or to one side or the other—who would dare to demand that we should still continue these terrible punishments?

There was, not long ago, in this House, a venerable old Gentleman who represented the University of Oxford, who constantly quoted in the discussion on this subject a certain verse of a certain chapter in the Book of Genesis. I am very glad that in the seven or eight years that have elapsed since this question was last discussed, we have advanced so far that nobody has now brought forward that argument. We have discussed it to-night by the light of proved experiments, of facts, and of reason. Seeing what has been done in this country by the amelioration of the Criminal Code, and what has been done in all other countries, is there any man with one particle of sense or the power of reason who believes that human life in this country is made more secure because ten or twelve men are publicly put to death every year?

The security of human life does not depend upon any such miserable and barbarous provision as that. The security for human life depends upon the reverence for human life; and unless you can inculcate in the minds of your people a veneration for that which God only has given, you do little by the most severe and barbarous penalties to preserve the safety of your citizens. If you could put down what it is that secures human life in figures and estimate it at 100, how much of it is to be attributed to your savage law, and how much of it to the reverence for human life implanted or existing in the human soul? No doubt 5 or 10 out of the 100 may be owing, for aught I know, to the influence of the law; but 90 or 95 per cent. is owing to that feeling of reverence for human life. Whenever you hang a man in the face of the public under the circumstances to which we are so accustomed in this country, if you do in the slightest degree deter from crime by the shocking nature of the punishment, I will undertake to say that you by so much—nay, by much more— weaken that other and greater security which arises from the reverence with which human life is regarded.

Since the notice of this Motion was given by my hon. Friend I took the liberty of writing to the Governors of three of the States of America in which capital punishment has for several years been abolished; and, with the permission of the House, I will read extracts from the answers which I have received. I think they are important in a discussion of this nature when we are attempting to persuade doubtful and timid people that we are not proposing a rash or dangerous change. In the State of Rhode Island, one of the small States of America, with a population of not more than 200,000, capital punishment has been abolished. The Governor, the Hon. J. Pye Smith, writing from the Executive Department, March 21, 1864, says:—

'1. The death penalty was abolished in this State in the year 1852. 2. I do not think its abolition has had any effect upon the security of life. 3. Is the law against the death penalty sustained by the public opinion of the State? Very decidedly. 4. Are convictions and punishments more certain than before the change was made? I think they are. 5. What is the punishment now inflicted on such criminals as were formerly punished with death? Imprisonment for life at hard labour. I have conversed with one Supreme Judge, State attorney, and warden of the State prison, and they support my own established views upon the subject.'

In a second letter, dated April 4, and which I received a few days ago, he says:—

'Our present able Chief Justice says:—"Although opposed to the present law when passed, I am equally opposed to a change in it until the experiment has been tried long enough to satisfy us that it has failed. I am clearly of opinion that the present state of the law is sustained by public opinion, and I believe it will continue to be until it is satisfactorily shown that crimes against life have been considerably increased in consequence of it. My observation fully justifies me in saying that conviction for murder is far more certain now in proper cases than when death was the punishment of it."'

Here is the answer which I received from the Hon. Austin Blair, the Governor of the State of Michigan:—

'Executive Office, Lancing, March 23, 1864.
'1. The death penalty for murder was abolished March 1, 1847, when the revised statutes of 1846 went into effect. 2. Life is not considered less secure than before; murders are probably less frequent in proportion to population. Twenty years ago the population of the State was 300,000, and we have now a population of about 900,000. Then it was chiefly agricultural, and now we have mines of copper, iron, coal, &c., bringing into proximity dissimilar classes, and increasing the probabilities of frequent crime. Before the abolition of the death penalty, murders were not unfrequent, but convictions were rarely or never obtained. It became the common belief that no jury could be found (the prisoner availing himself of the common law right of challenge) which would convict. Since the abolition there have been in seventeen years thirty-seven convictions. 3. There can be no doubt that public opinion sustains the present law and is against the restoration of the death penalty. 4. Conviction and punishment are now much more certain than before the change was made. Murder requires a greater amount of proof than any other crime, and it is found practically that a trial for murder excites no very unusual interest.'

It, therefore, does not make a hero of the criminal. The letter proceeds:—

'5. The punishment now is solitary confinement at hard labour for life. Since 1861 this class of prisoners have been employed as other prisoners, as it was found difficult to keep them at work in cells without giving them tools, and there was danger of their becoming insane. The reform has been successfully tried, and is no longer an experiment.'

The last letter is from the Hon. J. S. Lewis, the Governor of Wisconsin, and is dated Madison, March 29, 1864:—

'The evil tendency of public executions, the great aversion of many to the taking of life rendering it almost impossible to obtain jurors from the more intelligent portion of the community, the liability of the innocent to suffer so extreme a penalty and be placed beyond the reach of the pardoning power, and the disposition of courts and juries not to convict, fearing the innocent might suffer, convinced me that this relic of barbarism should be abolished. The death penalty was repealed in 1853. No legislation has since re-established it, and the people find themselves equally secure, and the public more certain than before. The population in 1850 was 305,000; in 1860 it was 775,000. With this large increase of population we might expect a large increase of criminal cases, but this does not appear to be the case.'

If you take these two States of Wisconsin and Michigan, which have been settled at a comparatively recent date, you will see that it was highly probable, as they are on the outskirts of advancing civilization, that crimes of violence would not be uncommon. But here, with the abolition of this punishment, crimes and violence are not more common than before; people are just as secure, the law is upheld by public opinion, and the elected Governors of three States, after the experience of these years, are enabled to write me letters like these, so satisfactory and so conclusive with regard to the effect of the experiment as it has been tried with them.

The special cases that have been mentioned to-night with regard to executions have not been by any means the most fearful that have occurred. There was a case last year at Chester of so revolting a nature that I should be afraid to state the details to the House. I think it is hardly conceivable that a Christian gentleman, a governor of a gaol, and a clergyman, another Christian gentleman, should be concerned in such a dreadful catastrophe as then took place. Sir, if there be fiends below, how it must rejoice them to discover that, after the law of gentleness and love has been preached on earth for eighteen hundred years, such a scene as that could be enacted in our day in one of the most civilized and renowned cities of this country. And these are cases which will happen again if this law remains; and all the difficulties which the right hon. Gentleman has alluded to to-night and on previous occasions are difficulties inseparable from the continuance of this punishment.

The right hon. Gentleman has referred to one or two cases; the noble Lord opposite (Lord Henry Lennox) has likewise referred to one or two. The case at Glasgow, the case at Derby, the recent case in London, and the recent case at Warwick, are cases which move whole populations; and, if that be so, how can any man argue that this law is in a satisfactory state, or that this punishment can be wisely and beneficially administered and executed in this country? Parliament, unfortunately—we need not disguise it, and I will not at any rate conceal it—Parliament has been very heedless upon this question. Secretaries of State have gone on from year to year hobbling, as it were, through the performance of their duties with great pain to themselves, and yet they have never had the courage to ask Parliament to consider whether the system might not be entirely abolished. Does not every man now feel that it is in opposition to the sentiment of what I will call—and I think I may say it without disparaging anybody—the most moral and religious population of this country, the men who have led the advance during the past century in every contest that we have had with ignorance, and crime, and cruelty, in whatsoever shape it has shown itself? And every day they are becoming more and more estranged from the spirit and operation of this law.

Whenever there are paragraphs floating about in the newspapers that on the 15th or the 25th of such a month such an one is to meet his doom for some crime, however foul, there is in every city, in every parish, and in almost every house in this country where there is any regard to humanity and to Christianity, a feeling of doubt as to whether this law is right, and a feeling of disgust and horror amongst hundreds of thousands of the best portion of our people. Now, merciful laws are, in my opinion, the very highest testimony to any Government, as I likewise think that they are the highest blessing a people can enjoy. I believe they give security to a Government, and they soften and humanise the people.

All the steps that have been taken in this direction have been so successful, that I wonder that even the hon. gentleman the late Lord Mayor of London should not himself have come to the conclusion that after all we could still sleep comfortably in our beds if men were not hanged; and that, if the law were gentle and merciful whilst it was just, we should find gradually growing up in the minds of all classes a greater dislike to crime and violence, and a greater reverence for human life.

Benjamin Franklin, a great authority on matters of this nature, said that the virtues are all parts of a circle; that whatever is humane is wise; whatever is wise is just; and whatever is wise, just, and humane, will be found to be the true interests of States, whether criminals or foreign enemies are the objects of their legislation. Would any one of us like to go back to the barbarism of that time when Charles Wesley wrote a note to the celebrated and excellent John Fletcher, the Vicar of Madeley, in 1776? We were then trying to keep the empire together, and neglecting this great work at home. He says:—

' A fortnight ago I preached a condemned sermon to about twenty criminals, and every one of them, I had good grounds to believe, died penitent. Twenty more must die next week.'

And there were then occasions on which twenty were hanged, not one of whom had been convicted of the crime of murder. Have we not from that time made great and salutary and satisfactory advances in this question? Is there any man who wants to turn back to the barbarism of that day? But if you turn back to the Secretaries of State of that day, or to the Judges of that day, or even to the Bishops of that day, you will find that they had just the same sort of arguments in favour of the barbarism in which they were then concerned that the right hon. Gentleman, I suppose forced by the necessities of his office, has offered to the House to-night.

I confess I wonder that all the right hon. Gentleman has

gone through in these painful cases has not driven him stark mad many times. I wonder that it has not driven him to the table of this House to propose, under the solemn feelings with which he must often have been impressed, that the House should take into consideration whether this vast evil—as I believe it to be—might not be put an end to. Is the Englishman worse than every other man? Is this nation worse than other nations? Cannot the lenient laws practised with perfect safety in every other—not every other, but in many other of the nations of the world—be practised in this nation, and at the same time leave us perfectly secure—at least as much so as we are at present? I say we may wash vengeance and blood from our code without difficulty and without danger.

The right hon. Gentleman is willing to appoint a Commission—he prefers it to a Committee, and I will not contest the point with him if the Commission be a fair Commission; but I should not like to see it a Commission of Judges. I do not wish to speak disrespectfully of Judges. I agree with what the right hon. Gentleman has said, that with the exception of a case or two, perhaps, in one's lifetime, we notice nothing on the bench but that which is honourable to the Judges of this country; and I would say that the Judges of this country may be compared with advantage probably with the Judges of any other country. But Judges are but men. Several of them, as a proof of that, have been Members of this House. And I am free to confess that the feelings I had when I was a schoolboy at York, and first went to an Assize trial, and saw a venerable old gentleman on the bench, and in his wig, were those of utter awe and astonishment; but those feelings have been considerably modified by my experience of many of the present Judges when they were Members of this House. But we know that Judges are like other men in this—they have trodden a certain path which has led them to the honourable position which they hold. They are there, not to make law, but to administer it; and they are disposed to adhere to the law, as they have studied it and administered it. Some of them are not desirous, perhaps, to express an opinion, like the noble Lord the father of the hon. and learned Member for Tiverton (Mr. Denman). They are strongly attached to that system which they have been administering; and, as I said at the beginning of the observations I have offered to the House, they have been in all past times—not all of them, but a majority of them—generally opposed to the amelioration of our Criminal Code.

Although, therefore, I believe that at this moment there are more Judges on the bench who are in favour of the abolition of capital punishment, yet I should not like the right hon. Gentleman to leave the inquiry into this question entirely or even to a majority of the members of the bench. There is no reason to believe that a Judge is more competent to give an opinion on this question than any other intelligent, educated, and observing man; nor would I admit that the right hon. Gentleman himself, who is in his person the whole bench of Judges, is more capable of giving an opinion than any other Member of this House who has paid long and careful attention to this subject. Therefore, I hope that if the right hon. Gentleman does appoint a Commission he will put upon it—I do not say men who have not an opinion on one side or the other, for men who have no opinion at all are not likely to give any worth hearing—but men in whom the House and the country, and those in the House who are against capital punishment, may have confidence, feeling that they will take evidence from every source whence it could be fairly offered to them, and that they will give to the House and the Government a fair opinion on that evidence in their report.

If that be done I am quite certain that the result will be a great improvement of the law, although it may not carry it to the point which my hon. Friend the Member for Dumfries has so long desired to carry it. But I should be very thankful if so much is accomplished; and if ever we come to that point, I have confidence too that even you Gentlemen opposite, who are so very timid, always fancying that the ice is going to break under you, will be induced to go further than you seem inclined to do now; and perhaps the ten or twelve wretched men who are now hanged annually may be brought down to three or four, and at last we may come unanimously to the opinion, that the security of public or private life in England does not depend upon the public strangling of three or four poor wretches every year. This Parliament is about to expire, I suppose, before very long—though some say it is to endure during another session; I should be glad indeed if it might be said of this Parliament at some future time, that it had dared to act upon the true lessons, and not upon the superstitions of the past; and that it might be declared to be the Parliament which destroyed the scaffold and the gallows, in order that it might teach the people that human life is sacred, and that on that principle alone can human life be secured.

THE PERMISSIVE BILL.

HOUSE OF COMMONS, JUNE 8, 1864.

From Hansard.

[The 'Permissive Bill' was a measure introduced by some of the friends of
Temperance, to enable a certain proportion of the population of a parish, by
vote, to shut up Public-houses, and to prohibit the sale of intoxicating
liquors within the parish.]

I THINK my hon. Friend the Member for Carlisle (Mr. Lawson) has at least no reason to complain of the manner in
which the House has listened to the statement which he has
made on behalf of his clients throughout the country. The
House has listened to his speech in a manner which proves
that this is a question which is getting more hold of the
mind of the country than it had some time ago, and that
it cannot be treated as the vision of a few wild enthu-
siasts. Everybody will agree that the evil which the hon.
Member has to some extent explained is a very grievous
one in almost every part of the country; and more—I believe
every Member will say that if any measures could be taken
that did not violate any of the recognised principles on which
this House acts, to help those who are making great exertions
to change the people of this country from their past and,

I fear, their present condition into a happier state, such
measures ought to be sanctioned.

I believe there are only two modes of remedy; the first
of which is the improvement and instruction of the people,
and the second, the special legislation of this House. I
am one of those who look rather to the improvement and
education of the people for a permanent remedy—and I
think that it is quite conclusive that this must be the sheet-
anchor, as it were, of this question. There are hon. Members
of this House older than I am, but I am old enough to
remember when among those classes with which we are
more familiar than with the working-people, drunkenness was
ten or twenty times more common than it is at present.
I have been in this House twenty years, and during that
time I have often partaken of the hospitality of various
Members of the House, and I may assert that during the
whole of those twenty years I have no recollection of having
seen one single person at any gentleman's table who has
been in the condition which would be at all fairly described
by saying that he was drunk. And I may say more—that
I do not recollect more than two or three occasions during
that time in which I have observed, by the thickness of
utterance, rapidity of talking, or perhaps a somewhat recklessness of conversation, that any gentleman had taken so
much as to impair his judgment. That is not the state of
things which prevailed in this country fifty or sixty years
ago. We know, therefore, as respects this class of persons,
who can always obtain as much of these pernicious articles
as they desire to have, because price to them is no object,
that temperance has made great way, and if it were possible
now to make all classes in this country as temperate as those
of whom I have just spoken, we should be amongst the very
soberest nations of the earth.

But it may be said after all this, that there is something
still to be done by special legislation—and I am not disposed

to contradict that; and if any Member were to contradict it, it would be going in the face of experience, and certainly in the face of the opinion which has been universally held by this House. All our legislation on this question has been special. My hon. Friend says he thinks no one would dare to propose to make the sale of intoxicating drinks free—as free for example as the sale of bread, potatoes, or any of the articles of ordinary consumption. If we required no taxes I do not know how we should treat this question; but, requiring taxes as we do, it has been thought in this country, and I suspect in most other countries too—certainly in many— that there is nothing upon which taxes can be levied with greater advantage (if I may use the term 'advantage' in connection with the levying of any taxes) as upon articles of an intoxicating quality. But having levied these taxes, and finding the consumption is large, the Government finds it also necessary to provide certain superintendence by the police; because, unfortunately, wherever the sale of these articles is considerable, there is found to be a state of things which is not favourable to obedience to the law, and which magistrates, policemen, and the law are called in to avert and prevent.

We have this special legislation now, and my hon. Friend says that not less than four hundred Acts of Parliament dealing with this question have been before the House: not all of them with a view of preventing the consumption of intoxicating liquors, but all showing what a constant and incessant atten- tion Parliament has been obliged to pay to this subject. Now we come to the system as we find it, and ask ourselves, Can anything more be done? Under the present system, if a man wishes to sell beer only, he gets six of his neighbours to sign a recommendation that he is a suitable and respectable man. I believe also the rent of his house has something to do with it, as indicating that he is a man not absolutely without means and character. But if he wishes to sell wine

and spirits he must ask the magistrates for a licence, and
the licence is renewable from year to year. I think it may
be generally said that this system is not satisfactory to
people throughout the country. There are many magistrates
who condemn the system of which they are a part; and in
many towns it is said—and I think upon inquiry we should
find it to be true—that the magistrates give licences too
freely; and men who live in quiet streets of a town are
angry with the magistrates for giving licences to houses
which are not needed. We also find that there is a great
diversity of action, for in some villages, towns, and districts,
public-houses are much more numerous than in others; and
at the same time there is a complaint that in giving licences
for the sale of beer the recommendation of six benevolent
neighbours is given more through kindness to the applicant
than kindness to the great bulk of the neighbourhood. In
some cases the number of beer-houses has been unnecessarily
and mischievously increased.

And now what does my hon. Friend propose? He proposes something that is entirely distinct, and to some
extent a revolutionary measure, with regard to this system.
He proposes that two-thirds of the rate-payers of any district, parish, or town shall have the power to decide
the whole of this question; and I think when the hon.
Gentleman stated that proposal, an hon. Gentleman on the
other side of the House, and an hon. Gentleman sitting near
me, made gestures as if they thought the rate-payers did
not represent the working-classes. But the working-classes
are ratepayers in a larger number than any other class,
for they are generally married and have families, and live
in houses that pay taxes; and therefore if you take the
opinion of the rate-payers of this country on any question,
you take in as clear a manner as possible the opinion of the
people of the country. Well, my hon. Friend proposes that
two-thirds shall decide;—but decide what? By this Bill,

they are to decide first of all whether any new licences shall be granted in the district to which the vote applies—that is, whether this Act shall be in force in the district—and they are to decide further whether any of the persons now licensed shall have those licences renewed at the expiration of the present year. ['No, no!' 'Hear, hear!']

That is what I understand by the Bill. I believe all licences are merely granted for selling drink from year to year. I think it was one of the statements of the licensed victuallers that the magistrates had the absolute control over them, and that there was no appeal from their decision, and every year they could refuse to renew any licences if they thought fit. It will thus be seen that my hon. Friend proposes a Bill which affects some scores of thousands of persons and some millions of property, the measure which he proposes being entirely different, I think, from anything which has ever been proposed or sanctioned by the House with regard to any other description of property or any other interest. Therefore, however sanguine I may be as to what I must call the violent success of his measure, and however desirous I may be to carry out his object, I do not think it likely that the House of Commons will consent to such a proposition as that.

What is meant by the representative system is not that you should have the vote of thousands of persons taken upon a particular question of legislation, but that you should have men selected from those thousands having the confidence of the majority of the thousands, and that they should meet and should discuss questions for legislation, and should decide what measures should be enacted ; and therefore in this particular question I should object altogether to disposing of the interest of a great many men, and of a great many families, and of a great amount of property—I should object altogether to allow such a matter to be decided by the vote of two-thirds of the rate-payers of any parish or town. By this

Bill they would have the power to shut up at once, or rather at the end of the current year, as far as the sale of these articles is concerned, every hotel, inn, public-house, and beer-shop throughout the country. I say throughout the country, but of course I allude to such subdivisions of the country as the Bill may indicate. There would of course be a difference, for some parishes would shut them up, and some would not; but that is not very much an argument against the Bill. But there might be, and I think there would be, in all proba-bility, sudden, capricious, and unjust action under this Bill, which would have a very unfortunate effect upon the interests of those immediately concerned; and I think it might also create throughout the country violent discussions on the question, and I am afraid might even produce a great and pernicious re-action against the very honest and good objects which my hon. Friend desires to carry out. For that reason, as a Member of this House, representing a very large consti-tuency, and having my sympathies entirely with those who are endeavouring to promote temperance amongst the people, and after much consideration on this subject, I have never yet seen my way at all to give a vote which would tend to pass a measure such as that now proposed to the House.

But then if there be persons who think that the sale of these articles is in itself absolutely evil and immoral—and I did not understand my hon. Friend to hold that opinion, or to have stated it to the House—but if there be persons of that opinion, they, of course, will not be influenced by any argu-ments of mine. I do not hold that opinion—and I think the friends of temperance throughout this country make a great mistake when they argue their cause on that ground. There is abundant ground on which to argue this question on which no man can assail or controvert them, and it is unfortunate for a great and good cause that any of its enthusiastic but illogical advocates should select arguments which cannot fairly be sustained.

Now, the question comes, if this Bill were disposed of,—is there nothing which the House could do to meet the growing opinion in many parts of the country that public-houses and beer-shops are often established with pernicious influence upon the district, and in far greater numbers than the fair wants of the people demand? I bring no charge against the magistrates. So far as I have seen, with some few exceptions of which we have heard, they perform their duty, and a disagreeable duty it is, as well as any body of men to whom you could intrust it. With regard to the householders, they are very likely to give recommendations with more regard to the persons themselves than to the wants of the public. Judging from the evidence brought before the committees of this House, it must be admitted that public opinion does not entirely agree with the mode which is at present in existence for the granting of licences, whether they be for public-houses or beer-houses; and looking at the course which the Government has taken—I do not mean this Government in particular, but the course Parliament has taken in past times—I do not see any reason why the public opinion of every city, town, and district should not have something to say with regard to this matter.

Some time ago, when I was down at Birmingham, a large number of persons connected with this question had an interview with me and with my hon. Colleague. We had a long discussion on the question, and I explained to them what I now wish to explain to the House—that although objecting to the Bill on the grounds which I have stated, yet it does appear to me that the House might proceed a step further than it has already done, and intrust to the ordinary local governing bodies of the cities, towns, and boroughs throughout the kingdom the decision of this question, with regard to the opening of public-houses and beer-shops, and the granting of licences within the limits of their jurisdiction. You cannot put this power into the hands of the Secretary of

State or the Lord Chancellor, as you do the appointment of magistrates ; and you cannot remove it from twenty magistrates and put it into the hands of some half-dozen men in the same neighbourhood.   You can make no change from where you are, unless you intrust to the municipal council, or some committee of the municipal council, in the various boroughs, the power of determining the number of licences for the sale of wine and spirits or beer.

If you were to intrust it to the Council, instead of to the full vote of the rate-payers, as proposed by the Bill, I think you would avoid everything like a sudden and violent interference with property, and you would also avoid the capricious action which might take place if two-thirds of the rate-payers were to judge this question, and you would give to the whole body of the rate-payers through their representatives in their municipal councils, the determination of a question which every day is becoming more important with the great masses of the people of this country.   I know no proposal which could be made from the point where we now stand to the point of the Bill of my hon. Friend except the one which I have suggested.   Generally, the municipal councils in this country perform their duties with admirable success, and there is no Bill passed in this century which has been more successful than the one which the House passed to reform the corporations.   If they had this further power, I think it would add to their influence and dignity ; and, in all probability, the opinions of the people would be fairly carried out in reference to this question.   But there is another question.   Hon. Gentlemen opposite may say that this could not be done in the rural districts, where there are no corporations, and therefore my suggestion could not apply. But I think if it were attempted in the towns, and it was found more advantageous and successful than the present system, something could be found before long to extend the new system to the agricultural districts as well : but if that should be found impracticable, it is no reason for debarring the towns from the benefit.

I should not have brought such a question as this before the House, and I am not so sanguine of the result of these changes as what I may call the Temperance party in this House.   I have not that faith in any act of the Legislature on this subject which my hon. Friend has.   I believe in the effects of the instruction of the people, and of the improvement which is gradually taking place amongst them.   I think that drunkenness is not on the increase, but rather is declining; and I hope, whether the law be altered or not, we shall find our working-classes becoming more and more sober than in past times. . But as I have on many occasions been before the public favouring the efforts of the advocates of temperance, I have felt bound to state the reasons why I cannot give my vote in favour of this Bill, and to suggest what the House might do by way of giving to the people through their municipal councils control over this question. By doing this you might promote temperance among the people, and at the same time avoid a great and manifest injustice to thousands of persons now engaged in this trade, whose property would be rendered uncertain if not altogether destroyed if the Bill of the hon. Gentleman should receive the sanction of the House.

ECCLESIASTICAL TITLES BILL.

HOUSE OF COMMONS, MAY 12, 1851.

From Hansard.

[The Ecclesiastical Titles Bill was a measure to prohibit Catholic Bishops from assuming any title from any place or territory within the United Kingdom. A Papal Edict had recently created an Archbishop of Westminster, and this caused a ferment or panic in the country, which was much stimulated by a letter from Lord John Russell, then Prime Minister, to the Bishop of Durham. The Bill passed by large majorities, but it has been wholly ineffectual, is now obsolete, and will probably shortly be repealed.]

I AM exceedingly glad that the discussion has taken the turn which it has now assumed; for as the proposition before the House is that the Speaker should leave the Chair, this appears to me a very fitting time to discuss the principle of the Bill, and the propriety of taking any further steps with regard to it. I was much struck with an observation of the right hon. Gentleman the Member for Ripon in a former debate, that it is an extremely dangerous thing for a Government to be legislating upon the idea that it is forced to do something with regard to a particular question, without knowing either exactly what it has to do, or how it ought to do it. There is great practical wisdom in that observation.

I will turn back to some of the proceedings connected with this question. The noble Lord at the head of the Govern-

ment commenced the fray by his celebrated letter; and any
stranger to the country who read that letter must have come
to the conclusion that some great outrage had been committed.
Within a week after the publication of that letter, the noble
Lord, the chief officers of the Crown, and some of the principal Judges, including the Lord High Chancellor and the
Lord Chief Justice of the Court of Queen's Bench, assembled
round the festive board of the chief magistrate of the City of
London; and there language was used which, to say the
least, should not have been employed by sedate and learned
men accustomed to administer justice, whether it was used in
seriousness or in joke.

I must here remark, however, that I am not at all
astonished at anything which takes place in connection with
such a question at the Mansion House of the City of London,
for, if I am not misinformed, the Mansion House was built
out of fines extorted from Nonjurors, from Protestant Dissenters, and, to a large extent, from the society of which I am
a member, between the passing of the Act of Uniformity and
the passing of the Act of Toleration. There is another curious
fact connected with that building. One hundred and ten
years ago, when a proposition was made to build it, the Earl
of Burlington of that day presented to the Common Council
an admirable design by an Italian architect; but the architect
being an Italian, and his name, ' Palladio,' possibly suggesting
Rome, his design, which was the best offered, was rejected
by the Corporation, though he had been dead 150 years.

I have observed almost all that has appeared in the
papers during the agitation of this question, and I have no
hesitation in saying that as yet there has been no logical
definition of the injury that has been inflicted on this
country, and no agreement as to any remedy which Parliament could provide. I may say the same for the leading
articles in the newspapers, from the *Times* down to the
humblest country paper. Not one has proposed an intelligible

remedy for the grievance. Certain specifics, indeed, have been proposed out of doors; but the noble Lord has not been so imprudent as to accept them. The celebrated Dr. Cumming, among the rest, proposed that Cardinal Wiseman should be packed off to Italy in a man-of-war, with Admiral Harcourt as commander. The choice was perhaps happy, because Admiral Harcourt is the son of a man who, while a bishop in the dominant Church, received no less than three-quarters of a million of money ; and therefore it is no wonder that his son should be hostile to any rival in so profitable a calling.

I will not allude particularly to the speeches made by certain distinguished individuals, to the burnings in effigy or to the threats of serving Cardinal Wiseman as a certain Austrian general had been served. I give the noble Lord credit for being too wise to follow such counsel. But after the noble Lord wrote his celebrated letter, he has had three months for quiet deliberation whether in Downing-street or Windsor; and at the end of that three months we have the noble Lord's speech, which is not about the Papal rescript, the real matter in hand, but about various matters that have occurred on the other side of the Channel. The noble Lord is now conscious of the difficulty, and cannot withdraw Ireland without overthrowing the whole speech upon which his legislation is founded.

The noble Lord objects to the synod of Thurles. I do not wish to see such synods, or anything else which interferes with education; but if the two Churches are compared, we must be driven to the conclusion that the Protestant bishops and clergy are quite as meddlesome in politics as the Catholics, and more especially upon this very question of national education. I have, while in the south of Ireland, spoken to a gentleman who is a county magistrate and a chairman of a board of guardians, and that gentleman has said that the Established clergy have committed a great mis-

take in so universally rejecting the national schools, as they
have by such conduct thrown them wholly into the hands
of the priests. We should not then judge too harshly of the
synod of Thurles for taking a different view of education from
them, more especially as at that synod the votes were equally
divided, which is more than could be said of the Established
clergy either in Ireland or in England. But the noble Lord
will have no bishops but his own bishops, of whom he is by
turns the tyrant and the vassal; while the bishops of Ireland,
in whom the people have confidence, are not to have any
opinion on this question of education, or, if they have, they
are not to express it. But the noble Lord has not been able
clearly to define the matter upon which he is going to
legislate. He has had to cite a great number of Acts, to
garnish with references to history, and menaces from other
countries, and to make up what lawyers call a cumulative case,
in order to establish even the slightest reason for legislation.

The noble Lord admits that the law has not been broken;
he cannot cite any instance in which the Catholic bishops of
Ireland have broken the law. I thought that the noble Lord
was going to admit that as the law has not been broken, no
offence has been committed, instead of which he is about to
ask for a stringent law to put down an offence which has
never been committed. There is one point on which the law
has been broken, and that is in the importation of the Bull;
but with that offence the noble Lord will not interfere. The
language of the Pope is complained of as offensive; but
have priests in power ever used any other? The language
is offensive—such language as might have been used by
Hildebrand, and very like what is used in our own legal
documents. I recollect a charge of libel being brought
against an unfortunate newspaper editor, in which he was
charged with every imaginable offence; but that was the
mere formal wording of the legal document. So it is with
the language of the Pope. Offensive, aggressive it is—

such as I despise and loathe; it is rather a form than a substance—but it is not a justification for the present attempt at legislation.   But the noble Lord says that there is an attack by a foreign Power on the supremacy of the Crown. The hon. Member for Oldham has truly observed that the Pope's being a temporal power is merely an accident.   The Pope is a priest, and it happens unfortunately that he is also a temporal prince; but if he were at Avignon, or Naples, or Brazil, or even in the town of Galway, still he would be Pope and priest, and would have precisely the same power over the Catholic world as he has at present.

The supremacy of the Queen is, in the sense used by the noble Lord, no better than a fiction.   There might have been such a supremacy down to the times of James II, but now there is no supremacy but that of the three estates of the realm, and the supremacy of the law.   The Queen is the chief of the Established Church; but that Church has not been assailed either in its wealth or power. The Queen has not the power of making Roman Catholic bishops, and therefore the making of them by the only Power on earth that has authority to make them, is no invasion of the prerogative of the Crown.   The noble Lord says that the Pope has ignored the Established Church of this country, and has abolished the see of Canterbury.   But the Pope has always done so; he looks upon the Church of England as an usurping Church, pretty much as the Church of England looks upon congregations of Dissenters.   Does not that Church, when appealing to the House on the plea of religious destitution, reckon up the population in a district, and the number of Church sittings, without taking into account the number of dissenting teachers, or of dissenting places of worship?   It is thus that one Church always treats another; and it is one of the unfortunate proofs, that so much as we have of Churches and of religions, the true spirit of Christianity has made very little way amongst the Churches of the world.

I am not one of those who think there is any strength in the
argument which is used so often, that bishops in ordinary
are not necessary for the effectual working of the Roman
Catholic Church. I am no friend to the bishops of any
Church. But my individual opinion has nothing whatever
to do with legislation on this question. I am not so pre-
sumptuous as to say to another Church that bishops are not
necessary for that Church; and if bishops are necessary
for the Anglican Church, who can say they are not necessary for the Church of Rome? We have heard much of
the changing of vicars-apostolic to bishops in ordinary,
and I wish on this subject to read an extract from a
letter which I have received from a constituent who is a
learned ecclesiastic of the Romish Church. I believe that
in that letter it is conclusively urged that the change from
vicars-apostolic to bishops in ordinary went far to free the
bishops from the arbitrary supremacy of the Pope, and to
place them under the control of a regularly-organised code of
laws. My correspondent says that the principal argument
against the bishoprics was founded on the assumption that
the bishops would be more under the control of the Pope
than the vicars-apostolic. That is wholly erroneous. The
bishop exercises his authority in virtue of his office, while
the vicar-apostolic acts as the mere delegate of the Pope, who
is the immediate bishop of the district. In both cases the
territory is marked out. In one case it is called a diocese,
and in the other a district, and in both cases the Pope confers
the jurisdiction. In both cases the jurisdiction extends to all
who belong to the Church, which includes, in the estimation
of the Church, all baptized persons; but it is not to be
exercised except over those who chose to submit to it. In
the case of the bishops, they are governed by laws regularly
enacted; while the vicars-apostolic are controlled solely by
the will of the Pope, who exercises as much power as he
thinks proper. The difference is this, a vicar-apostolic is

alone responsible to the Pope and to his will, whatever it might determine; but when a bishop in ordinary is appointed, he is relieved from the caprice—if I may say so—of the Pope, and is subject alone to those portions of the canon law that can be exercised in any country in accordance with the permission of the civil law of that country. It is asserted that the Roman Catholics of this country have suffered no grievance in being driven back again to the rule of vicars-apostolic. I beg to ask the people of this country, whether they would prefer to live under the ordinary constitution of the country, administered by its recognised tribunals; or under some special commission, with some exceptional state of the law, where liberty may be less secure than under the ordinary and recognised law of the State? I do not intend quoting further from the document I hold in my hand; but I think it only fairness to the gentleman who sent it that I should make use of it to this extent. I maintain that the course that has been taken in making these bishops in ordinary of vicars-apostolic is calculated to relieve the Roman Catholics in England from much of that ultramontane influence of which the House has heard so much: for if the bishops are natives here, and appointed with the consent of those over whom they will subsequently exercise control, it is reasonable to suppose that the Roman Catholic Church will become more national in character, than when ruled over by the Pope and the statutes of his council.

The noble Lord has designated the proceeding as an insult to the Crown, and an attack on the independence of the nation. I wish he could get rid of the silly and groundless fears he entertains on these points. To talk of this nation, its Crown and independence, being menaced by a petty sovereign or prince at Rome, is really too ludicrous. If England had not concurred in the invasion of Rome by the French, that temporal prince, the Pope, would probably be now no prince, there would be a republic established

at Rome, and, perhaps, the religious separated from the
political power for ever. But the country is misled by
these phrases, which are so misused by the noble Lord the
First Minister of the Crown. 'A foreign power has endangered the supremacy of the Crown, and attacked the independence of the country.' The whole matter is one of
idea, of sentiment, of such fine material that it is impossible
for an Act of Parliament to grapple with the case before
us. I admit the insult and offensiveness of the language—
it is repulsive to our feelings that such language should be
employed. But, admitting all that, I am at a loss to discover
how legislation can affect the question beneficially at all.
The noble Lord (Lord John Russell) has told us that this
Bill will meet the emergency, and no more. I think the
noble Lord is wise and prudent in not making it more stringent than it is. Of course the noble Lord consulted the law
officers of the Crown. It is well known that he consulted the
bishops; and I doubt not he consulted the noble Earl who
fills the office of Lord Lieutenant of Ireland.

The noble Lord informs the House that the Bill will meet
the emergency, and that he has proposed nothing that is not
required for the precise evil complained of; and yet, within a
few days after its first appearance, three-fourths of the Bill are
given up. After three months of discussion and consultation
with all these able and learned and pious men, with whom the
noble Lord has been conferring, he admits that he knows
nothing of the nature of his own Bill; and upon the occasion
of the second reading, consequently withdraws three-fourths
of it. I then argued that the noble Lord did not know
where he was hit, or the remedy for the wound of which
he complained; and the fact of the withdrawal of three-fourths
of the measure supports my argument. The noble Lord has
retained the clause forbidding the assumption of titles. Well,
assuming titles will be illegal by the Bill, what is the result?
At present the assumption is not legal, and titles assumed by

Roman Catholic ecclesiastics are looked upon as mere matters of courtesy, which give no status, or rank, or precedence over any other subject of the realm. But in any case the Roman Catholics only will submit to the authorities of these diguitaries—no matter whether bishops, cardinals, or archbishops.

But is there no effect produced by the Bill? Already the noble Lord has thrown over the Protestant feeling of the country, the sentiments of the Cummings, the M'Neiles, and the Stowells. It is not a question of Protestantism at present; it is a question of politics. I beg to ask the noble Lord, then, as a question of politics, who is injured by the Bill? The noble Lord does not touch the Pope. I believe the Pope acted very foolishly, and that Cardinal Wiseman also acted foolishly; but both will go unscathed. The true sufferers will be the wearer of the Crown, and the millions of subjects professing the Roman Catholic religion. Look at the speeches, the writings, and the denunciations of the last six months. Is it possible that all these could have occurred in the United Kingdom without producing a permanent evil as regards the harmony and the well-being and strength of the nation? Then take Ireland alone. There has been a great gulf heretofore existing between England and Ireland, a gulf created by past legislation. The noble Lord has helped to widen and deepen that gulf, and there is now a more marked separation between the countries than has existed at any period in the last twenty years. We have by our legislation taught 8,000,000 of our fellow-subjects that their priests are hated by the British Legislature, and that they themselves are treated with disrespect, and their loyalty denied by this House and the leading Minister of the country. That is an evil of great magnitude, and one which we are bound to take into consideration.

We were informed not long since that at the Thurles synod, half the prelates assembled were in favour of the colleges, and the other half against them. I doubt not, if a second synod were to take place, there will be an unanimous feeling against them. The noble Lord heretofore had a party amongst the ecclesiastics of the Church of Rome; but he has destroyed that party by his policy, and rendered them unanimous against the Protestant Government of that country. I ask any Gentleman here, not a Roman Catholic, what would be the effect of the recent proceedings on him if he were a member of that Church? Does the House suppose there is a Roman Catholic family in the empire, when assembled round the hearth, that does not entertain a greater reverence for the Pope now, than before these mischievous proceedings commenced? And does it not stand to reason that the missionary agencies of that Church, scattered over the kingdom for the conversion of Protestants, will take fresh hope from the paroxysm of terror and alarm into which the Protestants of England have thrown themselves? The apostles overthrew the Pagan worship of Rome; Luther, single-handed, wrested whole empires from the Pope; whilst here is a Church, endowed with millions, and having 15,000 learned clergymen for its guidance and control, thrown into a paroxysm of terror, and all that by a Church which, in these realms, has not the thousandth part of the advantages possessed by its opponents.

I wish the noble Lord had told the House where the gain lies. Is it in the Preamble of the Bill, which refers to the inviolable character of the Established Church in Ireland? Every one is aware that the Established Church in Ireland is not worth one good man raising his voice in its support; and the noble Lord well knows that it only waits the lifting of his own finger to ensure such a majority in that House as would suppress by Act of Parliament that Church for ever, notwithstanding its inviolable character. Is it as a matter of gratification to the ministers of the Established Church that the noble Lord introduced the measure—a matter of strife and rivalry between the Bishop of St. James's-square and the Archbishop of Golden-square? Is one to be suppressed for the satisfaction of the 'other? In such a case, there will be no great gain to the people, to political freedom, or to the Christianity of this country in suppressing one ecclesiastic, and conferring domination and power on the other.

In my opinion the noble Lord has made a great mistake. In the first place, he wrote a letter to the Bishop of Durham, and then consulted with the Bishop of London. A more unsafe man than the Bishop of London he could not have selected. Look at his character. He is an amphibious creature, reported by one to be a Puseyite, whilst another says he is on the high road to Rome. I am sorry to hear the amount of abuse that is lavished upon him; and yet the noble Lord 'rejoiced that he had the consent of that prelate.' That ecclesiastic, with twenty thousand excellent consolations, shed tears in presence of a deputation that waited on him. But doubtless they resembled the tears shed by the Syrian monk, who declared, according to the historian, that 'tears were as natural to him as perspiration.' However, it would appear that the said monk was less wise than the Bishop of London in one respect, for another historian relates of him that he feigned insanity that he might escape being made a bishop.

It is evident that the noble Lord at the head of Her Majesty's Government is in a quagmire, and he knows it well. It would be far better for the interests of the Crown, of the Kingdom, of this House, and of Christianity, if the Bill were withdrawn, instead of being proceeded with. There is no one in favour of the Bill except the noble Lord himself, for not one of his colleagues has really made a good fight for it. The Government supporters disagree; and even the law officers of the Crown give different accounts of the measure. The hon. Member for Midhurst made an excellent speech, not in favour of the Bill, but against Papal aggression; and concluded his speech with a request, that he should be permitted to substitute a new preamble and new clauses, which he was perfectly ready and willing to do. I doubt not when we go into Committee the hon. Gentleman will submit those clauses. But the Bill of the noble Lord is repudiated by all classes; and the press also repudiates it. It is well understood that the noble Lord is practising a cheat, a delusion on the people of England. The people have been clamouring for a resistance to the aggression of the Pope, but not for such resistance as this measure affords. They expect something that will be felt; but not the pretence of a measure, which, whilst it insults Roman Catholics, offers no defence to Protestants.

There is another remarkable point in this matter. I do not find any of the holy men of this House in favour of the Bill —men who are really attached to the Church of England. The hon. Members for Oxford University, for Kent, for Midhurst, not overlooking the Solicitor-General,—not one of them is to be found struggling in favour of the Bill. It has been said ' Multæ terricolis linguæ, cœlestibus una.' But it does not appear that the celestials in this House are more agreed about the matter than any of those who feel little regard for Protestantism or Catholicism. If the noble Lord cannot show a united Cabinet or party—if out of doors nobody is in favour of the Bill, and the press is almost unanimously against it—it is a fair ground for asking the House to proceed no further with the measure. If legislation be necessary at all, let it be substantial and to the purpose; if we are to obey the clamour out of doors, let us satisfy it by some substantial measure of legislation. It is said that there is a cry out of doors for a dissolution of Parliament, and I rather think some hon. Members are afraid of that. The hon. Member for Salford (Mr. Brotherton) has said that I and my Colleague do not speak the sentiments of our constituents; but, at least, we speak our sincere conviction. A reverend gentleman (the Rev. Hugh Stowell), one of the constituents of the hon. Member for Salford, whose Protestantism seems to be vituperation, and whose Christian charity clamour, has thanked God that he is represented by the hon. Member for Salford.   I am sure my hon. Friend must feel it humiliating to be patronised in such a manner.

But I will admit that many Members act in a manner opposed to the sentiments of a large number of their constituents. What of that? If there be any truth in the representative system, the 656 men returned to this House may be considered as of the foremost men of the country. It is not their duty to be the victims, subjects, and tools of a cry, but manfully and boldly to withstand it, if they believe it to be a hollow one. Of course, this language will not apply to hon. Members who conscientiously differ from me on this question ; but they must be very blind who do not know that the force of this cry, for which the noble Lord is largely responsible, is one not a few Members are disposed to yield to. We ought to resist the cry, to stem the torrent ; and it will be infinitely more honourable to go home to our avocations, if we have any, and abandon public life for ever, in defence of principles we have always held to be true, rather than be instruments of a cry to create discord between the Irish and English nations, and to perpetuate animosities which the last twenty-five years have done much to lessen. We are here to legislate calmly and deliberately, without reference to the passions and contending factions that may rage out of doors ; we are in a position to see that the course in which the noble Lord has been so recklessly dragging us is fruitful in discord, hatred, religious animosities—that it has separated Ireland from this country, has withdrawn her national sympathies from us, and has done an amount of mischief which the legislation of the next ten years cannot entirely, if at all, abate.

No one would have touched this Bill—certainly not the noble Lord—could he have foreseen all the difficulties that have arisen out of it. First of all, the Government has been broken up, though probably the noble Lord is patriotic enough to believe that that is not a national calamity. But the business of Parliament has been stopped for half a session; and we are not at the end of it yet; the Speaker has not left the chair; we are only on the brink, and about to plunge in. An hon. Gentleman has a proposition, to be supported by a large number, for a measure infinitely more stringent. The noble Lord will not carry his own measure but by the support of those who want one much more stringent. But they who want persecution will rather take a little than be entirely baffled. The noble Lord will not withdraw the Bill, because it will be humiliating to do so. But is it not very humiliating to go on with it; to be legislating for no practical good result; to pass a measure which the noble Lord knows will not satisfy those to appease whose clamour it is proposed, and which must produce the worst effects between England and Ireland? In 1829 a measure was passed—long delayed—which professed to give Roman Catholics all the liberty we ourselves enjoy. I will stand upon that Act. It is far better to have faith in the population of this country, to bind them to the Legislature and the Crown by a generous and confiding treatment, than to proceed in such a course as the House is now invited to enter on.

The noble Lord, I repeat, thinks there is great danger in this aggression of the Pope. How is there any danger? The Pope can have no authority, except over the Catholics. It is said there are 8,000,000 in England and Ireland; and should the number in England and Ireland increase to 20,000,000, there will be great danger of the Roman Catholic religion becoming the established religion of the country— should an Established Church exist so long. Therefore, the argument of danger supposes the conversion of the people; for it is only by this means that the country can, to any con-

siderable degree, come under the rule of the Pope.   The noble
Lord has drawn up an indictment against 8,000,000 of his
countrymen; he has increased the power of the Pope over
the Roman Catholics, for he has drawn closer the bonds
between them and their Church and the head of their Church.
The noble Lord has quoted Queen Elizabeth and the great
men of the Commonwealth, as though it were necessary now
to adopt the principles which prevailed almost universally
two hundred years ago.   Does the noble Lord forget that we
are the true ancients, that we stand on the shoulders of our
forefathers, and can see further?   We have seen the working
of these principles, and their result, and have concluded to
abandon them.

I have not touched on any matter purely religious; this
House is not the place for religious questions.   But reflecting
on the deep mysteries of religion, on my own doubts and
frailties, on the shortness of the present time, and on the awful
and unknown future—I ask what am I that I should judge
another in religious things, and condemn him to exclusion and
persecution?   I fear not for the country on questions like this.
England, with a united population—though the noble Lord
has done much to disunite them—cares nothing for foreign
potentates, be their combinations what they may.   England,
with her free press, her advancing civilisation, her daily and
hourly progress in the arts, sciences, industry, and morals,
will withstand any priestly attempts to subjugate the mind,
and successfully resist any menaces, whether coming from
Lambeth or from Rome.   I am one of a sect which has
invariably held the principles I now advocate, which has in
past years suffered greatly from those principles which the
noble Lord now wishes to introduce into our legislature.
I cannot do otherwise than raise my voice against such an
attempt, and ask the noble Lord to proceed no further.

ADMISSION OF JEWS TO PARLIAMENT.

HOUSE OF COMMONS, APRIL 15, 1853.

From Hansard.

ALTHOUGH this question has been discussed almost every session since I have had a seat in Parliament, I have never ventured to trouble the House with any observations upon it, and hoping, as I do most unfeignedly, that this may be the very last occasion on which it may be necessary to discuss it, I will ask the attention of the House for a very few moments while I state the opinions which I entertain upon it. I was once asked by an hon. Member on that (the Opposition) side of the House why I had not spoken upon the Jew Bill, and I gave him a candid answer. I told him that I had never heard anything in the shape of a fact or argument from the opponents of this measure, which, like facts and arguments on a great many questions which come before us, could be fairly grappled with, and which a man could undertake to lay hold of in the hope of answering it. I told him further, that it appeared to me that the opponents of this measure were actuated, I believed very honestly, by what was rather a sentiment than anything else; and the hon. Gentleman to whom I have alluded, not by any means one of the least distinguished amongst you, admitted that I was perfectly right, and that it was more a sentiment than anything else. A sentiment is, of course, difficult to argue against. This sentiment has gradually sunk down into a phrase, and we understand now that what is meant by that phrase is that we, on this side, are about to unchristianise the House of Commons.

Now I have endeavoured, in the course of these discussions, to trace whence this notion or feeling of unchristianising springs, and I think I can trace it backwards through the changes of the law, by which successive parties and sects, and sections of the people of this country, have, during the last 160 years, been admitted to full participation in the rights of citizenship. The very same feeling, though it was called something else, was in operation when you excluded the Roman Catholics from Parliament. The very same feeling under a somewhat different title was in operation when the Unitarians were subjected to oppressive statutes; and it was the very same spirit, however much you may attempt to disguise it, under which, previous to the repeal of the Test and Corporation Acts, the Dissenters of this country were excluded from municipal and other offices. It always seems to me to come from that appetite for supremacy which springs from the fact that we have had in this country a powerful and dominant Church, connected chiefly with a powerful ruling class, and that step by step the people of this country, one section after another, have wrested from that Church, and from that class, the rights of citizenship which we have claimed, and which we now enjoy.

Now what can be more marvellous than that any sane man should propose that doctrinal differences in religion should be made the test of citizenship and political rights? Doctrinal differences in religion, in all human probability, will last for many generations to come, and may possibly last so long as man shall inhabit this globe; but if you permit these differences to be the tests of citizenship, what is it but to admit into your system this fatal conclusion, that social and political differences in all nations can never be eradicated, but must be eternal? The hon. Baronet the Member for the University of Oxford (Sir R. H. Inglis) may be taken probably for as honest and consistent a representative of the opponents of this Bill as can be found in this House. I should like to ask whether there is any difference between the hon. Baronet the Member for the University of Oxford and Baron Rothschild in any matter which can affect citizenship or the duties of citizens, or in anything whatsoever of which the laws of this country can justly take cognizance as relating to the actions of the subjects of the Crown. I have watched the hon. Baronet for many years with great admiration—not with admiration for the principles which he holds, but with admiration for the manner in which he always maintains them. If all men who hold what I regard as sound principles in this House were to take the hon. Baronet for their model, sound principles would march on much faster than they do.

Take, for instance, what may be called the morality of politics, and you will find that the hon. Baronet draws nearly all his opinions from the very same source that Baron Rothschild draws his. We have discussed in this House the question of capital punishment. I find the hon. Baronet, with his accustomed bland dignity, quoting against me with perfect confidence the ninth chapter of the book of Genesis; and I have a strong suspicion that he takes his notions of the priesthood from the times of the book of Exodus. I think I have a distinct recollection that when the question of marriage with a deceased wife's sister was under discussion, the hon. Baronet referred the House with perfect confidence to the book of Leviticus. The hon. Baronet too, I think, will not dispute that his law of tithes comes from the very

same book.   If it be a question of oaths, although it has
been said by the highest authority, ' Ye have heard that it
hath been said in old times, Thou shalt not forswear thyself,
but shalt perform unto the Lord thy vows,' the ' swear not
at all' is disregarded, and the practice of the hon. Baronet—
a practice approved by his Church, and approved, I presume,
by a majority of this House—is precisely that which existed
in the time of the Old Testament Scriptures.   If the hon.
Baronet does not defend the practice of war, yet I know
writers who profess the same faith as the hon. Baronet who
have defended the practice of war, because they say it was,
if not inculcated, at least permitted, in the Old Testament.
I cannot see, if the hon. Baronet takes his public morality
from these writings, and if Baron Rothschild takes his from
the same source, and if the question of citizenship be not
a matter of doctrinal religion, but of the due performance
of our duties to each other and to the State—I cannot see
why the hon. Baronet should, for thirty or forty years, have
sat in this House, and Baron Rothschild, elected by the first
constituency of the kingdom, be shut out.

It would be as reasonable for a man to quarrel with his
own shadow, as for the hon. Baronet to quarrel with Baron
Rothschild on these grounds.   But what a ridiculous position
the House is placed in.   You have had not only Baron Rothschild, but another Member of his persuasion at that bar, and,
assuming he was a Christian, you allowed him to begin to
take the oath upon the Old Testament.   You made no objection to him until he came to the words ' on the true faith of
a Christian.'   If the oath had been taken with the words ' on
the faith of a Christian,' as you interpret them, on the Old
Testament, it could not possibly be a legal oath.   If it was
necessary for a man who took an oath in a court of law to
be a Christian, no Judge would allow an oath to be taken
on the Old Testament ; but would require it to be taken
on the New Testament, because the book must be the symbol

of the faith by which he affirmed. Well, you passed a Resolution that the seat for the City of London was full, and you put yourselves out of court with regard to the issuing of a new writ. If a man was an alien, and had been elected by a constituency, I presume that it would be competent for the House to appoint a Committee to examine into the petition charging him with being an alien, and upon the Report of the Committee that he was such, he would be excluded from the House, and a new writ would issue. But here you have no means of appointing a Committee for the purpose of interrogating Baron Rothschild as to whether he is a Jew or a Christian. He took one oath, and part of another. This House declared that the seat was full, and that a new writ for the City of London could not be issued; and then this House excluded the Member who was elected from his seat.

These facts lead me to the consideration of a second question, of as great importance as the original question which we are now discussing. This question has been discussed and decided upon within a very recent period in a great many divisions in this House, not less, I believe, than fourteen times. Whether it was before or after dinner—whatever the circumstances under which we were assembled — there was always a very large majority in favour of this Bill, from twenty-six, at the lowest, to more than one hundred at the highest. I want to ask hon. Gentlemen opposite whether they think, after the House of Commons in two, if not three Parliaments, within very recent years, has decided fourteen times in favour of the candidate elected by the City of London, that it is constitutional, after these incessant and oft-repeated expressions of opinion on the part of the constituencies of this country, that this question should longer remain unsettled?

I am told there is an awful power in another place. I do not mean Lords Temporal so much as Lords Spiritual.

I have no great opinion of Bishops in any case. But of all subjects, this is about the very last on which I should like to take the opinion of the Bishops of the Church of England. High titles, vast revenues, great power, conferred upon Christian ministers, are as without warrant to my mind in Scripture as in reason. I do not expect that they should be able to give an unbiassed, impartial judgment on a question like this. I understand that the noble Lord at the head of the Government—coming from the north may possibly account for it—is alarmed at the power of the bishops. I would not suggest how it is to be overcome; but probably there are means by which the Government can procure the passing of this Bill through the other House of Parliament. Now, that appears to be a question of some importance. Though hon. Gentlemen opposite have insisted on discussing this question, night after night, every session, for years past, let us have the subject thoroughly probed, if this is to be the last night.

The House of Commons has decided in favour of this Bill. Does any hon. Gentleman deny it? If the House of Commons represents the country, the country is in favour of this Bill. There is another estate of this realm, the most dignified of all, represented in this House by the Gentlemen who sit on that (the Ministerial) bench; that estate of the realm unites cordially with the House of Commons and with the people in this Bill. Fourteen times has this measure been carried by large majorities; repeatedly has it been sent to the other House, and each time has it been rejected, and on some occasions rejected in a manner which seemed to indicate contempt. Now, I ask the noble Lord the Member for the City of London if there is any remedy in the constitution for this state of things? The noble Lord had the opportunity of admitting the Jews by a Resolution of this House—he had a precedent of the most conclusive kind in the case of Mr. Pease—and although the law officers were not clear upon the law on that occasion, still the House of Commons, having once established a precedent of that nature, any person wishing to sustain the power of this House, and of one great branch of the Legislature, would have done wisely to have maintained the precedent, and to have relied on it in this case.

The noble Lord preferred what he thought a more constitutional course, and he asks this House to pass Bills for the purpose. Year after year this House has passed this measure, and I ask the noble Lord whether he thinks we are to go on year after year bombarding the Lords with this Jew Bill, with no other result than that it should be sent down again ? If the British constitution affords no remedy for this state of things, it is not worth all the boasting which the noble Lord and others have heaped upon it. There are two remedies for this evil. The one is the creation of new Peers. ['Hear!'] Do not for a moment imagine that I should recommend it. I think the remedy might be worse than the disease; but that is one of the remedies, as I understand it, which the constitution offers to the Crown in cases of this nature, provided the case be of sufficient magnitude. We know that this remedy has been threatened in our day, and threatened with some success.

There is another remedy. Some Gentlemen say, 'How can you expect the House of Lords to pass this Bill, when there is no ferment in the country?' I thought noblemen in that assembly were in an atmosphere so serene, that though disturbed occasionally by the contentions of prelates and the disputations of rival lawyers, they might be judged to be in that one place on the earth 'where the wicked cease from troubling, and the weary are at rest.' But we are told there is no ferment in the country. I have seen ferments in this country, and many others have. I do not much admire them. I would rather see the Houses of Legislature, whether the one or the other, taking these questions up in a broad, philosophic, generous spirit, and discussing and

settling them in that spirit, than that they should wait
until there is a ferment in the country approaching to
confusion, and then surrender, upon terms that shall be
humiliating to them, prejudices which, if given up in time,
might have been forgotten in the gratitude and the applause
of their countrymen. It is assumed, and properly and wisely,
that you will get no ferment up about the Jew Bill. I have
no objection to admit that the Jews, not being great in
numbers, and not free from some disadvantage, consequent
upon that prejudice so prevalent on the benches opposite,
will give occasion to no ferment before which those benches
will quail. ['Oh, oh!'] They will quail soon enough
when there is a ferment. ['Oh, oh!'] If that is doubted,
I refer you to the history of the last twenty-five years in proof
of what I say. But I want no ferment. I want argument
and sound principles of legislation to prevail within the
Houses of Parliament, and not the fear of anything that
may take place outside.

But now comes the case of the noble Lord who leads the
Government in this House. The noble Lord has worked
at this Bill for many years; he has induced this House to
abdicate the power which it possessed, by precedent, of
admitting the Jews to this House by a Resolution of this
House. He has recommended the constitutional course—a
good course if it should succeed—but I think he is bound to
take all the measures which are open to his Government for
the purpose of ensuring the success of this Bill; and I claim
it as one of those who have voted with him, I believe, on
every occasion, and done all that I could for the purpose of
securing the success of this measure. Now, if the Government would make up their minds that unless this Bill passes
during this session they would treat a defeat in the House
of Lords precisely as they would treat an important defeat
in this House; then no person could say hereafter that the
noble Lord and his Colleagues did not make every effort they

could be called on to make for the purpose of passing this Bill. I cannot say whether there is any other remedy than the creation of Peers, and agitation out of doors; but let it be a resolution on the part of the Government that this Bill shall pass—that they will make it a matter on which their existence, as a Government, shall be staked—and if it should not be passed, upon those persons be the responsibility of forming a Government who shall prevent this measure of justice to the Jewish population of this country.

I should have been glad if the noble Lord, with the great influence which he exercises in this House, had endeavoured to prevail on the House to abolish the whole system of oaths at the bar, and to have substituted some declaration which every honest man could take in an honest and conscientious spirit. These oaths are of no use—we know they are of no use; you make us affirm something that does not exist—and every man who takes an oath at the table, which I am happy to say I have never done, knows he is performing a farce which is ludicrous. ['Oh, oh!'] The fact is, that you are called on to affirm that you will not do something which it is impossible for you to do. Let us, then, get rid of this question, which has been discussed and decided year after year; and, above all, let us see that the Commons House of England is open to the Commons of England, and that every man, be his creed what it may, if elected by a constituency of his countrymen, may sit in this House, and vote on all matters which affect the legislation of this kingdom.

THE GOVERNMENT SCHEME
OF EDUCATION.

HOUSE OF COMMONS, APRIL 20, 1847.

From Hansard.

In rising to offer a few observations on this most interesting question, I am sensible that I have to defend men and principles which are not popular in this assembly. Nevertheless, being myself one of the Nonconformist body of this country, and being by birth, education, observation, and conviction, fully established in the opinions I hold, I am bound, though it may be in opposition to a Government sitting on the same side of the House as myself, to protest against the policy and principles now offered for the adoption of the House.

I listened with pleased attention to the speech of the right hon. Member for Edinburgh; and I read with due respect that of the noble Lord at the head of the Government. I admit the ability of those ·speeches; but there is nothing in which that ability is more displayed than in the skill with which they have evaded the question really in dispute between the Dissenting bodies and the Government by which this scheme of education is proposed. It is not the question before the House, in the scheme proposed, or in the Amendment moved by the hon. Gentleman the Member for Finsbury, whether the

State has any right or power to interfere with education in this country; it is not the question whether it is with secular education only that they have a right to interfere. The question is this:—what Minutes of Council are before us, what is their object, their tendency, and the effect they will produce upon the position of the Established Church and the Dissenting bodies in the United Kingdom?

The right hon. Gentleman the Member for Edinburgh spent three-fourths of the time he was on his legs in proving that the State has the power and the right, and that it is the duty of the State, to see to the education of its subjects. Judging from his speech, it was one of the simplest things imaginable; the proposition appeared to be so clear that he was astonished any one should doubt it; and with the right hon. Gentleman's opinions I was astonished he should take so much pains to enforce it. But if it be so clear a proposition that Government has the plain right to educate its subjects, it is somewhat extraordinary that with all the eminent statesmen in this country for some generations past, there has never been any bold and determined attempt to interfere with the education of the common people of England and Wales.

The right hon. Gentleman appeared to me to prove too much. He tried to prove that it was the duty of the Government to educate the people; but if it be the duty of Government to educate them, it must be the duty of the Government to enforce education. I do not know where the line can be drawn. If it be its solemn duty to afford opportunity for education, and to see that all the people are educated, it appears to me we must come inevitably to the conclusion, that Government has the power, and that it is also its right and its duty, to enforce education on all the people subject to its rule.

The noble Lord at the head of the Government objected to the Dissenters that they had supported the Committee of

Privy Council in 1839, whilst they oppose it in 1847; that
they were then in favour of this interference, and are now
against it. I admit that many, or at least, that some of the
Dissenters were in favour of it eight years ago. But we have
had some experience from 1839 to 1847. At that time the
Dissenters regarded the institution of the Committee of Privy
Council as a step leading away from that power which the
Church of England wished to usurp, of educating the whole
people; and the Dissenters hoped we were on the road at last
to overcome the pretensions which the Church of England
had so long asserted, that she was called upon and bound to
undertake the business of education, and that she ought to be
entrusted with the education of the people. But from 1839
to this year we have found no step taken by the Government which has not had a tendency to aggrandize the
Established Church. In 1839 the noble Lord proposed a
scheme which, from the opposition of the Established Church
and the Wesleyans, was withdrawn. In 1843, the right hon.
Baronet the late Secretary for the Home Department (Sir
James Graham) proposed a scheme of education in connection
with the Factories Bill—a scheme which was thought by
everybody to give undue power to the Established Church, and
which, in consequence of the opposition of the Dissenters, was
withdrawn. In 1847, the noble Lord comes forward with
another scheme. It has the same defect; its object, tendency,
and result will be to give increased and enormous power to the
clergy of the Established Church. It is a scheme of which
the Dissenters cannot avail themselves, in accordance with the
principles by which they are Dissenters; and, therefore, they
are bound now to step forward and protest against this as
against the former schemes. And I wonder not they have
come to the conclusion that it is dangerous to them as members of Dissenting bodies, and dangerous also to the civil
liberty of the people, that the State should interfere with
education, since the Government, it appears, is not able to

interfere without giving increased power to the clergy of an already dominant Church.

The right hon. Gentleman the Member for Edinburgh, and the noble Lord who has just sat down, have both failed to convey to the House any intimation that there is much doing in the cause of education by voluntary effort throughout the kingdom. If a man came to this House from any other country, and knew nothing of what was going on in England, he would have come to the conclusion that voluntary efforts had not only not succeeded, but had never even been attempted—so little would appear to have been done from the statements they made to the House. If these efforts have succeeded, few Members will say that any interference by the Government is desirable. If there be one principle more certain than another, I suppose it is this, that what a people is able to do for itself, that the Government should not attempt to do for it. For nothing tends so much to strengthen a people—to make them great and good—as the constant exercise of all their faculties for public objects, and the carrying on of all public works and objects by voluntary contributions among themselves.

I will just ask the attention of the House for a moment to what has been done during the last few years. The right hon. Gentleman the Member for Edinburgh said, we had been trying the voluntary principle ever since the Heptarchy; that the voluntary principle had been, in fact, for generations and ages on its trial; and the result was, that we had an enormous amount of intellectual destitution in the country. But it is not a fair statement to say, that we have been trying the voluntary system since the Heptarchy. We have not been trying the voluntary system to make rail-roads since the Heptarchy, but since the year 1830; and it would be as fair a statement to say that the voluntary system would never make railroads for this country, because it had not made railroads in fifteen or sixteen years, as to say that the voluntary system will not educate the people because it has not provided full means of education since 1790; many archbishops, bishops, and other distinguished members of the Established Church having opposed themselves to the effective education of the common people.

The House is not very fond, and I admire its judgment in this respect, of hearing statistics on a question of this kind; but it is a matter of figures as to what has been done. Looking to the statistics given by the friends and opponents of this measure, by Dr. Hook and Mr. Baines, and others who have made calculations on the subject, it appears that from the year 1818 to this time the progress has been something extraordinary. In 1818 there were 674,000 day-scholars in England and Wales; in 1833, there were 1,276,000; in 1847, there were 2,147,000. Thus, in 1818, the proportion was 1 in 17 to the population; in 1833, it was 1 in 11; in 1847, it was 1 in 8. The population has increased only 49 per cent. since that time, whilst the scholars in our day-schools have increased at least 210 per cent.; that is, leaving out of view the numbers who are Sunday scholars. I agree with the noble Lord who spoke last, that Sunday-school education is not all the children should have : but when you are complaining of the want, the destitution of education, it is fair that should be taken into account. In 1818, the Sunday scholars numbered 477,000; in 1833, they were more than 1,000,000; and from that time to this there has been a very rapid increase.

Now, look at Scotland. The right hon. Gentleman the Secretary at War, I think, is not in his place, or he could tell us something about the Church with which he is so honourably connected, I mean the Free Church of Scotland. If within three or four years they have raised more than 1,000,000*l.* sterling, if they have built or offered to build schools in some 600 or 700 parishes, what will the right hon. Member for Edinburgh say to this? I have been in their churches and chapels; and if there be one thing more honourable to the Scotchmen of this generation than another, it is the magnanimous and wonderful efforts which the members of that communion have made to constitute themselves a Church free from the trammels and embarrassments attendant on a connection with the State.

We will take Wales, and see what has been done there. In the *Carnarvon and Denbigh Herald* of the 21st of March, 1846, I find it stated, that

'About seven or eight years ago, in the seventy-three parishes of Anglesea, in which there were churches, there was not one Sunday-school connected with the Established Church, whilst there were in the county no fewer than 156 Sunday-schools kept by the various denominations of Dissenters.'

And the statement went on—

'There are now in the six counties of North Wales alone 1,022 places of public worship, in which Sunday-schools are regularly kept by Dissenters, and well attended, viz.—

Calvinistic Methodists	479 schools.
Independents	260 ,,
Baptists	81 ,,
Wesleyans	202 ,,

which were attended by upwards of 140,000 children altogether.'

With respect to Wales, there is this remarkable fact, that the education of the common people—of the labouring classes—has been altogether the work of the Dissenting communities in that part of the kingdom. There is not a Member of this House from Wales, on whatever side of the House he sits, who will deny that something like nine out of ten of the labouring classes in Wales who have received education within the last fifty years, have received that education at the hands of the Dissenting bodies. There is, I believe, a Commission of educational inquiry now at work in Wales. We have not their report yet; but I venture to foretell that when that report is printed it will establish the fact I have stated—that of late years, where the Church has educated one child in this part of the country, the Dissenting Churches have educated from eight to ten.

The noble Lord at the head of the Government appears to differ from his right hon. Colleague the Member for Edinburgh. From what he states, I understand he is of opinion that the voluntary principle has done a good deal—namely, it has provided schools sufficient for the wants of the population. The noble Lord said, speaking of his coming back to office—

'When, however, we came, being newly-appointed members of the Committee, to consider the state of education, it appeared to us that a very great number of schools had been built, and that there was no longer such a demand as there had been for money to build schools ; and that as various deficiencies in the management and conduct of the schools had been observed, it would be advisable to make Minutes, proposing a different distribution of the sum which might be voted by Parliament, and laying down in those Minutes what the application of that sum should be.'

So that we have the authority of the noble Lord for this fact, that the system hitherto pursued, the voluntary system, has provided schools in about sufficient abundance; and it is because the Government actually did not find that they had the means of distributing their grants for the building of schools, that they now come before the House and ask for powers to be allowed to spend the grants in improving the quality of the education. Is it likely, I ask, that the system which has built their schools for many of the population of this country, will be very long in improving the quality of the education given in them? is it likely that we shall have to wait long before it will be no more necessary to pay and pension the schoolmasters out of the public funds, than it is now to build schools for the accommodation of the children taught?

The noble Lord says—

' I do not understand, then, why any Dissenter should refuse to partake of this grant on the ground that part of this money is given to Church of England schools, these Church schools being supported by the subscriptions of individuals who are members of that Church.'

I think it was not very ingenuous of the noble Lord to make such a statement as this in his speech. He must know it is not because the Church of England receives money from this grant that Nonconformists object to the grant; but it is because Nonconformists themselves, in accordance with the principles by which they are so, cannot receive public money for the teaching of religion in their schools; and, therefore, they object to the State giving money as an advantage to the Church schools—an advantage by which they must profit, and which will certainly be most damaging to the Dissenting schools.

The right hon. Member for Edinburgh does not generally speak with great courtesy of Dissenters and Nonconformists. I have heard him speak in this House, I think, of the braying of Exeter Hall; and last night he spoke frequently of the clamour made out of doors. It is a very old story for Gentlemen in office—and there must be many comforts, conveniences, and pleasures, no doubt, connected with office, or men would not seek it so much—it is a common thing for men in office to say that any opposition to their plans made out of doors is clamour. But I ask whether it is likely that five hundred men, from all parts of the country, would come up to London, and take the trouble they have done, meeting all the hostility and obloquy heaped upon them, if they did not believe that there was something important in the Minutes to the interests of the different religious communities with which they are connected? And I think that the right hon. Gentleman is one of the last men in this House who should treat this movement as clamour, and condemn it as if it came from an unreasonable class of persons.

The right hon. Gentleman tells us that they are abandoning all the principles which the Nonconformists of past times ever taught; he tells us what republican statesmen and leaders in the United States have said, what has been done or held by Washington, Jefferson, and the commonwealth of Massachusetts. But is there any comparison between the United States and the United Kingdom? Is there any Established

Church in the United States? Has the commonwealth of Massachusetts, in every one of its parishes, a gentleman highly educated, well paid, connected by birth or standing with the aristocratic and privileged class, not influenced by the popular sentiment and the popular mind, but acting always in unison and conformity with the privileged class to which he is attached? Give us, if you please, the state of things which exists in the United States, and particularly in that State of Massachusetts. Free us from the trammels of your Church—set religion apart from the interference of the State—if you will make public provision for education, let it not depend upon the doctrines of a particular creed—and then you will find the various sects in this country will be as harmonious on the question of education as are the people of the United States of America.

Just recollect, when the whole of the Nonconformists are charged with clamour, what they mean by being Nonconformists. They object, as I understand, at least I object, to the principle by which the Government seizes public funds in order to give salaries and support to the teachers of all sects of religion, or of one sect of religion, for I think the one plan nearly as unjust as the other. Either the Nonconformists hold this opinion, or they are a great imposture. They object to any portion of the public money going to teachers of religion belonging either to the Established Church or to Dissenting bodies; they object to the receiving it for themselves. They find certain Minutes infringing on this principle. You wish to establish a system by which the young persons of this country shall be trained to certain religious tenets. In your Church schools, we are to have the Catechism taught, and the Liturgy taught, as well as the Scriptures read. All this is to be done under the cognizance and supervision of the clergyman of the parish. The children are to be examined by the clergymen and by inspectors appointed by the Government, who are also to be clergymen of the Church of England.

The Minutes do not say so; but under the compact entered into by the Government with the Church, they can appoint no inspector who is not palatable to the Archbishop of Canterbury. The inspector must be discharged if the Archbishop expresses an opinion unfavourable to him. Of course this is in Church of England schools only.

I admit that the noble Lord will not carry it the length of proposing this for Dissenting schools; he will not venture to do so. We are not yet sufficiently humiliated for that. No Government in this country durst attempt to carry that into effect. But if you had the power to carry out the spirit expressed in the Minutes, I say the Dissenting schools would not be free from interference by the clergymen of the State Church. I am prepared to contend that the powers given by these Minutes to the clergymen examiners are calculated to give a great increase of power to all the clergymen of the Established Church. They are made public officers with respect to schools. Now, the vicar of the parish enters the schools, and inquires about the children; but he has no more power than any other gentleman who may choose to visit it and do the same. But by your Minutes you empower him to enter under the authority of an inspector, who, by your compact with the Church, can only be a clergyman of the Established Church. I say these clergymen and inspectors are prone to meddle with everything. They will go there and examine the children in their books; they will interrogate the teachers as to their methods and their learning. Do you think, if they find a child whose brother or sister goes to a Dissenting chapel, the clergyman will not be zealous enough to use his influence to induce him to attend the church?

It is notorious that, in all parts of England, charities, never intended to be used for the promotion of particular religious opinions, but which are in the hands of the Established Church, are distributed with a view to the effect they may have in bringing an increase of attendance to the National schools or the churches of the Establishment. I know numbers of these cases myself; and I know that a child who did not bow down to the Church, or who refused to go to a National school, would find himself placed under the ban of the clergyman. All the inducements to him, which you boast of, to rise in the world and gain an honourable station in society, would be merely as the idle wind that blows, and would be of no avail whatever to obtain for him an honourable place in life. If anything were wanted to show the effect of these Minutes, look at the triumph your propositions have excited among the members of the Established Church, and the clergy especially. Was there ever a good measure for Nonconformists proposed that was received with an exulting shout of gratulation by the hon. Baronet below me (Sir R. H. Inglis), by the Bishops, and by all the clergy of the kingdom? I am wrong, perhaps, as regards the hon. Baronet; he did not loudly exult, but he took the measure meekly, he took it very thankfully.

I acknowledge that the Church is thankful for everything it can get, and it never loses anything for want of asking for it. I confess I am astonished that Churchmen throughout the country—I do not speak of the clergy, but the laity—have supported this measure, because I think they are as much interested as the Dissenters in opposing any extension of power on the part of the clergy. Nothing tends more to impede the progress of liberty, nothing is more fatal to independence of spirit in the public, than to add to the powers of the priesthood in matters of education. If you give them such increased powers by legislative enactment, you do more than you could effect by any other means to enslave and degrade a people subject to their influence.

There is yet another point to which I must advert. In the speech of the right hon. Member for Edinburgh, who dwelt with great emphasis on the impartiality which he attributed to this proposed system, the right hon. Gentleman said:—

' I do wish that, instead of using phrases of disparagement against the
scheme proposed, hon. Gentlemen would just answer me this plain question :—
Supposing in any one city there should be a school connected with the Church,
another connected with the Wesleyans, and another with the Presbyterians—
will any Gentleman distinctly point out to me what share of the public money
or what patronage is that which the school connected with the Church will
get, and which the other schools will not get ?'

That is the question to which the right hon. Gentleman asked
for an answer. If the right hon. Gentleman had looked over
the grants that have already been made, he would have found
that out of the sum of 149,000*l.*, which during the last three
years has been distributed by the Committee of the Privy
Council, the Church has received 141,000*l.* There never was
anything so impartial. ['Hear, hear!'] No doubt hon. Gentlemen opposite, who cheer, will say that the Dissenters might
have had it if they had asked for it. True, but the Dissenters
were of a different temper from that. They did not separate
from the Established Church that they should afterwards
come whining and asking the Government to support their
educational system. Their very principle is that the Government has no right to appropriate public funds for the purpose
of religious instruction. The right hon. Gentleman the
Member for Edinburgh knows right well that in times past
they have refused the public money for such a purpose, and
that in times to come they are likely to come still less forward
than hitherto to avail themselves of such support.

The right hon. Gentleman took us to the United States
last night, and I will ask him to accompany me there now for
a moment. The impartiality of your plan is like this.
Suppose at the present time in the United States—there
being no Established Church there—the Government were to
offer an endowment to the religious sects, and nine-tenths
having refused to accept it, the Government were to persist
in endowing the remaining one-tenth, while the others
protested against the principle of endowment altogether;
in that condition of things the plea of impartiality would

be as just and fair as that put forward in the present case by the right hon. Gentleman.   The Dissenters have not taken, and they will not take, this money; and it must be clear to those who know the history and understand anything of the principles of Nonconformity, that any Nonconformist who takes one sixpence of this grant for the purpose of teaching the tenets of his particular sect, can never afterwards, with any show of consistency and good faith, say one syllable against the domination and usurpation of the Established Church.

I think that in this year 1847 the time may be said to have come, when, although the members of the Established Church may not consider such scruples wise and prudent, the scruples which do exist and are conscientiously entertained by thousands and millions of our countrymen should be respected, and when the Government should pause before it holds out a great temptation to men to abandon their principles; and, in the event of their refusing to abandon them, offers an enormous advantage to the members of the Established Church.   With respect to the Roman Catholics, the right hon. Gentleman did not give a direct reply to the statement of the hon. Member for Finsbury on that part of the subject, when he read an extract from a speech of the noble Lord in 1839; and, as there has been some talk of the negotiations which have been going on with the Wesleyans during the last fortnight, I should be glad, if the right hon. Baronet the Secretary of State for the Home Department should think it worth while to notice anything I say, to receive an answer to this question—Have the Privy Council communicated with the authorities and dignitaries of the Roman Catholic Church with respect to the appointment of inspectors of Roman Catholic schools, or have they not?   If they have, then it follows of course that they must have had the intention, when these Minutes were laid upon the tables of both Houses of Parliament, to make grants to Roman Catholic schools.   That

would be something noble, something great, something to be
admired, in coming forward to offer this great boon to all
classes of the people without favour or distinction.

In this House I have often heard men taunt the Dissenters
with bigotry in their conduct towards the Roman Catholic
population; but let it be said that those Dissenters have
ever accorded and been willing to accord to their Roman
Catholic brethren all and everything they sought and could
conscientiously accept for themselves. Civil rights and privileges the Dissenters have been willing to grant to Catholics.
Many of them who have had seats in this House since 1829
would never have found admittance here had it not been
for the assistance they received in their struggle for civil
liberty at the hands of the Dissenting body. My honest
opinion is this, that when these Minutes were laid upon the
table, the Government intended, and most wisely, to open
these grants to all persons of all religious persuasions whatsoever.

The Government had no idea that there would be a disturbance about these Minutes. They were drawn up by a
very clever secretary, who, like other secretaries, is disposed
to magnify the importance of his office, and when drawn up
they were, no doubt, submitted to the oversight of the bishops
in the other House. The whole thing was comfortably concocted, and it was supposed the Dissenters would take it
without asking any questions. But the moment the Wesleyans evinced a disposition to join other Dissenters in resisting
the measure, it was feared that the opposition might grow too
formidable, and negotiations were entered into. Possibly the
Government did not make the first overture in this negotiation; but it often happens in these cases, as everybody
knows, that there is some convenient friend to make the
primary advance, and put the negotiation in train. At this
time the Wesleyans are supposed to be under the delusion
that the Roman Catholics are to be excluded; and if they

are, I am reminded of what has been said by a well-known writer, that it is sometimes as pleasant to be cheated as to cheat.

I am not now going to detain the House with any observations as to the construction of the Committee of the Privy Council, nor will I enter into particulars of the expenditure to be incurred, or of the bribes to be offered. This only I will remark, that I believe the last thing any reasonable man would do to elevate his fellow-man, is to make him a pensioner or recipient of the bounty of the Government. But the question is, whether the Nonconformists, forming so large a part of the population of this country, are to have their feelings and principles disregarded in the course of legislation you adopt—whether a new system of education is to be introduced in which you teach everybody's religion at everybody's expense? The Nonconformists deny your right to do this: they will not receive your money. You offer them that which is of no value to them; and the Church, less scrupulous, receives the gift. The consequence is that the schools of the Dissenters will stand at a great disadvantage as compared with the Church schools—the one class depending solely upon voluntary contributions, the other having certain bribes attached to it of provision for life, and for the maintenance of which the House is asked to vote at the expense of all.

I will say nothing now of the wonderful statesmanship which has chosen this particular season to open an arena of strife, and throw down an apple of discord amongst us when there was an appearance of concord and unanimity. I am sorry it has come to this; I am sorry, not because of the particular effect it may have upon this Government or that Government, but because I must ever regret to see discord and bitterness introduced upon religious subjects, and because I know that when once this strife begins, real interests, useful matters, are neglected; and men separate and stray aside from paths which they might tread together to the advantage of their common country.

I will now conclude; and if I have been betrayed into some warmth of expression, let it be remembered that I am a member of the Nonconformist body. My forefathers languished in prison by the acts of that Church which you now ask me to aggrandise. Within two years places of worship of the sect to which I belong have been despoiled of their furniture to pay the salary of a minister of the Established Church; and when I look back and see how that Church has been uniformly hostile to the progress of public liberty, it is impossible for me to withhold my protest against the outrage committed by the Government on the Nonconformist body for the sake of increasing the power of a political institution, which I believe is destined to fall before the growing Christianity and the extending freedom of the people.

CHURCH RATES ABOLITION BILL.

HOUSE OF COMMONS, APRIL 27, 1860.

From Hansard.

I FEEL somewhat indebted to the right hon. and learned Gentleman (Mr. Whiteside) for having come forward as a new advocate upon this question, for he has thrown, by that physical force oratory of which he is so great a master, some new light upon a question which has been worn almost threadbare. But I do not think that when his speech is read to-morrow it will persuade that great portion of the people who object to Church-rates that the system now existing should be permanently continued. I was not present at the opening of the learned Gentleman's speech, but when I entered the House he was telling us that the Nonconformists of the olden time were a much better class of men than the Dissenters of the present day; that they made no objections to the equity of Church-rates. That was a sentiment which was received with great enthusiasm by hon. Gentlemen opposite, who for the first time have appeared as decided admirers of the Nonconformists of the past. In answer to that it may be said that from the time of Queen Elizabeth down to the Act of Toleration the principles of religious freedom were little understood in this country. We know that not the Church only when it had the power, but many of the Nonconformists themselves, admitted that it was right not only to raise taxes for the support of a particular Church—their own Church—but that it was positively right to coerce those persons who held religious opinions different from their own. They had not advanced as far as the great body of the English people, including hon. Gentlemen opposite, and the party they represent, have now advanced, and therefore the learned Gentleman's argument goes for very little. But he has treated the House to a public reading of a large portion of the evidence of, I think, two gentlemen who were witnesses before the Committee of the House of Lords. I shall refer only to the evidence of one of these gentlemen— Mr. Bunting. I suspect that when the name of Bunting was mentioned there was a general impression that this was the evidence of a very distinguished man who, although not nominally, yet actually, was Bishop or Archbishop, and almost Pope, in the sect of which he was so distinguished a Member. But that is not the case. The learned Gentleman, not for the first time in his life as a counsel learned in the law, has been beholden for his brief to an attorney practising in Manchester. Mr. Bunting is not a minister of the Methodist Church, as I understand, but is in the profession of the law, and therefore I must strip him of any authority he has upon this matter in con- nection with the Methodist Church in consequence of his bearing the name of Bunting. I must say, further, that this Gentleman, although in some sort a Nonconformist, inas- much as I presume he attends a Methodist Chapel, is a politician of a peculiar kind, such as is not found very frequently among the Dissenting body. I dare say he agrees with the most obstructive, if I may use the term, Con- servative or Tory among hon. Gentlemen opposite, and if we had taken his opinion upon all those questions of policy which this House has decided in favour of popular rights and justice to the people of this country during the last twenty years, I have not the least doubt that Mr. Bunting would have been as conclusive in his evidence against all those concessions as he appears to have been upon the question of Church-rates. But the learned Gentleman did not treat the House quite fairly in stating the evidence of this Gentleman, because even he did not feel himself courageous enough to say that the Wesleyan body was in favour of Church-rates. I find he says, in answer to a question whether there was any likelihood of petitions being sent by them —:

'No : from a fear on the part of those who sympathize with the Church of England of eliciting an opinion to the contrary. There is among us a general agreement not to disturb questions which we do not consider essential. The opposition would, I believe, be from a minority in our own body.'

'A distinct minority ?—I think I should call it so.'

The House will see from this that although Mr. Bunting is not remarkable for great hesitation generally in his opinions upon this matter, yet he does hesitate to say that the Wesleyan body was with any sort of unanimity in favour of Church-rates. And I can give my testimony, living as I do in a neighbourhood where they are very numerous, and where their services have been very great, to the fact that when the question of Church-rates is mooted and contests take place, although a few leading men are anxious to keep the question quiet, because it is one which might disturb their body, as far as my observation goes, a very large number— I think a majority—who attend their chapels have generally acted with the party by which Church-rates were opposed.

But it must be borne in mind that the Wesleyan body is of a peculiar character, that its government is more strictly priestly than anything that exists in the Church of England, and almost beyond anything outside the Church of Rome. The Conference, composed of one hundred ministers, dominates

to a large extent not only over the private opinions and
individual action of the members, but also over what I
may call the corporate or sect action, and throughout
their numerous chapels in this country, unless the Conference were to give the order or its permission, we
should probably not find from any of these congregations
petitions presented to this House. But from this fact
may be traced an important series of circumstances—that
there have been from that body numerous secessions of very
noteworthy character, secessions which have not arisen from
any difference as to the doctrine, but simply as to the absolute
government of the Conference. Notwithstanding all this, as
I have said, great numbers of them—I believe a very great
majority—vote in opposition to Church-rates whenever a contest takes place, and do unite in sympathy upon this question
with the great body of Dissenters belonging to other sects.

I should not have said so much about this particular
body had it not been for the ˙ extraordinary importance
which the learned Gentleman has given to this part of
the subject. I find, however, that even from the Conference
Methodists there have been 135 petitions presented, from the
Methodist New Connection 97, from the Methodist Free
Church 164, from the Primitive Methodists 265, from the
Calvinistic Methodists 108, from the United Methodists, the
Methodist Reformers, and the Wesleyan Association 47;
making a total of more than 800 petitions which have been
presented from the whole body of Methodists in favour of this
Bill. Now, as to the other sects of Dissenters, I believe the
learned Gentleman has not been able to make out any kind of
case or show any difference of opinion among them upon this
question. I think he will admit that they are, with as much
unanimity as can ever be expected upon public questions, in
favour of a repeal of Church-rates. But if it be, as he says,
that this movement is merely the movement of a few busy,
meddling agitators belonging to those sects—whose numbers,

by the way, he has not given very accurately—if that be so, how comes it that throughout the country and in this House they have obtained so large a share of support? That fact is a very ugly one, and the right hon. and learned Gentleman passed it over. Even the Church, on whose behalf the learned Gentleman professes to speak, is itself not unanimous upon this question, and in all the parishes in towns and cities where Church-rates have been abolished, every Member who has been engaged in this question will admit that no inconsiderable number of those who regularly attend the services of the Church have joined those agitating, meddling Dissenters in their attempt to put an end to the system of Church-rates. I should say in those districts a large minority—I will not say a majority—of Churchmen have been as willing to get Church-rates abolished as Dissenters themselves.

I live in a town in which contests about Church-rates have been carried on in past years with a vigour and determination, and, if you like it, with an animosity which has not been surpassed in any other part of the kingdom. Hon. Gentlemen opposite, who profess to be in favour of what is called a stand-up fight, will be glad to hear that nothing could exceed the activity of their friends in that parish, nothing could exceed the profuseness with which they were willing to pay for a contest, in order that all might have to contribute to a Church which at that time they themselves were not willing adequately to support. The very last contest of this kind cost the Church party in the parish as much money as, if invested at the common rate of interest, would have supported the fabric of the church for ever. [A cry of 'How much?'] I can tell the hon. Gentleman what was the estimate formed, which I believe was never disputed, and which, judging from the expenditure on the other side, was not, I should say, very inaccurate. I believe that the expenditure would not be less than from 3,000*l.* to 4,000*l.* It is a large parish, probably ten miles square, and contains nearly 100,000 inhabitants; and I need not tell hon. Members that there is no class of people in England more determined and more unconquerable, whichever side they take, than are the people of the county from which I come.

What was the result of that struggle? The result was that the Church-rate was for ever entirely abolished in that parish. I have since seen several lists of candidates for the church-wardenship put forth by Churchmen, each of which claimed support upon the ground that they would never consent to the reimposition of a Church-rate; and the parish has been for many years upon this question a model of tranquillity. It would not be enough that it should be a model of tranquillity if the result had followed which the learned Gentleman foretold in such dolorous language, that religion would be uncared for, and that the Gospel would no longer be preached to the poor; but I will undertake to say that since that contest that venerable old parish church has had laid out upon it, in repairing and beautifying it, from money sub-scribed not altogether, but mainly by Churchmen, ten times, aye, twenty times as much as was ever expended upon it during a far longer period of years in which Church-rates were levied. During that period there were discussions about the graveyard, about the hearses, about the washing of the surplices, about somebody who had to sweep out the church. There were discussions of all sorts, of a most irritating and offensive character. The clock which was there for the benefit of the public no longer told the time, and, in fact, there was evidence of that sort of decay to which the learned Gentleman has pointed as the inevitable result of the abolition of Church-rates. Since the rate ceased to be levied the clock has kept time with admirable fidelity, and to such an extent has the liberality of Churchmen gone, that very lately they have put up another clock in a neighbouring church. I believe that in the parish of Rochdale the Church people have received far more benefit from the abolition of the Church-rate than the Dissenters have. They have found out, what they never knew before, that when placed upon the same platform as Dissenters, and obliged to depend upon their own resources, they are as liberal and zealous as other sects.

I wish that the learned Gentleman had told us, and I hope that some one who may follow him will do so, how it happens that year by year there has been growing in this House a power in opposition to Church-rates, while at the same time there has been less animosity throughout the country upon this question. I believe it has arisen from the growth of a better feeling on both sides, and from the fact that year by year there have been secessions from the supporters of Church-rates throughout the country, and that more and more without the action of Parliament the principle embodied in the clauses of the Bill of my hon. Friend has come to be acted upon. Now what is the real point between us?— because I believe that hon. Gentlemen opposite will agree with me that if it could be done it would be better that this question should be for ever disposed of. What is the question at issue between us? Does any man dispute the evils that have arisen? The right hon. and learned Gentleman has, in a speech of great vigour, endeavoured to throw ridicule and contempt upon the great body of the Dissenting population of this country. ['No, no!'] Well, at any rate, he has not refrained from expressions of harshness towards those whom he charges with being the movers in this question. But does he believe, or do any of you believe, that if those persons did not in the main possess the confidence of the great body of the Dissenters, they could in a week, a fortnight, or a month, stir them up from one end of the country to the other, and bring to your table the signatures of 500,000 of your countrymen? [Cries of '600,000.'] I am reminded that the number is 600,000, but in a matter of this kind I am not particular to 100,000 more or less. I say, then, is there any one here who disputes the evils which have arisen from these discussions? I confess that I have sometimes wished that I could speak in this House, even if it were for only one half hour, in the character of a member of the Church of England. If I could have done that I should have appealed to the House in language far more emphatic and impressive than I have ever been able to use as a Dissenter, in favour of the abolition of this most mischievous and obnoxious impost.

The right hon. and learned Gentleman has no plan. I think he was right in making that admission. I believe there are only two courses which can be pursued. One is to leave the law exactly as it is, a course which, if this matter did not touch a question of religion, I should not complain of, because it leaves the majority in every parish to decide for itself. The other plan is that of my hon. Friend the Member for Tavistock. You have tried every kind of contrivance. The right hon. Gentleman the Member for the University of Cambridge (Mr. Walpole) proposed a plan. The right hon. and learned Member for the University of Dublin was a Member of the Government by which that plan was proposed; and, as he now says that he has no plan, I presume that he has abandoned the plan of the right hon. Gentleman opposite. The right hon. Baronet the Home Secretary, and the right hon. Baronet the Chancellor of the Duchy of Lancaster, also tried plans. Indeed, there are in the House many who have aspired to legislate upon this subject, but have failed in these attempts at conciliation; and I think we must all feel conscious that we must either remain as we are, or adopt the Bill which is now before us. I confess that I am altogether against any kind of dodge by which this matter may be even temporarily settled. I think that if this Church be a national establishment, you cannot by law insist that its support shall be drawn from only a portion of the population. I agree with you altogether in that. If I were a Churchman I would never consent to it, and, not being a Churchman, I

wholly repudiate it.   The dissensions to which I have referred
have prevailed, prevail still, and cannot terminate as long as
this impost exists.   What is its natural and inevitable result?
It must be to create and stimulate the pride of supremacy in
the dominant Church, and at the same time produce what I
shall call the irritation of subjugation and injustice on the
part of that great portion of the people who support their own
ministers and places of worship, and who think that they
ought not to be called upon to support those of any other sect
or Church.   Now, is it necessary that this should continue?
I often have occasion in this House to give hope to hon.
Gentlemen opposite.   They are probably the most despairing
political party that any country ever had within its borders.
They despair of almost everything.   They despaired of agriculture.   Agriculture triumphs.   They despair of their Church,
yet whenever that Church has been left to its own resources
and to the zeal of its members its triumph has been manifest
to the country and to the world.   Are you made of different
material from the five millions of people who go to the Dissenting chapels of England and Wales?   You have your
churches,—I speak of the old ones, not of those recently
erected by means of voluntary contributions,—you have your
churches, which you call national, and you have them for
nothing.   You have your ministers paid out of property
anciently bequeathed or intrusted to the State for their use.
In that respect you stand in a far better position for undertaking what, if Church-rates are abolished, you must undertake, than do the great body of your Dissenting brethren.
Have you less zeal, have you less liberality, than they have?
Do not you continually boast in this House that you are
the owners of the great bulk of the landed property of the
country? Are you not the depositaries of political power, and
do you not tell us that when a Dissenter becomes rich he
always walks away from the chapel into your church? If this
be so, am I appealing in vain to you, or reasoning in vain

with you, when I try to encourage you to believe that if there
were no Church-rates the members of your church and your
congregations would be greatly improved, and that, as has
taken place in the parish in which I live, your churches would
be better supported by your own voluntary and liberal contributions, than they can ever be by the penny per pound issuing
from the pockets of men who do not attend your church, and
who are rendered ten times more hostile to it by the very
effort to make them contribute to its support.

I believe that Church-rates must before long be abolished.
Hence, I wish to afford some hope and consolation, if I
can, to hon. Gentlemen opposite. Mr. Osborne and Mr.
Bunting, from whom the right hon. and learned Member so
largely quoted, themselves belong to a body that has done
marvels in this country in erecting chapels, paying ministers,
establishing schools, raising the dead, if you like—for men
who were dead to religion have been made Christians; and
they have preached the Gospel to the poor in every county, I
might almost say in every parish, in the kingdom. Yet
they have not come to Parliament for grants of money; and,
although they have often come to me and others for contributions to their chapels and schools, they have never had any
·force of law to enable them to raise their funds. Throughout
England and Wales what would be the condition of your
population, your religious establishments, your education, if
it were not for the liberality of those sects of whom the right
hon. and learned Gentleman thinks fit to speak in disparaging
terms?

But I pass to his own country, and though I should
like to see Irish Members more frequently taking part in the
discussion of questions affecting England and Wales than
they do, I was surprised to find that the right hon. and
learned Gentleman made no reference whatever to what has
taken place in the island from which he himself comes. In
the year 1833 you abolished the vestry cess, the Church-rate

of Ireland; you abolished one-fourth of the tithe—that is, you took it from the Church and gave it to the landlord; you did many things which the Irish Church at that time, which many Gentlemen of the same party as the right hon. and learned Member denounced, just as you denounce the present Bill. Of course it will be said that the Earl of Derby has since then changed his opinions, and therefore the views he held at that period will have no authority with his followers now. But what has been the effect on that Church? Is there a man in this House with the slightest knowledge of what has occurred in Ireland during the last thirty years, who will not admit that the Irish Protestant Establishment would have been absolutely uprooted and separated from the State for ever long before now but for the large measure of change—I will say of reform—to which the Earl of Derby, as a Minister of that day, was a party? If that be true, what right has anybody to charge the hon. Member for Tavistock with a deadly hostility to the Church of England? I do not believe there is a man in this country at this moment who has any hostility to the Church of England as a Church. I never met with such a man. The right hon. and learned Gentleman has referred to a friend of mine who not long ago had a seat in this House, although he did not mention him by name. I allude to Mr. Miall. There is no man in England whose character for religion, morality, intelligence, or a persistent devotion to what he believes to be right stands higher than that of Mr. Miall. But Mr. Miall has not the smallest objection to the Church of England as a religious body, any more than he has to the Methodist Conference or any other denomination which teaches its own peculiar views of Christianity. What he objects to is that the Church should be, as it has been, so much of a political institution. And there can be no doubt but that among the clergy of the Establishment and the most thoughtful of her sons there is throughout the kingdom at this moment a deep sentiment at work which, altogether apart from Mr. Miall and the Liberation Society, is destined before many years are over to make great changes in the constitution and condition of that Church. And I undertake to say that, if their views, or those of Mr. Miall, were carried out by Parliament, the Church would still be a Church at least as great, as powerful, and as respected as it ever was at any period of its history. I believe it would, as effectually as it ever has done, raise to life those who are religiously dead, and at the same time, more extensively than it does now, preach the Gospel to the poor.

But the right hon. and learned Gentleman might have given us another lesson from Ireland. There the great body of the people—not the possessors of wealth—are in connection with the Roman Catholic Church. Many of us have been in Ireland. I have myself spent several weeks there, travelling from one part of the country to another. I saw chapels everywhere,—that great cathedrals had been built, that there were evidences of great zeal and wonderful liberality among a people at that time poor and dejected, and in a lower physical condition, I undertake to say, than could have been found in any other population in any Christian country of Europe. The Irish Catholics, without any assistance from the State except a paltry grant, which I believe many of them would gladly forego, have provided for all the religious wants of their people. And I venture to assert that religion — not now speaking of particular doctrines or forms—has there permeated even to the lowest class of society in a manner that is not equalled in this part of the kingdom, where your Church Establishment has for ages reigned almost supreme.

But if you are not satisfied with the case of Ireland, let us go to Wales. There you have a poor population who are mainly Dissenters. The Welsh Dissenters do not own the great estates. They have no ancient endowments, no grants from

Parliament. They do not even send representatives to this House—['Oh!']—representatives I mean of their peculiar views. Eight-tenths of the people of Wales have no connection with the Established Church. Yet, poor as they are, compared with the population of England, there is not a nook or corner of the Principality in which there are not a chapel, a school, and a minister, or in which you do not constantly see the influence of religious teaching on the character and habits of the people.

But go a little further north, to a land where men are not supposed to misunderstand their own interests. I refer to the country on the other side of the Tweed. You have an Established Church there. Many years ago you had two considerable secessions from its pale which became powerful sects. They have since united themselves, and their power has proportionately increased. But lately, within the recollection of every Member of this House, for it is but seventeen years ago, there was another great secession; and from what men fancied was the ruin of the Established Church of Scotland there arose a new Church, offering, I will say, to the world, an example of zeal and munificence such as has not been witnessed in this country during the lifetime of the present generation. Not long ago, while in Scotland—a country to which I am very glad to flee when we are liberated from attendance in this House—I took the pains to make some inquiry upon this question; and I found that the Free Church, which comprises probably not more than one-third of that portion of the population who pay any attention to religious matters, raised voluntarily, during the year when I made the inquiry, a larger sum than the whole annual emoluments of the Established Church of Scotland. It has built, I think, something like seven hundred churches throughout that part of the kingdom, and as many manses or dwellings for its ministers. It has also established schools in almost every parish. And I tell the House with the utmost sincerity that I believe I never questioned any man in Scotland as to the effect of the disruption who did not admit that, painful as it was, and utterly as he and many others might have opposed it, still it has been full of blessings to the people of that country. I believe the number of persons who frequent places of worship, the number of schools, and the number of scholars who attend them, are all far larger than ever they were before the last great secession. Bear in mind that, with the exception of a very few persons of high station in society, including one or two Members of the other House and two or three of this, the property of Scotland, as far as property is to be measured by the possession of the soil, has not gone with the Free Church at all. Yet you find throughout the whole of that country those vast results from a zeal, a religious fervour, a munificence, which are not a whit greater than would be exhibited under the same circumstances by members of the Church of England. But such a state of things, I say, must raise the character of the people of Scotland, high as it was before, still higher in the estimation of the Christian world.

Only one other point with regard to this voluntary question. Apart from the discussions and divisions, from Bills and clauses in this House, if I were to ask any´ hon. Member on the other side whether he believed that the Church of England was not, or would not, become as liberal as any other sect, I have no doubt he would at once say that to assert the contrary would be to slander and misrepresent the members of that Church. Well, I think so too, and the evidence lies in what the Church has been doing of late years. If you stand upon any eminence in the neighbourhood of any large town or city in England, you will see everywhere towers and spires indicating the temples that have been raised in recent days for the worship of God ; and so also, if you travel over the country, as you now rapidly do, you will see through the glass of the railway carriage one spire here, another there,

and a third yonder. I do not always admire their architecture, but some of them are beautiful objects in the land-
scape of which they form part. Well, this has all been
achieved, not by the votes of Parliament, for they have
ceased, but by exactly the same religious zeal, the same
Christian benevolence, which have distinguished the rest of
your countrymen, and which you, the richest and proudest of
them all, would surely, under the like circumstances, equally
display. I want to persuade you that this is a good Bill for
the Established Church. I am not about to try to take you
in by allowing you to suppose that I agree with you as to a
State Establishment for teaching religion. I agree on that
abstract question with Mr. Miall and the Liberation Society.
I believe it is an evil to the State and to religion; but that is
not a question for us to discuss now, or one which probably
this generation will ever be called on to decide. I say, the
abolition of these irritating levies of money in Ireland has
been of great advantage to the Established Church of Ireland.
I say, the more you remove your question of an Establishment
from that constant and irritating contest and discussion which
are inseparable from the continuance of these rates, the more
probably, for a long period of time, you will consolidate your
Church; and I am inclined to believe that its fall as a State
Establishment will never come from the assaults of those who
are without it, but will rather come from the strong differences
of doctrine among those within its pale.

I should like to ask hon. Gentlemen opposite to look
to a point in respect to which their Church is at a great
disadvantage as compared with Dissenting congregations.
I am in a position to observe both of them with great
impartiality, because I belong to a sect which is very
small, which some people say is decaying, although I believe its main principles are always spreading. I have no
particular sympathy with Wesleyans, Independents, or Bap-
tists, any more than I have with the congregations which

assemble in your churches. But have you not observed in
London, and more particularly in the country, where you
are more intimately acquainted with the circumstances—have
you not observed, that among the congregations of Dissenting
bodies there is a greater activity in all matters which belong
to their churches, and to objects which they unite together in
promoting as a religious community? Do not you find that
from the richest and the most influential man who enters a
chapel on a Sunday to the humblest of the congregation there
is, as it were, a chain of sympathy running through them all,
which gives to them a great strength, which combines them
together, which influences the humblest and the highest for
good, and which gives to the congregation a power which is
found to be greatly less existent in a congregation of the
Established Church? I have spoken of this to many persons
who differ from me on all these questions of Church establishments, Church-rates, and the like; but I never spoke to
any man in the habit of attending the Established Church
who did not admit to me that it is one of the things they
most deplore, that among the five hundred persons more or
less who attend any particular church there is infinitely less
sympathy, co-operation, union, and power of action than is
evinced among the various Dissenting communities in this
country almost without exception. But if you had none of
these rates to levy by law you would be placed—and it would
be a most material advantage—in the same position as are the
congregations of Dissenting bodies. You would be obliged,
of course, in the management of your congregational affairs,
to consult the members in general; you would have your
monthly or quarterly meetings; and thus you would know
who were your neighbours in church, and you would be united
together, as Dissenting congregations are. And I maintain
that your religious activity and life for all purposes of missionary work at home and abroad would be greatly increased
and strengthened; and so far your congregations, your

ministers, and your churches would be great gainers. Some hon. Gentlemen will say that I am a violent partisan on this question, and that I have partaken of the animosity which I stated to have existed in the parish in which I live. I do not deny that in times past I have taken a warm, and it may be occasionally, a too heated part in the contests and discussions on this question; but, so far as I am concerned, the feelings engendered by these strifes have been swept away; I am older than I was then; I make great allowance for men's passions, as I ask that they should make allowance for mine.

This question has now come to a crisis; and I ask the House to consider whether it would not be to the advantage of the Church, of morality, religion, and the public peace, that it should now be set at rest once and for ever. The right hon. and learned Gentleman—it is one of the faults of a high classical education—following the example of the right hon. Gentleman who delighted us all with a brilliant but most illogical speech last night, affrighted us with an account of what took place under the democracies of Greece, and asks us to follow the example of those who were believers in the paganism of ancient Rome. He says, Did not the Roman emperors, consuls, and people go in procession after the vile gods and goddesses which they worshipped? It is true they did, and I hope the right hon. and learned Gentleman regrets by this time that he asked us to follow an example of that kind. Rome has perished, and the religion which it professed has perished with it. The Christian religion is wholly different, and if there be one thing written more legibly than another in every page of that Book on which you profess that your Church is founded, it is that men should be just one to another, kind and brotherly one to another, and should not ask of each other to do that which they are not willing themselves to do. I say that this law of Church-rates is a law which violates, and violates most obviously and outrageously, every law of justice and of mercy which is written in that Book, and it is because I believe it does so that I am certain that it never can be of advantage to your Church, if your Church be a true Church; and, believing that, and feeling how much the interests and sympathies and wishes of millions of our countrymen are in favour of the abolition of this impost, I ask you to do what I am now ready to do—to give a cordial support to the third reading of this Bill of my hon. Friend.

LETTER TO DR. GRAY.

[The following letter on the Irish Church question was addressed to Dr. Gray, Editor of the *Freeman's Journal*, now Sir John Gray, M.P., October 25, 1852. The estimate of the property of the Irish Church is probably much too low, but this does not affect the argument, or the principle of the proposed arrangement.]

MY DEAR DR. GRAY,—I observe from the newspapers that the friends of 'religious equality' in Ireland are about to hold a conference in the city of Dublin with a view to consider the existing ecclesiastical arrangements of your country. My engagements will not permit me to be present at your deliberations, and, indeed, I am not sure that your invitations extend further than to Irishmen and Irish representatives; but I feel strongly disposed to address you on the great question you are about to discuss—a question affecting the policy and interests of the United Kingdom, but of vital importance to Ireland.

Let me say, in the first place, that I am heartily glad that any number of the Irish representatives should have resolved to grapple with a question which, in my opinion, must be settled on some just basis, if Ireland is ever to become tranquil and content. The case of the Catholic population of Ireland—and, in truth, it is scarcely more their case than that of every intelligent and just Protestant in the three kingdoms—is so strong, so unanswerable, and so generally admitted, that nothing is wanting to insure its complete success but the combination of a few able and honest men to concentrate and direct the opinion which exists. If such men are to be found among you—resolute, persevering, and disinterested—a great work is before them, and as certainly a great result. They will meet with insult and calumny in abundance; every engine of the 'supremacy' party will be in motion against them; they will be denounced as 'conspirators' against the institutions of the country, when, in fact, they combine only against a grievance which it is hard to say whether it is more humiliating in Ireland to endure, or disgraceful

M m 2

in England to inflict ; but against all this, having a right cause, and working it by right means, they will certainly succeed.

It would be to insult your understanding were I to imagine that you demand anything more or less than a perfect 'equality' before the law for the religious sects which exist in Ireland—that is, for the members or adherents of the Protestant Episcopalian, the Presbyterian, and the Roman Catholic Churches. So entirely is it felt that you are in the right in making this demand, that with regard to it your opponents dare not attempt an argument with you ; they prefer to say that you claim something else—namely, a supremacy as hateful as their own, and then they find it easy to contest the matter with you, writing and speaking, as they do, chiefly to a Protestant audience. On this point there should be no possibility of mistake ; and not only should the demand for 'equality' be unequivocal, but it appears to me most desirable that some mode of attaining it should be distinctly pointed out. We may, perhaps, imagine an 'equality' which would allow the Protestant Establishment to remain as it is, or, at least, to continue to be a State Church, building up at its side a Catholic Establishment ; and, to complete the scheme, a Presbyterian Establishment also, having a batch of Catholic prelates and of Presbyterian divines in the House of Lords ; but, in my opinion, any scheme of 'equality' of this description would be, and must necessarily be, altogether impracticable.

Lord John Russell, I think in 1843, expressed an opinion that the Protestant Church in Ireland should not be subverted, 'but that the Roman Catholic Church, with its bishops and clergy, should be placed by the State on a footing of equality with that Church.' He adopted the term 'equality,' and said that any plan he should propose would be 'to follow out that principle of equality, with all its consequences.' Lord Grey, in 1845, was, if possible, still more explicit, for he said, after expressing his opinion that 'the Catholics have the first claim' on the funds applied to ecclesiastical purposes in Ireland, 'you must give the Catholic clergy an equality also in social rank and position ;' and he went even further than this, and said, 'I carry my view on this subject as far as to wish to see the prelates of the Roman Catholic Church take their places in this House on the episcopal bench.' From this it appears that Lord John Russell and Lord Grey, seeing the enormous evil of the existing system, were ready to justify almost any measure that promised political and ecclesiastical equality to the Irish Catholics ; but they wished that equality to be obtained without the subversion of the Protestant Established Church in Ireland.

Of course, if all parties among the statesmen and the public of the United Kingdom were agreed, funds might be provided for the perpetual endowment and subjection to State control of the Irish Catholic and Presbyterian Churches, and some plan might be devised to secure them a representation in the House of Lords ;

but, happily for sound principles in civil government, and happily for religion itself, all parties are not agreed to do this, but are rather agreed that it shall not be done. The 'equality' which Lord John Russell would 'follow out with all its consequences' is a dream, and Lord Grey's bold idea of giving the Irish Catholics 'the first claim to the funds' and of placing their bishops in the House of Lords is not less impracticable. To have two Established Churches in Ireland, the one Protestant and the other Catholic; to have in the House of Lords Protestant and Catholic bishops, elbowing each other on the 'right reverend bench,' guarding the temporal and spiritual interests of two Churches which denounce each other as idolatrous or heretical, would be an inconsistency so glaring, that it would go far to overthrow all reverence for Governments and Churches, if not for Christianity itself. The scheme is surely too absurd to be seriously thought of, and if there be a statesman bold enough to propose it, he will find no support in the opinion of the English public, except from that small section with whom religion goes for nothing, and Churches and priests are tolerated as machinery in the pay and service of the Government.

But there is an 'equality' which is attainable without inconsistency, which would meet with favour among large classes in every part of Great Britain, and which, I think, if fairly proposed, would be well received by many of the more enlightened and just Protestants in Ireland. It is an 'equality' which must start from this point, that henceforth there must be no Church in Ireland in connection with the State. The whole body of English Dissenters, the United Presbyterian Church of Scotland, and the Catholic population of the United Kingdom, might be expected cordially to welcome such a proposition; and it is difficult to understand how the Presbyterians of the North of Ireland, or the Free Church of Scotland, or the adherents of the Wesleyan Conference in England, could, with any consistency or decency, oppose it; and I am confident that a large number of persons connected with the Established Churches in the three kingdoms, who are enlightened enough to see what is right, and just enough to wish it to be done, would give their support to any Minister who had the courage to make such a measure the great distinguishing act of his administration. But, if this principle were adopted—that is, the principle that henceforth there must be no Church in Ireland in connection with the State— there would still be a question as to the appropriation of the large funds now in the hands of the Irish Established Church.

There are two modes of dealing with these funds, either of which may be defended, but one of them seems to offer facilities which do not belong to the other. The most simple plan would be to absorb the revenues of the Established Church as the livings become vacant, and to apply them in some channel not ecclesiastical, in which the whole population of Ireland could participate. The objections to this plan are, that it would be hard upon the Protestant Episcopalians, after having pampered them so long with a munificent support, to throw them at once on their resources, and that to withdraw the Regium Donum from the Presbyterians of the North, when they have no other provision made for their religious wants, would be to create a just discontent among them. There is some force in this, inasmuch as upon one generation would be thrown the burden of the creation and support of a religious organisation which, in voluntary churches, is commonly the work of successive generations of their adherents, and the argument may be considered almost irresistible when it is offered to a Government which does not repudiate, but rather cherishes, the principle of a State Church.   But whatever may be the inconveniences of this plan, they are, in my estimation, infinitely less than those which are inseparable from a continuance of the present system.

There is, however, another mode of settlement which, though open to some objection, is probably more likely to obtain a general concurrence of opinion in its favour in Ireland, and to which, I think, a great amount of consent might be obtained in England and Scotland.   Your present ecclesiastical arrangements are briefly these :—The Protestant Episcopal Church has 500,000*l.* per annum entrusted to it, or a principal sum, at twenty years' purchase, of 10,000,000*l.* sterling.   The Presbyterian Church or Churches have 40,000*l.* per annum, or, estimated at the same rate, a principal sum of 800,000*l.*   The Roman Catholic Church has 26,000*l.* per annum, or a principal sum of 520,000*l.*   I will say nothing about the exact proportions of population belonging to each Church, for I do not wish to give opportunity for dispute about figures.   It is sufficient to say, what everybody knows to be true, that the Irish population is Catholic, and that the Protestants, whether of the Episcopalian or Presbyterian Church, or of both united, are a small minority of the Irish people.   I will admit the temporary hardship of at once withdrawing from the Protestant sects all the resources which the State has hitherto provided for them ; but, at the same time, no one can deny, and I cannot forget, the hardship to which the Catholics have been subjected, inasmuch as they, the poorest portion of the people, and by many times the most numerous, have been shut out from almost all participation in the public funds applied to ecclesiastical purposes in Ireland.   Is it not possible to make an arrangement by which the menaced hardship to the Protestants may be avoided, and that so long endured by the Catholics, in part at least, redressed ?   And can this be done without departing from the principle, 'that henceforth there must be no Church in Ireland in connection with the State ?'   Let an Act be passed to establish a 'Church Property Commission' for Ireland, and let this Commission hold in trust, for certain purposes, all the tithes and other property now enjoyed by the Established Church ; let it, in fact, become possessed of the 10,000,000*l.* sterling, the income from which now forms the revenues of that Church, as the livings and benefices become vacant. It would be desirable to offer facilities to the landed proprietors to purchase the tithes at an easy rate, in order that funds might be in hand to carry out the other arrangements of the scheme.

I have estimated the total value at 10,000,000*l.* ; it might not reach that sum if the tithes were sold at a low rate ; but whether it were 10,000,000*l.* or only 8,000,000*l.* would not affect the practicability or the justice of this proposition. Let this Commission be empowered and directed to appropriate certain portions of this fund as a free gift to each of the three Churches in Ireland —to the Protestant Episcopalian, the Presbyterian, and the Roman Catholic Church. Whatever is thus given must be a free gift, and become as much the private property of the respective sects or churches as is the property of the Free Church in Scotland, or that of the Wesleyan Methodists in England. It must no longer be a trust from the State, liable to interference or recall by the State, or the 'equality' and independence of the Irish sects will not be secured.

There comes now the question of the amounts to be thus given. · From some inquiries I have made I have arrived at the conclusion that if in each parish in Ireland there was a house and a small piece of land, say from ten to twenty acres, in the possession of the Roman Catholic Church, that would be all the provision that would be required or wished for, as the general support of its ministers would be derived, as at present, from the voluntary contributions of their flocks. There are in round numbers about 1,000 parishes in Ireland. In many of them there is now a provision up to the standard above stated in the possession of the Roman Catholic Church, but I will assume that in all of them such provision would have to be made. 1,000*l.* for each parish, taking one parish with another, would amply make up any deficiency, and this amount throughout the parishes of Ireland would require the sum of 1,000,000*l.* sterling to be appropriated from the general fund ; and this should be made over absolutely and for ever to the Roman Catholics of Ireland, in such hands and in such manner as the funds of their Church raised by voluntary effort are usually secured.

Under an arrangement of this kind, of course, the special grant to the college of Maynooth would be withdrawn. The Presbyterians, under the operation of this act, would lose their annual grant of 40,000*l.* ; but, in place of it, assuming that they have an organisation and a system of government which would enable them to hold and administer funds for the use of their Church, a portion of the general fund should be set apart for them, equal to the production of a revenue of like amount with that they now receive by grant from Parliament. This should also be given to them absolutely and for ever, and they should become henceforth a voluntary and independent Church.

The Protestant Episcopalians should be treated as liberally as the

Presbyterians, with whom, it is estimated, they are about on a par in point of numbers. Assuming that they could and would form themselves into a Free Episcopal Church, the Commission would be empowered to grant them a sum equal to that granted to the Presbyterians, and which would be about the same in amount as that granted to the Catholics. And further, so long as they undertook to keep the churches in repair, they might be permitted to retain possession of them at a nominal rent, for their own use only ; and that when or where they had no congregation sufficient to maintain the church, then the buildings should be at the disposal of the Commission to let or sell, as might be thought best. In the case of the Protestant Episcopalians, as with the Presbyterians and the Catholics, whatever sum is given to them must be given absolutely and for ever, that thenceforth they may rely on their own resources and become a voluntary and independent Church.

The State would thus have distributed about 3,000,000*l.* of the original fund, and would have relinquished all claims upon it for ever ; and it would be the duty of the Commission to take care that those grants were applied, in the first instance, for the purposes and in the manner intended by the Act. The remaining 5,000,000*l.* or 7,000,000*l.*, as the case might be, might, and in my opinion ought, to be reserved for purposes strictly Irish, and directed to the educational and moral improvement of the people, without respect to class or creed. This fund would extend and perfect the educational institutions of the country ; it would establish and endow free libraries in all the chief towns of Ireland, and would dispense blessings in many channels for the free and equal enjoyment of the whole population. Of course there will be objections started to this scheme, as there will be to any scheme which attempts to remedy an injustice which has lasted for centuries. The 'Church party' may, and probably will, denounce it as a plan of spoliation most cruel and unholy ; but no man who proposes to remedy Irish ecclesiastical wrongs can expect to find favour with the sect whose supremacy he is compelled to assail. We must hope that State patronage has not so entirely demoralised the members of the Protestant Episcopalian sect, either in England or Ireland, as to leave none among them who are able to see what is just on this question, and who are willing that what is just should be done. I believe there are many intelligent and earnest Churchmen, and some eminent politicians connected with the Established Church, who would welcome almost any proposition which afforded a hope of a final settlement of this question.

From Scotland, and probably from certain quarters in England, we may hear of the great crime of handing over 1,000,000*l.* sterling to the Roman Catholics of Ireland. It will, perhaps, be insisted upon that to add to the means of a Church whose teaching is held to be 'erroneous' is a grievous national sin ; and many will honestly doubt the wisdom of a scheme which proposes such an appropriation of a portion of a great public fund. Now, there is not a man in the United Kingdom more averse to religious endowments by the State than I am. I object to the compulsory levying of a tax from any man to teach any religion, and still more to teach a religion in which he does not believe ; and I am of opinion that, to take a Church into the pay of the State, and to place it under the control of the State, is to deaden and corrupt the Church, and to enlist its influence on the side of all that is evil in the civil government. But in the plan now suggested the Irish sects or Churches would be left entirely free, as is the Free Church in Scotland, or the Wesleyan Methodist Church in England. The grants once made, each Church would possess absolutely its own funds, just as much as if they were the accumulations of the voluntary contributions and liberality of past generations of its members, and thus would be avoided the damage to religion and to civil government which is inseparable from what is called the union of Church and State ; whilst the sum granted to each Church, being equal to a provision of about 40,000*l.* per annum, would be too small to create any important corporate influence adverse to the public interest.

As to the complaint that the sum of 1,000,000*l.* is proposed to be given to the Irish Catholics, I will ask any man with a head to comprehend and a heart to feel, to read the history of Ireland, not from the time of Henry VIII, but from the accession of William III, and if he insists upon a settlement of this question by grants to the Protestant sects, and by the refusal of any corresponding grant to the Roman Catholics, I can only say that his statesmanship is as wanting in wisdom as his Protestantism lacks the spirit of Christianity. If, for generations, a portion of the Protestants of Ireland, few in number but possessing much wealth, have enjoyed the large ecclesiastical revenues of a whole kingdom ; and if, during the same period, the Roman Catholics, the bulk of the population, but possessing little wealth, have been thrown entirely on their own limited resources, and under circumstances of political and social inferiority, can it be possible, when an attempt shall be made to remedy some of the manifold injustice of past times, that any Englishman or any Scotchman will be found to complain of the impartiality of the Government, and in his zeal for Protestantism, to forget the simple obligations of justice ?

But it may be objected that it is contrary to sound policy to make grants of public money to any public body, or corporation, or sect, not submitting to State control—that, in fact, a Church receiving anything from the State should be a State Church. No one is more sensible of the weight and soundness of this argument than I am ; but observe the peculiarities of this case. I start from the point that ' henceforth there shall be no Church in Ireland in connection with the State.' I have to free the Protestant Episco-

palian sect and the Presbyterians from their State connection ; and
to make the Irish sects voluntary Churches for the future. I propose an appropriation of about one-third of existing ecclesiastical
property in Ireland, with a view to soften the apparent severity of
the change to the sects heretofore paid by the State, and to make
some amends to that majority of the Irish population, the injustice
of whose past treatment is admitted by all the world. The Protestants of Ireland have done hitherto little for themselves, because
the bounty of the State has paralysed their exertions, or made
exertion unnecessary. The Catholics have done much for themselves ; but they are in great poverty, and our existing ecclesiastical
legislation has been felt, and is now felt, by them to be grievously
unjust. Would it not be worth the concession of the sum I have
suggested, and of the deviation from ordinary rule which I venture
to recommend, to obtain the grand result which is contemplated by
the change now proposed ? I have said that there will be objections
to this scheme and to every scheme. The grievance is centuries
old, and around it are entwined interests, prejudices, fanaticism,
animosities, and convictions. It is a desperate evil, and whoever
waits till the remedy is pleasant to everybody may and will wait
for ever. The object in view is the tranquillity of Ireland. The
means are simple, but altogether novel in that unhappy country—
to do full and impartial justice to her whole population. I propose
to leave the Presbyterians as well circumstanced as they are now,
with this exception, that all future extension of their organisation
must be made at their own cost ; and I would place the Protestant Episcopalians in as good a position as the Presbyterians.
The Catholics only could have any ground of complaint, owing to
their numbers so far exceeding those of the Protestant sects ; but
in the application of the remainder, and much the largest portion
of the funds, for educational or other purposes, they would participate exactly in proportion to their numbers ; and I have a strong
belief that, so far as they are concerned, such an arrangement as is
now suggested would be accepted as a final settlement of a most
difficult and irritating question.

As you know, I am neither Roman Catholic, Protestant Episcopalian, nor Presbyterian, nor am I an Irishman. My interest in
this matter is not local or sectarian. I have endeavoured to study
it, and to regard it as becomes an Englishman loving justice and
freedom, anxious for the tranquillity of Ireland, the welfare of the
Empire, and the honour of the Imperial Government. I believe
that statesmanship does not consist merely in preserving institutions, but rather in adapting them to the wants of nations, and
that it is possible so to adapt the institutions of Ireland to the
wants and circumstances of Ireland, that her people may become as
content as the people of England and Scotland are, with the mild
monarchy under which we live. Some experience and much reflection have convinced me that all efforts on behalf of industry

and peace in Ireland will be in great part unavailing until we eradicate the sentiment which is universal among her Catholic population—that the Imperial Government is partial, and that to belong to the Roman Catholic Church is to incur the suspicion or the hostility of the law. A true ' equality' established among the Irish sects would put an end to this pernicious but all-pervading sentiment ; and Catholics, whether priests or laymen, would feel that the last link of their fetters was at length broken. Supremacy on the one hand, and a degrading inferiority on the other, would be abolished, and the whole atmosphere of Irish social and political life would be purified. Then, too, Christianity would appeal to the population, not as a persecuting or a persecuted faith, with her features disfigured by the violence of political conflict, but radiant with the divine beauty which belongs to her, and speaking with irresistible force to the hearts and consciences of men.

I know not if the statesman be among us who is destined to settle this great question, but whoever he may be he will strengthen the monarchy, earn the gratitude of three kingdoms, and build up for himself a lasting renown. I am sensible that in writing this letter, and in expressing the views it contains, I run the risk of being misunderstood by some honest men, and may subject myself to misrepresentation and abuse. It is under a solemn sense of duty to my country, and to the interests of justice and religion, that I have ventured to write it. I have endeavoured to divest myself of all feeling of preference for, or hostility to, any of the Churches or sects in Ireland, and to form my judgment in this matter upon principles admitted by all true statesmanship, and based on the foundations of Christian justice. If I should succeed in directing the attention of any portion of those most deeply interested to some mode of escape from the difficulties with which this question is sur-rounded, I shall willingly submit to the suspicions or condemnation of those who cannot concur with me in opinion. I wish this long letter were more worthy of its purpose. As it is, I send it to you, and you may make whatever use of it you think will be likely to serve the cause of ' religious equality' in Ireland.

Believe me to be, very truly yours,

JOHN BRIGHT.

Rochdale,
October 25, 1852.

INDEX.

A.

December, 1868.

16, BEDFORD STREET, COVENT GARDEN, LONDON.

MACMILLAN AND CO.'S

List of Publications.

Æschyli Eumenides.

The Greek Text with English Notes, and an Introduction. By
BERNARD DRAKE, M.A. 8vo. 7s. 6d.

AIRY.—*Works by* G. B. AIRY, M.A. LL D. D.C.L. *Astronomer
Royal, &c.*

*Treatise on the Algebraical and Numerical Theory of
Errors of Observations and the Combination of Observations.*

Crown 8vo. 6s. 6d.

Popular Astronomy.

A Series of Lectures delivered at Ipswich. 18mo. cloth, 4s. 6d.
With Illustrations. Uniform with MACMILLAN'S SCHOOL CLASS
BOOKS.

*An Elementary Treatise on Partial Differential
Equations.*

With Stereoscopic Cards of Diagrams. Crown 8vo. 5s. 6d.

On the Undulatory Theory of Optics.

Designed for the use of Students in the University. Crown
8vo. 6s. 6d.

On Sound and Atmospheric Vibrations,

With the Mathematical Elements of Music. Designed for the
use of Students of the Universities. Crown 8vo. 9s.

Algebraical Exercises.

Progressively arranged by Rev. C. A. JONES, M.A. and C. H.
CHEYNE, M.A. Mathematical Masters in Westminster School.
18mo. 2s. 6d.

2000 12.68.

Alice's Adventures in Wonderland.
> By LEWIS CARROLL. With Forty-two Illustrations by TENNIEL. 14th Thousand. Crown 8vo. cloth. 6s.

ALLINGHAM.—*Laurence Bloomfield in Ireland.*
> A Modern Poem. By WILLIAM ALLINGHAM. Fcap. 8vo. 7s.

ANSTED.—*The Great Stone Book of Nature.*
> By DAVID THOMAS ANSTED, M.A. F.R.S. F.G.S. Fcap. 8vo. 5s.

ANSTIE.—*Stimulants and Narcotics, their Mutual Relations.*
> With Special Researches on the Action of Alcohol, Æther, and Chloroform on the Vital Organism. By FRANCIS E. ANSTIE, M.D. M.R.C.P. 8vo. 14s.

Neuralgia, and Diseases which resemble it.
> 8vo.   [In the Press.

Aristotle on Fallacies ; or, the Sophistici Elenchi.
> With a Translation and Notes by EDWARD POSTE, M.A. 8vo. 8s. 6d.

ARNOLD.—*Works by* MATTHEW ARNOLD.
New Poems. Second Edition.
> Extra fcap. 8vo. 6s. 6d.

A French Eton ; or, Middle-Class Education and the State.
> Fcap. 8vo. 2s. 6d.

Essays in Criticism.
> *New Edition.* Extra fcap. 8vo. 6s.

Schools and Universities on the Continent.
> 8vo. 10s. 6d.

BAKER.—*Works by* SIR SAMUEL W. BAKER, M.A. F.R.G.S.
The Nile Tributaries of Abyssinia, and the Sword Hunters of the Hamran Arabs.
> With Portraits, Maps, and Illustrations. *Third Edition.* 8vo. 21s.

The Albert N'yanza Great Basin of the Nile, and Exploration of the Nile Sources. New and cheaper Edition.
> With Portraits, Maps, and Illustrations. Two Vols. crown 8vo. 16s.

Cast up by the Sea ; or, The Adventures of Ned Grey.
> With Illustrations. Crown 8vo.

BARWELL.—*Guide in the Sick Room.*
> By RICHARD BARWELL, F.R.C.S. Extra fcap. 8vo. 3s. 6d.

BARNES.—*Poems of Rural Life in Common English.*
By the Rev. W. BARNES, Author of "Poems of Rural Life in the Dorset Dialect." Fcap. 8vo. 6s.

BATES AND LOCKYER.—*A Class-Book of Geography. Adapted to the recent programme of the Royal Geographical Society.*
By H. W. BATES and J. N. LOCKYER, F.R.G.S. [In the Press.

BAXTER.—*National Income.*
By R. DUDLEY BAXTER, M.A. With Coloured Diagram. 8vo. 3s. 6d.

BAYMA.—*Elements of Molecular Mechanics.*
By JOSEPH BAYMA, S. J. 8vo. 10s. 6d.

BEASLEY.—*An Elementary Treatise on Plane Trigonometry.*
With a Numerous Collection of Examples. By R. D. BEASLEY, M.A. *Second Edition.* Crown 8vo. 3s. 6d.

BELL—*Romances and Minor Poems.*
By HENRY GLASSFORD BELL. Fcap. 8vo. 6s.

BERNARD.—*The Progress of Doctrine in the New Testament.*
In Eight Lectures preached before the University of Oxford. By THOMAS DEHANY BERNARD, M.A. *Second Edition.* 8vo. 8s. 6d.

BERNARD.—*Four Lectures on Subjects connected with Diplomacy.*
By MOUNTAGUE BERNARD, M.A., Chichele Professor of International Law and Diplomacy, Oxford. 8vo. 9s.

BERNARD (ST.).—*The Life and Times of St. Bernard, Abbot of Clairvaux.*
By J. C. MORISON, M.A. *New Edition.* Crown 8vo. 7s. 6d.

BESANT.—*Studies in Early French Poetry.*
By WALTER BESANT, M.A. Crown 8vo. 8s. 6d.

BIRKS.—*Works by* THOMAS RAWSON BIRKS, M.A.
The Difficulties of Belief in connexion with the Creation and the Fall.
Crown 8vo. 4s. 6d.

On Matter and Ether ; or, the Secret Laws of Physical Change.
Crown 8vo. 5s. 6d.

BLAKE.—*The Life of William Blake, the Artist.*
By ALEXANDER GILCHRIST. With numerous Illustrations from Blake's Designs and Fac-similes of his Studies of the "Book of Job." Two Vols. Medium 8vo. 32s.

BLAKE.—*A Visit to some American Schools and Colleges.*
By SOPHIA JEX BLAKE. Crown 8vo. 6s.

Blanche Lisle, and other Poems.
By CECIL HOME. Fcap. 8vo. 4s. 6d.

BOOLE.—*Works by the late* GEORGE BOOLE, F.R.S. *Professor of Mathematics in the Queen's University, Ireland, &c.*

A Treatise on Differential Equations.
New Edition. Edited by I. TODHUNTER, M.A. F.R.S. Crown 8vo. 14s.

Treatise on Differential Equations.
Supplementary Volume. Crown 8vo. 8s. 6d.

A Treatise on the Calculus of Finite Differences.
Crown 8vo. 10s. 6d.

BRADSHAW.—*An Attempt to ascertain the state of Chaucer's Works, as they were Left at his Death,*
With some Notices of their Subsequent History. By HENRY BRADSHAW, of King's College, and the University Library, Cambridge. [In the Press.

BRIGHT.—*Speeches on various Questions of Public Policy.*
By JOHN BRIGHT, M.P. Edited by PROFESSOR THOROLD ROGERS. 2 vols. 8vo. 25s.

BRIMLEY.—*Essays by the late* GEORGE BRIMLEY, M.A.
Edited by W. G. CLARK, M.A. With Portrait. *Cheaper Edition.* Fcap. 8vo. 3s. 6d.

BROOK SMITH.—*Arithmetic in Theory and Practice.*
For Advanced Pupils. Part First. By J. BROOK SMITH, M.A. Crown 8vo. 3s. 6d.

BRYCE.—*The Holy Roman Empire.*
By JAMES BRYCE, B.C.L. Fellow of Oriel College, Oxford. *A New Edition, revised and enlarged.* Crown 8vo. 9s.

BUCKNILL.—*The Mad Folk of Shakespeare.*
Psychological Lectures by J. C. BUCKNILL, M.D. F.R.S. Second Edition. Crown 8vo. 6s. 6d.

BULLOCK.—*Works by* W. H. BULLOCK.

Polish Experiences during the Insurrection of 1863-4.
Crown 8vo. With Map. 8s. 6d.

Across Mexico in 1864-5.
With Coloured Map and Illustrations. Crown 8vo. 10s. 6d.

BURGON.—*A Treatise on the Pastoral Office.*
Addressed chiefly to Candidates for Holy Orders, or to those who
have recently undertaken the cure of souls. By the Rev. JOHN
W. BURGON, M.A. 8vo. 12s.

BUTLER (ARCHER).—*Works by the Rev.* WILLIAM ARCHER
BUTLER, M.A. *late Professor of Moral Philosophy in the
University of Dublin.*

Sermons, Doctrinal and Practical.
Edited, with a Memoir of the Author's Life, by THOMAS WOOD-
WARD, M.A. Dean of Down. With Portrait. *Seventh and
Cheaper Edition.* 8vo. 8s.

A Second Series of Sermons.
Edited by J. A. JEREMIE, D.D. Regius Professor of Divinity at
Cambridge. *Fifth and Cheaper Edition.* 8vo. 7s.

History of Ancient Philosophy.
Edited by WM. H. THOMPSON, M.A. Master of Trinity College,
Cambridge. Two Vols. 8vo. 1l. 5s.

*Letters on Romanism, in reply to Dr. Newman's Essay
on Development.*
Edited by the Dean of Down. *Second Edition,* revised by
Archdeacon HARDWICK. 8vo. 10s. 6d.

BUTLER (MONTAGU).—*Sermons preached in the Chapel of
Harrow School.*
By H. MONTAGU BUTLER, Head Master. Crown 8vo. 7s. 6d.

BUTLER (GEORGE).—*Works by the Rev.* GEORGE BUTLER.

Family Prayers.
Crown 8vo. 5s.

Sermons preached in Cheltenham College Chapel.
Crown 8vo. 7s. 6d.

CAIRNES.—*The Slave Power; its Character, Career, and
Probable Designs.*
Being an 'Attempt to Explain the Real Issues Involved in the
American Contest. By J. E. CAIRNES, M.A. *Second Edition.*
8vo. 10s. 6d.

CALDERWOOD.—*Philosophy of the Infinite.*
> A Treatise on Man's Knowledge of the Infinite Being, in answer to Sir W. Hamilton and Dr. Mansel. By the Rev. HENRY CALDERWOOD, M.A. Professor of Moral Philosophy at Edinburgh. *Second Edition.* 8vo. 14s.

Cambridge Senate-House Problems and Riders, with Solutions.

1848—1851.—*Problems.*
> By FERRERS and JACKSON. 15s. 6d.

1848—1851.—*Riders.*
> By JAMESON. 7s. 6d.

1854.—*Problems and Riders.*
> By WALTON and MACKENZIE, M.A. 10s. 6d.

1857.—*Problems and Riders.*
> By CAMPION and WALTON. 8s. 6d.

1860.—*Problems and Riders.*
> By WATSON and ROUTH. 7s. 6d.

1864.—*Problems and Riders.*
> By WALTON and WILKINSON. 10s. 6d.

Cambridge Lent Sermons.—
> Sermons preached during Lent, 1864, in Great St. Mary's Church, Cambridge. By the BISHOP of OXFORD, Rev. H. P. LIDDON, T. L. CLAUGHTON, J. R. WOODFORD, Dr. GOULBURN, J. W. BURGON, T. T. CARTER, Dr. PUSEY, DEAN HOOK, W. J. BUTLER, DEAN GOODWIN. Crown 8vo. 7s. 6d.

Cambridge Course of Elementary Natural Philosophy, for the Degree of B.A.
> Originally compiled by J. C. SNOWBALL, M.A., late Fellow of St. John's College. *Fifth Edition,* revised and enlarged, and adapted for the Middle-Class Examinations by THOMAS LUND, B.D. Crown 8vo. 5s.

Cambridge and Dublin Mathematical Journal.
> The Complete Work, in Nine Vols. 8vo. Cloth. 7l. 4s. Only a few copies remain on hand.

Cambridge Characteristics in the Seventeenth Century.
> By JAMES BASS MULLINGER, B.A. Crown 8vo. 4s. 6d.

CAMPBELL.—*Works by* JOHN M'LEOD CAMPBELL.
Thoughts on Revelation, with Special Reference to the Present Time.
Crown 8vo. 5s.

The Nature of the Atonement, and its Relation to Remission of Sins and Eternal Life.
Third Edition. With an Introduction and Notes. 8vo. 10s. 6d.

CARTER.—*King's College Chapel : Notes on, its History and present condition.*
By T. J. P. CARTER, M.A. Fellow of King's College, Cambridge. With Photographs. 8vo. 5s.

Catullus.
Edited by R. ELLIS. 18mo. 3s. 6d.

CHALLIS.—*Creation in Plan and in Progress :*
Being an Essay on the First Chapter of Genesis. By the Rev. JAMES CHALLIS, M.A. F.R.S. F.R.A.S. Crown 8vo. 3s. 6d.

CHATTERTON.—*Leonore; a Tale.*
By GEORGIANA LADY CHATTERTON. *A New Edition.* Beautifully printed on thick toned paper. Crown 8vo. with Frontispiece and Vignette Title engraved by JEENS. 7s. 6d.

CHEYNE.—*Works by* C. H. H. CHEYNE, B.A.
An Elementary Treatise on the Planetary Theory.
With a Collection of Problems. Crown 8vo. 6s. 6d.

The Earth's Motion of Rotation (including the Theory of Precession and Nutation).
Crown 8vo. 3s. 6d.

Choice Notes on St. Matthew, drawn from Old and New Sources.
Crown 8vo. 4s. 6d.

CHRISTIE (J. R.).—*Elementary Test Questions in Pure and Mixed Mathematics.*
Crown 8vo. 8s. 6d.

Church Congress (Authorized Report of) held at Wolverhampton in October, 1867.
8vo. 3s. 6d.

CHURCH.—*Sermons preached before the University of Oxford.*
By R. W. CHURCH, M.A. late Fellow of Oriel College, Rector of Whatley. Extra fcap. 8vo. 4s. 6d.

CICERO.—*The Second Philippic Oration.*
With an Introduction and Notes, translated from KARL HALM.
Edited, with Corrections and Additions, by JOHN E. B. MAYOR,
M.A. *Third Edition.* Fcap. 8vo. 5s.

CLARK.—*Four Sermons preached in the Chapel of Trinity
College, Cambridge.*
By W. G. CLARK, M.A. Fcap. 8vo. 2s. 6d.

CLAY.—*The Prison Chaplain.*
A Memoir of the Rev. JOHN CLAY, B.D. late Chaplain of the
Preston Goal. With Selections from his Reports and Correspondence, and a Sketch of Prison Discipline in England. By
his Son, the Rev. W. L. CLAY, M.A. 8vo. 15s.

The Power of the Keys.
Sermons preached in Coventry. By the Rev. W. L. CLAY, M.A.
Fcap. 8vo. 3s. 6d.

Clergyman's Self-Examination concerning the Apostles' Creed.
Extra fcap. 8vo. 1s. 6d.

CLOUGH.—*The Poems of Arthur Hugh Clough,*
sometime Fellow of Oriel College, Oxford. With a Memoir by
F. T. PALGRAVE. *Second Edition.* Fcap. 8vo. 6s.

COLENSO.—*Works by the Right Rev. J. W. COLENSO, D.D.
Bishop of Natal.*

The Colony of Natal.
A Journal of Visitation. With a Map and Illustrations. Fcap.
8vo. 5s.

Village Sermons.
Second Edition. Fcap. 8vo. 2s. 6d.

Four Sermons on Ordination and on Missions.
18mo. 1s.

Companion to the Holy Communion,
Containing the Service and Select Readings from the writings of
Professor MAURICE. *Fine Edition* morocco, antique style, 6s.
Common paper, 1s.

Letter to His Grace the Archbishop of Canterbury,
Upon the Question of Polygamy, as found already existing in
Converts from Heathenism. *Second Edition.* Crown 8vo. 1s. 6d.

Connells of Castle Connell.
By JANET GORDON. Two Vols. Crown 8vo. 21s.

COOPER.—*Athenae Cantabrigienses.*
By CHARLES HENRY COOPER, F.S.A. and THOMPSON COOPER,
F.S.A. Vol. I. 8vo. 1500—85, 18s. Vol. II. 1586—1609, 18s.

COPE.—*An Introduction to Aristotle's Rhetoric.*
With Analysis, Notes, and Appendices. By E. M. COPE, Senior Fellow and Tutor of Trinity College, Cambridge. 8vo. 14s.

COTTON.—*Works by the late* GEORGE EDWARD LYNCH COTTON, D.D. *Bishop of Calcutta.*

Sermons and Addresses delivered in Marlborough College during Six Years.
Crown 8vo. 10s. 6d.

Sermons, chiefly connected with Public Events of 1854.
Fcap. 8vo. 3s.

Sermons preached to English Congregations in India.
Crown 8vo. 7s. 6d.

Expository Sermons on the Epistles for the Sundays of the Christian Year.
Two Vols. Crown 8vo. 15s.

COX.—*Recollections of Oxford*
By G. V. Cox, M.A. late Esquire Bedel and Coroner in the University of Oxford. Crown 8vo. 10s. 6d.

CRAIK.—*My First Journal.*
A Book for the Young. By GEORGIANA M. CRAIK, Author of "Riverston," "Lost and Won," &c. Royal 16mo. Cloth, gilt leaves, 3s. 6d.

CURE.—*The Seven Words of Christ on the Cross.*
Sermons preached at St. George's, Bloomsbury. By the Rev. E. CAPEL CURE, M.A. Fcap. 8vo. 3s. 6d.

DALTON.—*Arithmetical Examples progressively arranged; together with Miscellaneous Exercises and Examination Papers.*
By the Rev. T. DALTON, M.A. Assistant Master at Eton College. 18mo. 2s 6d.

DANTE.—*Dante's Comedy, The Hell.*
Translated by W. M. ROSSETTI. Fcap. 8vo. cloth. 5s.

DAVIES.—*Works by the Rev.* J. LLEWELYN DAVIES, M.A. *Rector of Christ Church, St. Marylebone, &c.*

Sermons on the Manifestation of the Son of God.
With a Preface addressed to Laymen on the present position of the Clergy of the Church of England; and an Appendix, on the Testimony of Scripture and the Church as to the Possibility of Pardon in the Future State. Fcap. 8vo. 6s. 6d.

DAVIES.—*The Work of Christ; or, the World Reconciled to God.*
With a Preface on the Atonement Controversy. Fcap. 8vo. 6s.

Baptism, Confirmation, and the Lord's Supper.
As interpreted by their outward signs. Three Expository Addresses for Parochial Use. Fcap. 8vo. Limp cloth. 1s. 6d.

Morality according to the Sacrament of the Lord's Supper.
Crown 8vo. 3s. 6d.

The Epistles of St. Paul to the Ephesians, the Colossians, and Philemon.
With Introductions and Notes, and an Essay on the Traces of Foreign Elements in the Theology of these Epistles. 8vo. 7s. 6d.

DAWSON.—*Acadian Geology, the Geological Structure, Organic Remains, and Mineral Resources of Nova Scotia, New Brunswick, and Prince Edward Island.*
By J. W. DAWSON, LL.D. F.R.S. F.G.S. *Second Edition*, revised and enlarged, with Geological Maps and Illustrations. 8vo. 18s.

DAY.—*Properties of Conic Sections proved Geometrically.*
By the Rev. H. G. DAY, M.A. Head-Master of Sedburgh Grammar School. Crown 8vo. 3s. 6d.

Days of Old; Stories from Old English History.
By the Author of "Ruth and her Friends." *New Edition*, 18mo. cloth, gilt leaves. 3s. 6d.

Demosthenes, De Corona.
The Greek Text with English Notes. By B. DRAKE, M.A. *Third Edition*, to which is prefixed ÆSCHINES AGAINST CTESIPHON, with English Notes. Fcap 8vo. 5s.

DE TEISSIER.—*Works by* G. F. DE TEISSIER, B.D.

Village Sermons.
Crown 8vo. 9s.

Second Series.
Crown 8vo. 8s. 6d.

The House of Prayer; or, a Practical Exposition of the Order for Morning and Evening Prayer in the Church of England.
18mo. extra cloth. 4s. 6d.

DE VERE.—*The Infant Bridal, and other Poems.*
By AUBREY DE VERE. Fcap. 8vo. 7s. 6d.

DILKE.—*Greater Britain.*
A Record of Travel in English-speaking Countries during 1866-7. (America, Australia, India.) By CHARLES WENTWORTH DILKE. Two Vols. 8vo. 28s.

DODGSON.—*Elementary Treatise on Determinants.*
By C. L. DODGSON, M.A. 4to. 10s. 6d.

DONALDSON.—*A Critical History of Christian Literature and Doctrine, from the Death of the Apostles to the Nicene Council.*
By JAMES DONALDSON, LL.D. Three Vols. 8vo. cloth. 31s.

DOYLE.—*The Return of the Guards, and other Poems.*
By Sir FRANCIS HASTINGS DOYLE, Professor of Poetry in the University of Oxford. Fcap. 8vo. 7s.

DREW.—*Works by* W. H. DREW, M.A.

A Geometrical Treatise on Conic Sections.
Third Edition. Crown 8vo. 4s. 6d.

Solutions to Problems contained in Drew's Treatise on Conic Sections.
Crown 8vo. 4s. 6d.

Early Egyptian History for the Young.
With Descriptions of the Tombs and Monuments. *New Edition,* with Frontispiece. Fcap. 8vo. 5s.

EASTWOOD.—*The Bible Word Book.*
A Glossary of Old English Bible Words. By J. EASTWOOD, M.A. of St. John's College, and W. ALDIS WRIGHT, M.A. Trinity College, Cambridge. 18mo. 5s. 6d. Uniform with Macmillan's School Class Books,

Ecce Homo.
A Survey of the Life and Work of Jesus Christ. 23d Thousand. Crown 8vo. 6s.

Echoes of Many Voices from Many Lands.
By A. F. 18mo. cloth, extra gilt. 3s. 6d.

ELLICE.—*English Idylls.*
By JANE ELLICE. Fcap. 8vo. cloth. 6s.

ELLIOTT.—*Life of Henry Venn Elliott, of Brighton.*
By JOSIAH BATEMAN, M.A. Author of "Life of Daniel Wilson, Bishop of Calcutta," &c. With Portrait, engraved by JEENS. Crown 8vo. 8s. 6d.

Essays on Church Policy.
Edited by the Rev. W. L. CLAY, M.A. Incumbent of Rainhill, Lancashire. 8vo. 9s.

Essays on a Liberal Education.
By Various Writers. Edited by the Rev. F. W. FARRAR, M.A. F.R.S. &c. *Second Edition.* 8vo. 10s. 6d.

EVANS.—*Brother Fabian's Manuscript, and other Poems.*
By SEBASTIAN EVANS. Fcap. 8vo. cloth. 6s.

FARRAR.—*The Fall of Man, and other Sermons.*
By the Rev. F. W. FARRAR, M.A. late Fellow of Trinity College, Cambridge. Fcap, 8vo. 6s.

FAWCETT.—*Works by* HENRY FAWCETT, M.P.
The Economic Position of the British Labourer.
Extra fcap. 8vo. 5s.

Manual of Political Economy.
Second Edition. Crown 8vo. 12s.

Fellowship: Letters addressed to my Sister Mourners.
Fcap. 8vo. cloth gilt. 3s. 6d.

FERRERS.—*A Treatise on Trilinear Co-ordinates, the Method of Reciprocal Polars, and the Theory of Projections.*
By the Rev. N. M. FERRERS, M.A. *Second Edition.* Crown 8vo. 6s. 6d.

FLETCHER.—*Thoughts from a Girl's Life.*
By LUCY FLETCHER. *Second Edition.* Fcap. 8vo. 4s. 6d.

FORBES.—*Life of Edward Forbes, F.R.S.*
By GEORGE WILSON, M.D. F.R.S.E., and ARCHIBALD GEIKIE, F.R.S. 8vo. with Portrait. 14s.

FORBES.—*The Voice of God in the Psalms.*
By GRANVILLE FORBES, Rector of Broughton. Crown 8vo. 6s. 6d.

FOX.—*On the Diagnosis and Treatment of the Varieties of Dyspepsia, considered in Relation to the Pathological Origin of the different Forms of Indigestion.*
By WILSON FOX, M.D. Lond. F.R.C.P. Holme Professor of Clinical Medicine at University College, London, and Physician to University College Hospital. *Second Edition.* Demy 8vo. 7s. 6d.

On the Artificial Production of Tubercle in the Lower Animals.
4to. 5s. 6d.

FREELAND.—*The Fountain of Youth.*
Translated from the Danish of Frederick Paludan Müller. By
HUMPHREY WILLIAM FREELAND, late M.P. for Chichester.
With Illustrations designed by Walter Allen. Crown 8vo. 6s.

FREEMAN.—*History of Federal Government from the Foun-
dation of the Achaian League to the Disruption of the
United States.*
By EDWARD A. FREEMAN, M.A. Vol. I. General Introduction.
—History of the Greek Federations. 8vo. 21s.

FRENCH.—*Notes on the Characters in Shakespeare's Plays.*
By G. R. FRENCH. [In the Press.

FROST.—*The First Three Sections of Newton's Principia.*
With Notes and Problems in Illustration of the Subject. By
PERCIVAL FROST, M.A. *Second Edition.* 8vo. 10s. 6d.

FROST AND WOLSTENHOLME.—*A Treatise on Solid Geo-
metry.*
By the Rev. PERCIVAL FROST, M.A. and the Rev. J. WOLSTEN-
HOLME, M.A. 8vo. 18s.

The Sicilian Expedition.
Being Books VI. and VII. of Thucydides, with Notes. By the
Rev. P. FROST, M.A. Fcap. 8vo. 5s.

FURNIVALL.—*Le Morte Arthur.*
Edited from the Harleian M.S. 2252, in the British Museum.
By F. J. FURNIVALL, M.A. With Essay by the late HERBERT
COLERIDGE. Fcap. 8vo. 7s. 6d.

GALTON.—*Meteorographica, or Methods of Mapping the
Weather.*
Illustrated by upwards of 600 Printed Lithographed Diagrams.
By FRANCIS GALTON, F.R.S. 4to. 9s.

GEIKIE.—*Works by* ARCHIBALD GEIKIE, F.R.S. *Director of
the Geological Survey of Scotland.*

Story of a Boulder; or, Gleanings by a Field Geologist.
Illustrated with Woodcuts. Crown 8vo. 5s.

*Scenery of Scotland, viewed in connexion with its
Physical Geology.*
With Illustrations and a New Geological Map. Crown 8vo.
10s. 6d.

Elementary Lessons in Physical Geology. [In the Press.

GIFFORD.—*The Glory of God in Man.*
By E. H. GIFFORD, D.D. Fcap. 8vo. 3s. 6d.

Globe Editions :
  The Complete Works of William Shakespeare.
    Edited by W. G. CLARK and W. ALDIS WRIGHT. Ninety-first
    Thousand. Globe 8vo. 3s. 6d. ; paper covers, 2s. 6d.
  Morte DArthur.
    SIR THOMAS MALORY'S Book of KING ARTHUR and of his noble
    KNIGHTS of the ROUND TABLE. The Edition of Caxton, revised
    for Modern use. With an Introduction by SIR EDWARD
    STRACHEY, Bart. Globe 8vo. 3s. 6d.
  The Poetical Works of Sir Walter Scott.
    With Biographical Essay by F. T. PALGRAVE.
  The Poetical Works and Letters of Robert Burns.
    Edited, with Life, by ALEXANDER SMITH. Globe 8vo. 3s. 6d.
  The Adventures of Robinson Crusoe.
    Edited, with Introduction, by HENRY KINGSLEY. Globe 8vo.
    3s. 6d.
  Goldsmith's Miscellaneous Works.
    With Biographical Essay by PROF. MASSON. Globe 8vo. 3s. 6d.
    Other Standard Works are in the Press.
Globe Atlas of Europe.
    Uniform in Size with MACMILLAN'S GLOBE SERIES. Containing
    Forty-Eight Coloured Maps on the same scale, Plans of London
    and Paris, and a Copious Index. Strongly bound in half morocco,
    with flexible back, 9s.
GODFRAY.—*An Elementary Treatise on the Lunar Theory.*
    With a brief Sketch of the Problem up to the time of Newton.
    By HUGH GODFRAY, M.A. *Second Edition revised.* Crown 8vo.
    5s. 6d.
  *A Treatise on Astronomy, for the Use of Colleges
  and Schools.*
    By HUGH GODFRAY, M.A. 8vo. 12s. 6d.
Golden Treasury Series :
    Uniformly printed in 18mo. with Viguette Titles by Sir NOEL
    PATON, T. WOOLNER, W. HOLMAN HUNT, J. E. MILLAIS,
    ARTHUR HUGHES, &c. Engraved on Steel by JEENS. Bound
    in extra cloth, 4s. 6d. ; morocco plain, 7s. 6d. ; morocco extra,
    10s. 6d. each volume.
  *The Golden Treasury of the Best Songs and Lyrical
  Poems in the English Language.*
    Selected and arranged, with Notes, by FRANCIS TURNER PAL-
    GRAVE.
  The Children's Garland from the Best Poets.
    Selected and arranged by COVENTRY PATMORE.

Golden Treasury Series—continued.

The Book of Praise.
From the Best English Hymn Writers. Selected and arranged by Sir ROUNDELL PALMER. *A New and Enlarged Edition.*

The Fairy Book: the Best Popular Fairy Stories.
Selected and rendered anew by the Author of "John Halifax, Gentleman."

The Ballad Book.
A Selection of the choicest British Ballads. Edited by WILLIAM ALLINGHAM.

The Jest Book.
The choicest Anecdotes and Sayings. Selected and arranged by MARK LEMON.

Bacon's Essays and Colours of Good and Evil.
With Notes and Glossarial Index, by W. ALDIS WRIGHT, M.A.
** Large paper copies, crown 8vo. 7s. 6d. ; or bound in half morocco, 10s. 6d.

The Pilgrim's Progress
From this World to that which is to Come. By JOHN BUNYAN.
** Large paper copies, crown 8vo. cloth, 7s. 6d.; or bound in half morocco, 10s. 6d.

The Sunday Book of Poetry for the Young.
Selected and arranged by C. F. ALEXANDER.

A Book of Golden Deeds of all Times and all Countries.
Gathered and Narrated anew by the Author of "The Heir of Redclyffe."

The Poetical Works of Robert Burns.
Edited, with Biographical Memoir, by ALEXANDER SMITH. Two Vols.

The Adventures of Robinson Crusoe.
Edited from the Original Editions by J. W. CLARK, M.A.

The Republic of Plato.
Translated into English with Notes by J. LL. DAVIES, M.A. and D. J. VAUGHAN, M.A.

The Song Book.
Words and Tunes from the best Poets and Musicians, selected and arranged by JOHN HULLAH.

La Lyre Française.
Selected and arranged, with Notes, by GUSTAVE MASSON.

Tom Brown's School Days.
By an OLD BOY.

GREEN.—*Spiritual Philosophy.*
> Founded on the Teaching of the late SAMUEL TAYLOR COLE-RIDGE. By the late JOSEPH HENRY GREEN, F.R.S. D.C.L. Edited, with a Memoir of the Author's Life, by JOHN SIMON, F.R.S. Two Vols. 8vo. cloth. 25s.

Guesses at Truth.
> By TWO BROTHERS. With Vignette Title and Frontispiece. *New Edition.* Fcap. 8vo. 6s.

GUIZOT, M.—*Memoir of M. de Barante.*
> Translated by the Author of "John Halifax, Gentleman." Crown 8vo. 6s. 6d.

Guide to the Unprotected
> In Every Day Matters relating to Property and Income. By a BANKER'S DAUGHTER. *Third Edition.* Extra fcap. 8vo. 3s. 6d.

HAMERTON.—*A Painter's Camp in the Highlands.*
> By P. G. HAMERTON. *New and Cheaper Edition,* one vol. Extra fcap. 8vo. 6s.

Etching and Etchers.
> A Treatise Critical and Practical. By P. G. HAMERTON. With Original Plates by REMBRANDT, CALLOT, DUJARDIN, PAUL POTTER, &c. Royal 8vo. Half morocco. 31s. 6d.

HAMILTON.—*On Truth and Error.*
> Thoughts on the Principles of Truth, and the Causes and Effect of Error. By JOHN HAMILTON. Crown 8vo. 5s.

HARDWICK.—*Works by the Ven.* ARCHDEACON HARDWICK.
Christ and other Masters.
> A Historical Inquiry into some of the Chief Parallelisms and Contrasts between Christianity and the Religious Systems of the Ancient World. *New Edition,* revised, and a Prefatory Memoir by the Rev. FRANCIS PROCTER. Two vols. crown 8vo. 15s.

A History of the Christian Church.
> Middle Age. From Gregory the Great to the Excommunication of Luther. Edited by FRANCIS PROCTER, M.A. With Four Maps constructed for this work by A. KEITH JOHNSTON. *Second Edition.* Crown 8vo. 10s. 6d.

A History of the Christian Church during the Reformation.
> Revised by FRANCIS PROCTER, M.A. *Second Edition.* Crown 8vo. 10s. 6d.

Twenty Sermons for Town Congregations.
> Crown 8vo. 6s. 6d.

HELPS.—*Realmah.*
> By ARTHUR HELPS. Two vols. crown 8vo. 16s.

HEMMING.—*An Elementary Treatise on the Differential and Integral Calculus.*
By G. W. HEMMING, M.A. *Second Edition.* 8vo. 9s.

HERSCHEL.—*The Iliad of Homer.*
Translated into English Hexameters. By Sir JOHN HERSCHEL, Bart. 8vo. 18s.

HERVEY.—*The Genealogies of our Lord and Saviour Jesus Christ,*
As contained in the Gospels of St. Matthew and St. Luke, reconciled with each other, and shown to be in harmony with the true Chronology of the Times. By Lord ARTHUR HERVEY, M.A. 8vo. 10s. 6d.

HERVEY (ROSAMOND). *Works by* ROSAMOND HERVEY.

The Aarbergs.
Two vols. crown 8vo. cloth. 21s.

Duke Ernest,
A Tragedy ; and other Poems. Fcap. 8vo. 6s.

HILL (FLORENCE).—*Children of the State. The Training of Juvenile Paupers.*
Extra fcap. cloth. 5s.

Historical Selections.
A Series of Readings from the best Authorities on English and European History. Selected and Arranged by E. M. SEWELL and C. M. YONGE. Extra fcap. 8vo. 6s.

HISTORICUS.—*Letters on some Questions of International Law.*
Reprinted from the *Times*, with considerable Additions. 8vo. 7s. 6d. Also, ADDITIONAL LETTERS. 8vo. 2s. 6d.

HODGSON.—*Mythology for Latin Versification.*
A Brief Sketch of the Fables of the Ancients, prepared to be rendered into Latin Verse for Schools. By F. HODGSON, B.D. late Provost of Eton. *New Edition*, revised by F. C. HODGSON, M.A. 18mo. 3s.

HOLE.—*Works by* CHARLES HOLE, M.A. *Trinity College, Cambridge.*

A Brief Biographical Dictionary.
Compiled and arranged by CHARLES HOLE, M.A. Trinity College, Cambridge. In pott 8vo. neatly and strongly bound in cloth. *Second Edition.* 4s. 6d.

Genealogical Stemma of the Kings of England and France.
In One Sheet. 1s.

B

HORNER.—*The Tuscan Poet Guiseppe Giusti and his Times.*
By SUSAN HORNER. Crown 8vo. 7s. 6d.

HOWARD.—*The Pentateuch ;*
Or, the Five Books of Moses. Translated into English from the
Version of the LXX. With Notes on its Omissions and Inser-
tions, and also on the Passages in which it differs from the
Authorized Version. By the Hon. HENRY HOWARD, D.D.
Crown 8vo. GENESIS, One Volume, 8s. 6d. ; EXODUS AND
LEVITICUS, One Volume, 10s. 6d. ; NUMBERS AND DEUTER-
ONOMY, One Volume, 10s. 6d.

HOZIER.—*The Seven Weeks' War ;*
Its Antecedents and its Incidents. By H. M. HOZIER. With
Maps and Plans. Two Vols. 8vo. 28s.

HUMPHRY.—*The Human Skeleton (including the Joints).*
By G. M. HUMPHRY, M.D., F.R.S. With Two Hundred and
Sixty Illustrations drawn from Nature. Medium 8vo. 1l. 8s.

HUXLEY.—*Lessons in Elementary Physiology.*
With numerous Illustrations. By T. H. HUXLEY, F.R.S.
Professor of Natural History in the Royal School of Mines.
Uniform with Macmillans' School Class Books. *Second Edition.*
18mo. 4s. 6d.

Hymni Ecclesiæ.
Fcap. 8vo. 7s. 6d.

IRVING.—*Annals of our Own Time.*
A Diurnal of Events, Social and Political, which have happened
in or had relation to the Kingdom of Great Britain from the
Accession of Queen Victoria to the present Year. By JOSEPH
IRVING. 8vo.   [In the Press.

JAMESON.—*Works by the Rev. F. J. JAMESON, M.A.*

Life's Work, in Preparation and in Retrospect.
Sermons preached before the University of Cambridge. Fcap.
8vo. 1s. 6d.

Brotherly Counsels to Students.
Sermons preached in the Chapel of St. Catharine's College,
Cambridge. Fcap. 8vo. 1s. 6d.

JEVONS.—*The Coal Question.*
By W. STANLEY JEVONS, M.A. Fellow of University College,
London. *Second Edition, revised.* 8vo. 10s. 6d.

JONES.—*The Church of England and Common Sense.*
By HARRY JONES, M.A. Fcap. 8vo. 3s. 6d.

JONES.—*Algebraical Exercises,*
Progressively Arranged by the Rev. C. A. JONES, M.A. and
C. H. CHEYNE, M.A. Mathematical Masters in Westminster
School. 18mo. 2s. 6d.

Journal of Anatomy and Physiology.
> Conducted by Professors Humphry and Newton, and Mr. Clark of Cambridge ; Professor Turner, of Edinburgh ; and Dr. Wright, of Dublin. Published twice a year. Price to subscribers, 14s. per annum. Price 7s. 6d. each Part. Vol. 1. containing Parts I. and II. Royal 8vo. 16s. Part III. 6s.

Juvenal, *for Schools.*
> With English Notes. By J. E. B. Mayor, M.A. *New and Cheaper Edition.* Crown 8vo. [In the Press.

Keary.—*The Little Wanderlin,*
> And other Fairy Tales. By A. and E. Keary. 18mo. 3s. 6d.

Kempis (Thos. A).—*De Imitatione Christi. Libri IV.*
> Borders in the ancient style, after Holbein, Durer, and other old Masters, containing Dances of Death, Acts of Mercy, Emblems, and a variety of curious ornamentation. In white cloth, extra gilt. 7s. 6d.

Kennedy.—*Legendary Fictions of the Irish Celts.*
> Collected and Narrated by Patrick Kennedy. Crown 8vo. 7s. 6d.

Kingsbury.—*Spiritual Sacrifice and Holy Communion.*
> Seven Sermons preached during the Lent of 1867 at St. Leonard's-on-Sea, with Notes. By T. L. Kingsbury, M.A. late Rector of Chetwynd. Fcap. 8vo. 3s. 6d.

Kingsley.—*Works by the Rev. Charles Kingsley, M.A. Rector of Eversley, and Professor of Modern History in the University of Cambridge.*

The Roman and the Teuton.
> A Series of Lectures delivered before the University of Cambridge. 8vo. 12s.

Two Years Ago.
> Fourth Edition. Crown 8vo. 6s.

" Westward Ho ! "
> Fifth Edition. Crown 8vo. 6s.

Alton Locke.
> New Edition. With a New Preface. Crown 8vo. 4s. 6d.

Hypatia.
> Fourth Edition. Crown 8vo. 6s.

Yeast.
> Fifth Edition. Crown 8vo. 5s.

Hereward the Wake—Last of the English.
> Crown 8vo. 6s.

KINGSLEY (*Rev.* CHARLES).—*The Saint's Tragedy.*
Third Edition. Fcap. 8vo. 5*s.*

Andromeda,
And other Poems. *Third Edition.* Fcap. 8vo. 5*s.*

The Water Babies.
A Fairy Tale for a Land Baby. With Two Illustrations by Sir
NOEL PATON, R.S.A. *Third Edition.* Crown 8vo. 6*s.*

The Heroes ;
Or, Greek Fairy Tales for my Children. With Coloured Illustrations. *New Edition.* 18mo. 4*s.* 6*d.*

Three Lectures delivered at the Royal Institution on the
Ancien Regime.
Crown 8vo. 6*s.*

The Water of Life,
And other Sermons. Fcap. 8vo. 6*s.*

Village Sermons.
Seventh Edition. Fcap. 8vo. 2*s.* 6*d.*

The Gospel of the Pentateuch.
Second Edition. Fcap. 8vo. 4*s.* 6*d.*

Good News of God.
Fourth Edition. Fcap. 8vo. 4*s.* 6*d.*

Sermons for the Times.
Third Edition. Fcap. 8vo. 3*s.* 6*d.*

Town and Country Sermons.
Extra fcap. 8vo. New Edition. 6*s.*

Sermons on National Subjects.
First Series. *Second Edition.* Fcap. 8vo. 5*s.*
Second Series. *Second Edition.* Fcap. 8vo. 5*s.*

Discipline,
And other Sermons. Fcap. 8vo. 6*s.*

Alexandria and her Schools.
With a Preface. Crown 8vo. 5*s.*

The Limits of Exact Science as applied to History.
An Inaugural Lecture delivered before the University of Cambridge. Crown 8vo. 2*s.*

Phaethon ; or, Loose Thoughts for Loose Thinkers.
Third Edition. Crown 8vo. 2*s.*

David.
Four Sermons : David's Weakness—David's Strength—David's
Anger—David's Deserts. Fcap. 8vo. cloth. 2*s.* 6*d.*

KINGSLEY.— *Works by* HENRY KINGSLEY.
Austin Elliot.
New Edition. Crown 8vo. 6s.

The Recollections of Geoffry Hamlyn.
Second Edition. Crown 8vo. 6s.

The Hillyars and the Burtons: A Story of Two Families.
Crown 8vo. 6s.

Ravenshoe.
New Edition. Crown 8vo. 6s.

Leighton Court.
New Edition. Crown 8vo. 6s.

Silcote of Silcotes.
Three Vols. Crown 8vo. 31s. 6d.

KIRCHHOFF.—*Researches on the Solar Spectrum and the Spectra of the Chemical Elements.*
By G. KIRCHHOFF, of Heidelberg. Translated by HENRY E. ROSCOE, B.A. Second Part. 4to. 5s. with 2 Plates.

KITCHENER.—*Geometrical Note Book,*
Containing Easy Problems in Geometrical Drawing, preparatory to the Study of Geometry. For the Use of Schools. By F. E. KITCHENER, M.A., Mathematical Master at Rugby. 4to. 2s.

LANCASTER.—*Works by* WILLIAM LANCASTER.
Præterita.
Poems. Extra fcap. 8vo. 4s. 6d.

Studies in Verse.
Extra fcap. 8vo. 4s. 6d.

Eclogues and Mono-dramas; or, a Collection of Verses.
Extra fcap. 8vo. 4s. 6d.

LATHAM.—*The Construction of Wrought-iron Bridges.*
Embracing the Practical Application of the Principles of Mechanics to Wrought-Iron Girder Work. By J. H. LATHAM, Civil Engineer. 8vo. With numerous detail Plates. *Second Edition.* [Preparing.

LATHAM.—*Black and White: A Three Months' Tour in the United States.*
By H. LATHAM, M.A. Barrister-at-Law. 8vo. 10s. 6d.

LAW.—*The Alps of Hannibal.*
By WILLIAM JOHN LAW, M.A. Two vols. 8vo. 21s.

Lectures to Ladies on Practical Subjects.
　Third Edition, revised. Crown 8vo. 7s. 6d.

LEMON.—*Legends of Number Nip.*
　By MARK LEMON. With Six Illustrations by CHARLES KEENE.
　Extra fcap. 8vo. 5s.

LIGHTFOOT.—*Works by* J. B. LIGHTFOOT, D.D. *Hulsean Professor of Divinity in the University of Cambridge.*

　St. Paul's Epistle to the Galatians.
　　A Revised Text, with Notes and Dissertations. *Second Edition,
　　revised.* 8vo. 12s.

　St. Paul's Epistle to the Philippians.
　　A Revised Text, with Notes and Dissertations. 8vo. 12s.

Little Estella.
　And other Fairy Tales for the Young. Royal 16mo. 3s. 6d.

LIVERPOOL.—*The Life and Administration of Robert Banks,
Second Earl of Liverpool.*
　Compiled from Original Documents by PROFESSOR YONGE.
　3 vols. 8vo. 42s.

LOCKYER.—*Elementary Lessons in Astronomy. With
numerous Illustrations.*
　By J. NORMAN LOCKYER, F.R.A.S. 18mo. 5s. 6d.

LUCKOCK.—*The Tables of Stone.*
　A Course of Sermons preached in All Saints', Cambridge, by
　H. M. LUCKOCK, M.A., Vicar. Fcap. 8vo. 3s. 6d.

LUDLOW and HUGHES.—*A Sketch of the History of the
United States from Independence to . Secession.*
　By J. M. LUDLOW, Author of "British India, its Races and its
　History," "The Policy of the Crown towards India," &c.
　To which is added, "The Struggle for Kansas." By THOMAS
　HUGHES, Author of "Tom Brown's School Days," "Tom Brown
　at Oxford," &c. Crown 8vo. 8s. 6d.

LUSHINGTON.—*The Italian War,* 1848-9, *and the Last
Italian Poet.*
　By the late HENRY LUSHINGTON. With a Biographical Preface
　by G. S. VENABLES. Crown 8vo. 6s. 6d.

LYTTELTON.—*Works by* LORD LYTTELTON.
　The Comus of Milton rendered into Greek Verse.
　　Extra fcap. 8vo. *Second Edition.* 5s.
　*The Samson Agonistes of Milton rendered into Greek
　Verse.*
　　Extra fcap. 8vo. 6s. 6d.

MACKENZIE.—*The Christian :Clergy of the First Ten Centuries, and their Influence on European Civilization.*
> By HENRY MACKENZIE, B.A. Scholar of Trinity College, Cambridge. Crown 8vo. 6s. 6d.

MACLAREN.—*Sermons preached at Manchester.*
> By ALEXANDER MACLAREN. *Second Edition.* Fcap. 8vo. 4s. 6d. A Second Series in the Press.

MACLAREN.—*Training, in Theory and Practice.*
> By ARCHIBALD MACLAREN, Oxford. With Frontispiece, and other Illustrations. 8vo. Handsomely bound in cloth. 7s. 6d.

MACLEAR.—*Works by* G. F. MACLEAR, B.D. *Head Master of King's College School, and Preacher at the Temple Church :—*

A History of Christian Missions during the Middle Ages.
> Crown 8vo. 10s. 6d.

The Witness of the Eucharist; or, The Institution and Early Celebration of the Lord's Supper, considered as an Evidence of the Historical Truth of the Gospel Narrative and of the Atonement.
> Crown 8vo. 4s. 6d.

A Class-Book of Old Testament History.
> With Four Maps. *Fourth Edition.* 18mo. 4s. 6d.

A Class-Book of New Testament History.
> Including the connexion of the Old and New Testament. *Second Edition.* 18mo. 5s. 6d.

A Class-Book of the Catechism of the Church of England.
> Second Edition. 18mo. cloth. 2s. 6d.

A Shilling Book of Old Testament History.
> 18mo. cloth limp. 1s.

A Shilling Book of New Testament History.
> 18mo. cloth limp. 1s.

A First Class-Book of the Catechism of the Church of England, with Scripture Proofs for Junior Classes and Schools.
> 6d.

MACMILLAN.—*Works by the Rev.* HUGH MACMILLAN.

Bible Teachings in Nature.
Second Edition. Crown 8vo. 6s.

Foot-notes from the Page of Nature.
With numerous Illustrations. Fcap. 8vo. 5s.

Macmillan's Magazine.
Published Monthly, price One Shilling. Volumes I. —XVIII. are now ready, 7s. 6d. each.

MACMILLAN & CO.'S *Six Shilling Series of Works of Fiction.*

KINGSLEY.—*Works by the* REV. CHARLES KINGSLEY, M.A.
Westward Ho !
Hypatia.
Hereward the Wake—Last of the English.
Two Years Ago.

Works by the Author of " The Heir of Redclyffe."
The Heir of Redclyffe.
Dynevor Terrace ; or, The Clue of Life.
Heartsease ; or, The Brother's Wife.
The Clever Woman of the Family.
Hopes and Fears; or, Scenes from the Life of a Spinster.
The Young Stepmother ; or, A Chronicle of Mistakes.
The Daisy Chain.
The Trial : More Links of the Daisy Chain.

KINGSLEY.—*Works by* HENRY KINGSLEY.
Geoffry Hamlyn.
Ravenshoe.
Austin Elliot.
Hillyars and Burtons.
Leighton Court.

TREVELYAN.—*Works by* G. O. TREVELYAN.

Cawnpore.

Competition Wallah.

MISCELLANEOUS.

The Moor Cottage.
By MAY BEVERLEY.

Janet's Home.

Tom Brown at Oxford.
By the Author of "Tom Brown's School Days.

Clemency Franklyn.
By the Author of "Janet's Home."

A Son of the Soil.

Old Sir Douglas.
By HON. MRS. NORTON.

McCOSH.—*Works by* JAMES McCOSH, LL.D. *Professor of Logic and Metaphysics, Queen's College, Belfast, &c.*

The Method of the Divine Government, Physical and Moral.
Ninth Edition. 8vo. 10s. 6d.

The Supernatural in Relation to the Natural.
Crown 8vo. 7s. 6d.

The Intuitions of the Mind.
A New Edition. 8vo. 10s. 6d.

An Examination of Mr. J. S. Mill's Philosophy.
Being a Defence of Fundamental Truth. Crown 8vo. 7s. 6d.

Philosophical Papers.
1. Examination of Sir W. Hamilton's Logic. II. Reply to Mr. Mill's. Third Edition. III. Present State of Moral Philosophy in Britain. 8vo. 3s. 6d.

MANSFIELD.—*Works by* C. B. MANSFIELD, M.A.

Paraguay, Brazil, and the Plate.
With a Map, and numerous Woodcuts. With a Sketch of his Life, by the Rev. CHARLES KINGSLEY. Crown 8vo. 12s. 6d.

A Theory of Salts.
A Treatise on the Constitution of Bipolar (two membered) Chemical Compounds. Crown 8vo. cloth. 14s.

MARKHAM.—*A History of the Abyssinian Expedition.*
Including an Account of the Physical Geography, Geology, and Botany of the Region traversed by the English Forces. By CLEMENTS R. MARKHAM, F.R.G.S. With a Chapter by LIEUT. PRIDEAUX, containing a Narrative of his Mission and Captivity. With Maps, &c. 8vo.

MARRINER.—*Sermons preached at Lyme Regis.*
By E. T. MARRINER, Curate. Fcap. 8vo. 4s. 6d.

MARSHALL.—*A Table of Irregular Greek Verbs.*
8vo. 1s.

MARTIN.—*The Statesman's Year Book for* 1869. By FREDERICK MARTIN. (*Sixth Annual Publication.*)
A Statistical, Mercantile, and Historical Account of the Civilized World for the Year 1868. Forming a Manual for Politicians and Merchants. Crown 8vo. 10s. 6d.

MARTINEAU.—*Biographical Sketches,* 1852–68.
By HARRIET MARTINEAU.

MASSON.—*Works by* DAVID MASSON, M.A. *Professor of Rhetoric and English Literature in the University of Edinburgh.*

Essays, Biographical and Critical.
Chiefly on the English Poets. 8vo. 12s. 6d.

British Novelists and their Styles.
Being a Critical Sketch of the History of British Prose Fiction. Crown 8vo. 7s. 6d.

Life of John Milton.
Narrated in connexion with the Political, Ecclesiastical, and Literary History of his Time. Vol. I. with Portraits. 8vo. 18s.

Recent British Philosophy.
A Review, with Criticisms, including some Comments on Mr. Mill's Answer to Sir William Hamilton. *New and Cheaper Edition.* Crown 8vo. 6s.

MAUDSLEY.—*The Physiology and Pathology of the Mind.*
By HENRY MAUDSLEY, M.D. *New and Revised Edition.* 8vo. 16s.

MAURICE.—*Works by the Rev.* FREDERICK DENISON MAURICE, M.A. *Professor of Moral Philosophy in the University of Cambridge.*

The Conscience.
Lectures on Casuistry, delivered in the University of Cambridge. 8vo. 8s. 6d.

MAURICE.—*The Claims of the Bible and of Science.*
A Correspondence on some Questions respecting the Pentateuch.
Crown 8vo. 4*s.* 6*d.*

Dialogues on Family Worship.
Crown 8vo. 6*s.*

The Patriarchs and Lawgivers of the Old Testament.
Third and Cheaper Edition. Crown 8vo. 5*s.*
This volume contains Discourses on the Pentateuch, Joshua,
Judges, and the beginning of the First Book of Samuel.

The Prophets and Kings of the Old Testament.
Second Edition. Crown 8vo. 10*s.* 6*d.*
This volume contains Discources on Samuel I. and II.; Kings I.
and II.; Amos, Joel, Hosea, Isaiah, Micah, Nahum, Habakkuk,
Jeremiah, and Ezekiel.

The Gospel of the Kingdom of Heaven.
A Series of Lectures on the Gospel of St. Luke. Crown 8vo. 9*s.*

The Gospel of St. John.
A Series of Discourses. *Third and Cheaper Edition.* Crown
8vo. 6*s.*

The Epistles of St. John.
A Series of Lectures on Christian Ethics. *Second and Cheaper
Edition.* Crown 8vo. 6*s.*

*The Commandments considered as Instruments of
National Reformation.*
Crown 8vo. 4*s.* 6*d.*

*Expository Sermons on the Prayer-book. The Prayer-
book considered especially in reference to the Romish
System.*
Second Edition. Fcap. 8vo. 5*s.* 6*d.*

Lectures on the Apocalypse,
Or Book of the Revelation of St. John the Divine. Crown 8vo.
10*s.* 6*d.*

What is Revelation?
A Series of Sermons on the Epiphany; to which are added
Letters to a Theological Student on the Bampton Lectures of
Mr. MANSEL. Crown 8vo. 10*s.* 6*d.*

Sequel to the Inquiry, "What is Revelation?"
Letters in Reply to Mr. Mansel's Examination of "Strictures on
the Bampton Lectures." Crown 8vo. 6*s.*

Lectures on Ecclesiastical History.
8vo. 10*s.* 6*d.*

MAURICE.—*Theological Essays.*
Second Edition.   Crown 8vo.   10s. 6d.

The Doctrine of Sacrifice deduced from the Scriptures.
Crown 8vo.   7s. 6d.

The Religions of the World,
And their Relations to Christianity.   *Fourth Edition.*   Fcap.
8vo.   5s.

On the Lord's Prayer.
Fourth Edition.   Fcap. 8vo.   2s. 6d.

On the Sabbath Day;
The Character of the Warrior; and on the Interpretation of
History.   Fcap. 8vo.   2s. 6d.

Learning and Working.
Six Lectures on the Foundation of Colleges for Working Men.
Crown 8vo.   5s.

The Ground and Object of Hope for Mankind.
Four Sermons preached before the University of Cambridge.
Crown 8vo.   3s. 6d.

Law's Remarks on the Fable of the Bees.
With an Introduction by F. D. MAURICE, M.A.   Fcap. 8vo.
4s. 6d.

MAYOR.—*A First Greek Reader.*
Edited after Karl Halm, with Corrections and Additions.   By
JOHN E. B. MAYOR, M.A.   Fcap. 8vo.   6s.

Autobiography of Matthew Robinson.
By JOHN E. B. MAYOR, M.A.   Fcap. 8vo.   5s. 6d.

MERIVALE.—*Sallust for Schools.*
By C. MERIVALE, B.D.   *Second Edition.*   Fcap. 8vo.   4s. 6d.
*** The Jugurtha and the Catalina may be had separately, price
2s. 6d. each.

Keats' Hyperion rendered into Latin Verse.
By C. MERIVALE, B.D.   *Second Edition.*   Extra fcap. 8vo.
3s. 6d.

MISTRAL, F.—*Mirelle, a Pastoral Epic of Provence.*
Translated by H. CRICHTON.   Extra fcap. 8vo.   6s.

*Modern Industries: A Series of Reports on Industry and
Manufactures as represented in the Paris Exposition
in 1867.*
By TWELVE BRITISH WORKMEN.   Crown 8vo.   1s.

MOORHOUSE.—*Works by* JAMES MOORHOUSE, M.A.
Some Modern Difficulties respecting the Facts of Nature and Revelation.
Fcap. 8vo. 2s. 6d.

The Hulsean Lectures for 1865.
Crown 8vo. 5s.

MORGAN.—*A Collection of Mathematical Problems and Examples.*
By H. A. MORGAN, M.A. Crown 8vo. 6s. 6d.

MORISON.—*The Life and Times of Saint Bernard, Abbot of Clairvaux.*
By JAMES COTTER MORISON, M.A. *New Edition, revised.*
Crown 8vo. 7s. 6d.

MORLEY, JOHN.—*Edmund Burke—a Historical Study.*
Crown 8vo. 7s. 6d.

MORSE.—*Working for God,*
And other Practical Sermons. By FRANCIS MORSE, M.A.
Second Edition. Fcap. 8vo. 5s.

MULLINGER.—*Cambridge Characteristics in the Seventeenth Century.*
By J. B. MULLINGER, B.A. Crown 8vo. 4s. 6d.

MYERS.—*St. Paul.*
A Poem. By F. W. H. MYERS. *Second Edition.* Extra fcap.
8vo. 2s. 6d.

NETTLESHIP.—*Essays on Robert Browning's Poetry.*
By JOHN T. NETTLESHIP. Extra fcap. 8vo. 6s. 6d.

New Landlord, The.
Translated from the Hungarian of MAURICE JOKAI by A. J.
PATTERSON. Two vols. crown 8vo. 21s.

Northern Circuit.
Brief Notes of Travel in Sweden, Finland, and Russia. With a
Frontispiece. Crown 8vo. 5s.

NORTON.—*The Lady of La Garaye.*
By the Hon. Mrs. NORTON. With Vignette and Frontispiece.
Sixth Edition. Fcap. 8vo. 4s. 6d.

O'BRIEN.—*Works by* JAMES THOMAS O'BRIEN, D.D. *Bishop of Ossory.*

An Attempt to Explain and Establish the Doctrine of Justification by Faith only.
Third Edition. 8vo. 12s.

Charge delivered at the Visitation in 1863.
Second Edition. 8vo. 2s.

OLIPHANT.—*Agnes Hopetoun's Schools and Holidays.*
By Mrs. OLIPHANT. Royal 16mo. gilt leaves. 3s. 6d.

OLIVER.—*Lessons in Elementary Botany.*
With nearly 200 Illustrations. By DANIEL OLIVER, F.R.S. F.L.S. 18mo. 4s. 6d.

OPPEN.—*French Reader,*
For the Use of Colleges and Schools. By EDWARD A. OPPEN. Fcap. 8vo. 4s. 6d.

ORWELL.—*The Bishop's Walk and the Bishop's Times.*
Poems on the Days of Archbishop Leighton and the Scottish Covenant. By ORWELL. Fcap. 8vo. 5s.

Our Year.
A Child's Book, in Prose and Verse. By the Author of "John Halifax, Gentleman." Illustrated by CLARENCE DOBELL. Royal 16mo. 3s. 6d.

PALGRAVE.—*History of Normandy and of England.*
By Sir FRANCIS PALGRAVE. Completing the History to the Death of William Rufus. Vols. I. to IV. 8vo. each 21s.

PALGRAVE.—*A Narrative of a Year's Journey through Central and Eastern Arabia,* 1862-3.
By WILLIAM GIFFORD PALGRAVE (late of the Eighth Regiment Bombay N.I.) *Fourth and Cheaper Edition.* With Map, Plans and Portrait of Author, engraved on Steel by JEENS. Crown 8vo. 7s. 6d.

PALGRAVE.—*Works by* FRANCIS TURNER PALGRAVE, M.A. *late Fellow of Exeter College, Oxford.*

The Five Days' Entertainments at Wentworth Grange.
Small 4to. 9s.

PALGRAVE.—*Essays on Art.*
> Mulready—Dyce—Holman Hunt—Herbert—Poetry, Prose, and
> Sensationalism in Art—Sculpture in England—The Albert Cross,
> &c. Extra fcap. 8vo. 6s.

Sonnets and Songs.
> By WILLIAM SHAKESPEARE. GEM EDITION. With Vignette
> Title by JEENS. 3s. 6d.

Original Hymns.
> Second Edition, enlarged. 18mo. 1s. 6d.

PALMER.—*The Book of Praise:*
> From the Best English Hymn Writers. Selected and arranged
> by SIR ROUNDELL PALMER. With Vignette by WOOLNER.
> 18mo. 4s. 6d. *Large Type Edition*, demy 8vo. 10s. 6d. ;
> morocco, 21s.

A Hymnal.
> Chiefly from the BOOK OF PRAISE. In various sizes.
> A.—In royal 32mo. cloth limp. 6d.
> B.—Small 18mo. larger type, cloth limp. 1s.
> C.—Same Edition, fine paper, cloth. 1s. 6d.

An Edition with Music, Selected, Harmonized, and Composed by
JOHN HULLAH. Square 18mo. 3s. 6d.

PARKINSON.—*Works by* S. PARKINSON, B.D.

A Treatise on Elementary Mechanics.
> For the Use of the Junior Classes at the University and the
> Higher Classes in Schools. With a Collection of Examples.
> *Third Edition, revised.* Crown 8vo. 9s. 6d.

A Treatise on Optics.
> *Second Edition, revised.* Crown 8vo. 10s. 6d.

PATMORE.—*Works by* COVENTRY PATMORE.

The Angel in the House.
> Book I. The Betrothal.—Book II. The Espousals.—Book III.
> Faithful for Ever. With Tamerton Church Tower. Two vols.
> fcap. 8vo. 12s.
>
> ** A New and Cheap Edition, in one vol. 18mo. beautifully
> printed on toned paper, price 2s. 6d.

The Victories of Love.
> Fcap. 8vo. 4s. 6d.

Phantasmagoria and other Poems.
> By LEWIS CARROLL.

PHEAR.—*Elementary Hydrostatics.*
> By J. B. PHEAR, M.A. *Third Edition.* Crown 8vo. 5s. 6d.

PHILLIMORE.—*Private Law among the Romans.*
From the Pandects. By JOHN GEORGE PHILLIMORE, Q.C. 8vo. 16s.

Philology.
The Journal of Sacred and Classical Philology. Four Vols. 8vo. 12s. 6d. each.

The Journal of Philology. New Series. Edited by W. G. CLARK, M.A. JOHN E. B. MAYOR, M.A. and W. ALDIS WRIGHT, M.A. No. I. 8vo. 4s. 6d. (Half-yearly.)

PLATO.—*The Republic of Plato.*
Translated into English, with Notes. By Two Fellows of Trinity College, Cambridge (J. Ll. Davies, M.A. and D. J. Vaughan, M.A.). With Vignette Portraits of Plato and Socrates engraved by JEENS from an Antique Gem. (Golden Treasury Series.) *New Edition*, 18mo. 4s. 6d.

Platonic Dialogues, The.
For English Readers. By the late W. WHEWELL, D.D. F.R.S. Master of Trinity College, Cambridge. Vol. I. *Second Edition*, containing *The Socratic Dialogues*, fcap. 8vo. 7s. 6d.; Vol. II. containing *The Anti-Sophist Dialogues*, 6s. 6d.; Vol. III. containing *The Republic*, 7s. 6d.

Plea for a New English Version of the Scriptures.
By a Licentiate of the Church of Scotland. 8vo. 6s.

POTTER.—*A Voice from the Church in Australia :*
Sermons preached in Melbourne. By the Rev. ROBERT POTTER, M.A. Extra fcap. 8vo. 4s. 6d.

Practitioner (The), a Monthly Journal of Therapeutics.
Edited by FRANCIS E. ANSTIE, M.D. and HENRY LAWSON, M.D. 8vo. Price 1s. 6d.

PRATT.—*Treatise on Attractions, La Place's Functions, and the Figure of the Earth.*
By J. H. PRATT, M.A. *Third Edition.* Crown 8vo. 6s. 6d.

PRESCOTT.—*The Threefold Cord.*
Sermons preached before the University of Cambridge. By J. E. PRESCOTT, B.D. Fcap. 8vo. 3s. 6d.

PROCTER.—*Works by* FRANCIS PROCTER, M.A.

A History of the Book of Common Prayer :
With a Rationale of its Offices. *Seventh Edition, revised and enlarged.* Crown 8vo. 10s. 6d.

PROCTER AND G. F. MACLEAR, B.D.—*An Elementary History of the Book of Common Prayer. New Edition.*
18mo. 2s. 6d.

Psalms of David chronologically arranged.
An Amended Version, with Historical Introductions and Explanatory Notes. By FOUR FRIENDS. Crown 8vo. 10s. 6d.

PUCKLE.—*An Elementary Treatise on Conic Sections and Algebraic Geometry, with numerous Examples and Hints for their Solution,*
Especially designed for the Use of Beginners. By G. HALE PUCKLE, M.A. Head Master of Windermere College. *Third Edition, enlarged.* Crown 8vo. 7s. 6d.

PULLEN.—*The Psalter and Canticles, Pointed for Chanting,*
With Marks of Expression, and a List of Appropriate Chants. By the Rev. HENRY PULLEN, M.A. 8vo. 5s.

RALEGH.—*The Life of Sir Walter Ralegh, based upon Contemporary Documents.*
By EDWARD EDWARDS. Together with his LETTERS, now first Collected. With Portrait. Two Vols. 8vo. 32s.

RAMSAY.—*The Catechiser's Manual;*
Or, the Church Catechism Illustrated and Explained, for the Use of Clergymen, Schoolmasters, and Teachers. By ARTHUR RAMSAY, M.A. *Second Edition.* 18mo. 1s. 6d.

RAWLINSON.—*Elementary Statics.*
By G. RAWLINSON, M.A. Edited by EDWARD STURGES, M.A. Crown 8vo. 4s. 6d.

Rays of Sunlight for Dark Days.
A Book of Selections for the Suffering. With a Preface by C. J. VAUGHAN, D.D. 18mo. *New Edition.* 3s. 6d. Morocco, old style, 7s. 6d.

Reform.—Essays on Reform.
By the Hon. G. C. BRODRICK, R. H. HUTTON, LORD HOUGHTON, A. V. DICEY, LESLIE STEPHEN, J. B. KINNEAR, B. CRACROFT, C. H. PEARSON, GOLDWIN SMITH, JAMES BRYCE, A. L. RUTSON, and Sir GEO. YOUNG. 8vo. 10s. 6d.

Questions for a Reformed Parliament.
By F. H. HILL, GODFREY LUSHINGTON, MEREDITH TOWNSEND, W. L. NEWMAN, C. S. PARKER, J. B. KINNEAR, G. HOOPER, F. HARRISON, Rev. J. E. T. ROGERS, J. M. LUDLOW, and LLOYD JONES. 8vo. 10s. 6d.

REYNOLDS.—*A System of Medicine. Vol. I.*
> Edited by J. RUSSELL REYNOLDS, M.D. F.R.C.P. London.
> PART I. GENERAL DISEASES, or Affections of the Whole
> System. § I.—Those determined by agents operating from
> without, such as the exanthemata, malarial diseases, and their
> allies. § II.—Those determined by conditions existing within
> the body, such as Gout, Rheumatism, Rickets, &c. PART II.
> LOCAL DISEASES, or Affections of particular Systems. § I.—
> Diseases of the Skin. 8vo. 25s.

REYNOLDS.—*A System of Medicine. Vol. II.*
> PART II. § I.—Diseases of the Nervous System. A. General
> Nervous Diseases. B. Partial Diseases of the Nervous System.
> 1. Diseases of the Head. 2. Diseases of the Spinal Column.
> 3. Diseases of the Nerves. § II.—Diseases of the Digestive
> System. A. Diseases of the Stomach. 8vo. 25s.

Notes of the Christian Life.
> A Selection of Sermons by HENRY ROBERT REYNOLDS, B.A.
> President of Cheshunt College, and Fellow of University College,
> London. Crown 8vo. 7s. 6d.

REYNOLDS.—*Modern Methods of Elementary Geometry.*
> By E. M. REYNOLDS, M.A. Mathematical Master in Clifton
> College. Crown 8vo. 3s. 6d.

Ridicula Rediviva.
> Being old Nursery Rhymes. With Coloured Illustrations by
> J. E. ROGERS. 9s.

ROBERTS.—*Discussions on the Gospels.*
> By the Rev. ALEXANDER ROBERTS, D.D. *Second Edition,
> revised and enlarged.* 8vo. 16s.

ROBERTSON.—*Pastoral Counsels.*
> By the late JOHN ROBERTSON, D.D. of Glasgow Cathedral.
> New Edition. With Biographical Sketch by the Author of
> "Recreations of a Country Parson." Extra fcap. 8vo. 6s.

ROBINSON CRABB.—*Life and Reminiscences.*   [In the Press.

ROBY.—*A Latin Grammar for the Higher Classes in
Grammar Schools, based on the "Elementary Latin
Grammar."*
> By H. J. ROBY, M.A.   [In the Press.

ROBY.—*Story of a Household, and other Poems.*
> By MARY K. ROBY. Fcap. 8vo. 5s.

ROMANIS.—*Sermons preached at St. Mary's, Reading.*
> By WILLIAM ROMANIS, M.A. *First Series.* Fcap. 8vo. 6s.
> Also, *Second Series.* 6s.

ROSCOE.—*Lessons in Elementary Chemistry, Inorganic and Organic.*
By H. E. ROSCOE, F.R.S. *Eighth Thousand.* 18mo. 4s. 6d.

ROSSETTI.—*Works by* CHRISTINA ROSSETTI.
Goblin Market, and other Poems.
With Two Designs by D. G. ROSSETTI. *Second Edition.* Fcap. 8vo. 5s.

The Prince's Progress, and other Poems.
With Two Designs by D. G. ROSSETTI. Fcap. 8vo. 6s.

ROSSETTI.—*Works by* WILLIAM MICHAEL ROSSETTI.
Dante's Comedy, The Hell.
Translated into Literal Blank Verse. Fcap. 8vo. 5s.

Fine Art, chiefly Contemporary.
Crown 8vo. 10s. 6d.

ROUTH.—*Treatise on Dynamics of Rigid Bodies.*
With Numerous Examples. By E. J. ROUTH, M.A. *New Edition.* Crown 8vo. 14s.

ROWSELL.—*Works by* T. J. ROWSELL, M.A.
The English Universities and the English Poor.
Sermons preached before the University of Cambridge. Fcap. 8vo. 2s.

Man's Labour and God's Harvest.
Sermons preached before the University of Cambridge in Lent, 1861. Fcap. 8vo. 3s.

RUFFINI.—*Vincenzo ; or, Sunken Rocks.*
By JOHN RUFFINI. Three vols. crown 8vo. 31s. 6d.

Ruth and her Friends.
A Story for Girls. With a Frontispiece. *Fourth Edition.* Royal 16mo. 3s. 6d.

SCOTT.—*Discourses.*
By A. J. SCOTT, M.A. late Professor of Logic in Owens College, Manchester. Crown 8vo. 7s. 6d.

Scouring of the White Horse.
Or, the Long Vacation Ramble of a London Clerk. By the Author of "Tom Brown's School Days." Illustrated by DOYLE. *Eighth Thousand.* Imp. 16mo. 8s. 6d.

SEATON.—*A Hand-Book of Vaccination.*
By EDWARD C. SEATON, M.D. Medical Inspector to the Privy Council. Extra fcap. 8vo. 8s. 6d.

SELKIRK.—*Guide to the Cricket Ground.*
By G. H. SELKIRK. With Woodcuts. Extra Fcap. 8vo. 3s. 6d.

SELWYN.—*The Work of Christ in the World.*
By G. A. SELWYN, D.D. Bishop of Lichfield. *Third Edition.* Crown 8vo. 2s.

SHAKESPEARE.—*The Works of William Shakespeare. Cambridge Edition.*
Edited by WM. GEORGE CLARK, M.A. and W. ALDIS WRIGHT, M.A. Nine Vols. 8vo. cloth. 4l. 14s. 6d.

Shakespeare's Tempest.
With Glossarial and Explanatory Notes. By the Rev. J. M. JEPHSON. 18mo. 1s. 6d.

SHAIRP.—*Kilmahoe, and other Poems.*
By J. CAMPBELL SHAIRP. Fcap. 8vo. 5s.

SHIRLEY.—*Elijah ; Four University Sermons.*
I. Samaria. II. Carmel. III. Kishon. IV. Horeb. By W. W SHIRLEY, D.D. Fcap. 8vo. 2s. 6d.

SIMPSON.—*An Epitome of the History of the Christian Church.*
By WILLIAM SIMPSON, M.A. *Fourth Edition.* Fcap. 8vo. 3s. 6d.

SMITH.—*Works by* ALEXANDER SMITH.

A Life Drama, and other Poems.
Fcap. 8vo. 2s. 6d.

City Poems.
Fcap. 8vo. 5s.

Edwin of Deira.
Second Edition. Fcap. 8vo. 5s.

SMITH.—*Poems by* CATHERINE BARNARD SMITH.
Crown 8vo. 5s.

SMITH.—*Works by* GOLDWIN SMITH.

A Letter to a Whig Member of the Southern Independence Association.
Extra fcap. 8vo. 2s.

Three English Statesmen ; Pym, Cromwell, and Pitt.
A Course of Lectures on the Political History of England. Extra fcap. 8vo. *New and Cheaper Edition.* 5s.

SMITH.—*Works by* BARNARD SMITH, *M.A. Rector of Glaston, Rutland, &c.*

Arithmetic and Algebra.
Tenth Edition. Crown 8vo. 10s. 6d.

Arithmetic for the Use of Schools.
Ninth Edition. Crown 8vo. 4s. 6d.

A Key to the Arithmetic for Schools.
Fifth Edition. Crown 8vo. 8s. 6d.

Exercises in Arithmetic.
With Answers. Cr. 8vo. limp cloth, 2s. 6d. Or sold separately as follows :—Part I. 1s. Part II. 1s. Answers, 6d.

School Class Book of Arithmetic.
18mo. 3s. Or sold separately, Parts I. and II. 10d. each. Part III. 1s.

Keys to School Class Book of Arithmetic.
Complete in One Volume, 18mo. 6s. 6d. ; or Parts I. II. and III. 2s. 6d. each.

Shilling Book of Arithmetic for National and Elementary Schools.
18mo. cloth. Or separately, Part I. 2d. ; II. 3d. ; III. 7d.

Answers to the Shilling Book of Arithmetic.
18mo. 6d.

Key to the Shilling Book of Arithmetic.
18mo. 4s. 6d.

Examination Papers in Arithmetic.
In Four Parts. 18mo. 1s. 6d. With Answers, 1s. 9d.

Key to Examination Papers in Arithmetic.
18mo. 4s. 6d.

SMITH.—*Hymns of Christ and the Christian Life.*
By the Rev. WALTER C. SMITH, M.A. Fcap. 8vo. 6s.

SMITH.—*Obstacles to Missionary Success among the Heathen.*
The Maitland Prize Essay for 1867. By W. S. SMITH, M.A. Fellow of Trinity College, Cambridge. Crown 8vo. 3s. 6d.

SMITH.—*A Treatise on Elementary Statics.*
By J. H. SMITH, M.A. Gonville and Caius College, Cambridge Royal 8vo. 5s. 6d.

SMITH.—*A Treatise on Elementary Trigonometry.*
Royal 8vo. 5s.

A Treatise on Elementary Hydrostatics.
Royal 8vo. 4s. 6d.

SNOWBALL.—*The Elements of Plane and Spherical Trigo-nometry.*
By J. C. SNOWBALL, M.A. *Tenth Edition.* Crown 8vo. 7s. 6d.

Social Duties considered with Reference to the Organization of Effort in Works of Benevolence and Public Utility.
By a MAN OF BUSINESS. Fcap. 8vo. 4s. 6d.

SPENCER.—*Elements of Qualitative Chemical Analysis.*
By W. H. SPENCER, B.A. 4to. 10s. 6d.

Spring Songs.
By a WEST HIGHLANDER. With a Vignette Illustration by GOURLAY STEELE. Fcap. 8vo. 1s. 6d.

STEPHEN.—*General View of the Criminal Law of England.*
By J. FITZ-JAMES STEPHEN. 8vo. 18s.

STRATFORD DE REDCLIFFE.—*Shadows of the Past, in Verse.*
By VISCOUNT STRATFORD DE REDCLIFFE. Crown 8vo. 10s. 6d.

STRICKLAND.—*On Cottage Construction and Design.*
By C. W. STRICKLAND. With Specifications and Plans. 8vo. 7s. 6d.

Sunday Library for Household Reading. Illustrated.
Monthly Parts, 1s ; Quarterly Vols. 4s. Gilt edges, 4s. 6d.
Vol. I.—The Pupils of St. John the Divine, by the Author of "The Heir of Redclyffe."
Vol. II.—The Hermits, by PROFESSOR KINGSLEY.
Vol. III.—Seekers after God, by the Rev. F. W. FARRAR.
Vol. IV.—England's Antiphon, by GEORGE MACDONALD, LL.D.

SWAINSON.—*Works by* C. A. SWAINSON, D.D.

A Handbook to Butler's Analogy.
Crown 8vo. 1s. 6d.

The Creeds of the Church in their Relations to Holy Scripture and the Conscience of the Christian.
8vo. cloth. 9s.

The Authority of the New Testament,
And other Lectures, delivered before the University of Cambridge. 8vo. cloth. 12s.

TACITUS.—*The History of Tacitus translated into English.*
By A. J. CHURCH, M.A. and W. J. BRODRIBB, M.A. With a Map and Notes. 8vo. 10s. 6d.

The Agricola and Germany.
By the same Translators. With Map and Notes. Fcap. 8vo. 2s. 6d.

TAIT AND STEELE.—*A Treatise on Dynamics.*
With numerous Examples. By P. G. TAIT and W. J. STEELE. *Second Edition.* Crown 8vo. 10s. 6d.

TAYLOR.—*Words and Places;*
Or, Etymological Illustrations of History, Ethnology, and Geography. By the Rev. ISAAC TAYLOR. *Second Edition.* Crown 8vo. 12s. 6d.

TAYLOR.—*The Restoration of Belief.*
New and Revised Edition. By ISAAC TAYLOR, Esq. Crown 8vo. 8s. 6d.

TAYLOR (C.).—*Geometrical Conics.*
By C. TAYLOR, B.A. Crown 8vo. 7s. 6d.

TEBAY.—*Elementary Mensuration for Schools,*
With numerous Examples. By SEPTIMUS TEBAY, B.A. Head Master of Queen Elizabeth's Grammar School, Rivington. Extra fcap. 8vo. 3s. 6d.

TEMPLE.—*Sermons preached in the Chapel of Rugby School.*
By F. TEMPLE, D.D. Head Master. *New and Cheaper Edition.* Crown 8vo. 7s. 6d.

THORPE.—*Diplomatarium Anglicum Ævi Saxonici.*
A Collection of English Charters, from the Reign of King Æthelberht of Kent, A.D. DC.V. to that of William the Conqueror. With a Translation of the Anglo-Saxon. By BENJAMIN THORPE, Member of the Royal Academy of Sciences, Munich. 8vo. cloth. 21s.

THRING.—*Works by* EDWARD THRING, M.A. *Head Master of Uppingham.*

A Construing Book.
Fcap. 8vo. 2s. 6d.

A Latin Gradual.
A First Latin Construing Book for Beginners. 18mo. 2s. 6d.

The Elements of Grammar taught in English.
Fourth Edition. 18mo. 2s.

THRING.—*The Child's Grammar.*
>   *A New Edition.* 18mo. 1s.

Sermons delivered at Uppingham School.
>   Crown 8vo. 5s.

School Songs.
>   With the Music arranged for Four Voices. Edited by the Rev.
>   EDWARD THRING, M.A. and H. RICCIUS. Small folio. 7s. 6d.

Education and School.
>   *Second Edition.* Crown 8vo. 6s.

A Manual of Mood Constructions.
>   Extra fcap. 8vo. 1s. 6d.

THRUPP.—*Works by the Rev. J. F. THRUPP.*

The Song of Songs.
>   A New Translation, with a Commentary and an Introduction.
>   Crown 8vo. 7s. 6d.

Introduction to the Study and Use of the Psalms.
>   Two Vols. 8vo. 21s.

Psalms and Hymns for Public Worship.
>   Selected and Edited by the Rev. J. F. THRUPP, M.A. 18mo.
>   2s. Common paper, 1s. 4d.

The Burden of Human Sin as borne by Christ.
>   Three Sermons preached before the University of Cambridge in
>   Lent, 1865. Crown 8vo. 3s. 6d.

THUCYDIDES.—*The Sicilian Expedition:*
>   Being Books VI. and VII. of Thucydides, with Notes. By the
>   Rev. PERCIVAL FROST, M.A. Fcap. 8vo. 5s.

TOCQUEVILLE.—*Memoir, Letters, and Remains of Alexis de
Tocqueville.*
>   Translated from the French by the Translator of "Napoleon's
>   Correspondence with King Joseph." With numerous Additions.
>   Two vols. Crown 8vo. 21s.

TODD.—*The Books of the Vaudois.*
>   The Waldensian Manuscripts preserved in the Library of Trinity
>   College, Dublin, with an Appendix by JAMES HENTHORN TODD,
>   D.D. Crown 8vo. cloth. 6s.

TODHUNTER.—*Works by* ISAAC TODHUNTER, M.A. F.R.S.

Euclid for Colleges and Schools.
New Edition. 18mo. 3s. 6d.

Algebra for Beginners.
With numerous Examples. New Edition. 18mo. 2s. 6d.

Key to Algebra for Beginners.
Crown 8vo. 6s. 6d.

Mechanics for Beginners.
With numerous Examples. 18mo. 4s. 6d.

Trigonometry for Beginners.
With numerous Examples. 18mo. 2s. 6d.

A Treatise on the Differential Calculus.
With numerous Examples. Fourth Edition. Crown 8vo. 10s. 6d.

A Treatise on the Integral Calculus.
With numerous Examples. Third Edition. Crown 8vo. 10s. 6d.

A Treatise on Analytical Statics.
Third Edition. Crown 8vo. 10s. 6d.

A Treatise on Conic Sections.
Fourth Edition. Crown 8vo. 7s. 6d.

Algebra for the Use of Colleges and Schools.
Fourth Edition. Crown 8vo. 7s. 6d.

Plane Trigonometry for Colleges and Schools.
Third Edition. Crown 8vo. 5s.

A Treatise on Spherical Trigonometry for the Use of Colleges and Schools.
Second Edition. Crown 8vo. 4s. 6d.

Critical History of the Progress of the Calculus of Variations during the Nineteenth Century.
8vo. 12s.

Examples of Analytical Geometry of Three Dimensions.
Second Edition. Crown 8vo. 4s.

A Treatise on the Theory of Equations.
Second Edition. Crown 8vo. 7s. 6d.

Mathematical Theory of Probability.
8vo. 18s.

Tom Brown's School Days.
> By an OLD BOY. Fcap. 8vo. 5s.
> Golden Treasury Edition, 4s. 6d.
> PEOPLE'S EDITION, 2s.
> Illustrated Edition.

Tom Brown at Oxford.
> By the Author of "Tom Brown's School Days." *New Edition.*
> Crown 8vo. 6s.

Tracts for Priests and People. (By various Writers.)
> THE FIRST SERIES, Crown 8vo. 8s.
> THE SECOND SERIES, Crown 8vo. 8s.
> The whole Series of Fifteen Tracts may be had separately, price
> One Shilling each.

TRENCH.—*Works by* R. CHENEVIX TRENCH, D.D. *Archbishop of Dublin.*

Notes on the Parables of Our Lord.
> *Tenth Edition.* 8vo. 12s.

Notes on the Miracles of Our Lord.
> *Eighth Edition.* 8vo. 12s.

Synonyms of the New Testament.
> *New Edition.* One vol. 8vo. cloth. 10s. 6d.

On the Study of Words.
> *Twelfth Edition.* Fcap. 8vo. 4s.

English Past and Present.
> *Sixth Edition.* Fcap. 8vo. 4s. 6d.

Proverbs and their Lessons.
> *Fifth Edition.* Fcap. 8vo. 3s.

*Select Glossary of English Words used **formerly** in Senses different from the present.*
> *Third Edition.* Fcap. 8vo. 4s.

On some Deficiencies in our English Dictionaries.
> *Second Edition.* 8vo. 3s.

Sermons preached in Westminster Abbey.
> *Second Edition.* 8vo. 10s. 6d.

The Fitness of Holy Scripture for Unfolding the Spiritual Life of Man :
> Christ the Desire of all Nations; or, the Unconscious Prophecies
> of Heathendom. Hulsean Lectures. Fcap. 8vo. *Fourth Edition.*
> 5s.

TRENCH (R. CHENEVIX)—*On the Authorized Version of the New Testament.*
Second Edition. 8vo. 7s.

Justin Martyr, and other Poems.
Fifth Edition. Fcap. 8vo. 6s.

Gustavus Adolphus.—Social Aspects of the Thirty Years' War.
Fcap. 8vo. 2s. 6d.

Poems.
Collected and arranged anew. Fcap. 8vo. 7s. 6d.

Poems from Eastern Sources, Genoveva, and other Poems.
Second Edition. Fcap. 8vo. 5s. 6d.

Elegiac Poems.
Third Edition. Fcap. 8vo. 2s. 6d.

Calderon's Life's a Dream :
The Great Theatre of the World. With an Essay on his Life and Genius. Fcap. 8vo. 4s. 6d.

Remains of the late Mrs. Richard Trench.
Being Selections from her Journals, Letters, and other Papers. *New and Cheaper Issue.* With Portrait. 8vo. 6s.

Commentary on the Epistles to the Seven Churches in Asia.
Third Edition, revised. 8vo. 8s. 6d.

Sacred Latin Poetry.
Chiefly Lyrical. Selected and arranged for Use. *Second Edition.* Corrected and Improved. Fcap. 8vo. 7s.

Studies in the Gospels.
Second Edition. 8vo. 10s. 6d.

Shipwrecks of Faith :
Three Sermons preached before the University of Cambridge in May, 1867. Fcap. 8vo. 2s. 6d.

A Household Book of English Poetry.
Selected and Arranged with Notes. By the ARCHBISHOP OF DUBLIN. Extra fcap. 8vo. 5s. 6d.

TRENCH (REV. FRANCIS).—*Brief Notes on the Greek of the New Testament (for English Readers).*
Crown 8vo. cloth. 6s.

TREVELYAN.—*Works by* G. O. TREVELYAN, M.P.

The Competition Wallah.
New Edition. Crown 8vo. 6s.

Cawnpore,
Illustrated with Plan. Second Edition. Crown 8vo. 6s.

TUDOR.—*The Decalogue viewed as the Christian's Law.*
With Special Reference to the Questions and Wants of the Times.
By the Rev. RICH. TUDOR, B.A. Crown 8vo. 10s. 6d.

TULLOCH.—*The Christ of the Gospels and the Christ of Modern Criticism.*
Lectures on M. RENAN's " Vie de Jésus." By JOHN TULLOCH, D.D. Principal of the College of St. Mary, in the University of St. Andrew. Extra fcap. 8vo. 4s. 6d.

TURNER.—*Sonnets.*
By the Rev. CHARLES TENNYSON TURNER. Dedicated to his Brother, the Poet Laureate. Fcap. 8vo. 4s. 6d.

Small Tableaux.
By the Rev. C. TURNER. Fcap. 8vo. 4s. 6d.

TYRWHITT.—*The Schooling of Life.*
By R. ST. JOHN TYRWHITT, M.A. Vicar of St. Mary Magdalen, Oxford. Fcap. 8vo. 3s. 6d.

Vacation Tourists ;
And Notes of Travel in 1861. Edited by F. GALTON, F.R.S. With Ten Maps illustrating the Routes. 8vo. 14s.

Vacation Tourists ;
And Notes of Travel in 1862 and 1863. Edited by FRANCIS GALTON, F.R.S. 8vo. 16s.

VAUGHAN.—*Works by* CHARLES J. VAUGHAN, D.D. *Vicar of Doncaster.*

Notes for Lectures on Confirmation.
With suitable Prayers. Sixth Edition. Fcap. 8vo. 1s. 6d.

Lectures on the Epistle to the Philippians.
Second Edition. Crown 8vo. 7s. 6d.

Lectures on the Revelation of St. John.
Second Edition. Two vols. crown 8vo. 15s.

VAUGHAN (CHARLES J.).—*Epiphany, Lent, and Easter.*
A Selection of Expository Sermons. *Third Edition.* Crown 8vo. 10s. 6d.

The Book and the Life,
And other Sermons, preached before the University of Cambridge. *New Edition.* Fcap. 8vo. 4s. 6d.

Memorials of Harrow Sundays.
A Selection of Sermons preached in Harrow School Chapel. With a View of the Chapel. *Fourth Edition.* Crown 8vo. 10s. 6d.

St. Paul's Epistle to the Romans.
The Greek Text with English Notes. Crown 8vo. 5s. *New Edition in the Press.*

Twelve Discourses on Subjects connected with the Liturgy and Worship of the Church of England.
Fcap. 8vo. 6s.

Lessons of Life and Godliness.
A Selection of Sermons preached in the Parish Church of Doncaster. *Third Edition.* Fcap. 8vo. 4s. 6d.

Words from the Gospels.
A Second Selection of Sermons preached in the Parish Church of Doncaster. *Second Edition.* Fcap. 8vo. 4s. 6d.

The Epistles of St. Paul.
For English Readers. Part I. containing the First Epistle to the Thessalonians. *Second Edition.* 8vo. 1s. 6d. Each Epistle will be published separately.

The Church of the First Days.
Series I. The Church of Jerusalem. *Second Edition.*
   ,, II. The Church of the Gentiles. *Second Edition.*
   ,, III. The Church of the World. *Second Edition.*
Fcap. 8vo. cloth. 4s. 6d. each.

Life's Work and God's Discipline.
Three Sermons. Fcap. 8vo. cloth. 2s. 6d.

The Wholesome Words of Jesus Christ.
Four Sermons preached before the University of Cambridge in November, 1866. Fcap. 8vo. cloth. 3s. 6d. *New Edition in the Press.*

Foes of Faith.
Sermons preached before the University of Cambridge in November, 1868.

VAUGHAN.—*Works by* DAVID J. VAUGHAN, M.A. *Vicar of St. Martin's, Leicester.*

Sermons preached in St. John's Church, Leicester,
During the Years 1855 and 1856. Crown 8vo. 5s. 6d.

Sermons on the Resurrection.
With a Preface. Fcap. 8vo. 3s.

Three Sermons on the Atonement.
1s. 6d.

Sermons on Sacrifice and Propitiation.
2s. 6d.

Christian Evidences and the Bible.
New Edition. Revised and enlarged. Fcap. 8vo. cloth. 5s. 6d.

VAUGHAN.—*Memoir of Robert A. Vaughan,*
Author of "Hours with the Mystics." By ROBERT VAUGHAN, D.D. *Second Edition.* Revised and enlarged. Extra fcap. 8vo. 5s.

VENN.—*The Logic of Chance.*
An Essay on the Foundations and Province of the Theory of Probability, with special reference to its application to Moral and Social Science. By the Rev. J. VENN, M.A. Fcap. 8vo. 7s. 6d.

Village Sermons.
By a NORTHAMPTONSHIRE RECTOR. With a Preface on the Inspiration of Holy Scripture. Crown 8vo. 6s.

Vittoria Colonna.—Life and Poems.
By MRS. HENRY ROSCOE. Crown 8vo. 9s.

Volunteer's Scrap Book.
By the Author of "The Cambridge Scrap Book." Crown 4to. 7s. 6d.

WAGNER.—*Memoir of the Rev. George Wagner,*
late of St. Stephen's, Brighton. By J. N. SIMPKINSON, M.A. *Third and Cheaper Edition.* 5s.

WALLACE.—*The Malay Archipelago : The Home of the Orang Utan and the Bird of Paradise.*
A Narrative of Travel. With Studies of Man and Nature. By ALFRED RUSSEL WALLACE. With Maps and Illustrations.

WARREN.—*An Essay on Greek Federal Coinage.*
By the Hon. J. LEICESTER WARREN, M.A. 8vo. 2s. 6d.

WEBSTER.—*Works by* AUGUSTA WEBSTER.

Dramatic Studies.
Extra fcap. 8vo. 5s.

A Woman Sold,
And other Poems. Crown 8vo. 7s. 6d.

Prometheus Bound, of Æschylus,
Literally Translated into English Verse. Extra fcap. 8vo. 3s. 6d.

Medea of Euripides,
Literally Translated into English Verse. Extra fcap. 8vo. 3s. 6d.

WESTCOTT.—*Works by* BROOKE FOSS WESTCOTT. B.D.
Examining Chaplain to the Bishop of Peterborough.

A General Survey of the History of the Canon of the New Testament during the First Four Centuries.
Second Edition, revised. Crown 8vo. 10s. 6d.

Characteristics of the Gospel Miracles.
Sermons preached before the University of Cambridge. *With Notes.* Crown 8vo. 4s. 6d.

Introduction to the Study of the Four Gospels.
Third Edition. Crown 8vo. 10s. 6d.

The Gospel of the Resurrection.
Thoughts on its Relation to Reason and History. *New Edition.* Fcap. 8vo. 4s. 6d.

The Bible in the Church.
A Popular Account of the Collection and Reception of the Holy Scriptures in the Christian Churches. *Second Edition.* 18mo. 4s. 6d.

History of the English Bible.
Crown 8vo. 10s. 6d.

Westminster Plays.
Lusus Alteri Westmonasterienses, Sive Prologi et Epilogi ad Fabulas in Sti Petri Collegio : actas qui Exstabant collecti et justa quoad licuit annorum serie ordinati, quibus accedit Declamationum quæ vocantur et Epigrammatum Delectus. Curantibus J. MURE, A.M., H. BULL, A.M., C. B. SCOTT, B.D. 8vo. 12s. 6d.

IDEM.—Pars Secunda, 1820—1865. Quibus accedit Epigrammatum Delectus. 8vo. 15s.

WILSON.—*Works by* GEORGE WILSON, M.D.

Counsels of an Invalid.
Letters on Religious Subjects.   With Vignette Portrait.   Fcap.
8vo.   4s. 6d.

Religio Chemici.
With a Vignette beautifully engraved after a Design by Sir
NOEL PATON.   Crown 8vo.   8s. 6d.

WILSON (GEORGE).—*The Five Gateways of Knowledge.*
New Edition.   Fcap. 8vo.   2s. 6d.   Or in Paper Covers, 1s.

The Progress of the Telegraph.
Fcap. 8vo.   1s.

WILSON.—*An English, Hebrew, and Chaldee Lexicon and
Concordance.*
By WILLIAM WILSON, D.D. Canon of Winchester.   *Second
Edition.*   4to.   25s.

WILSON.—*Memoir of George Wilson,* M.D. F.R.S.E.
Regius Professor of Technology in the University of Edinburgh.
By HIS SISTER.   *New Edition.*   Crown 8vo.   6s.

WILSON.—*Works by* DANIEL WILSON, L.L.D.

Prehistoric Annals of Scotland.
New Edition.   With numerous Illustrations.   Two Vols. demy
8vo.   36s.   .

Prehistoric Man.
New Edition.   Revised and partly re-written, with numerous
Illustrations.   One vol. 8vo.   21s.

WILSON.—*A Treatise on Dynamics.*
By W. P. WILSON, M.A.   8vo.   9s. 6d.

WILSON.—*Elementary Geometry.*
PART I.—Angles, Triangles, Parallels, and Equivalent Figures,
with the application to Problems.   By J. M. WILSON, M.A.
Fellow of St. John's College, Cambridge, and Mathematical
Master at Rugby.   Extra fcap. 8vo.   2s. 6d.

WINSLOW.—*Force and Nature.   Attraction and Repulsion.*
The Radical Principles of Energy graphically discussed in their
Relations to Physical and Morphological Development.   By C.
F. WINSLOW, M.D.   8vo.   [In the press.

WOLLASTON.—*Lyra Devoniensis.*
By T. V. WOLLASTON, M.A. Fcap. 8vo. 3s. 6d.

WOLSTENHOLME.—*A Book of Mathematical Problems.*
Crown 8vo. 8s. 6d.

WOODFORD.—*Christian Sanctity.*
By JAMES RUSSELL WOODFORD, M.A. Fcap. 8vo. cloth. 3s.

WOODWARD.—*Works by the Rev.* HENRY WOODWARD, *edited by his Son,* THOMAS WOODWARD, M.A. *Dean of Down.*

Essays, Thoughts and Reflections, and Letters.
Fifth Edition. Crown 8vo. 10s. 6d.

The Shunammite.
Second Edition. Crown 8vo. 10s. 6d.

Sermons.
Fifth Edition. Crown 8vo. 10s. 6d.

WOOLLEY.—*Lectures delivered in Australia.*
By the late JOHN WOOLLEY, D.C.L. Crown 8vo. 8s. 6d.

WOOLNER.—*My Beautiful Lady.*
By THOMAS WOOLNER. With a Vignette by ARTHUR HUGHES.
Third Edition. Fcap. 8vo. 5s.

Words from the Poets.
Selected by the Editor of "Rays of Sunlight." With a Vignette
and Frontispiece. 18mo. Extra cloth gilt. 2s. 6d. *Cheaper
Edition,* 18mo. limp. 1s.

Worship (The) of God and Fellowship among Men.
Sermons on Public Worship. By PROFESSOR MAURICE, and
Others. Fcap. 8vo. 3s. 6d.

WORSLEY.—*Christian Drift of Cambridge Work.*
Eight Lectures. By T. WORSLEY, D.D. Master of Downing
College, Cambridge. Crown 8vo. cloth. 6s.

WRIGHT.—*Works by* J. WRIGHT, M.A.
Hellenica;
Or, a History of Greece in Greek, as related by Diodorus
and Thucydides, being a First Greek Reading Book, with
Explanatory Notes Critical and Historical. *Third Edition,*
WITH A VOCABULARY. 12mo. 3s. 6d.

D

The Seven Kings of Rome. ·
An Easy Narrative, abridged from the First Book of Livy by the omission of difficult passages, being a First Latin Reading Book, with Grammatical Notes. Fcap. 8vo. 3s.

A Vocabulary and Exercises on the "Seven Kings of Rome."
Fcap. 8vo. 2s. 6d.

. The Vocabulary and Exercises may also be had bound up with "The Seven Kings of Rome." Price 5s.

A Help to Latin Grammar;
Or, the Form and Use of Words in Latin, with Progressive Exercises. Crown 8vo. 4s. 6d.

David, King of Israel.
Readings for the Young. With Six Illustrations. Royal 16mo. cloth, gilt. 3s. 6d.

YOUMANS.—Modern Culture,
Its True Aims and Requirements. A Series of Addresses and Arguments on the Claims of Scientific Education. Edited by EDWARD L. YOUMANS, M.D. Crown 8vo. 8s. 6d.

𝕎orks by the 𝔄uthor of

"THE HEIR OF REDCLYFFE."

The Prince and the Page. A Book for the Young. 18mo. 3s. 6d.

A Book of Golden Deeds. 18mo. 4s. 6d. Cheap Edition, 1s.

History of Christian Names. Two. Vols. Crown 8vo. 1l. 1s.

The Heir of Redclyffe. Seventeenth Edition. With Illustrations. Crown 8vo. 6s.

Dynevor Terrace. Third Edition. Crown 8vo. 6s.

The Daisy Chain. Ninth Edition. With Illustrations. Crown 8vo. 6s.

The Trial: More Links of the Daisy Chain. Fourth Edition. With Illustrations. Crown 8vo. 6s.

Heartsease. Tenth Edition. With Illustrations. Crown 8vo. 6s.

Hopes and Fears. Third Edition. Crown 8vo. 6s.

The Young Stepmother. Second Edition. Crown 8vo. 6s.

The Lances of Lynwood. With Coloured Illustrations. *Second Edition.* Extra fcap. cloth. 4s. 6d.

The Little Duke. New Edition. 18mo. cloth. 3s. 6d.

Clever Woman of the Family. Crown 8vo. 6s.

Danvers Papers ; an Invention. Crown 8vo. 4s. 6d.

Dove in the Eagle's Nest. Two vols. Crown 8vo. 12s.

Cameos from English History. From Rollo to Edward II. Extra fcap. 8vo. 5s.

Book of Worthies. [In the Press.

ELEMENTARY SCHOOL CLASS BOOKS.

The Volumes of this Series of ELEMENTARY SCHOOL CLASS BOOKS *are handsomely printed in a form that, it is hoped, will assist the young Student as much as clearness of type and distinctness of arrangement can effect. They are published at a moderate price, to insure an extensive sale in the Schools of the United Kingdom and the Colonies.*

Euclid for Colleges and Schools.
By I. TODHUNTER, M.A. F.R.S. 18mo. 3s. 6d.

Algebra for Beginners.
By I. TODHUNTER, M.A. F.R.S. 18mo. 2s. 6d.

Key to Algebra for Beginners.
Crown 8vo. 6s. 6d.

The School Class Book of Arithmetic.
By BARNARD SMITH, M.A. Parts I. and II. 18mo. limp cloth, price 10d. each. Part III. 1s. ; or Three Parts in one Volume, price 3s.
KEY TO CLASS BOOK OF ARITHMETIC.
Complete, 18mo. cloth, price 6s. 6d. Or separately, Parts I. II. & III. 2s. 6d. each.

Mythology for Latin Versification.
A Brief Sketch of the Fables of the Ancients, prepared to be rendered into Latin Verse for Schools. By F. HODGSON, B.D. *New Edition.* Revised by F. C. HODGSON, M.A. Fellow of King's College, Cambridge. 18mo. 3s.

A Latin Gradual for Beginners.
A First Latin Construing Book. By EDWARD THRING, M.A. 18mo. 2s. 6d.

Shakespeare's Tempest.
The Text taken from "The Cambridge Shakespeare." With Glossarial and Explanatory Notes. By the Rev. J. M. JEPHSON. 18mo. cloth limp. 1s. 6d.

Lessons in Elementary Botany.
The Part on Systematic Botany based upon Material left in Manuscript by the late Professor HENSLOW. With nearly Two Hundred Illustrations. By DANIEL OLIVER, F.R.S. F.L.S. 18mo. cloth. 4s. 6d.

Lessons in Elementary Physiology.
With numerous Illustrations. By T. H. HUXLEY, F.R.S. Professor of Natural History in the Government School of Mines. 18mo. 4s. 6d.

Popular Astronomy.
A Series of Lectures delivered at Ipswich. By GEORGE BIDDELL AIRY, Astronomer Royal. 18mo. cloth. 4s. 6d.

Lessons in Elementary Chemistry.
By HENRY ROSCOE, F.R.S. Professor of Chemistry in Owens College, Manchester. With numerous Illustrations. 18mo. cloth. 4s. 6d.

An Elementary History of the Book of Common Prayer.
By FRANCIS PROCTER, M.A. 18mo. 2s. 6d.

Algebraical Exercises.
Progressively arranged by Rev. C. A. JONES, M.A. and C. H. CHEYNE, M.A. Mathematical Masters in Westminster School. 18mo. cloth. 2s. 6d.

The Bible in the Church.
A Popular Account of the Collection and Reception of the Holy Scriptures in the Christian Churches. By BROOKE FOSS WESTCOTT, B.D. 18mo. 4s. 6d.

The Bible Word Book.
A Glossary of Old English Bible Words. By J. EASTWOOD, M.A. and W. ALDIS WRIGHT, M.A. 18mo. 5s. 6d.

MACMILLAN AND CO. LONDON.